THE EASTER REBELLION

POBLACHT NA H EIREANN.

THE PROVISIONAL GOVERNMENT
OF THE
IRISH REPUBLIC
TO THE PEOPLE OF IRELAND.

IRISHMEN AND IRISHWOMEN: In the name of God and of the dead generations from which she receives her old tradition of nationhood, Ireland, through us, summons her children to her flag and strikes for her freedom.

Having organised and trained her manhood through her secret revolutionary organisation, the Irish Republican Brotherhood, and through her open military organisations, the Irish Volunteers and the Irish Citizen Army, having patiently perfected her discipline, having resolutely waited for the right moment to reveal itself, she now seizes that moment, and, supported by her exiled children in America and by gallant allies in Europe, but relying in the first on her own strength, she strikes in full confidence of victory.

We declare the right of the people of Ireland to the ownership of Ireland, and to the unfettered control of Irish destinies, to be sovereign and indefeasible. The long usurpation of that right by a foreign people and government has not extinguished the right, nor can it ever be extinguished except by the destruction of the Irish people. In every generation the Irish people have asserted their right to national freedom and sovereignty : six times during the past three hundred years they have asserted it in arms. Standing on that fundamental right and again asserting it in arms in the face of the world, we hereby proclaim the Irish Republic as a Sovereign Independent State, and we pledge our lives and the lives of our comrades-in-arms to the cause of its freedom, of its welfare, and of its exaltation among the nations.

The Irish Republic is entitled to, and hereby claims, the allegiance of every Irishman and Irishwoman. The Republic guarantees religious and civil liberty, equal rights and equal opportunities to all its citizens, and declares its resolve to pursue the happiness and prosperity of the whole nation and of all its parts, cherishing all the children of the nation equally, and oblivious of the differences carefully fostered by an alien government, which have divided a minority from the majority in the past.

Until our arms have brought the opportune moment for the establishment of a permanent National Government, representative of the whole people of Ireland and elected by the suffrages of all her men and women, the Provisional Government, hereby constituted, will administer the civil and military affairs of the Republic in trust for the people.

We place the cause of the Irish Republic under the protection of the Most High God, Whose blessing we invoke upon our arms, and we pray that no one who serves that cause will dishonour it by cowardice, inhumanity, or rapine. In this supreme hour the Irish nation must, by its valour and discipline and by the readiness of its children to sacrifice themselves for the common good, prove itself worthy of the august destiny to which it is called.

Signed on Behalf of the Provisional Government,

THOMAS J. CLARKE.

SEAN Mac DIARMADA,   THOMAS MacDONAGH,

P. H. PEARSE,   EAMONN CEANNT,

JAMES CONNOLLY,   JOSEPH PLUNKETT

The Proclamation of the Irish Republic

THE EASTER REBELLION

Max Caulfield

GILL & MACMILLAN

Gill & Macmillan Ltd
Goldenbridge
Dublin 8
with associated companies throughout the world
© Max Caulfield 1963, 1995
0 7171 2293 X
Index compiled by Helen Litton
Print origination
Carrigboy Typesetting Services
Printed by ColourBooks Ltd, Dublin

A catalogue record is available for this book from the British Library.

1 3 5 4 2

Contents

Illustrations

Preface to 1995 edition

This book was first written over thirty years ago, when I had the great advantage of being able to interview many of the survivors of the Rising. Their testimony seems as fresh today as it did then. In other respects, however, our understanding of Easter Week has changed. Biographies of some of the leaders have given us a greater insight into the personalities involved. Memoirs and more general studies of the period have altered or amended points of view previously taken for granted.

This new edition of *The Easter Rebellion* takes account of these changes and incorporates them in the text. In general, I have tried to keep amendments to the minimum, in order to retain the immediacy and—as I hope—the fluency of the original narrative.

The bibliography has been revised and extended.

Max Caulfield
London, 1995

Acknowledgments

So many people gave of their time and trouble towards the making of this book that it is almost invidious to single any out.

Both in England and in Ireland, I was received with great courtesy and hospitality by everyone in a position to help with the research. Many people went to great trouble to look up documents or write accounts of their recollections.

In Dublin one was almost washed away with hospitality, but I would particularly like to thank Mr. Michael MacDonagh, then editor of the *Dublin Sunday Review*, Mr. Erskine Childers, jun., and Mr. Desmond Ryan, an historian of the Rebellion himself, who went to great trouble to put me in touch with sources and to advise in general. Mr. William Cosgrave went to exceeding trouble to show me over the site of the battle at the South Dublin Union and General Richard Mulcahy aided me with personal recollections and several interesting documents. No one could have been more helpful than Mr. Frank Robbins, who gave me much information and helped me with sources in relation to the Irish Citizen Army. Nor could anyone have been of greater assistance than Commandant Brennan Whitmore who not only gave me the benefit of his most lucid interpretation of events but has allowed me access to his personal memories.

Magnificent hospitality was shown me by Mr. James Doyle at his farm in Wexford, and by Mr. Thomas Walsh at his home in Dublin. Both Jack Shouldice and his brother Frank went to immense trouble to procure me every possible detail of the fighting in North King Street and have left me with warm memories of Dublin. Mr. Garry Holohan, Mr. Thomas Sherrin and Mr. Joseph Brady all put themselves to a great deal of inconvenience.

My inquiries were no less well assisted in England. My researches took me into a belt of country with which I was not very well acquainted, and it was interesting to note the character and habits and social nature of the people *vis-à-vis* their counterparts in Ireland. Here, away from the acerbities of London, I found the same kind of warm-hearted courtesy and hospitality, particularly in Nottinghamshire and Derbyshire. I am exceedingly grateful to Captain Frank Pragnell of Nottingham, Major William Foster of Southwell, Colonel J. S. Oates of Besthorpe, Nottinghamshire, and Colonel M. C. Martyn, of Wentworth, Yorkshire, for the trouble and time they took to give

me their accounts and lend me books and documents. I am particularly
indebted to Captain A. E. Slack of Chesterfield, Derbyshire, whose enthusiasm
and cheerfulness gave me many valuable leads to sources.

My thanks, too, to the staffs of the Imperial War Museum, the British
Museum and the National Library of Ireland whom I put to considerable
inconvenience.

London, 1963.

AUTHOR'S NOTE

A word of explanation to Irish friends who may feel that I should not have
described the Easter week happenings as a "Rebellion".

I am fully aware of the connotation. But in extenuation, I would point out
that it was thus described at the time and it has been my endeavour to retain
the atmosphere of events as well as I can. Similarly, the rebellion was widely—
if erroneously—believed to be the work of Sinn Fein. This illusion was current
not just in government and Castle circles but among large numbers of the public. Again, I have retained contemporary references to Sinn Fein which, while
historically anachronistic, are at least authentic. There are, of course, some references to the organization which are specific to Arthur Griffith's political
movement. I trust that these are self-evident in the text and are distinguishable
from more casual uses of the term.

Again, in calling Sean MacDiarmada by his name in English, for example, I
am trying not only to make things easier for non-Irish and non-Gaelic-speak-
ing readers, but seeking to avoid the illogicality of calling a man by a Gaelic
Christian name and an anglicized surname.

In the case of men such as Presidents de Valera and O'Kelly, I have retained
the form in which they were known throughout the world.

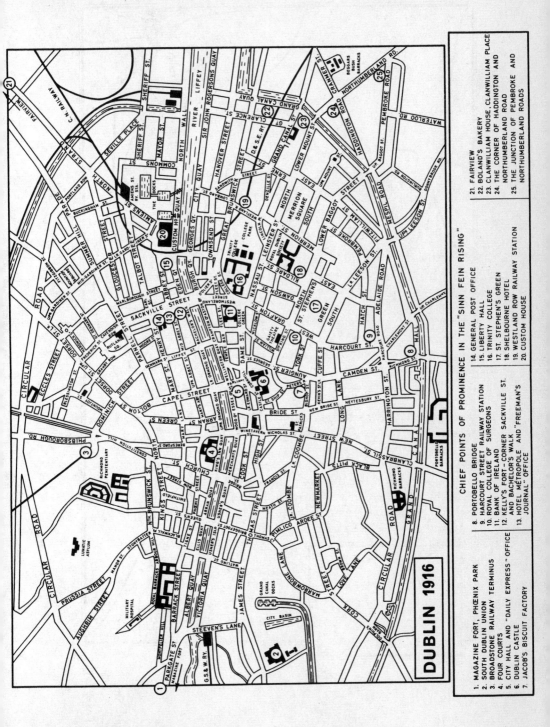

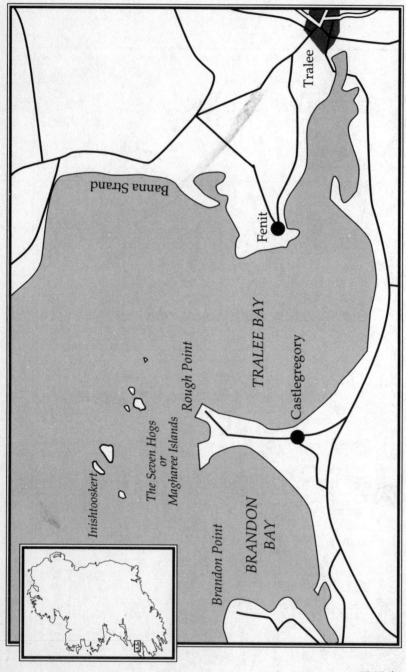

Banna Strand
and
Tralee Bay

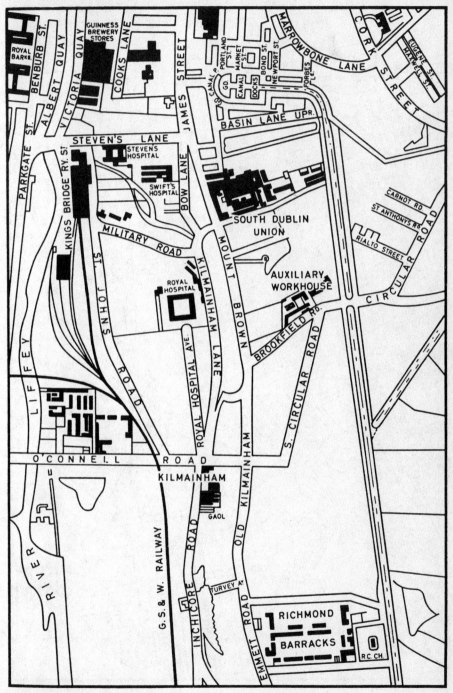

The South Dublin Union area

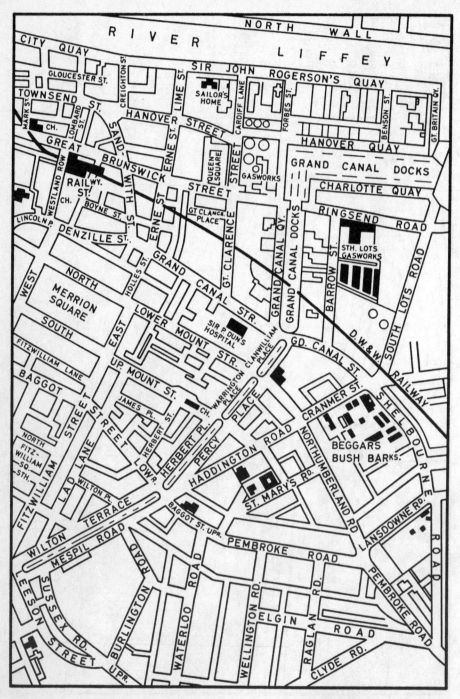

The Mount Street Bridge area

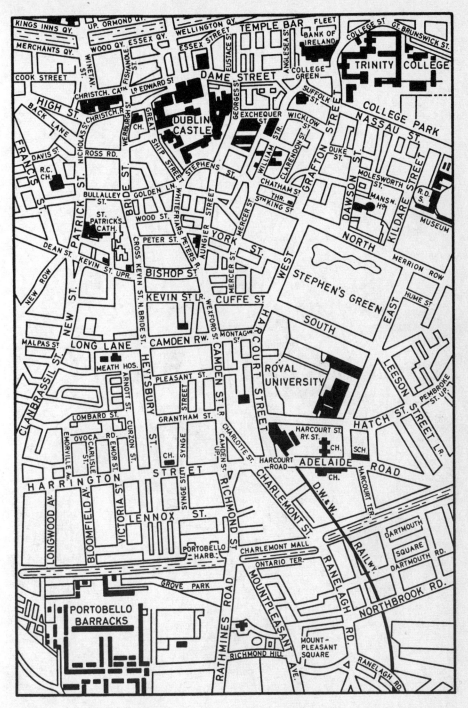

The Stephen's Green and Dublin Castle area

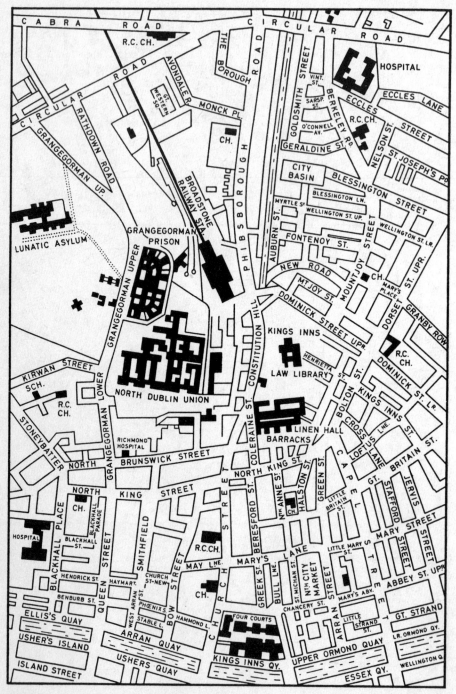

The Four Courts and North King Street area

1

AT FOUR MINUTES past noon on Easter Monday, April 24th, 1916, a Red Cross nurse, returning to duty at the wartime hospital in Dublin Castle, paused at the main gate and half-jokingly asked the policeman on duty, "Is it true that the Sinn Feiners are going to take the Castle?"

"Ah, no, miss," said Constable James O'Brien of the Dublin Metropolitan Police. "I don't think so. Aren't the authorities making too much fuss?"

So the nurse smiled and went her way, passing out of sight through a stone archway which led into Upper Castle Yard, an archway imposingly surmounted by a large statue of Justice, which stood—significantly, said Dubliners of rebellious sympathies—with her *back* to the city. Upper Castle Yard itself was a two hundred and eighty by one hundred and thirty-foot quadrangle enclosed by the various Crown administrative offices and the Irish State Apartments, among them the gilded Throne Room, with its exquisitely curved ceiling, and the age-worn St. Patrick's Hall, where for centuries the Irish Viceroys had given magnificent levees. It was in this room that new Knights of the Illustrious Order of St. Patrick were installed; here, also, that Victoria and Albert danced quadrilles on the occasion of their state visit to Dublin. Of the rather indifferent set of panels decorating the ceiling, the most significant was a painting showing the Irish chieftains paying homage to their feudal overlord, King Henry II, a measure of the time England had wielded paramount influence in Ireland. Here, then, in and around this short perimeter, lay the heart of British power in the subjugated sister island.

Less than a minute later, Mr. H. S. Doig, editor of the Dublin *Mail & Express*, whose windows faced the Castle Gate, heard one of his staff say, "Good God! The Citizen Army are parading in spite of MacNeill's letter." Doig, who was busy writing a leader on Shakespeare's Tercentenary, rose from his chair and saw a small detachment of armed men and women just about to break ranks. He noted that they were wearing the dark green uniforms and the Boer-like slouch hats of the Irish Citizen Army. He watched O'Brien confront them with his hand up and thought he was telling them, "Now, boys, you shouldn't be here at all." Then, to his surprise, the Citizen Army stepped back and raised their rifles. There was the crack of a bullet and the big policeman crashed to the ground, shot through the brain. For a moment, the rebels hesitated, almost as though they were stunned themselves by this abrupt expression of violence.

Then Doig heard their leader roaring, "Get in! Get in!" and saw them surge forward.

Inside the Gate, the military sentry fired once, then dived for cover as the rebels returned his fire. Quickly a number of them succeeded in reaching the archway and launching an assault on the Guardroom. Behind them, and still under the eyes of the astonished Doig, a priest who happened to be passing up Cork Hill, rushed in and began gesturing wildly in an obvious attempt to dissuade the main force from further action, but they simply ignored him and pressed on with their attack. Left standing in utter bewilderment—Irishmen, after all, rarely disobeyed Catholic clergy—the priest finally caught sight of O'Brien's body lying beside the Gate and at once ran over and knelt down to administer the last rites. Even as he did so, the rebels opened up a general, if rather haphazard fire on the Castle in support of their advanced comrades.

Within that enormous, straggling complex of buildings, in a fusty Victorian office scarcely twenty-five yards from where O'Brien now lay dead, Sir Matthew Nathan, His Majesty's Under-Secretary for Ireland, Major Ivor Price, the Military Intelligence Officer, and Mr. A. H. Norway, Secretary of the Post Office, had already risen to their feet in some alarm. They had been sitting discussing in detail a plan to arrest the leaders of Sinn Fein, following a decision reached at a conference held the previous night with the Lord Lieutenant, Lord Wimborne, at the Vice-Regal Lodge, Phoenix Park. This had marked the culmination of a series of incidents over the week-end, which had begun with the arrest of Sir Roger Casement after he had landed from a German submarine, and had reached an apparent climax with the cancellation of the special manoeuvres called for Easter Sunday by the Irish Volunteers—exercises which had been clearly intended, as it had now become obvious, only to cloak something much more serious. Although the conference had decided that the danger of real trouble in Ireland had almost entirely receded, still it had been considered advisable to take punitive measures if only on a kind of *pour encourager les autres* basis. After all, an overt attempt at rebellion *had* been made, and the conspirators ought to be locked away at once—as indeed, if the truth were admitted, they should have been a long time ago.

Before the arrests could be made, however, it had been constitutionally necessary to obtain the permission of the Chief Secretary, Mr. Augustine Birrell, who was in London. A cable had been dispatched to him the previous night, therefore, immediately after the conference, and his reply had just been received—or not much more than an hour before—agreeing to the arrests. Sir Matthew had waited until the arrival of Major Price at 11.45 a.m. before telephoning Mr. Norway at the newly-renovated and remodelled General Post Office in Sackville Street (which had just been reopened to the public) inviting him to join in the discussions. Mr. Norway (rather fortunately in the light of events) had left his office at approximately 11.50 a.m. and had arrived at the Castle almost precisely at noon. The three men were hardly settled down to their talks, therefore, when the sound of the shots penetrated their seclusion.

"They've commenced it!" shouted Price, leaping to his feet and running from the room, tugging at his revolver. In Upper Castle Yard he was in time to see half-a-dozen rebels breaking their way into the Guardroom. He emptied his revolver in their direction, then deciding that there was little he could do without assistance, rushed back to Sir Matthew's office.

Inside the Guardroom the six soldiers on duty had been heating a saucepan of stew for their midday meal when they were rudely disturbed by the shots. Reaching for their rifles, they were about to rush outside at the double when a home-made bomb, lobbed through the window, landed right in the middle of them. It failed to explode but created such panic that when the insurgents broke in they had no difficulty in forcing a surrender. Within seconds, the six soldiers had been laid flat on the floor, trussed up with their own puttees, and the rebel party, under the command of Citizen Army Sergeant Tom Kain, were crouching under the windows, quietly planning their next move.

Among the several mistakes made by the insurgents during the course of the subsequent week, their decision not to press forward with their attack on Dublin Castle still ranks as one of the most difficult to understand. Possibly, as has been argued, their orders were *not* to capture the Castle, because of difficulty in defending it against counter-attack. Possibly they were simply overawed at the idea of taking a fortress which had defied the Irish for almost seven hundred years. But, more probably, they were afraid of blundering into the considerable military forces with which the Castle was normally garrisoned. Clearly they never guessed that the place lay almost entirely at their mercy; that fewer than twenty-five soldiers—and these were idling away their time in Ship Street barracks round the corner—were all that stood between them and an epic moment in Irish history. Yet they were aware that there was an excellent holiday card at Fairyhouse races (including the Irish Grand National) and might be presumed to have known that the garrison would be below strength. In fact, there were only two officers on duty in Dublin Castle that morning.

There were sixty-seven war-wounded soldiers in the Red Cross hospital but none of these, of course, could have fought. The Castle, to all intents and purposes, indeed, lay entirely in the hands of its civil servants, most of whom had spent their morning idly gazing out at a blue sky and at wisps of trailing cloud, envying holiday-makers who were even then enjoying themselves on the beaches at Dalkey and Malahide.

But instead of reinforcing Kain and ordering him to take the Castle—and if necessary burn it down—John Connolly (no relation of James Connolly), leader of the rebel detachment, decided to split his forces—acting on his original orders. He sent one party to occupy the premises of Henry & James, outfitters, on the corner of Cork Hill and Parliament Street, which directly faced the Castle Gate; another to charge up the stairs of the *Mail & Express* offices on the other corner and eject the startled Doig and his staff at bayonet point, while the main body, under his own command, turned aside to break into the City Hall, using a specially-impressed key to open the main door.

Meanwhile, in Sir Matthew's office, Major Price had set about the hasty task of organizing the Castle's defences. His first job, even while he waited for the rebels to break down the door and slaughter them all without mercy, was to summon every available soldier from Ship Street barracks. Sir Matthew himself took a revolver from his desk and prepared to assist in selling their lives dearly—fortunately, it proved to be quite an unnecessary gesture, for the rebels inexplicably failed to put in an appearance. In their stead, the military party from Ship Street turned up at the double, although Price was somewhat taken aback to count only twenty-five men where he had expected to see two hundred, the normal garrison strength. He at once reached for Sir Matthew's private telephone which gave a direct line to Irish Command H.Q. at Parkgate, conscious that someone had blundered badly in not doubling the garrison that morning. In his excitement he had difficulty at first in disentangling the wires, but finally he managed to sort them out. For perhaps three full seconds he held the receiver to his ear, waiting. Then a wild look suddenly crossed his face and, turning to Sir Matthew, he exclaimed in desperation, "My God! They've cut the wires!"

Bugler William Oman of the Irish Citizen Army had sounded the "fall-in" for the main rebel army at exactly 11.30 that morning. The notes had risen stickily into the calm air of Beresford Place, which abuts the River Liffey, and had sounded hoarsely along the dingy corridors of Liberty Hall, headquarters of the Irish Transport and General Workers' Union, and its militant offshoot, the Citizen Army. Sergeant Frank Robbins, who was trying on a new pair of trousers at the time, had them only half on when he heard the call. There was a sudden rush of feet along the rough boards outside the door and, heart in mouth, Robbins, who was only twenty, slung his bandolier over his shoulder, took up his rifle, and went racing down the stairs, still buttoning his trousers. He found the place in an uproar. There were bicycles parked everywhere, in some cases a dozen deep; girls were rushing about, carrying haversacks stuffed with food and medical supplies; wives and sweethearts were thrusting cigarettes or chocolates upon their men as they said farewell.

Outside in the big square in front of Liberty Hall, two hundred and fifty men and boys at the most were feverishly shuffling themselves into an orderly double column. One of them, Tommy Keenan, was only twelve years old. Behind them, bisected by the ugly Loop Line railway bridge which links termini at Amiens Street and Westland Row, rose Gandon's graceful Custom House, in the sunlight a dazzlingly white-and-shadowed affair of slender dome and sweeping perpendiculars. Over the Liffey, mirrored as a lake now, swung the lazy, drifting gulls, like flowing polka dots.

Despite the enhancing effect of a glorious morning, the rebel army hardly looked an inspiring one. Fewer than a fourth of its members wore the dark green uniform of the Citizen Army or the heather green of the Irish Volunteers. One or two had tried to give themselves a military appearance by covering their legs with puttees or leggings; some had put on riding breeches; but all that most of them had been able to do was to sling a bandolier over their right shoulder or tie a yellow brassard around their left arm. Their armaments, too, looked appallingly primitive. In the bright sunlight, the high gleam of pikes caught the eye a great deal more readily than the dull glint of rifles; when there was a stir among the Kimmage men, for instance, the pikes were seen to jink in the air like the halberds of a Tudor army. For that matter, the rifles themselves seemed only a trifle less antique. There were a few modern short Lee-Enfields (filched or bought clandestinely from the military when no officer was looking); some Italian Martinis (smuggled in from the Continent among the blocks of Carrara marble) and the odd Lee-Metford (come from God knows where!). There were plenty of single-barrelled shotguns; but the predominant weapon was the brute-like Howth Mauser—so called because it had formed part of a cargo of German rifles landed at Howth in July 1914, from Erskine Childers' yacht *Asgard*. This rifle, manufactured for the Prussian forces of 1870, was a single-loader, firing a soft-nosed lead bullet which struck with all the effect of a dum-dum. In action, it would be discovered that it drilled a neat hole in a man as it entered but tore out the other side like a plate, and its use would anger the British Army and lead to an accusation against the rebels of firing outlawed bullets. In short, these men, like almost any army of rebels anywhere, looked a forlorn and rather desperate lot.

No one, certainly, realized this better than James Connolly, commander of all the rebel forces in Dublin city. As he clattered down the broad sweeping stair-case of Liberty Hall, a stocky little man in the full uniform of a Commandant-General, his bandy legs encased in highly-polished leggings, ready to lay down his life for the principles in which he so passionately believed, he stopped for a moment to say good-bye to his friend William O'Brien. In a half-whisper, so that the men nearby would not overhear him, he added, "Bill, we're going out to be slaughtered."

"Is there no hope at all?" asked O'Brien, who knew the question was super-fluous.

"None whatever," Connolly answered cheerfully and, slapping O'Brien's shoulder, strode on.

At 11.50 precisely, the first body of rebels to move off turned smartly in obedience to Connolly's sharp order, "Left turn! Quick march!" Twenty-eight men and eight boys, comprising a detachment under Citizen Army Captain Richard MacCormack, marched towards Butt Bridge. They had gone only a short distance when Connolly ran after them, shouting, "No, not that way, Mac!—you'll get slaughtered! Fighting might have broken out in some places already. You'd better take a short cut and be as quick as you can!" MacCormack at once wheeled his column and led them up Eden Quay. With Robbins in the column was James Fox, aged nineteen. A few minutes before they moved off, an old man had pushed his way forward, leading a young man by the hand. "Frank Robbins," Patrick Fox had said, "here's my lad—will you take him with you? I'm too old for the job myself."

It was 11.55 a.m. before Pearse himself finally made an appearance, followed by the pale-faced figure of his younger brother Willie. Preceding them was the bizarre and dying figure of Joseph Plunkett, his throat still swathed in bandages as a result of an operation for glandular tuberculosis three weeks earlier, who had to be helped down the steps by his A.D.C. Michael Collins. A filigree bangle glittered on Plunkett's wrist and two enormous antique rings clustered upon his fingers. By this time MacCormack's column had crossed O'Connell Bridge, marching at the double; the Castle detachment under John Connolly had followed; then John Heuston, aged nineteen, leading a party of twelve young men, all of about his own age, had tramped off to occupy the Mendicity Institution, up-river on the south bank. Until that moment there had been no perceptible thinning of the main body, but as forty men under Commandant Michael Mallin moved off to occupy St. Stephen's Green—his second-in-command, Lieutenant Countess Markievicz flamboyantly following with her own troop of women and Boy Scouts—its numbers suddenly depreciated alarmingly. Hardly one hundred and fifty men, in fact, were left to shuffle their feet in Beresford Place—the total of the grand army with which Patrick Pearse intended to establish the headquarters of an Irish Republic in the General Post Office in Sackville Street.

From the steps of Liberty Hall Patrick Henry Pearse, thirty-six-year-old Commander-in-Chief and President of the Provisional Government, gazed out over the shabbily-thin ranks and, beyond them, two drays laden with an astonishing assortment of weapons and work-implements, including pickaxes, sledges and crow-bars and some brand-new wicker-hampers, to where a closed cab hung funereally about on the outskirts, stuffed to the roof with similar junk. For a moment he studied the men's faces intently. Not content with a soldier's normal equipment, many of them were carrying two rifles, one over each shoulder, or a rifle and a pickaxe, or a shotgun and a pike. Captain Brennan Whitmore, a member of Plunkett's staff, wondered how they hoped to defend themselves if they were called upon suddenly to do battle but, before he could raise the issue, a dusty touring car swung round into Beresford Place and halted amid cheers. Down from the running-board stepped The O'Rahilly, Treasurer of the Irish Volunteers. No one there knew it, but The O'Rahilly had, in fact, spent the previous twenty-four hours doing his best, in the light of what had happened during the week-end, to prevent a Rising—his efforts taking him in a wild night drive to the provincial Commandants in Cork, Kerry, Limerick and Tipperary with orders from Professor Eoin MacNeill, President of the Volunteers, not to obey Pearse's instructions. Now, however, he leaped eagerly up the steps of Liberty Hall to shake hands with Pearse and Plunkett, gasping out the explanation, "Well, I've helped to wind up the clock—I might as well hear it strike!" Delighted Volunteers and Citizen Army men began to load weapons, implements and home-made bombs into his car.

The time was just two minutes to twelve. Pearse, his thoughts fixed intently upon sombrely magnificent ambitions whose realization now seemed imminent, took his place at the head of the column. He was followed by Plunkett, his Chief-of-Staff and the mercurial brain behind the military planning and strategy of the Rebellion, who dramatically unsheathed a sabre as he took up his position. Then Connolly, having satisfied himself that all was in readiness, placed himself between Pearse and Plunkett, and behind the three Commandant-Generals (as they had ranked themselves) came the rest of the column in orthodox fours. Captain Brennan Whitmore took the extreme left and next to him stood Michael Collins, who, until recently, had been an employee of the Post Office in London. Further back stood Sean T. O'Kelly, who would one day find himself President of Ireland, and still farther back young Thomas MacEvoy, aged seventeen, a grocer's assistant, who marched into insurrection blithely believing that he was taking part in an ordinary route march. Captain Michael O'Reilly, Brigade deputy-adjutant, tightened his grip on the magnificent sword which had cost him all of thirty bob and hoped that the words with which he had comforted his wife and four children ("Don't worry now, when I come back, I'll be Minister of Defence") would prove prophetic. In the column, too, were Connolly's fifteen-year-old son Rory, and his loyal secretary Winifred Carney, the only woman in the entire procession. The rear—behind the closed cab, the drays and The O'Rahilly's motor-car—was brought up by two motor-cyclists, young Jack Plunkett (youngest of the three Plunkett brothers) and Volunteer Fergus O'Kelly who had been ordered by Joseph Plunkett to set up a wireless transmitter. Connolly snapped out, "By the left, quick march!", a command which drew ironical cheering and clapping from a crowd of urchins and grown-ups who had been watching them parade.

The rebels stepped out briskly and, considering their weird impedimenta, quite impressively. Their disciplined look was not surprising. Most of them had been exposed to some form or degree of military training. Many had been drilling regularly with the Volunteers for the previous three years, while a number had actually served with the British Army; one, Major John MacBride, had fought with the Boers. They had an appreciation of order and discipline, therefore, despite their ridiculous paraphernalia, despite even the pikes.

Yet as Volunteer Patrick Colwell clattered up Abbey Street, he had no idea where they were all marching to, or, indeed, exactly what they were marching for. None of the officers had bothered to inform him, but he presumed, as young MacEvoy and several others had, that this was only an ordinary route march, or, at best, a tactical exercise. He was a Kimmage man—in other words, one of the fifty-six young men who for the past three months had been living it rough, sleeping eight to a mattress in some cases, in an old mill on the farm of Count Plunkett at Kimmage. They were Irishmen who had left their homes and jobs in places like Glasgow, Liverpool and London when conscription had been introduced into Great Britain, believing that if they had to fight for anybody, then they would rather fight for Ireland. At Kimmage, where the Plunketts had set up a crude arsenal, they had made weapons. Eventually they had attempted a field gun, using twelve feet of rainwater piping bound with copper wire, and a heavy chain. To test it, they had stuffed a charge of gun-powder into the breech, rammed the ammunition—pieces of metal of every description, including old razor blades—down the muzzle, and had touched it off. The gun, of course, had blown up immediately, scattering metal over a wide area and almost killing Count Plunkett's daughter as she emerged from the door of the farmhouse. From then on they had confined their activities to the less complicated, if more unrewarding, tasks of making six-foot pikes, or hammering out crude bayonets, or even manufacturing home-made bombs from such unpromising materials as old tea canisters and tobacco tins.

That morning, all fifty-six of them, led by their captain, George Plunkett, had marched from Kimmage to the suburb of Harold's Cross and had there, somehow or other, squeezed aboard a tram-car. The conductor was flabbergast-ed when Plunkett asked him for fifty-seven tuppenny tickets ("Why bother to pay, anyway," he had expostulated, "when you've already captured the tram?"). Meanwhile, Volunteer James Brennan had moved up inside the vehicle until he was standing beside the driver. He then prodded the man gently in the back with a shotgun and ordered him to keep going without stopping until they reached O'Connell Bridge.

"I've more sense than to argue with a gun," the driver replied, and cheer-fully did as he was told to do. Several passengers, however, loudly voiced complaints, some insisting that they should be allowed to get off. One large woman, struck several times in the face by the swinging equipment, finally lost her temper and shouted at the conductor, "I demand that you put these men off!"

"In that case," the conductor replied with what patience he could still sum-mon, "would you mind doing it yourself, ma'am. As you can see, I'm rather busy."

The long march up Abbey Street, for all its subsequent significance in Irish history, passed fleetingly for most of the men in the column that morning. When the front ranks reached Sackville Street, people halted on the kerbs to let them march through. One or two raised a cheer, but for the most part, they were greeted with an indifference which had become almost endemic in Dublin. There always seemed to be men marching about the streets; yet noth-ing of bloody consequence had yet happened.

The mainstream of traffic halted as Connolly led his forces out into the great street. He took them across to the far side, then marched them briskly up towards Nelson Pillar. Some British cavalry officers standing outside the Metropole Hotel grinned broadly as they marched past. From the main door of the General Post Office, Second Lieutenant A. D. Chalmers of the 14th Royal Fusiliers caught sight of them and paused long enough to say to a friend, "Look at that awful crowd!" Then he pushed his way inside to send a telegram to his wife in London.

Thirty seconds later, the rebels had drawn abreast of the great building—a Palladian structure with Ionic columns supporting a stupendous classical pediment surmounted by the figures of Hibernia, Mercury, and Fidelity (known colloquially as the Three Apostles). Suddenly, in the hoarse, bitten-off shout of a regimental sergeant-major, Connolly gave the command, "Company halt! Left turn!" Then, as his men obeyed him, he let loose a shout aflame with the pent-up passion of a lifetime:

"The G.P.O. . . . charge!"

The whole incongruous column broke formation to hurl itself towards the great façade, rifles, pikes and bayonets swinging in short, bright, menacing arcs. They swept through the main doorway in a cheering, triumphant mob and spilled out over the marble floor. Behind the counters the staff froze at their positions, while the public, who had been drifting leisurely about the splendid office, halted bewildered. Lieutenant Chalmers, on the other hand, did not even bother to look round, and the first he knew of the rebel occupation was when he felt something sharp prod his backside. He turned to find a pike pointed straight at him, held by a scowling rebel who looked determined to run him through. He might easily have been spitted upon the archaic weapon had not Captain O'Reilly warned the pikeman sternly, "That's not at all necessary."

Then Connolly shouted, "Everybody out!"

Not surprisingly, no one took the order seriously. Indeed, a woman's voice could be heard loudly insisting that she wanted to buy stamps. But suddenly the staff stampeded; some, in their hurry, vaulting the counters, others running out without waiting to grab their hats or coats. Mr. D. A. Stoker, a Grafton Street jeweller, who had been standing outside the G.P.O. and had seen the rebels charge, actually decided to follow them into the building under the impression that they were making only a dummy attack. He managed to fight his way through the crowd flooding out, only to be brought up short by a youth who punched a revolver into his stomach.

"Get out!" said the youth.

"What's up?" asked Stoker incredulously.

"Hands up or I'll blow your heart out!" And Stoker found himself forced back towards the door.

Michael Collins left Plunkett, so ill that he had to support himself by leaning his arm on a wooden ledge, and crossed to the telegram counter where he informed Chalmers that he was a prisoner and would be searched. Chalmers, much concerned with retaining his dignity, submitted gracefully. Then, while Brennan Whitmore kept him covered, Collins crossed to a telephone booth in the centre of the office and yanked out the flex. With this he bound the Englishman, then lifting him on to his back, staggered across to the telephone booth and dumped him down inside it facing out towards Sackville Street.

Constable Dunphy of the D.M.P., also taken prisoner, had remained standing white-faced at the telegram counter, a rifle pointed at his chest, while Collins dealt with Chalmers. When he saw the big-shouldered Volunteer officer striding back, he called out, "Please don't shoot me. I've done no harm."

"We don't shoot prisoners," replied Collins curtly and ordered two Volunteers to take him upstairs and lock him in a room. As Dunphy was led away, he heard James Connolly ordering the rebels to "Smash the windows and barricade them."

For several minutes afterwards, the big main office was a place of furious destruction. Glass showered on the pavements outside as men drove their rifle butts through the great windows. Inevitably, a man staggered out of the mêlée, holding up a bleeding wrist. Pearse, exhilarated as anyone else, beamed at The O'Rahilly, then suddenly frowned as the latter informed him, "We haven't seized the telegraph instrument room yet." Pearse turned to a Volunteer named Michael Staines and ordered him to "Take six or seven men and occupy the second floor."

Staines led a small party up the wide staircase, meeting some girl telegraphists on their way down. One girl knew him and yelled, "That's the stuff to give them, Michael!" When the party reached the landing they found themselves looking down the muzzles of seven rifles. Instinctively a Volunteer fired and his shot luckily dropped the sergeant of the guard. The entire guard at once dropped their weapons.

"We've no ammunition!" shouted a corporal.

Staines checked their guns and ammunition pouches and found that this was true. He thereupon backed the six soldiers against a wall, and ordered two of his men to take the wounded sergeant to hospital. The sergeant, however, suddenly sat up and declared he had no intention of quitting his post. "Ah'm on guard here until sax o'clock this evening and I dinna leave ma post until ah'm relieved," he declared.

Staines did not argue. Leaving a guard on the obstinate Scot, he pushed on into the instrument room. The staff had left—except for the woman supervisor, another indomitable Scot. She, too, resolutely refused to leave.

"All right," rasped Staines impatiently. "Stay if you like, but don't touch those instruments!"

"Can't I send out these death telegrams?" the woman asked, pointing to a sheaf of messages.

"No. Some of my men will do that."

"Oh, then, in that case . . . !" she said, and angrily flounced past him.

Downstairs, the ground floor had by now become a shambles; tables, chairs, desks—anything solid or heavy—having been pushed under the windows. All along the front and sides of the big office the massive window-frames were empty. Men were standing on tables or desks, knocking out the upper panes. Others were busy piling books, ledgers, pads of money orders and even correspondence files into the empty window-frames, then flattening themselves down behind their piles to check what protection they gave. Brennan Whitmore, standing on a table, paused for a moment to wipe the sweat from his face. Beside him, Michael Collins smashed out a pane and a woman outside cried, "Glory be to God! Would you look at them smashing all the lovely windows!" Collins laughed boisterously, such an infectious laugh that within a moment half the Post Office was also laughing its head off. In the middle of the uproar somebody accidentally let off a shot, which ploughed its way into the ceiling.

Miss Carney had settled herself on a high stool behind the brass grille of a stamp counter where, an enormous Webley within reach, she began typing Connolly's orders. Sean T. O'Kelly stood by himself in the middle of the big room, waiting to be assigned duties, for although he held the rank of captain, he was not a military man, and had no idea how to initiate orders. On first entering the building, he had kept close to his protégé Pearse, having volunteered to act as his A.D.C. His duties, however, had proved light. All he had done was accompany Pearse upstairs for a talk with Tom Clarke and Sean MacDermott, fellow-members of the Provisional Government, then accompany him downstairs again.

"Are you busy, Sean?" shouted James Connolly.

"No, not at all," replied O'Kelly hopefully.

"Well, will you go to Liberty Hall and bring me back a couple of flags?"

"Glad to," said O'Kelly, and after being instructed where to find them, trotted off.

He returned shortly, carrying the traditional green flag of Ireland and the Republican tricolour of green, white and orange (signifying the union of Catholic Ireland with Protestant and Orange Ulster).

"Here!" said Connolly to a Volunteer officer. "Have these hoisted up on the flagpoles."

O'Kelly sauntered outside to view the effect. He watched the tiny figures of Volunteers suddenly appear above the massive tympanum bearing the Royal Arms of England, watched them move across to the left-hand corner of the roof and fumble around there for a moment. The big crowd standing behind him in Sackville Street gazed up in fascination, anxious not to miss a move which might cast light on this whole extraordinary and rather puzzling affair. For an instant the flag rested at the top of the flagpole, a dark, nondescript blob, then it broke out jerkily at the masthead—only to flap down listlessly in the warm midday air. A few half-hearted, half-mystified cheers greeted its appearance. It was not until a sudden breeze stirred it gently that anybody could make out what it was—a green flag on which was written in bold Gaelic lettering, half-gold, half-white, the quite incredible legend:

IRISH REPUBLIC

2

IRELAND—which has probably the oldest continuing national conscious-ness of any nation in Western Europe—had always been a puzzle and a source of continual anxiety, not only to Dublin Castle, but to every English Government for centuries. Not that England was in Ireland for any reason other than for Ireland's own good—or so Englishmen liked to think. As far back as the reign of Henry II, Pope Adrian IV, the only Englishman ever to sit on the throne of St. Peter, had recognized the chaotic state of the country and the inability of the Irish to govern themselves, and had issued a Bull bestowing the island upon those who could undoubtedly run it better. Yet, good Catholics though they were—and few had been more tenacious over the centuries for what they believed—the Irish had somehow or other never been able to accept the legality of England's conquest.

They had almost rid themselves of the incubus during the reign of the first Elizabeth, but the eventual failure of the great Hugh O'Neill, Earl of Tyrone, after years of continual victories, had led in the end to the break-up of that ancient Gaelic order whose roots lay in pre-historic society. Worse, it had led to a policy of annexation and colonization by successive English governments so that eventually two Irelands emerged—that of the English landowners (the Anglo-Irish) and that of the dispossessed natives. But although appar-ently well and truly tamed by the end of the sixteenth century, twice in the seventeenth and again in the eighteenth century the country had risen in rebellion. Napoleon, indeed, was to lament that he had not attacked England by landing in Ireland, where he would have been warmly received, instead of wasting his time in Egypt. By the 1840s, however, such was the way in which war, waste and conquest and the stoutly-resisted Act of Union with England and Scotland of 1801 had operated upon the country, that the Irish had become the poorest people in Europe. Even the Duke of Wellington could say: "There never was a country in which poverty existed to so great a degree." This was the age of the Anglo-Irish rakes; rapacious landlords who, on the one hand built elegant Palladian mansions and Grecian temples, planted innumerable avenues of glorious trees opening onto vistas of glitter-ing fountains, and on the other gulped down such oceans of claret in the evenings that they could only sprawl senseless in their own vomit; an age when rich men quarrelled and duelled at the rear of coffee houses, gamed and wenched in common ale houses and, for bloody excitement, matched gor-geously-apparelled fighting cocks; erecting the whole grand edifice of extrav-agant living upon rents which rose higher and higher even as the population of the country mounted. This was a time when Ireland presented "the extra-ordinary spectacle of a country in which wages and employment, practically speaking, did not exist. There were no industries; there were very few towns; there were almost no farms large enough to employ labour . . . greens were unknown, bread was unknown, ovens were unknown. The butcher, the baker, the grocer, did not exist; tea, candles and coals were unheard of." (*The Reason Why*, by Cecil Woodham-Smith.) Men lived on patches of land for which they paid preposterous rents and grew potatoes as their only crop. On this diet alone the population somehow managed to thrive—from some four millions in the second half of the eighteenth century, it grew to over eight millions by the 1840s. Then the crop failed; and, within ten years, two mil-lion Irish had vanished—either into the towns and prairies of America or into their coffins. By the start of the twentieth century a further two millions had emigrated, leaving the population at half its pre-Famine level.

Three times in the bustling, expanding nineteenth century—a time of unparalleled misery for the farming people of Ireland—the wilder spirits made a protest in arms. Each was hardly more than a skirmish, a brush with authority, a puny thing bordering on farce. Their objective, stripped of all qualifications and reservations, was the end of English rule. The twentieth century, however, opened with hope. There seemed an excellent chance that a Home Rule Bill might at last be granted; and this, it was felt on both sides of the Irish Sea, small measure of local government though it might be, would appease all Irish national sentiment. In addition, the attractions of English social and commercial order, now that they were being more fully extended to Ireland, had helped to soften many of the more bitter memories. The lifting of penalties against Catholics; the disestablishment of the Protestant Church of Ireland; the efforts of Englishmen such as the Liberal Gladstone, with his three attempts to push Home Rule Bills through Parliament, and of the Tory George Wyndham, whose Land Act had converted the peasants into a class of small proprietors, had all had their inevitable effect. The Famine became only a dark remembrance; the land agitation, with its evictions and boycotts, a matter for history. Great Protestant names such as Wolfe Tone, Robert Emmet, Dean Swift, Oliver Goldsmith and Charles Stewart Parnell became enshrined as those of national heroes and adornments. Catholic Irishmen received their own university. Self-governing boards, divorced from the control of Dublin Castle, were set up in various counties. Wealthy people began to act and think as the English upper classes did, and the British Army found a fertile recruiting ground among those of a more idle and less imagi-native character. In the minds of the majority of English and Irish people, therefore, in the first decade of the twentieth century, Ireland had at last become an integral part of the United Kingdom; Dublin as much a British city as Manchester or Leeds, Edinburgh or Cardiff. A sixth of the House of Commons at Westminster were Irish members and Home Rule had become the great moral touchstone of British politics. At long last it began to look as though the two countries were about to embark upon a new era of mutual respect and goodwill.

There were only three things amiss with this otherwise beautifully ordered picture. The British Conservative Party were against any kind of independence for Ireland; the Protestant Orangemen, who had enjoyed a local majority in the four north-eastern counties since the great Plantation of 1603 (when the lands of the Irish had been seized and given to the English or Scottish settlers), believed that Home Rule meant Rome Rule—to which hell, of course, was preferable; and there were young men in the rest of Ireland who still resented any integration of their country at all into Britain's political and economic structure and the consequent disappearance of their own nationality. The seeds of action lay with the Conservatives. As far back as 1885 when Gladstone was preparing his Home Rule Bill, Lord Randolph Churchill, father of Sir Winston, had offered the opinion that, "if the G.O.M. [Grand Old Man, i.e., Gladstone] went for Home Rule, the Orange card would be the one to play. Please God it may turn out the ace of trumps and not the two." Gladstone, of course, did go for Home Rule and the Tories played their trump. The north Irish Orangemen (a society named for the Protestant champion, William of Orange, who defeated James II at the Battle of the Boyne in 1690) were stirred to fury by a succession of demagogic meetings and made it plain that they would not stomach Home Rule at any price. The House of Lords, as might have been expected, adopted a similar attitude and Gladstone's Bill was aborted.

In 1905, however, an Irishman of Welsh descent called Arthur Griffith, round-faced, pince-nezed, brushily-moustached, a journalist by trade, inspired by ideas which had enabled Hungary to achieve autonomy within the Austro-Hungarian empire, published a revolutionary proposal. The Hungarians had gained their objectives by refusing to send representatives to the parliament in Vienna; the Irish should follow their example and ignore Westminster. Members of Parliament could begin by withdrawing from Westminster and setting up an Irish Council; after that, Irish courts, banks, a civil service, a stock exchange, could be established to function alongside their British counterparts until the latter withered away through lack of use. The King of England, of course, could remain King of Ireland—in a Dual Monarchy—but that would be all. Griffith named this policy Sinn Fein (pronounced Shinn Fain) whose literal meaning is "Ourselves"—that is, "We rely on ourselves."

His proposals were received enthusiastically by several disparate groups of Irishmen who at that time were vaguely groping towards a better Ireland. All, at least, were anxious to make sure that Ireland did not lose its separate identity. There were those who wanted to see a revival of the Gaelic language (Gaelic had ceased to be the spoken language of most of the country at the beginning of the nineteenth century) and of the native culture of the Golden

Age. Others merely looked for a political and economic policy which would lift Ireland from her trough of poverty. Still others could only recall the misdeeds of England down through the centuries and feel themselves less than men because they were not free to rule themselves. All found in the principles of Sinn Fein some expression of their aspirations. Far more important for Ireland eventually, however, was the interest displayed in Griffith and his ideas by two militant organizations. The first was the Irish Republican Brotherhood, a secret society formed in the United States in 1857 and intimately linked with Clan na Gael, an open Irish-American organization. The second was the Irish Transport and General Workers' Union; housed in the worst slums in Europe and paid farcical wages, the victims of police oppression and frequent brutality, these trade unionists, militant and tough, supported the idea of a separate Ireland. Yet everything might have remained just a matter of talk and argument and general old blether if it had not been for two significant developments.

When, in 1911, the Liberal Party again found itself in power in Great Britain, it had a majority so small (forty-three) that, without the support of the Irish Party's eighty-four members, it would not have found it possible to govern at all. As the price of his support John Redmond, leader of the Irish Party, demanded that the Government introduce another Home Rule Bill; this time it could not fail as Gladstone's had, because concurrent legislation—the Parliament Bill—would be introduced making it impossible for the Lords to block any measure which had passed the Commons three times. The Tories responded to this development with a terrible vehemence. They enlisted the services of Sir Edward Carson, K.C., who set about arousing a new generation of Orangemen. In a grand gesture of sheer theatricality "King" Carson persuaded 80,000 Belfastmen to sign a Solemn League and Covenant against Home Rule, some of them in their own blood (many Englishmen did the same later). Then he organized them into the Ulster Volunteers, an independently armed, drilled and disciplined body—probably the most significant action to occur in Ireland since the eighteenth century. Finally, with the direct encouragement of Mr. Bonar Law, the Canadian-born leader of the Conservative Party (whose forebears had been born in Ulster), he and his Orangemen pledged themselves to resist Home Rule by force. They announced that they would fight the United Kingdom in order to *remain part* of the United Kingdom—which was being a great deal more Irish than the Irish themselves. They even went so far as to set up the skeleton of their own Provisional Government to take over and administer "Ulster" as an integral part of the United Kingdom.

Suddenly civil war threatened not only Ireland but even Great Britain herself. British Army officers debated whether to refuse any orders which directed them to take action against Ulster. Churchill, First Lord of the Admiralty and—in contradistinction to his father—a supporter of Home Rule, ordered the Third Battle Squadron to stations off the west coast of Scotland, reportedly threatening that if Belfast showed fight, he "would have the town in ruins in twenty-four hours." In the Curragh, Co. Kildare (the main camp for the British Army in Ireland), fifty-eight senior officers "mutinied", that is, they declared they would accept dismissal rather than fight against Ulster. And then the Orangemen smuggled in 3,000 German rifles and 3,000,000 rounds of ammunition.

The time was April 1914. In Berlin, Kaiser Wilhelm II and his advisers watched the unfolding drama with keenest interest. Deep in the mire of unresolvable Irish politics, irregular armies stumping about all over the place threatening civil war or revolution, the regular armed forces mutinous and disobedient, the two great political parties ready to fling themselves at each other's throat, England appeared to have her hands much too full to intervene with the dramatic situation then unfolding in the Balkans. In August, therefore, the Kaiser cast the fatal die in support of his ally, the Austrian Emperor— a month after a conference of all parties concerned with Ireland, called by King George at Buckingham Palace, had broken down in immutable intransigence.

Long before this, of course, the southern Irish had delightedly responded to the challenge thrown down by "King" Carson. "There is only one thing more ridiculous than the sight of an Orangeman with a rifle and that is a Nationalist without one," declared Pearse. If it were legal for Orangemen to take up arms and defy the Government, then surely it must be legal for southern Catholics to take them up in its defence. The South decided to form its own "armies".

In the field first were the Dublin trade unionists. Led by James Larkin, a great hulking man of extraordinary eloquence, and James Connolly, his first lieutenant, they formed the Irish Citizen Army. Originally intended to be simply a protective force against the Dublin Metropolitan Police, it was not until Larkin went to America in 1914, leaving Connolly to take command, that the Citizen Army began to be trained seriously as a revolutionary body. At his headquarters in Liberty Hall Connolly pored over the great insurrectionary battles of Paris and Moscow. He set up a rifle club, to which his men contributed sixpence a week. He bought guns illegally from British soldiers of the Dublin garrison. He got his women helpers to stitch and sew the Army's dark green uniforms. He led route marches through the streets of Dublin in defiance of the police, and mounted dummy attacks against prominent public buildings. With the assistance of ex-regular army N.C.O.s and reservists, he rapidly made his Citizen Army a small, tough, creditably efficient force.

The poets and professors, the intellectuals and professional men—all the "advanced nationalists"—but above all, the Irish Republican Brotherhood, were also stirred to action. In November 1913, they founded the Irish Volunteers, electing Eoin MacNeill, the eminently respectable Professor of Early Irish History at University College Dublin, President of the Executive Committee and Chief of Staff. But, without MacNeill's knowledge, three key members of the I.R.B., Patrick Pearse, Sean MacDermott and Eamonn Ceannt, managed to get themselves elected to the Committee. Cynically they planned to take over the whole organization eventually, and use it as a revolutionary weapon. Left to themselves, they had little hope of gaining sufficient adherents to form even the tiniest of "armies", for most Irishmen had forsworn methods of violence. Joining the Volunteers, however, appeared to be a different matter—violence seemed only implicit—and by the end of 1913 membership had risen to 10,000. Redmond, jealous of the organization's increasing power and influence, demanded a share in its control and, when his nominees were finally admitted to the Executive Committee, membership quickly reached 160,000. The Volunteers, in fact, appeared to be such a respectable body—their field commander was Colonel Maurice Moore, brother of the novelist, George Moore—that when they marched through the streets of Dublin in their light-green uniforms and their stiff-peaked caps (or those of them who could afford a uniform), the Castle authorities, if they hardly relished the sight, could discover little cause for alarm. Particularly as the organization had few arms and little hope of getting more following the embargo which had been imposed after the Orangemen's exploit.

Yet, a month before general war broke out in Europe, the Volunteers managed to run in 1,500 Mauser rifles and 49,000 rounds of ammunition (most of it "explosive" stuff outlawed by international convention and therefore unusable). This cargo was landed at Howth, the landing being followed by an incident when regular troops opened fire on a crowd of jeering women and children—an incident which looked likely to spark off an explosion. By now, too, Parliament had passed Home Rule and the Bill needed only the formality of the Royal Assent. Mr. Asquith's Government suddenly found itself facing a dilemma which had long been inevitable; either they had to impose the Bill on the whole country at once—and therefore clash with the Orangemen; or, by means of an Amending Bill, exclude "Ulster" for the time being—in which case they could expect trouble from the already incensed Irish Volunteers. Before the shotguns could go off in Ireland, however, a greater cataclysm was to divert men's minds elsewhere. On August 4th, 1914, the Kaiser at last launched his armies against defenceless Belgium.

In the House of Commons that dark and dreadful day, Sir Edward Grey, the Foreign Secretary, felt able to announce: "The one bright spot in the very dreadful situation is Ireland. The position in Ireland—and this is a thing I should like to be clearly understood abroad, is not a consideration among the things we have to take into account."

Grey had every reason to believe that what he said was true. The Ulster leaders, through Bonar Law, had at once pledged themselves to call off their Home Rule revolt and to support the Government loyally—at least for the duration. John Redmond was driven to feel he could only say something equally generous. So he jumped to his feet to suggest that Britain could safely withdraw her forces from Ireland and leave the defence of the island to the

Volunteers. This announcement was misinterpreted by an emotionally-charged Commons as a pledge of absolute Irish support for the war. As for the contentious Home Rule Bill—well, all parties were agreed that it should be deferred, and the arguments about it dropped.

Redmond had no doubts as to where Ireland's real interests lay. He believed that Irishmen should support Britain and the British Empire to the hilt—thereby demonstrating a loyalty and friendship which was certain to be rewarded when the guns were eventually stilled. His subsequent recruiting speeches proved persuasive enough. Some two divisions of Irish troops voluntarily agreed to go to France.

Yet power to speak for Ireland was already passing from the parliamentarians. At a meeting held on September 5th, 1914, the Supreme Council of the Irish Republican Brotherhood decided upon an insurrection and agreed to accept whatever assistance Germany was prepared to render them. No specific date for an uprising was fixed other, it was agreed, than that it should take place (1) if the Germans invaded Ireland, (2) if the English tried to force conscription on the country or (3) if the war looked like coming to an end. The insurrection was to be accompanied by a declaration of war on Britain and a demand that the Provisional Government be represented as the envoys of a belligerent nation at the Peace Conference which must inevitably follow the end of international hostilities.

British authority in Ireland at this time rested primarily upon the shoulders of three men. The first was young Ivor Churchill Guest, Baron Wimborne, a Liberal peer who had only recently been appointed Lord Lieutenant (or Viceroy) and who, as the Monarch's personal representative, lived in opulent state at Vice-Regal Lodge, driving through Dublin in an open carriage escorted by Household Cavalry and Hussars. Like the Sovereign, however, he possessed no executive authority and functioned only as a figure-head—a role against which he kicked frequently and vociferously.

The two men who really bossed Ireland, in fact, were the Chief Secretary, Mr. Augustine Birrell, a genial politician and litterateur, and his assistant Sir Matthew Nathan, the Under-Secretary, a former Governor of Hong Kong and an ex-Chairman of the Board of Inland Revenue. Until the war broke out Birrell had appeared to be handling Ireland with a quite superlative skill, possessing as he did a genuine regard for the country and its people—a feeling reciprocated by most Irishmen. In his seven years of office he had pushed fifty-six Bills through Parliament dealing specifically with improvements in Irish agriculture, housing and education. He had given Catholics their first university. And invariably he had treated North and South, Catholic and Protestant alike, refusing to countenance the invidious distinctions which former Chief Secretaries had done. In addition, he enjoyed a reputation for geniality and wit in a country bursting with genial wits. When he proclaimed that "Orangemen have no more religion than a billiard ball," all Southern

Ireland burst with laughter. The worst his Irish opponents could say of him was that he was "trying to kill Home Rule with kindness."

The chief difficulty facing Dublin Castle by 1916 was the fierce opposition by the Irish people to any threat of military conscription. Young Irishmen evinced an understandable reluctance to sacrifice their lives for a nation towards which they felt no loyalty. Those who appreciated exactly what the struggle between Germany and Great Britain was about wanted no part of it; while the attitude of the rest is perhaps best summed up in a statement issued by Bishop O'Dwyer of Limerick after a party of Irish men and women emigrating to America had been jeered and cat-called at Liverpool docks as shirkers: "Their crime is that they are not ready to die for England. Why should they? What have they or their forebears ever got from England that they should die for her? This war may be just or unjust, but any fair-minded man will admit that it is England's war, not Ireland's." It was a view which became more popular as Britain's military position grew increasingly parlous and the enormous wastage of manpower on the battlefields of France caused British politicians and military leaders to cast about for new sources of manpower. In England thousands of young men of military age had to be exempted from duty because they were skilled workers; the Irish, for the most part, were technologically unskilled, and would therefore make ideal cannon fodder. In the last weeks of 1915 over two thousand young men, apprised of these facts, enrolled in the Irish Volunteers, and it became increasingly clear that any attempt to introduce conscription would be resisted, if necessary, with violence.

By now Redmond and his party had broken away and had formed their own organization, the National Volunteers, which, rather ironically, attracted by far the larger number of members. The rump, still calling themselves the Irish Volunteers, rapidly grew more vocal and belligerent under the direction of the I.R.B. Organizers such as MacDermott stumped the country, spreading violent anti-British and anti-recruiting propaganda, helping to break up recruiting meetings and promising young hotheads that a "day of action" was coming soon. Newspapers and magazines—they included publications such as the *Spark, Honesty, Scissors & Paste*—published material which Dublin Castle could only regard as out and out pro-German propaganda. Plunkett's *Irish Review*, for instance, described the war as a "blessing" and said that it "approved" the possible "conquest" of Ireland by Germany. Alongside defaced British recruiting posters, fresh newspaper bills appeared all over Dublin announcing "England's Last Ditch", "England's Growing Hypocrisy" and similar sentiments.

Mr. Birrell, as a member of the Imperial Cabinet, naturally found it incumbent to spend most of his time in London. His visits to Dublin had become increasingly rare and were, in fact, generally undertaken only at holiday times, drawing a complaint from the *Irish Times* that he was not earning his £4,000 a year salary. In Dublin Sir Matthew Nathan, upon whom the day-to-day running of the country devolved, tried to do what he could to keep agitation within bounds—short of attempting to disarm the Volunteers or arrest their leaders. He closed down one seditious newspaper after another, only to find them reopening under other names. He prosecuted full-time organizers of the Irish Volunteers such as Terence MacSwiney for seditious utterances, only to see an Irish magistrate let him off with a shilling fine. He banned the import of all arms and ammunition, only to discover that he had no means of preventing English firms importing what they liked (on one occasion an innocent looking case labelled "Hardware" dispatched from a reputable firm in Sheffield to a respectable firm in Dublin was found to contain five hundred bayonets). But, on the whole, he set his course by Mr. Birrell's policy, which was to do as little as possible to upset the delicate balance of order in Ireland. Yet he had himself seen proof that the Volunteers were growing increasingly more cocksure. On St. Patrick's Day, 1916 they had commandeered the entire centre of Dublin to stage a march past their Chief of Staff, behaving on this occasion with the contemptuous assurance of men who believed they could seize the whole city if they wanted to.

And then, on the night of March 20th, the guns finally blazed. The incident occurred in the town of Tullamore, about 45 miles from Dublin. The trouble had begun on the 19th when some young men jeered the 7th Leinster Regiment as it departed for France. The crowd turned on them and the following night, waving Union Jacks, converged on a local nationalist hall and stoned it. The defenders replied with shots, which brought the local police to the scene, and in the ensuing fracas some thirty shots were exchanged. Even Sir Matthew was shaken. Major-General L. B. Friend, G.O.C. Irish Command, at once ordered a detachment of infantry to stand by to raid Liberty Hall. But before General Friend could precipitate a widespread clash of arms, Mr. Birrell had dispatched an angry countermanding order from London.

Even when Major Price, early in April, produced a copy of a letter which had fallen into his hands, written by an advanced nationalist to a friend abroad and hinting at an early insurrection, Sir Matthew had no hesitation in writing in the margin: "The outbreak in the summer I look upon as vague talk." The Chief Secretary was more emphatic. "The whole letter is rubbish!" he wrote in the margin. He could foresee nothing but a few small outbreaks of home-made bomb-throwing, he said. Yet drills and marches became more frequent; noisy demonstrations were staged against the deportation of minor figures; articles were published in the Irish Volunteers' official organ or Connolly's *Workers' Republic* telling men how to fight in the streets or to conduct guerrilla warfare in open country.

From his imposing suite in Phoenix Park, where he could gaze out of the graceful windows and glimpse, over the tops of the trees, a memorial to yet another man of destiny, Wellington, who had actually been born in the country, Lord Wimborne almost daily bombarded Nathan with reminders that they were all sitting on a powder-keg. Repeatedly Sir Matthew replied that it was not possible to bring charges which would stick in any court; that there was nothing in the Defence Regulations designed to cover the situation. Sir Matthew probably hoped that the storm would blow itself out. Yet these hopes should have been dashed finally on Spy Wednesday, April 19th, 1916. On that day a Dublin newspaper attempted to publish a document which it claimed had been copied from the official files of the Castle. It gave specific details of a directive signed by General Friend, ordering an extensive swoop on all Volunteer premises in Dublin. The censor killed the story at once, but that afternoon an Alderman Kelly, who was handed the document by the newspaper's editor, read it out to a meeting of the Dublin Corporation. His action produced immediate uproar, the document being regarded as proof that the Castle desired to provoke an insurrection so that the British Government might be absolved from its obligation to implement Home Rule when the war ended. Sir Matthew, of course, realized that the document was a forgery, but did not guess its portent. The document, in fact, was not really directed at the Castle at all and indeed came near to achieving its real end. Professor MacNeill—who, all along, had been adamantly against any violence unless the Government *first* moved against the Volunteers—convinced that there was a crisis at hand, issued a general order to all Volunteers to stand ready to defend themselves and their arms. The right atmosphere for violence had thus been shrewdly induced.

Sir Matthew should have understood what was happening particularly in view of an Admiralty message which had flopped onto his desk five days before; this had stated baldly that "a German ship and escort had left on the 12th, was due to arrive on the 21st, and that a rising had been planned for Easter Eve," but had added, "the Admiralty is sceptical of such an intention."

Wimborne had found the message so vague that he was left with the impression that the ship was coming from America. Anyhow, he did nothing. Nathan, of course—as usual—decided to take no action. The casual manner in which the message arrived, too, did nothing to help either man. General Friend received it from General Stafford, C.-in-C. Southern Ireland, who got it, again apparently quite casually, from the Admiral Commanding at Queenstown. No one appreciated that it was a vital intercept of messages passing between Clan na Gael in New York and the German Foreign Office in Berlin, an intercept secured by Naval Intelligence's Room 40—that famous room where Captain (later Admiral Sir) Reginald Hall and his brilliant team of cypher experts had cracked the German codes; where everything passing between the German Embassy in Washington and the Foreign Office in the Wilhelmstrasse had long been an open book.

3

PHYSICALLY, for heroes, the men who led the Irish insurrection were a quite extraordinary bunch. One would be hard put to find a more unlikely-looking collection of revolutionaries anywhere. Clarke was a small, frail man, broken in health after fifteen years of confinement in an English jail and aged fifty-eight; Pearse, tall and full of the dignity of his own destiny, was squint-eyed; MacDermott, dark-haired and almost handsome, limped as a result of polio; and Plunkett was a helpless figure suffering from glandular tuberculosis of the throat who was about to die anyway. Of the three remaining members of the Provisional Government, only James Connolly possessed that robust health and tough, overpowering dynamism which are the usual marks of a true leader. Without Clarke and MacDermott, however, it is highly unlikely that there would have been any insurrection at all, for these two men were its main architects—Clarke the old revolutionary master, MacDermott his zealous pupil. In his own person Clarke was a living link with the revolutionary effort of the previous generation, the dynamitards of the 1880s. Sunken-cheeked, wearing cheap glasses and with a drooping, seedy moustache, he looked for all the world like a downtrodden clerk or, at the best, a petty shopkeeper—which is exactly what he was. Yet he was the most singularly dedicated of all the rebel leaders and generated enormous driving force. On his release from an English prison in the 1890s he had gone to the United States, where he might easily have remained for the rest of his life. Once home again, he had become the focal point, the doyen, the old man of wisdom, the ancient prophet, the unresting force.

His greatest friend and ally was Sean MacDermott, who had begun life as a barman. MacDermott proved to be an intelligent and articulate speaker, possessing splendid energy and zeal. Perhaps his greatest asset, however, was his simple charm—years later, he was still remembered in Dublin as "a delightful man." Yet he was also a person of hard and practical common sense. As a paid organizer of the Irish Volunteers (salary £150 per annum), he travelled about the countryside speaking on the aims of Sinn Fein and the I.R.B., and enrolling young men. It was a key position which enabled him to appoint members of the Brotherhood to many of the top Volunteer commands. When the rising came, such men, it was intended, would take their orders directly from Pearse and, if necessary, ignore MacNeill.

Thomas MacDonagh was a Professor of English at the National University and a stylish minor poet and dramatist whose presence among the rebel leaders has helped to lend the Irish Rebellion, in retrospect, a certain poetic ambience. By nature he was an excitable and temperamental little man given too much perhaps to exaggerated gestures and mannerisms, often maybe a trifle too flamboyant, even arrogant. His moods alternated between gloom and high exultation; psychological jargon today might classify him a manic-depressive. Normally, however, his conversation was rapid and full of learning and wit, though perhaps his poetry reveals more truly the man. It shows him inwardly as full of gloom, as one who had the death wish. Indeed, he once wrote a poem called "The Suicide."

He was not, at the outset, a man who particularly wanted to be a rebel. When Irish Home Rule once again became an important issue in British politics he was a happily-married man with a young son, Donagh (later a well-known playwright), and a predominating interest in European literature plus a half-hearted one in the revival of the Gaelic language. The attempts of the Conservative Party to block Home Rule, however, utterly incensed him and finally drove him along the path which led to the firing squad.

Joseph Mary Plunkett's father was a Papal Count and Director of the National Museum among many other honours and emoluments. The Plunketts had antecedents—a forebear was Saint Oliver Plunkett; kinsmen were Sir Horace Plunkett who reorganized Irish agriculture at the beginning of the century and Lord Dunsany, the writer. Plunkett and his two brothers, George and John, were imaginative and talented boys; early in life Joseph discovered an aptitude for excellent minor poetry. As boys they played a great deal with toy soldiers, and it was while planning imaginary military campaigns in the drawing-room that Joseph is said to have worked out the basis of the rebel strategy in Easter Week—although it is more probable that he found inspiration in earlier plans made by the United Irishmen in the eighteenth century and by Robert Emmet. Certainly he fancied himself as a military thinker. When he left Berlin in 1915, after paying a secret visit there to negotiate a cargo of arms, an exasperated member of the German General Staff was heard to declare: "That blowhard Plunkett! Imagine! He was trying to tell us how to conduct the war!"

Eamonn Ceannt (Edmund Kent) remains, perhaps, the most shadowy of all the rebel leaders. By trade he was a £300-a-year employee in the Treasurer's Department of the Dublin Corporation; a zealous and sensitive man who possessed a passionate love for the Gaelic language and for the uileann pipes. Dressed in a saffron kilt, he once gave a recital for the Pope.

Towering above all the others, however, stood Patrick Pearse and James Connolly—Pearse the young dreamer and idealist of whom many who knew him say, as of a saint: "He would never have made a success of anything in this life"; Connolly the tough socialist, the iron-willed man who would probably have gone out in rebellion with only a hundred men. At forty-six, Connolly was a thickset, round-faced, big-moustached, bandy-legged man, capable of producing the most blistering language, either with his pen or his tongue, and revelling in sheer audacity. From the age of eleven he had been forced to earn his own living, and his education, while not inconsiderable, came wholly as the result of voracious reading on his own account. When James Larkin, the Irish trade union pioneer, left Dublin for America in 1914, Connolly inherited both the Irish Transport and General Workers' Union and the infant Citizen Army, which marched under the proud banner of the Plough and the Stars. His first action when he became boss of Liberty Hall was to hang a banner outside, declaring: "We serve neither King nor Kaiser, only Ireland." A staunch believer in the equality of women, he would brook no distinctions in Liberty Hall; he even chose a woman to be one of his army commanders—Constance, Countess Markievicz, daughter of Sir Henry Gore-Booth, Bart., and a friend of the poet W. B. Yeats. By 1915 Connolly had converted part of Liberty Hall into a munitions factory, where he made bayonets, steel bars (for forcing doors) and bombs. His speeches and writings, meanwhile, underlined his determination to use them. So much so that the Republican Brotherhood became concerned. Scared that he might stage a small-scale effort on his own before they were ready ("What could he do by himself but stage a riot?" demanded Pearse, exasperated), they asked Connolly to meet them. The talks, held in a house in South Dublin, lasted for three days and in the end Connolly became a member of the Brotherhood and agreed that preparation for an insurrection should be conducted as a joint operation. Yet, strangely, the only result of this agreement was that, instead of becoming more discreet, Connolly's behaviour became increasingly reckless.

On Palm Sunday, April 16th, he staged an elaborate ceremony at which the old flag of Ireland—a golden harp upon a green background—was hoisted on to the roof of Liberty Hall. That day the entire Citizen Army paraded in full dress, while thousands of Dubliners cheered and wept openly as Miss Molly O'Reilly, her long red tresses dancing in the wind, climbed out on to the parapet and hauled on the lanyard which sent the flag billowing in the wind.

That night he delivered a last lecture to his troops on tactics. "I'm going to fight the way I want, not the way the enemy wants," he announced. "It'll be a new way, one the soldiers haven't been trained to deal with. We'll use the rooftops for a start. But remember this; if you do snipe your man, don't get enthusiastic and stand up and cheer, for if you do it'll probably be the last cheer you'll ever give." Then he reminded them: "The odds against are a thousand to one. But if we *should* win, hold on to your rifles because the Volunteers may have a different goal. Remember, we're out not only for political liberty but for economic liberty as well. So hold on to your rifles!"

It sounds incredible that Pearse went into battle knowing that Connolly had these reservations; yet Patrick Henry Pearse remains a most improbable insurgent leader. The thirty-six-year-old son of an Englishman (the family originally spelt the name Pierce), but born of an Irish mother, Pearse was an introspective idealist who, even from childhood, seems to have foreseen his tragic destiny. While still a boy, he once knelt down on a prie-dieu with his adoring brother Willie and swore an oath to some day "free Ireland or die fighting the English!" He grew up tall and well built, with a slightly stooping head and deep, profound eyes—the left one marred by a slight cast. What greatness, if any, he possessed was rarely apparent to anyone at first meeting: he was inclined to remain aloof and reserved unless he happened to be addressing a large body of people when the burning passion within him would then flood forth. It was largely because of his oratorical gifts that he eventually became prominent in nationalist politics. In private life he was an ascetic, neither drinking nor smoking, and normally restricting his social pleasures to the delights of good conversation and the tumultuous subject of Irish independence. Once MacDonagh managed to lure him to a music hall and, out of sheer irreverence, insisted on breaking into his embarrassed reveries with comments on the physical attractiveness of the young ladies on the stage.

"Begad, Pat, isn't that a fine leg?" said MacDonagh.
"Like the limb of an angel," agreed Pearse.
"What fine eyes, Pat," said MacDonagh.
"Indeed, indeed, the eyes of an angel," replied Pearse.
"Beautiful lassies," persisted MacDonagh, desperately.
"Angels, angels, every one," echoed Pearse, reverently.

Yet he had once managed to fall in love—and indeed treasured the memory of the girl all his life—his lost, drowned love, a young university student who had lost her life while bathing.

"O lovely head of the woman I loved
In the middle of the night I remember thee;
But reality returns with the sun's awakening
Alas, that the slender worm gnaws thee tonight."

And in a poem called "I Have Not Garnered Gold" he wrote:

"In love I got but grief
That withered my life."

Early in life he had become fascinated with the Gaelic language and with that lost culture of Ireland which once produced such visual masterpieces as the Book of Kells and the Cross of Cong. In young manhood he liked to dress himself as a tramp and go into far Connacht to study the ancient language and the people who still spoke it, and to take down some of the old songs and stories. He became rapt in this "beauty of the Irish world" until finally this half-legendary society dominated his very life and thoughts.

His great work was the establishment of St. Enda's, an experimental, bilingual school at Rathfarnham. He founded it as a protest against the existing National School system which, he said, was an English one, and not a very good English one at that, complaining that it was intended simply to turn all Irishmen into good little Britons. He described it as a worse offence against Ireland "even than the Famine", insisting that Irish education must possess a soul of its own, that it ought to mould Irish character as the English public school system moulded upper-class English character. In pursuit of his theories he covered the walls of St. Enda's with murals depicting the deeds of ancient Irish heroes, blazoning across them, too, the words attributed to Cuchulain (accurately echoing his own ambitions): "I care not though I were to live but one day and one night provided my fame and my deeds live after me." Here, then, he practised the most modern methods of bi-lingual teaching, dreaming that some day everybody in Ireland would speak two tongues, English and Irish; yet, even so, failure haunted him, and the school was deeply in debt when he marched out into Sackville Street. Shortly before Easter, 1916, confiding to a friend that he might be forced to close the school, he confessed that he hated the idea because he did not want to be pointed out in the streets of Dublin as a failure.

In 1912 Sean T. O'Kelly arranged for him to be formally enrolled in the I.R.B. By 1914, when the war had begun in Europe and the Home Rule Bill lay suspended, Pearse was declaring: "If the English trick us again there'll be war in Ireland; yes, by God! even if I have to lead it myself!" And shortly afterwards he wrote: "The European war has brought about a crisis which may contain, as yet hidden within it, the moment for which the generations have been waiting. It remains to be seen whether, if that moment reveals itself, we shall have the sight to see and the courage to do; or whether it shall be written of this generation, alone of all the generations of Ireland, that it had none among it who dared to make the ultimate sacrifice."

On another occasion he declared: "My God, rather than go on living as we are, I would prefer to see Dublin in ruins." Yet behind this bloody intention remained the gentle scholar: "Wouldn't it be a grand thing to have no ambition whatever and to be a clerk with £2 a week? Yes, I should enjoy that—no worries and at ease among my books."

Like Connolly, he realized from the outset that an insurrection was certain to prove a failure in a military sense. One afternoon in the winter of 1915, when he was standing in his own bedroom on the first floor of St. Enda's gazing out at the magnificent view which extended west to the Dublin mountains, his mother entered. He called her over and said: "How beautiful is all that has been created by God, mother! Look at the slanting sun and the play of its shadow on the hills." Then he moved to the middle of the room, talking about the flowers, the trees and the beautiful streams which ran through the grounds of the house.

"Soon, mother, that will be no more for me . . . for us. The day is coming when I shall be shot . . . swept away like that . . . and my colleagues, shot like me."

"And Little Man, our Willie?" asked his mother.

"Willie? Shot like the others, mother. We will all be shot."

In January 1916, as Director of Organization, he issued instructions to all battalions of the Irish Volunteers to prepare for special manoeuvres at Easter. As a result, MacNeill asked him directly if he were planning an insurrection and, on receiving an assurance that he was not, returned to his medieval studies. He should have known his man better. He should have remembered Pearse's words at the graveside of O'Donovan Rossa, an old Fenian whose body had been brought back from America in 1915 for burial: "Life springs from death and from the graves of patriot men and women spring living nations. The Defenders of this Realm have worked well in secret and in the open. They think they have pacified Ireland. They think they have purchased half of us and intimidated the other half. They think they have foreseen everything, think they have provided against everything; but the fools, the fools, the fools!—they have left us our Fenian dead, and while Ireland holds these graves, Ireland unfree shall never be at peace."

Up until Thursday, April 20th, then, the great insurrection promised to be a really serious and impressive affair. If every Irish Volunteer answered the call, 10,000 would be in action. If, in addition, once the fighting had started, Redmond's National Volunteers would join in—as was hoped—then there would be over 100,000 men under arms.

Yet, as events transpired, Pearse and Connolly were to march into action with only two hundred men of the Citizen Army and less than a tenth of the full membership of the Irish Volunteers. Plunkett's military plan for Dublin alone, on the other hand, called for at least 5,000 men. In addition, they were to march out short of modern rifles and ammunition and without even a machine-gun. Until Holy Thursday, however, they had every reason to believe that once the fighting began they would have plenty of material, for they looked forward to receiving a substantial cargo of arms and ammunition, *including artillery*, from Germany. Besides which, they still hoped—against admittedly forlorn hope—that the Germans might land an expeditionary force.

The original overall plan had hinged primarily on the successful landing of the German arms in the south-west of Ireland and the denial of the ports of Dublin and Kingstown to the Government by the deployment of at least one German submarine—whose efforts they themselves intended to reinforce by sinking blockships. The arms themselves were earmarked for the provincial battalions, most of which were even more abysmally supplied than the Dublin units (in the County Limerick, for instance, some Volunteers possessed only enough ammunition to sustain a five-minute action). When the provincial battalions had been at least satisfactorily armed, their task then was to establish a line based roughly on the River Shannon and from there advance upon Dublin, reducing military and police barracks piecemeal as they marched. Although an ambitious strategy, this was considered feasible enough because the British Army in wartime Ireland stood well below full strength.

In the capital itself the principal buildings were to be seized and a series of fortresses established in an inverted crescent across the southern suburbs of the city, commanding the roads and railways by which military reinforcements would enter the capital. If pressure ultimately proved to be too strong, these fortress garrisons were to fall back upon G.H.Q., and in case that, too, eventually failed to hold, a line of retreat would be held open northwards as far as the County Tyrone, where a link up with northern units would be made and the fight developed into guerrilla warfare in open country. As a socialist, Connolly, of course, firmly believed that a capitalist government would never dare to use artillery because of damage to property, and this view eventually became a cardinal tenet of rebel strategy. Joyously, therefore, his Citizen Army could parade through the streets of Dublin in the week before Easter, bravely singing:

> "We've got the guns and ammunition
> We know how to use them well,
> And when we meet the Saxon
> We'll drive them all to hell.
> We've got to free our country
> And to avenge all those who fell,
> And our cause is marching on.
> Glory, glory to old Ireland,
> Glory, glory to our sireland,
> Glory to the memory
> Of those who fought and fell,
> And we still keep marching on."

4

A BORED BRITISH seaman patrolling the south-west of Ireland during Easter, 1916, finally summed up his desolate environment as "nothing but rocks, sea and Sinn Feiners." The British Admiralty, however, knew a great deal better than that.

On February 10th, 1916, Von Skal, a member of the German Ambassador's staff in Washington, had sent a dispatch to an agent in Rotterdam containing an extract from a letter written by John Devoy from New York and intended for the German Government. In this Devoy, a former Fenian and the head of Clan na Gael, had reported: "Unanimous opinion is that action cannot be postponed much longer. It has therefore been decided to begin action on Easter Saturday. Unless entirely new circumstances arise you must have your arms and ammunition landed between Good Friday and Easter Saturday. Expect German help immediately after." On March 4th the German Foreign Office replied by cable to its Washington Embassy: "Between 20th and 23rd April, two or three steamers could land 20,000 rifles, ten machine-guns with ammunition in Tralee Bay. Irish pilot boat to meet trawlers at dusk north of island of Inishtooskert at entrance of Tralee Bay and show two green lights close to each other at short intervals." Three weeks later another cable had reaffirmed that "three trawlers with a small cargo steamer capable of carrying 1,400 tons will be sent." This message also stated that, beginning from April 8th, Mauen wireless station would broadcast every midnight the codeword "Finn"—meaning that the cargo had started—or the word "Bran" if a hitch had occurred. In reply to this Devoy had dispatched urgent messages on March 18th, 19th and 20th asking that Easter Sunday be fixed as the date for the delivery of arms and inquiring about the possibility of a submarine being sent to Dublin Bay. There was also a suggestion that Germany should try to land troops "possibly from an airship." This had drawn the tart reply from Berlin: "Sending German submarines to Dublin harbour impossible. Landing troops equally out of the question."

On March 21st, the German Admiralty had finally decided to send only one ship, and had selected the man to command her. He was Lieutenant Karl Spindler of the Imperial Naval Reserve; the ship was the *Libau* (formerly the *Castro*, an impounded Allied vessel). On April 9th, the *Libau*, masquerading as the *Aud*, a neutral Norwegian, set sail from Lubeck. Three days later Sir Roger Casement, with two companions, left Wilhelmshaven in a submarine.

Admiral Sir Lewis Bayley, C.-in-C. Queenstown, had a shrewd idea of what was impending, thanks to Room 40. From St. Patrick's Day (March 17th) onwards, in fact, he had instituted special precautions along the west coast of Ireland. He had ordered an array of sloops to lie out to sea in a wide intercepting arc and smaller craft to constantly scour every inlet and river mouth along the highly indented coastline. On Holy Thursday, in addition, he dispatched the cruiser H.M.S. *Gloucester*, plus three destroyers of the Grand Fleet, to watch for any vessel acting suspiciously.

The *Aud* took her time about reaching Ireland. First steaming through the Kattegat and the Skaggerak, she then steered up the North Sea to where the meridian of Greenwich intersects the Arctic Circle, in order to evade British blockage patrols. On her run down towards Ireland she was scrutinized by a British warship but not stopped, the disguise working perfectly. Passing Rockall, she again came under surveillance, but was once more allowed to proceed. At 4.15 p.m. on April 20th she finally reached Inishtooskert, a small uninhabited island in the north-west corner of Tralee Bay, where she was due to rendezvous with Casement's U-boat. Spindler saw nothing of the submarine, however, and after a half-hour's wait steamed into the Bay. When dusk fell he began flashing a signal towards the shore but to his consternation received no reply from the darkened, sleeping Fenit. For some hours he sailed about the Bay, repeating the signal at intervals, but when the coastline still stubbornly remained in darkness he finally dropped anchor at 1.30 a.m. in the lee of Inishtooskert, realizing that somehow or other the plans had miscarried.

Then, as Good Friday dawned, his luck at last ran out. An armed trawler, *Setter II*, spotting him, drew alongside. Spindler kept his head admirably, however, and decided to try bluffing the Englishman. He explained to *Setter's* captain that he had been forced to anchor because his engine had broken down. Then he showed forged papers, which appeared convincing enough. Finally, he opened up part of his cargo and showed pots and pans catalogued in the ship's manifest. The suspicions of the Englishman were lulled and he bade Spindler a cheery good-bye and resumed patrol. The German, grateful for his escape, decided to wait until darkness, then move out into the Atlantic and make for Lisbon. Soon after 1 p.m., however, he received another palpable shock. He saw a small steamer racing towards him from the north end of Tralee Bay, a gun poised on her fo'c'sle. The newcomer was the armed trawler *Lord Heneage* whose skipper, Lieutenant W. H. A. Bee, R.N.R., had just picked up a message from Loop Head signalling station telling him that a suspicious vessel had been sighted in Tralee Bay. A second message from the Smerwick station, relaying the information that the foreigner was heaving things overboard, had confirmed Bee's suspicions. But, now, as the furious Bee bore down, Spindler raised his anchor and ordered full speed ahead, and despite his chief engineer's warning, "If you go on like this the boilers will burst," he kept at it until he began to pull away from his pursuers. In desperation the *Lord Heneage* opened fire at long range, Bee, meanwhile, sparking out a message to Admiral Bayley, "Suspicious vessel sighted south of Tearaght, steering south-west." At 4.30 p.m. two sloops, *Zinnia* and *Bluebell*, hastened to intercept. At 5.40 p.m. *Bluebell* sighted the *Aud* racing towards the south-west, and at 6.15 both vessels closed in, but *Zinnia*, finding nothing more than a three-island tramp steamer, apparently built for the Baltic timber trade, flying the Norwegian flag and with the Norwegian colours painted on her sides, signalled her to proceed. *Zinnia's* Commander, Lieutenant-Commander G. F. Wilson, R.N., however, decided to shadow the stranger for a while pending further orders from Admiral Bayley. These, when they arrived, were specific, "If *Aud* sighted she is to be brought into port for examination." Wilson at once asked Spindler to show his papers, but the German pretended not to understand and Wilson, considering him a tiresome fellow, ordered *Bluebell* to escort him into Queenstown. He did not know this Spindler, however; he was still far from finished.

"I am bound for Genoa," signalled the German ingenuously. "May I proceed?"

"Wait," replied *Bluebell.*

"Why?" demanded Spindler.

"Follow me to Queenstown, course S.60," replied *Bluebell.*

For the third time Spindler tried to pretend that he did not understand instructions but, his patience by now exhausted, Lieutenant Martin Hood, *Bluebell's* skipper, fired a shell which just cleared the German's bows and, this time, Spindler obeyed. At 9.25 next morning, the day calm and beautiful and both ships just off the Daunt Rock Lightship outside Queenstown Harbour, he played his last card. Suddenly he halted. *Bluebell* immediately backed a cable's length to find out what was wrong, and then saw Spindler lowering his boats. Scrambling into them were his crew, dressed now in German naval uniform. Then the smoke of an explosion burst into the air from charges laid in the *Aud's* hold. Within ten minutes the ship had gone down. And with her, too, had sunk 20,000 rifles, 1,000,000 rounds of ammunition and ten machine-guns, part of the spoils of Hindenburg's victory over the Russians at Tannenberg—and the last hope the insurgents had of entering the conflict on something like equal terms, so far as small arms, anyway, were concerned.

What had gone wrong?

The two green lights, which should have blinked out at Spindler as he sailed up and down Tralee Bay, still hung idly in the Rink, the Volunteers' drill-hall in the town of Tralee itself.

Three weeks before Spindler's arrival, Patrick Cahill, Vice-Commandant of the Tralee Battalion of the Volunteers, had travelled up to Dublin to obtain the two green fishing lamps from Sean MacDermott. On his return Austin Stack, his Commandant, had told him to leave them hanging in the Rink, adding that they would not be needed until sometime between afternoon on Holy Saturday and the early hours of Easter Monday. So certain was

Stack that the German ship would not arrive before this that he did not even engage the pilot, Mr. Matt. O'Leary of Castlegregory, until Holy Thursday— the day the *Aud* actually sailed in. Indeed, as Mr. O'Leary tramped home after agreeing to take on the job, he spotted a large, two-masted vessel lying about a mile off Inishtooskert. However, he had been told that the German ship would be a small one and that she would not arrive before Easter Sunday at the earliest, so he presumed that this was a British decoy ship and went on home and forgot all about it.

The blame for the mistake can hardly be laid at Mr. O'Leary's door. The real culprits in this affair were undoubtedly the rebel leaders and the German Admiralty who, between them—aided and abetted by admittedly complex difficulties in communication—had managed to get their timings muddled.

Direct communication between Dublin and Berlin was not possible, of course, in wartime. Officially Ireland, as part of the United Kingdom, was the enemy of Germany. The conspirators, therefore, had been forced to send their messages, and to receive the answers, through John Devoy, the seventy-year-old head of Clan na Gael. Realizing that the British Government would probably break their codes if they used the Atlantic cables, the insurgents had hit upon a much more cumbersome, if seemingly safer, method of getting their messages through; they employed emissaries. Early in March, Tommy O'Connor, a steward on an Atlantic liner, had carried a message to Devoy giving Berlin the date of the rising. In this message a clear request had been made to the Germans to land their arms sometime between dusk on Holy Thursday and dawn on Easter Monday. But in the first week of April, Pearse and his colleagues had had second thoughts. If the arms were to arrive on Holy Thursday, they decided, Dublin Castle would know all about them long before Easter Sunday. The alternative was to ask the Germans to delay the landing until after the insurrection (timed to start at 6.30 p.m. on Easter Sunday in Dublin, 7 p.m. in the provinces) had started. Accordingly they sent Joseph Plunkett's niece, Philomena, to New York with urgent fresh instructions. She did not arrive in Manhattan until April 14th, exactly five days after the *Aud* had left Lubeck, and two days after Casement had quit Wilhelmshaven. When they received the frantic countermanding message from Devoy, the German Admiralty—behaving in a rather more off-handed manner than one would have expected of a service trying to raise a revolution in the enemy's rear—decided that, as the *Aud* had no wireless, there was nothing that they could usefully do and informed Devoy accordingly. The old man swore that he dispatched a messenger to Ireland to warn Pearse of this mishap, but there is no record that such a message was ever received; and, indeed, Pearse and his colleagues continued to act as though their plans were still fitting neatly together. As an example of their belief that the Germans had received their urgent message and would be by now acting on it, it was not until Good Friday that Plunkett sent three specialists to Kerry with orders to dismantle the Government radio at Valentia and set up their own transmitter in a remote spot in order to contact the arms ship as she sailed down the west coast. Yet they can scarcely escape reprimand for not ordering Austin Stack and his men to keep watch in Tralee Bay from Thursday onwards—as a simple, indeed elementary, precaution against ordinary human fallibility.

While Spindler was sailing aimlessly up and down Tralee Bay between Inishtooskert Island and Fenit Pier, the German submarine *U.19* had begun cautiously nosing her way inshore, aboard her Sir Roger Casement and his two companions, Robert Monteith of the Irish Republican Brotherhood and Sergeant Daniel Bailey of the Royal Irish Rifles—Bailey was one of that handful of Irish prisoners of war in Germany who had been induced to join Sir Roger's so-called Irish Brigade. For some reason which he never revealed to his passengers, Lieutenant Weisbach, commander of *U.19*, did not attempt to talk to Spindler or even signal his presence after he had sighted him off his starboard beam just before dusk, and for an hour and a half afterwards, sought the two green lights independently, while Casement and his companions stood in the conning tower straining their eyes into the darkness. The night was a murky one, with the sea calm. Quite an ideal one, Monteith thought, for running guns ashore. But as time passed and neither lights nor pilot could be discerned, he heard the Germans begin swearing into the night. Casement's face gradually took on a "cold, drawn and hopeless" look. Then, finally, apparently anxious for the safety of his ship, Weisbach told Casement that he could no longer stay in the vicinity, and that he intended running deep into Tralee Bay and landing him and his companions somewhere along the deserted shore. The climax of Casement's tragedy was now fast approaching.

Meantime, in Dublin, events of an equally critical nature—so far as the rebels were concerned—were occurring. Earlier that same evening, while Bulmer Hobson, Secretary of the Irish Volunteers, was working late at his office in Dawson Street, two prominent Volunteer officers, J. J. O'Connell and Eimer Duffy, broke in on him with some startling news.

"Several of the country companies have received orders to take part in an insurrection next Sunday," exploded O'Connell.

Hobson was astonished at the news. "We must see MacNeill at once!" he said, and led the way downstairs to his car. The party at once drove to Rathfarnham and at 11 p.m. knocked on the door of a large Victorian villa in Woodtown Park, where MacNeill greeted them in his pyjamas. Utterly incensed that an attempt appeared to be under way to usurp his prerogative, MacNeill thundered, "My authority must not be flouted, I must see Pearse and tell him what I think of him." And although it was by then well past midnight, he insisted that Hobson drive him over to St. Enda's.

"I've just learned that you've issued orders for an insurrection!" he accused Pearse immediately when they were led into the I.R.B. leader's study.

Thrown off balance by the intrusion, Pearse was for once at a loss for words but finally he did admit, "Yes, a rising is intended."

MacNeill at once flew into a temper, and for the next few minutes berated Pearse with a blistering and highly unacademic flow of abuse. Pearse managed to interrupt the torrent long enough to get out the words, "Yes, you've been deceived. But it was necessary!"

"Well, there'll be no rising!" replied MacNeill. "There'll be no waste of lives for which I'm directly responsible. I'll not allow a half-armed force to be called out. I can promise you this; I'll do everything I can to stop a rising—everything, that is, short of ringing up Dublin Castle." And with a final angry flourish of his fist, MacNeill stamped out of Pearse's study and marched down the steps to the waiting car.

Behind him he left a chastened and dejected Pearse slumped down wearily at his desk. Through the great picture-window under which he sat, night obscured the low Dublin mountains and the rushing streams which worked their way down and across the school grounds—grounds where his hero, Robert Emmet, had once walked when he had paid court to Sarah Curran more than a century before. After a while his mother entered the room.

"Is there anything wrong, Pat?" she asked gently.

"Nothing, Mother, nothing much," replied Pearse. "I've had some trouble with MacNeill, that's all. But it'll all come right in the end, you'll see. So don't worry." And with that he rose and got ready to go into Dublin. By the time he left, he had fought the last battle with his conscience; had made the fatal decision from which there could be no turning back.

At 2.30 a.m. on Good Friday, 1916 *U.19* finally hove to a mile or so offshore and a small, tub-like collapsible boat was lowered into the water. Sir Roger, looking down at it, murmured encouragingly, "Well, it'll be a much greater adventure going ashore in this cockle-shell, anyway." Then he jumped in and took a seat in the stern, while Monteith and Bailey slipped into the front seats. All three donned lifebelts and strapped their coats and kits to the seats—each kit containing a Mauser pistol, a pair of Zeiss binoculars and sheath knife. From the conning tower there were shouts of good luck and then *U.19* edged away to become merely a shadow in the night, then to be lost altogether in the darkness.

The three men thought that with luck they ought to be able to land safely, despite the fact that the coastline was well patrolled by police and government agents. Their hope was to reach Tralee shortly after breakfast and contact Commandant Austin Stack. To begin with, all went well, and after they had been rowing for almost an hour, Casement suddenly leaned forward and declared he could see the coast ahead. Just at this moment, the sea grew rough, great green hissing caverns opening up all around them, and even as he shouted, "Only two hundred yards more," a giant wave curled up behind them and overturned the boat. Probably they would all have drowned had it not been for the lifebelts. As it was, Monteith managed to touch the flatbottom, which at once miraculously righted itself, and somehow or other they managed to scramble aboard. Wet, miserable and exhausted, they allowed themselves to be carried ashore. When the boat grounded only Monteith and Bailey had enough strength left to crawl from it. Monteith, up to his waist in water, held the craft steady while Bailey unstrapped the coats and kits and then carried them ashore. Casement was too weak to struggle and had to be helped ashore by Bailey while Monteith tried to scuttle the boat with his knife. This proving impossible, he gave up the attempt and, stumbling out of the water, found his companions stretched upon the sand. Casement was hardly conscious. He lay half-in, half-out of the water and the sea lapped against him and sometimes broke over him. His eyes were closed and without his beard, shaved off before departure, Monteith thought he looked like a sleeping child. The latter, who was to regret for the rest of his life that he did not leave him to die by the water's edge, lifted him up and chafed his legs and body in order to revive him. Eventually Casement came round and after a while had recovered sufficiently to move about by himself and restore his circulation fully.

Sir Roger Casement, of course, was among the most distinguished and famous Irishmen of his day. Born at Sandycove, Co. Dublin of Ulster Protestant stock, he had won fame in the opening years of the century by courageously exposing the atrocities committed against natives by rubber planters in the Belgian Congo and the Putamayo area of Peru. Retiring from the British consular service in 1912, he had become a founder-member of the Irish Volunteers and served on the governing committee. But, early in 1914, he had left Ireland for the United States, hoping by lectures, cajolery and charm, plus his own great personal prestige, to raise funds for the organization.

By this time he had swung round violently to the view that the Irish insurrectionary movement had no alternative but to seek Germany as an ally. When war broke out in 1914, he travelled to Berlin where he told the German Foreign Office something which they already knew—that a group of nationally-minded Irishmen, having organized themselves into an armed and disciplined body, hoped to rise in rebellion soon. Underlining the advantages Germany would gain from an insurrection in Ireland, he pressed them to send an expeditionary force. The German Government, however, reacted quite lukewarmly and Casement suggested as an alternative that at least they should send some experienced officers to Ireland. Led by German officers, the raw Volunteers might evolve into a really serious embarrassment for the British Army. This suggestion, also, was left pretty much in the air by the Germans.

Then in March 1916, while lying ill in a Munich sanatorium, his hopes of raising a strong Irish Brigade from among Irish-born prisoners moribund, he was told that the date of the rebellion had at last been decided upon. He left hospital at once, and got into touch with Monteith, who informed him that the Germans had decided not only *not* to send an expeditionary force to

Ireland but that they even had no intention of sending artillery. Angered beyond measure after all the years he had spent in desperate effort, Casement stormed into both the German Foreign Office and the Admiralty and demanded much greater support. "All they want is cheap Irish blood," he complained bitterly to Monteith.

Thoroughly annoyed in turn, the German General Staff finally turned on Casement, their spokesman, Captain Nadolny, bluntly informing him that Germany had no idealistic interest in Irish freedom. "Indeed, if it were not for our hopes of a military diversion, we would not even send the rifles," he explained cynically. "As it is, we may well cancel the shipment altogether and leave your countrymen in the lurch." Staggered by such a show of Germanic ruthlessness, Casement decided to return to Ireland as soon as possible and make it plain that a Rebellion would receive little serious support from Germany. On April 12th, therefore, two days before Miss Plunkett was destined to arrive in Manhattan, he set sail from Wilhelmshaven. Such were his feelings that he lightheartedly noted in his diary that evening, "Left Wicklow [code name for Wilhelmshaven] in Willie's yacht."

It was the last time he would ever again feel even so remotely happy.

At 4 a.m. on Good Friday, the collapsible was discovered floating on the tide. For no particular reason John MacCarthy, a farmer, had awakened at two o'clock that morning and, recalling what day it was, had decided to do something he had never done in his life before—rise and walk to a holy well along Banna Strand to say his prayers. Sighting the collapsible on his way back, he called Pat Driscoll, a neighbour, who helped him to drag it in. They found a dagger lying in the bottom and, in the sand nearby, tied with cord, a box containing 1,000 rounds of ammunition. Further up the beach they later found MacCarthy's small daughter playing with three loaded revolvers. Their most significant discovery, however, was the footprints of three men in the sand. As there was no sign of the men, MacCarthy asked Driscoll to fetch the police.

Sergeant Thomas Hearn and Constable Bernard Reilly spent the better part of that morning making a search of the neighbourhood. It was almost 1 p.m. when they finally reached a prehistoric castle known locally as MacKenna's Fort, a circular stone ruin surrounded by a trench, the interior thick with bushes. Working cautiously round this fort, Reilly sighted a crouching man, swiftly covered him with his rifle and threatened to shoot unless he surrendered.

"That's a nice way to treat an English visitor," Casement shouted as he rose to his feet. "I'm not armed, you know, I won't do you any harm."

Reilly called over the sergeant.

"What are you doing here, anyway?" demanded Hearn when he joined them.

"What's your authority for asking me that?" countered Casement aggressively.

"I can ask you any questions I like," said Hearn. "I could arrest you under the Defence Regulations. What's your name?"

"Richard Morten, of Denham, Buckinghamshire," lied Casement. "I'm an author."

"Oh," said Hearn, "What books have you written?"

"One on the life of St. Brendan the Navigator," replied Casement. But Hearn had noticed that his trousers were wet and that there was sand on his boots, so he ordered Reilly to search him. The constable found a slip of paper in Casement's waistcoat. On it there was writing in a strange language.

"This isn't Irish, anyway," said Reilly, puzzled.

"Well, I've no idea what it is," muttered Casement. "I've never seen it before."

He was at once taken to the police station at Ardfert, where a second and more thorough search disclosed that he had five sovereigns and eleven shillings in English money in his possession. But apart from the arms and ammunition found near the collapsible, the only really incriminating evidence against him consisted of two sheets of typewritten paper which he had tried to dispose of as he was being led away from MacKenna's Fort. These bore a series of numbers in a foreign script and phrases to correspond with them, which clearly indicated some kind of a code; the phrases included "await further instructions", "further ammunition needed" and "send another ship to".

Sergeant Hearn, still ignorant, of course, of his prisoner's real identity, telephoned Tralee for further instructions. Monteith and Bailey, who had left Casement shortly after they landed in order to seek help from Commandant Austin Stack, were actually in the town at this time but knew nothing of Casement's capture. The Tralee authorities ordered the prisoner to be sent forward at once, then the following morning, after consultation with the Castle, put him on the train for Dublin, *en route* for the Tower of London. And eventually, after a trial which would have world-wide publicity, the scaffold in Pentonville Prison.

5

BACK IN DUBLIN, Patrick Pearse, faced with the wreckage of all his plans following MacNeill's midnight visit and his threat to prevent a Rebellion, sought out MacDermott and MacDonagh, with the result that early on Good Friday morning all three called on the Chief of Staff at his home. They found the professor still in bed; he agreed to talk, but only with MacDermott, insisting that he would have nothing more to do with Pearse under any circumstances. Ushered into MacNeill's bedroom, MacDermott made no attempt to dissimulate. German arms were about to be landed in Kerry, he revealed, and MacNeill must bow to reason (MacDermott, of course for his part, did not know that Spindler had been lying in Tralee Bay for the past twelve hours).

"I'm against a Rising and I intend to do everything I can to stop one," insisted the professor stubbornly.

"Look," pointed out MacDermott, "the fact is that we control the Volunteers and we won't let you. But anyhow, it's too late for you to interfere now. Hostilities are inevitable."

MacNeill considered this point. An arms landing in Ireland now was certain to bring the wholehearted wrath of the authorities down on them. No government could be expected to show leniency in the circumstances. Bloody force undoubtedly would be used if necessary, and probably the whole Sinn Fein movement would be disarmed.

"Well," he said finally, "if we have to fight or be suppressed, then I suppose I'm ready to fight."

MacDermott went down to tell the others, leaving MacNeill to dress. When MacNeill came down and entered the drawing-room he at once approached Pearse and shook hands. Then, to show that full amity had been restored, he invited them all to stay to breakfast.

A dispatch, informing Sir Matthew Nathan that the *Aud* had scuttled herself, landed on the Under-Secretary's desk shortly after ten o'clock on the morning of April 22nd (Holy Saturday). It lay beside one reporting the arrest of a certain "Richard Morten" in Kerry and another which said that Commandant Austin Stack, trying to secure "Morten's" release, had also been arrested. Even Sir Matthew Nathan suddenly appreciated that he had a crisis on his hands.

He was interrupted by a telephone call from Vice-Regal Lodge.

Although Lord Wimborne had found it an easy enough matter to work with Nathan without actually falling out with him, the latter's supine attitude towards the current campaign of sedition in Ireland had always annoyed him. It appeared to him a thoroughly ridiculous suggestion that just because Britain had her hands full in Europe, peace in Ireland had to be purchased at any price. Firm action by the Government—possibly the arrest of the Sinn Fein leaders, or the disarming of the Volunteers, or the introduction of conscription—ought, in his opinion, to have been taken several months ago. As it was, thousands of shirkers were simply getting away with it. Conscription had worked in England. It had languished in Ireland only because Birrell and Nathan had continued to behave with pusillanimity. At a time when the Empire needed every man it could get, a policy of restraint could only be construed as weakness.

Speaking now from his regally-magnificent residence in Phoenix Park, Baron Wimborne made no attempt to conceal his anxiety. These three reports certainly clinched matters, he insisted. It would now be possible to charge the Sinn Feiners with "hostile association with the enemy" under the Defence Regulations. All the necessary evidence was available to prove that they were hand in glove with the Germans. Sir Matthew listened carefully, but after a short conversation, resolutely refused to hold out any hope that, even now, he would take action.

Twice again that day, Sir Matthew Nathan was to be allowed golden chances to act with decision, yet on both occasions he hesitated. The first came when he motored the one and a half miles to Vice-Regal Lodge, carrying with him the sensational news that "Richard Morten" was none other than Sir Roger Casement. It was a climactic moment for the British Imperial interest in Ireland when the two men sat down together in the Vice-Regal drawing-room to talk over what they should do next. Casement's arrest, plus the scuttling of the *Aud*, was certainly proof that the Sinn Feiners were in league with the Germans. Yet . . .

And here Sir Matthew had paused. Did not the loss of the *Aud*, he suggested tentatively, really mean that there would be no uprising now? With their arms and ammunition at the bottom of the sea, their most distinguished leader under arrest, would not even the Sinn Feiners realize that the game was up? Sir Matthew, studying the Lord Lieutenant's expression, saw that this line of argument was producing a good effect. Nevertheless he was agreeably surprised—aware as he was of His Excellency's very strong views on the subject—when Lord Wimborne nodded his head in agreement and said he fully concurred that a rebellion must now be considered unlikely. Indeed, added Wimborne, stroking his beard reflectively, all this probably marked the complete collapse of the Sinn Fein movement.

And on this brave note of Imperial optimism, Sir Matthew gravely bowed and took his leave.

Neither man, of course, had guessed correctly. By mid-afternoon, Pearse and his colleagues had been apprised of the full extent of the disaster, yet far from considering a change in plans had decided that it was now more than ever imperative to go ahead with them. Dublin Castle, they believed, was certain to order their arrests and thereby destroy, in a single blow, the whole of the carefully built-up movement for national independence.

It was at this point that The O'Rahilly dramatically intervened. His decision to take a hand in the events could scarcely have been less welcome to Pearse, although even he could hardly have foreseen its far-reaching consequences.

Handsome and empirically gallant, if sometimes a little impetuous, The O'Rahilly had first irrupted into the affair late on Friday evening. Angered by the news that the I.R.B. had kidnapped Bulmer Hobson—although a member of the I.R.B., Hobson was opposed to any form of uprising, and was a strong MacNeill supporter—he broke in upon Pearse as he sat alone in his study at St. Enda's. His entrance was entirely theatrical for he held a revolver in his hand.

"Whoever kidnaps me will have to be a quicker shot," he declared, waving the weapon in an alarming manner in front of the startled Pearse.

The I.R.B. chief had stared up at the enraged face looming above the revolver-barrel and countered icily, "No one wants to kidnap you, man—sit down and throw away that gun!"

And, a trifle shamefacedly, The O'Rahilly had lowered the revolver and sat down. With the weapon resting over his knee, he had then launched into a prolonged discussion, in a vivid effort to dissuade Pearse from violent action. The I.R.B. chief, for his part, argued back with equal passion. In the end, they were unable to agree. Pearse's arguments, insisted The O'Rahilly, were those of a poet and idealist, not of a practical man of affairs.

He was still burning with furious anger when he woke up on Saturday morning; so furious, indeed, that he decided that at all costs he would have to stop Pearse. He drove out to Woodtown Park, hoping to talk MacNeill into the belief that "the insurrection *could* and *should* be averted." He found the Volunteer Chief of Staff in a "terribly agitated" state. The skimpy press reports from Kerry relating to the capture of a man who had landed from a German submarine had persuaded the ostrich-minded professor that something had gone seriously wrong down there, and that the I.R.B.'s hopes of substantial German aid might well have already foundered. Fretfully he paced the room as The O'Rahilly enumerated the reasons why he should step in and exert his supreme authority against the proposed Rising. In the end MacNeill promised to act. He declared that he would ask all Volunteer staff officers to meet him at Dr. James O'Kelly's house on the Rathgar Road at 9.30 that evening. Then, while The O'Rahilly waited beside him, he sat down and began writing a series of countermanding orders for dispatch to all battalions in the country, certain, at least in his own mind, that he still had the power—and the means—to prevent a Rebellion.

At fifteen minutes past six that evening, hoping to force MacNeill's resolve with additional moral support, The O'Rahilly brought two Volunteer officers, O'Loughlin and Fitzgibbon, who had just returned from Kerry, out to the house to see him. They possessed full details of the capture of Casement and the scuttling of the *Aud* and their accounts had the desired effect. Pearse, decided MacNeill, must be given a last chance. Would The O'Rahilly drive him over to St. Enda's?

The Volunteer Chief of Staff was received by the I.R.B. chief alone in the long hall of the Georgian house, where they held a short but animated conversation. Then, still arguing fiercely, they came out together to the head of the steps. Neither man made any attempt to conceal his bitterness.

Angrily—almost rudely—Pearse shouted, "We've used your name and influence for all they're worth—now we don't need you any more. It's no use your trying to stop us. Our plans are laid and they'll be carried out."

"Your plans are so well laid," MacNeill retorted acidly, "that the police at Ardfert have already upset them. Anyway, I'm still Chief of Staff of the Irish Volunteers and I'm going to forbid tomorrow's mobilization."

"Our men, at least, will never obey you," declared Pearse passionately.

"Well, if they don't, then that's your responsibility," answered MacNeill. Then he added, "If you should want to see me again I'll be at Doctor O'Kelly's house on the Rathgar Road from nine o'clock tonight." And with that he turned abruptly on his heel and strode down to the waiting car.

But when ten o'clock had passed and there was still no word from Pearse, MacNeill indicated that the countermanding order, which had been prepared, should be dispatched at once. This read:

WOODTOWN PARK
RATHFARNHAM
CO. DUBLIN
22 April, 1916.

Volunteers completely deceived. All orders for special action are hereby cancelled, and on no account will action be taken.

Signed: Eoin MacNeill,
Chief of Staff.

At once, The O'Rahilly jumped into a taxi and drove off in the whirlwind tour that was to take him through Cork, Kerry and Tipperary, before he ended up in Limerick city the following morning. Other couriers quickly scattered out from Dublin by train and taxi. Then finally at 10.20 p.m. MacNeill took the irrevocable step; he sat down and composed an announcement for publication in a Dublin Sunday newspaper:

"Owing to the very critical position, all orders given to Irish Volunteers for tomorrow, Easter Sunday, are hereby rescinded and no parades, marches, or other movement of Irish Volunteers will take place. Each individual Volunteer will obey this order strictly in every particular."

And to make certain that this was published, he personally cycled down to the *Sunday Independent* offices to speak to the editor. He had cast the die. Now freedom must await their children's generation.

Elsewhere in Dublin, however, the other main actors in the drama had gone about their business unconcerned—as was Pearse it seems—or ignorant—as was Sir Matthew Nathan.

Sir Matthew paid a final visit to Vice-Regal Lodge that evening, only to discover that Lord Wimborne had again, like a weathercock, changed his noble mind. He now wanted an immediate swoop on Liberty Hall—under the impression, apparently, that this was the headquarters of all subversion and that if he raided it he was bound to catch all the plotters together. Sir Matthew, palpably unnerved at this suggestion, could only repeat his earlier advice against "precipitate action", adding that he was not prepared to accept responsibility for a raid which could easily set the country alight. And still balancing the pros and cons of the argument in his mind, he had taken his leave again and returned to Dublin Castle.

Pearse, quite unperturbed by MacNeill's threat, left St. Enda's with the intention of spending the night in Dublin and thus avoiding arrest if the Government, tipped off by a traitor, perhaps, swooped at the last minute. Before leaving he called his boys together for a last farewell. His parting words were generous and indicative of what he hoped for the future: "Always remember. If you're ever free, it's the son of an Englishman who will have freed you."

The morning of Easter Sunday, April 23rd, 1916 dawned with all the soft beauty of an Irish spring. The altars of the Dublin churches, immaculate in their adornments of starched white linen and solid gold candelabra, looked even more richly-hued because of immense sprays of Easter lilies. Among the communicants were hundreds of Irish Volunteers, many in full uniform.

Nora Connolly returned from Mass to Liberty Hall, to find her father up and dressed in his Commandant-General's uniform and quietly singing to himself:

"We've another saviour now,
    That saviour is the sword."

Nora had arrived in Dublin early that morning after a frantic all-night train journey from the North, a journey caused by the arrival of MacNeill's order late on Saturday night at Dungannon, where hundreds of Volunteers had gathered for Sunday's mobilization. Nora had left at once for Dublin to see her father and find out what was happening. On her arrival Connolly had reassured her, "Pray God, Nora, if there's no Rising, may an earthquake swallow up Ireland," and had then calmly gone back to bed.

Dutifully, Nora set about preparing breakfast for the members of the Provisional Government, who soon began to turn up. It was some time before Pearse himself arrived; he had stayed to have breakfast at Sean T. O'Kelly's house where he and Willie had spent the night. While the Provisional Government were still eating, a Citizen Army girl entered the room, carrying a copy of the *Sunday Independent*.

"Look, Mr. Connolly," she said. "The *Independent* says 'No manoeuvres today'!"

"What's that?" shouted Connolly, rising to his feet and grabbing the paper from her. His face paled as he read MacNeill's announcement.

"Let me see it," said Pearse. He glanced down the paragraph, then said to Connolly, "I knew nothing about this."

By now the other leaders had risen to their feet and Connolly led the way into the Council Room where they all sat down, Tom Clarke taking the chair. Clarke put forward the first proposal, which was that they should go ahead with their plans as they had been already worked out, arguing that once the fighting had begun that evening in Dublin, Volunteers throughout the country would inevitably join in. Pearse said he disagreed and MacDermott, for once deserting his old friend and mentor, supported him. Connolly finally cast his vote in favour of postponing the insurrection until the following day at noon, arguing that it would be impossible to get enough men out now anyway. No question of abandoning their daring—their suicidal—idea was ever considered, and eventually the fateful decision was agreed. At approximately 1 p.m. the agonizing conference ended.

When it was over, and Tom Clarke was returning to his tobacconist's shop in Great Britain Street, he confided to his bodyguard, Vice-Commandant Piaras Beaslai, "MacNeill has ruined everything—all our plans. I feel like going away to cry."

That afternoon Dublin looked her most serene and lovely—as all spacious and well-ordered cities used to do before the advent of motor-cars. Open deck tram-cars, rattling along on four sets of tramlines, were almost the only mechanical means of travel to be seen in Sackville Street. In St. Stephen's Green crowds of leisurely people strolled about, the men in respectable bowlers, the women in wide hats and ground-sweeping skirts. Great trees rustled gently over the pavements, casting shade broken by shifting discs of sunlight. At the "hazards" cab-horses munched peacefully. . . .

Meanwhile, in Liberty Hall, despite an early hitch, flatbed presses were rolling off copies of the Proclamation of the Republic, the three printers, Christopher Brady, Michael Molloy and William O'Brien, faced with a shortage of type, using sealing wax to turn a capital F into a capital E. By mid-afternoon they had run off a thousand copies. Countess Markievicz grabbed one while the ink was still wet upon it and, from the front steps, read it out to the small crowd gathered there, with characteristic hauteur disregarding the detectives who mingled among them.

That evening Lord Wimborne decided to make a last attempt to carry out his duty, despite Sir Matthew's continued opposition. At 7 p.m. when the latter returned to Vice-Regal Lodge accompanied by Colonel H. V. Cowan, military commander in Dublin during the Commander-in-Chief's absence in London, His Excellency asked Cowan his opinion about raiding Liberty Hall.

"Well, sir, I couldn't get in without fighting my way in," said Cowan. "And to do that I'd need a field gun. The nearest, unfortunately, is at Athlone."

"How many men have you available?" asked Wimborne.

"There are always four hundred standing to arms in Dublin barracks," replied Cowan.

Wimborne hesitated. Then, with an almost theatrical gesture, he called his private secretary and told him to cancel his official trip to Belfast the following day.

"I'm not leaving Dublin until I've secured the arrest of these Sinn Feiners," he declared.

"In that case, I'd like to consult with some of my staff as well as the Commissioner of the Metropolitan Police," said Cowan. "May I return at ten o'clock?"

"Yes, all right," said Wimborne grimly.

At ten o'clock, then, Sir Matthew once again drove into Phoenix Park. Stepping down from the running-board outside Vice-Regal Lodge, he was quickly ushered into the drawing-room where he found six men, including the Lord Lieutenant, waiting.

"I want between sixty and a hundred of the ringleaders arrested tonight," began Wimborne, as soon as the group had seated itself.

"On what charge?" demanded Sir Matthew, immediately on his mettle. "To hold them on a charge of 'hostile association' would need the agreement of the Home Secretary."

"They could be kept on remand," insisted Wimborne. "Anyway, I'll sign the warrants and accept full responsibility." And having thus steamrollered his way through Sir Matthew's first objection, he got down smartly to the real business of the meeting. The obstacles to the actual physical arrest of the Sinn Feiners were formidable, he agreed. An immediate raid on Liberty Hall was, of course, out of the question. As Cowan had pointed out, the loss of life, without artillery, would be high. Major Price then remarked that it was unlikely that all the Sinn Feiners would be together under one roof anyway. For more than an hour the six men continued their discussions, until it was decided to put into operation a plan proposed by the Commissioner of Police. This involved a joint military-police swoop on the homes of the Sinn

Fein leaders about 2 o'clock some morning when they were certain to be fast asleep. The raid, however, could not be carried out at once for it would take a couple of days at least to make the necessary arrangements.

It was well after midnight before the conference finally broke up. The agreement was that Nathan would cable Birrell first thing in the morning and that, meanwhile, the military and police would begin making their preparations.

In the early hours of Easter Monday, MacDonagh issued a final order to the Dublin battalions of the Irish Volunteers: "The four city battalions will parade for inspection and route march at 10 a.m. today. Commandants will arrange centres. Full arms and equipment and one-day's rations."

In Liberty Hall a whistle blew and the sleeping men sprang to their feet, their rifles at the ready. But it proved to be only a false alarm. Outside, the streets lay dark and empty, the Liffey glistening under the gas-light. Across Beresford Place, the splendid bulk of the Custom House rose in outline against the stars.

Under the portico of the General Post Office, stray city cats rubbed themselves against torn newsbills echoing far-off battles at Kut-el-Amara and Verdun.

At 2 a.m. scouts posted near British barracks reported that all was quiet within. The city slept and had no premonitions.

6

VOLUNTEER Garry Holohan's idea was to explode five bags of gelignite in the Magazine Fort in Phoenix Park as a signal that the Rebellion had started. What he intended to do was not really very spectacular, not very violent; not in a world deeply inured to violence. For this was the 265th day of the second year of the First World War; the 65th day of the battle of Verdun. Along the Meuse before this day was over, the Germans would use flame guns against the French, explode infernal mines near Souchez and win a bloody footing in British trenches. At Loos, Arras, and Ypres there would be a series of spectacular artillery duels, while farther along the front, historic French châteaux would be systematically pounded to rubble. It was not a world, therefore, where there was much latitude to indulge delicate susceptibilities.

Nevertheless, on the Home Front affairs would continue to function in an atmosphere of near-normality. In England, for instance, their Majesties would spend the holiday, as usual, at Windsor. In Brighton and Southend piers and cafés would be packed with Londoners who had swarmed in from early morning. Hampstead Heath, Epping Forest, Hampton Court and Box Hill would all be well patronized—although it would be too cold for picnicking. Only along Carlton Terrace might tangible reminders of the war still be glimpsed in the spectacle of convalescent officers sitting out in wicker chairs or propped up in beds at open windows enjoying the sun. In Ireland, despite a few scarcely-felt food shortages, it would prove even more difficult to imagine there was trouble in the world, although the recruiting posters— or what remained of them after Sinn Fein sympathizers had torn them— offered these reminders:

The Irishmen
in the
Trenches
are calling for
YOU.
Ask yourself squarely
Whether you are justified
in turning a deaf ear to
THEM.

Why not
JOIN THE ARMY
For the period
of the war?
You will like it.
Your pals will like it.
The Kaiser will hate it!

Apart from the Fairyhouse race meeting, the Spring Show of the Royal Dublin Society would open at Ballsbridge. In the afternoon, for those who did not mind spending the holiday indoors, St. John Ervine was offering a matinée performance of Yeats's *Cathleen ni Houlihan* at the Abbey. That night, too, the D'Oyly Carte Opera Company were due to open a season at the Gaiety—in fact, four theatres in all proposed to give Dubliners, and the many visitors from England and out of town, a chance to enjoy themselves and forget their troubles.

Holohan still lay in bed at half-past nine when he was aroused by his friend Paddy Daly. Daly was an expert on the Magazine Fort; six months earlier he had wangled himself a job with Sir Patrick Shortall's building firm when it was carrying out extensive repairs there and had seized the chance to map the interior and learn the drill of the guard. He had also found out exactly where the keys to the high-explosive store were kept.

"Get up for God's sake!" said Daly. "Don't you know we're going out at twelve?"

"But surely the Rebellion isn't until this evening?" protested Holohan.

"That's all a mistake," said Daly. "Get up!"

Holohan got out of bed at once while Daly left to mobilize other men. Holohan knew that his first job was to get hold of Volunteer Tim Roche and get him to "commandeer" a car and have it waiting near the Fort, with its engine running, by half-past eleven; next, to help out Paddy Daly with the mobilization. Obviously he had misunderstood Sean MacDermott's remark when he had spoken to him on Sunday in Liberty Hall. MacDermott had said, "Everything is off for twenty-four hours," and Holohan had taken this too literally, it seemed. Still smarting at his blunder, he cycled off to see Roche. He arranged things with Roche, then started to help with the mobilization. But by 11.05 a.m. he realized it was going badly. He had found only three men at home when he called and he decided to go to Liberty Hall and report to Commandant Connolly. Connolly heard him with sympathy, and gave him a note to the four City Commandants allocating him a man from each battalion. By 11.45, he had picked up a further four men; the last, a lad named Barney Mellowes, begged him for a chance to say good-bye to his mother.

"There isn't time!" Holohan roared in exasperation. "For God's sake, man, jump on a tram at once!"

He turned towards home then, certain that the idea of blowing up the Fort would have to be abandoned. Even as he passed through St. Stephen's Green, in fact, he saw Commandant MacDonagh's men already mobilizing to seize Jacob's biscuit factory. But when he reached home no less than thirty young men were waiting for him. Paddy Daly was with them, issuing final instructions. The party would split into three detachments, the first and second going to Phoenix Park by tram, the third travelling by bicycle. All would meet on the football ground near the Fort, and would pretend that they were going to play a match.

At five minutes past twelve Holohan and Daly stopped briefly at Whelan's shop near the Four Courts and bought a football. At twelve-fifteen they cycled into Phoenix Park and rode towards Thomas's Hill on whose brow squatted the Fort, a low stone structure. Roche was waiting in the drive-way—but with a jaunting-car instead of a motor. He explained that he had managed to steal a car all right, but on the way up to the Park had driven it straight into a lamp-post. He had jumped out unhurt and hailed a passing jaunting-car. Holohan, glancing at the jarvey as he idly flicked away the flies from his nag, wondered what chance they stood of getting away safely; still, there was nothing he could do about it now.

The rest of the lads had gathered beside the fence encircling the Fort. Holohan punted the ball up the hill and the young men began scrambling for it. The time, Holohan noticed, was just 12.17 and down in the city—and all over Ireland, he hoped—the Rebellion would have already started.

After kicking it about for a moment or so, someone booted the ball round the corner of the Fort to the east side where the sentry guarded the main gate. Another kick landed it beside the sentry. Before the man knew what was hap-pening several young men had leaped on him and brought him down.

Daly led the way inside. Once in the long passageway, which ran the com-plete length of the building, he turned right into the guardroom. Holohan went straight on until he emerged into a bright quadrangle where he saw a raised platform, scarcely four feet high and accessible by steps at each corner, running round the walls. A soldier was standing with his back towards him, partially screened by a small hut. Yanking out his automatic, Holohan shout-ed, "Surrender."

The soldier turned. But for the hut he could probably have picked Holohan off there and then. Instead, he shifted right to get in a better shot, then sud-denly changed his mind and jabbed out his bayonet. Holohan squeezed his automatic twice and saw the man go down, clutching at his side. As Barney Mellowes raced in from the right, the wounded man cried out, "Sirs, sirs, don't shoot me! I'm an Irishman myself and the father of five children."

"Don't worry, we won't," Mellowes assured him and they lifted him up. Blood was welling from his thigh and, when they stood him on his feet, he collapsed again immediately.

"We'll just have to leave him," said Holohan. Turning to the wounded man, he said, "Don't worry—we'll let your pals know." With that he jumped down from the parapet and, followed by Mellowes, raced back across the quadrangle. Inside the guardroom he found ten military prisoners guarded by rebels. All were young and frightened; one was weeping copiously.

"One of your chaps is hurt," Holohan said, jerking his thumb towards the quadrangle. He asked a young rebel where Daly was and was told he was in the small arms store.

Holohan found Daly in a room opening off the main passageway; with him were Holohan's brother Pat and a lad called Edward Martin. Daly had

had wretched luck. After overpowering the guard, he had rounded up Mrs. Isabel Playfair, wife of the Fort's Commander (who was with an Irish regiment in France), and her two boys and girl, and had warned her that he was going to blow up the Fort. He had allowed her six minutes to get clear. Then with success apparently in his grasp, he had reached up for the key to the high-explosives store only to find that the hook was empty. Unbelievably, the Officer-in-Charge had put it in his pocket and taken it with him to the Fairyhouse races. Daly, foiled, had been forced to content himself with the key to the small-arms store instead. By the time Holohan arrived, he had placed the five bags of gelignite next to the wall of the high-explosives store and had then piled belts of small-arms ammunition on top of them, hoping that with luck the resulting explosion would blast through the wall and trigger off the lot. Holohan, who had been trained to handle explosives, was asked to set the fuses. When he had done this the party returned to the guardroom, where Daly warned the prisoners, "When we let you outside—don't try to follow us or raise the alarm!" Then he ordered that the captured military rifles—which lay stacked neatly in a long rack—were to be taken outside. Finally he nodded to Holohan, and together they shepherded the disarmed soldiers out through the doors. Once outside, he barked, "Now clear off!" An order the red-faced prisoners obeyed with alacrity. Down the slope of St. Thomas's Hill streamed the young rebels, holding the captured rifles on high and singing *The Soldier's Song* at the top of their voices. On reaching the foot, they dumped the rifles in the well of the jaunting-car, and a handful climbed aboard while the rest scattered through Phoenix Park.

"Gee up now!" yelled Daly, and the jarvey, in terror of his life, whipped up his nag and drove off at a fast trot towards the Islandbridge gate, Holohan following on his bicycle. Then as the high outside-car swayed over the cindery road, a boy was noticed running some distance ahead.

"That's young Playfair," shouted Daly. "Stop him!"

Holohan sighted the boy as he ran through the park gate and out into the middle of the road to speak to a policeman on traffic duty. Immediately he pushed down hard on the pedals. There were two military barracks close by—Islandbridge and the Royal Barracks—and so they could be easily intercepted. Young Playfair turned left down a road leading towards the city and at the gate Holohan swerved left after him, ignoring the policeman, who made no attempt, anyhow, to stop him. By the time Playfair reached the corner of Islandbridge Road, Holohan had substantially narrowed the gap. Turning the corner, he saw the boy running diagonally across the road, making for a row of large houses. For the first time Playfair looked round and saw Holohan following him. He reached the first house and was battering on the door when Holohan leaped from his bicycle, and drawing his revolver from his pocket, took aim. Holohan saw a desperate face glance back at him from the doorway. Then the door opened and for a moment a woman stood framed in the hallway. It was over in an instant; Holohan fired three times and the boy (who was barely seventeen years of age), his hands clawing out frantically at the still-opening door, crumpled up on the step, dying.

Almost at that moment, behind Holohan somewhere, back towards the Park, there was a sudden dull explosion. It was not very loud; not loud enough, certainly, to be heard any distance away.

Across the river, in the South Dublin Union, Commandant Eamonn Ceannt again looked at his watch, waiting impatiently for the signal. When five minutes passed and there was still no sound, he shrugged his shoulders philosophically. "Ah, well, it hasn't worked," he commented, and strode off to attend to his dispositions.

A big bang might well have cheered Ceannt, for he faced an almost impossible task. The South Dublin Union (or Workhouse) sprawled over some fifty-two acres, the better part of it wide lawns and open fields, the whole enclosed by a stone wall. It was an amazing ramification of streets, alleyways and courtyards, studded with residences, halls, dormitories, wards, sheds and even two churches; in fact, it was a small town. Even its population that morning—excluding officials and insurgents—amounted to some 3,282 souls, which is larger than most Irish towns. Ceannt had mobilized the Fourth Battalion at eleven o'clock that morning in Emerald Square, a small square of workmen's cottages in south-west Dublin, an area of tall distilleries and factories, with the concomitant debris of back-to-back terrace houses, sleazy-looking pubs and small huckster shops, all dominated by the giant complex of Guinness's Brewery. Of a nominal battalion strength of seven hundred only one hundred and twenty of his men had turned out. Nominal volunteer strengths, of course, normally meant very little; they varied a great deal according to political shifts. Whenever the British Army launched a fresh recruiting campaign in Ireland or the British Government hinted that it might impose conscription, then there was an upsurge in attendances. When things became quiet they fell off again, although the hard core of enthusiasts, to be fair, rarely varied. These were the men who, for diverse reasons, regarded the Volunteers as the mainspring of their existence. Many of these men had enrolled in the organization because they were genuine patriots; others simply because they enjoyed drilling or learning to fire a rifle; but others had joined from baser motives—a belief that membership of the Volunteers might someday lead to a good job or that it was the best way to prevent conscription. There were saints and sinners in the organization. Even so, Ceannt realized, under more auspicious circumstances at least five hundred men would have turned out for him.

Those who *had* reported for duty, however, had responded with magnificent spirit to his brief and deliberately unemotional address: "Today you're going into action! An Irish Republic has been declared and we are marching on the South Dublin Union." Most of them, he knew, had waited a long time to hear such words; he had no need to add anything in the way of heroics.

At 11.35 a.m the Battalion had moved off; Ceannt, tall and lean, leading a party of ten cyclists by a back route while Lieutenant William Cosgrave, a Dublin city councillor who lived in the district, led the main party (under the command of Vice-Commandant Cathal Brugha, the small but ferocious son of a Yorkshireman), through side streets in order to avoid being seen by the police and perhaps challenged. Nearing the Union, small parties dropped off at what were intended to be three main outposts—Jameson's Distillery in Marrowbone Lane (which was occupied by Captain James Murphy with twenty men); Watkin's Brewery in Ardee Street (seized by a pugnacious little man called Con Colbert, with about the same number); and Roe's Distillery in James Street (which was broken into by Captain Thomas MacCarthy, again with approximately twenty men). From a strategic viewpoint, the Union and its outposts constituted an important rebel position; military movements along the Quays could be interfered with and a loose command exercised over the Kingsbridge Railway Station and the Royal Hospital, Kilmainham. Kingsbridge was the terminus for trains from the Curragh, the British Army's main camp in Ireland; the Royal Hospital, one of the most architecturally-pleasing buildings in the city, the headquarters of the British Commander-in-Chief.

Ceannt waited until noon before approaching the back entrance with his cyclists; this was at Rialto Bridge, one of the many small bridges which cross the Grand Canal. (Dublin had two main canals—one called the Royal threads its way through the northern suburbs; the other, the Grand, through the southern, both running from west to east in a line roughly parallel to the Liffey.) He encountered no opposition beyond a porter who refused to hand over the keys. Ceannt simply brushed the man aside and took them from their rack. Courageously the porter made an attempt to telephone the police, only to discover that the line had been cut. Leaving a party of nine volunteers under Captain George Irvine to guard the Rialto entrance, Ceannt marched half a mile through the Union Grounds to the front gate, where he rejoined Cathal Brugha and the main party. As he did so, the strains of a military band, borne on the breeze, reached the Union from Richmond Barracks. "They don't know yet," smiled Ceannt happily, but he had hardly spoken when the music suddenly stopped. "Oh, that's ominous," he remarked.

His overall plans for the defence of the Union were based, of course, on the assumption that he would have a great many more men. Brugha had already barricaded the main gate and sent a party to occupy the offices arching over it—which took up most of the Union's short frontage on James Street. Tunnelling through the party walls had already commenced and very shortly it would be possible for men to traverse the whole frontage without leaving cover. Ceannt now decided to deploy a further thirty-eight officers and men throughout the Union grounds, a gesture of extraordinary prodigality perhaps, considering the circumstances. His principal problem, however, was how to prevent British troops moving into the centre of Dublin by the south-western suburbs. These forces, in the opening stages anyway, were likely to march in from either Richmond or Islandbridge Barracks—possibly both—moving along the southern bank of the Liffey. In this event they could be fired on from Roe's Distillery. If, instead, they chose the parallel inland route, along Old Kilmainham, and along the slight rise of Mount Brown, they must pass right in front of the Union, and before reaching it could be fired on from close range as they marched some five hundred yards alongside open fields on their right called MacCaffrey's Estate—a part of the Union grounds. At the foot of Mount Brown lay Brookfield Road leading to Rialto Bridge and the South Circular Road and if the military swung right here they would certainly outflank the Union, but in that case they would run into fire from Murphy's men holding Jameson's Distillery.

Eamonn Ceannt, however, was not a man to let the enemy outflank him without making at least a stubborn effort to prevent them. So he first placed an officer and four men at the extreme point of MacCaffrey's Estate (at the corner of Mount Brown and Brookfield Road), where they gained concealment from a low wall which dropped steeply on the other side to the pavement. Back nearer the Union, and well-hidden behind thick hedges, he placed another officer and eight men. Irvine and his party, of course, already held the Rialto Gate and also a three-hundred-foot-long tin shed used by the Union authorities to house male lunatics. A single Volunteer daringly took up a suicidal position in a shallow trench facing the gate. In addition, he now sent an officer and five men to guard the Canal wall at the rear of the Union, and dispatched another five Volunteers to guard the eastern boundary wall. Finally, he placed eight Volunteers in the big isolated permanent building known as Hospital 2–3, two hundred and fifty yards from the Rialto Gate, two men occupying the ground floor, six the upper.

Cosgrave, critical of these dispositions, remarked to Vice-Commandant Brugha, "Look, isn't this hopeless? Surely we can't hope to hold the whole Union—we haven't got the men."

"Well, what do you suggest then?" asked Brugha sarcastically.

Cosgrave pointed to the Night Nurses' Home, a solid, three-storey, stone-built structure situated on the west side of the main courtyard and lying at right-angles to James Street. "It's the strongest building in the Union," he suggested. "And it's in the right position. From the back we could control MacCaffrey's, Mount Brown, Brookfield Road and even the Rialto Gate."

"Get the men in at once," said Brugha. "Ceannt will want to make that headquarters."

By 12.25 p.m., when Daly's five bags of gelignite eventually blew up, the Battalion had already started establishing its defences. In the front offices the work of breaking through the party walls was showing progress; inside the Nurses' Home most of the windows had been smashed and the frames well barricaded; in the Rialto sheds, the Union Wardmaster herded his lunatic charges into the last of the six dormitories and Irvine began throwing up protecting mattresses at the windows.

At the bottom of MacCaffrey's Estate Section-Commander John Joyce lay behind the low wall and stared intently up at Old Kilmainham. For ten minutes now he and three other men under Lieutenant William O'Brien had been suffering a great deal of abuse from a bunch of separation women (British Army wives who received separation allowances while their husbands were serving in France). One Volunteer angrily shouted, "Oh, go to hell!" but suddenly, the women stopped screaming abuse and scattered, one shouting, "Yez'll bate it now, me boyos. Here come the military!"

"Remember," warned O'Brien calmly, "for God's sake don't fire till I tell you—d'ye hear that!"

A few moments later Joyce caught a glimpse of khaki figures coming down into the dip in the road, barely three hundred yards away. They were marching with all the cheerful precision of the British Army and their bayonets were gleaming brightly in the midday sun.

Other Volunteer Battalions, meanwhile, had been enjoying comparable successes and could claim with some degree of truth that they had achieved their principal objectives.

At 11.45 a.m. Commandant Edward Daly, commanding the First Volunteer Battalion, walked out of Colmcille Hall into the bright sunlight, escorted by his aides, and saluted his men briskly. Although it was a moment when heroics could have been excused, Daly chose deliberately to address his men in a matter-of-fact tone. "I have to tell you, men, that you will shortly be going into action," he announced without flourish. "At twelve o'clock today, the flag of the Irish Republic is to be raised—now I don't want any cheering, and I also want to make it clear," and here his eyes had strayed anxiously over his desperately thin ranks, "that if anybody wants to withdraw now, then he is at liberty to do so." For fully five seconds there was no movement in the ranks. Then Volunteer John Alwright shouted hoarsely, "Well, I don't like this," and stepped out. When nobody else moved, the quick frown vanished from Daly's face and he almost looked cheerful as he gave the command, "Left turn, quick march!"

Daly's principal objective was the Four Courts, the home of Ireland's Judiciary, where a great dome, sixty-four feet in diameter, rising like a giant upturned saucer, looms massively over the River Liffey. His real problem, however, was to decide which outposts he should seize, for with the small forces available, he could not hold many. He decided to dispose of twenty men under Lieutenant Joseph MacGuinness in the Four Courts itself; then he split the rest of his forces into five small parties and ordered them to occupy positions in the surrounding streets. He himself marched up Church Street to the Convent of St. John, where he set up temporary headquarters.

The Angelus bell was ringing as MacGuinness led his party towards the Four Courts. They did not anticipate much resistance, and indeed they met none; all the Volunteers, in fact, were to marvel that day at the ease with which a city, even a capital like Dublin, steel-ringed with military barracks, could be taken over. Those who were aware of the efforts that had been made to persuade the Germans to send an expeditionary force could only feel a sense of despair when they realized how easily they could have seized all Ireland. MacGuinness, ignoring twenty D.M.P.s watching him from the Bridewell Police Station, marched to the Chancery Place entrance of the Four Courts where Lieutenant Thomas Allen, revolver in hand, ordered a policeman to hand over the keys. They entered the building with less difficulty than if they had been litigants. Volunteer Charles Beavan and a three-man party made their way to the front of the building and occupied the Lord Chancellor's Chambers facing up-river, smashing the tall windows and barricading them with leather-tooled books from the Chancellor's Library.

In the surrounding streets other rebels had begun erecting barricades. Along the Quay, a lorry blocked Church Street Bridge; in Hammond Lane, bedsteads were linked across the road to make a crude fence; in other streets, squaresetts or cobbles were prised up and built into a wall. Everywhere broken bottles and glass lay scattered over the roads to prevent a cavalry charge. Trams were halted at the entrance to Church Street and the passengers made to alight; one tram was heaved over on its side, blocking most of the street. The main effort, however, was concentrated at the intersection of Church Street and North King Street. The latter runs roughly parallel to the river, the former intersecting at right-angles. The whole constitutes an area of narrow streets, small houses, pubs and little shops. Here the insurgents soon learned that a rebellion is likely to prove something more than a matter of simple heroics; that it is mainly hard and back-breaking effort—and it guarantees no immunity from insults. There was plenty of foul language when the poor people of the area saw their possessions being dragged out to make barricades.

"But the Republic will repay you, ma'am!" Lieutenant Jack Shouldice assured everyone. Although it seemed to have little effect. People's sympathies were divided. Some helped when they heard that a Republic had been declared; others became hostile. Patrick Kelly of "C" Company had to draw his revolver to protect himself against women of the neighbourhood when he halted a regular soldier who wanted to walk through the rebel-held area. From their doorways, they hurled abuse at him, and then advanced menacingly.

"Go on, can't ye—take away his gun!" they shouted to the soldier. "Take away his gun and he'll run!" But the soldier, warned by a look in Kelly's eye, shrugged his shoulders and turned back and the women themselves came no further.

Then, suddenly, into all this blundered the regular cavalry. A troop of the 5th and 12th Lancers, part of the 6th Cavalry Reserve Regiment stationed at Marlborough Barracks (Phoenix Park), had been sent down that morning to the North Wall railway terminus to escort a small ammunition convoy. Pearse and Connolly had just begun their march on the G.P.O. when the troop began trekking back along the quays, five low carts loaded with rifles, rifle-grenades and bombs rumbling along noisily in their midst. Their lances bobbed disdainfully, their hooves clattered spiritedly. A small rebel party, left behind in Liberty Hall to guard reserves of food and ammunition, watched a perfect target approaching, but Lieutenant Frank Thornton had been given orders to avoid action until the main forces of the Republic had consolidated themselves in the Post Office. To his chagrin, therefore, Thornton was forced to allow the convoy to pass. And unaware that behind the silent windows of Liberty Hall, rifle-barrels stood trained on them, the Lancers trekked proudly on. At O'Connell Bridge, rebel scouts acting under orders similar to Thornton's, permitted them to pass without hindrance and a little arrogantly the troopers clattered across Lower Sackville Street; then, harness and accoutrements jingling martially, they made their way along Bachelor's Walk. They had gone only a short distance when a man yelled at Second Lieutenant Hunter, officer-in-charge, "Look out for yourselves! The Sinn Feiners are out— they're up ahead!" Discounting this as a piece of proverbial Irish nonsense, Hunter continued his disdainful march, confident in the capacity of British cavalry to overawe rebels anywhere, a confidence forged long ago in many a foreign clime. To Daly's men, hard at work erecting barricades around the Four Courts, the Lancers proved a startling sight. In sheer panic, the men at the Church Street barricade knelt in the roadway and loosed off a fusillade.

Six or seven troopers fell immediately while their animals plunged and reared wildly in terror. Lieutenant Hunter wheeled his horse and yelled to his men to make for a side street. A handful unheedingly rode towards Chancery Place, hoping to take refuge in the Four Courts, only to come under heavy fire from Volunteer James Byrne, guarding the gate, whose Howth rifle, with its reverberating echo, sounded like a small cannon. The main body rode into Charles Street and galloped towards Ormonde Market, only to be turned back by further insurgent fire. For a few moments of sheer chaos they milled around in the narrow street, all order and discipline vanished. Then Hunter, bravely rallying them, ordered them to break into the Collier Dispensary and the Medical Mission opposite it. They did so; then, once inside, they were able to unload the ammunition carts and bring the boxes in.

Meanwhile, in the streets nearby, wounded or unhorsed troopers had begun surrendering to the rebels. Two lone troopers, lost in a maze of back streets, galloped wildly down North King Street; then, spotting rebels ahead, shot off their carbines. One bullet hit a child, killing her instantly. Alerted, the rebels at Church Street corner fired a ragged volley as the Lancers swerved right, hooves flying wildly. At the corner of North Brunswick Street, Section-Commander Philip Walsh and Commandant Daly both shot at them. Daly dropped one Lancer, while Walsh carried the other man out of the saddle and brought him sprawling into the gutter. Volunteers at once rushed from cover and grabbed the loose horses; Daly slapped one on the rump and sent it back down Church Street with the intention of creating confusion among any cavalry following.

Triumphantly the dead trooper's lance was borne back to the corner of North King Street, where it was stuck into a manhole in the centre of the road and the tricolour of the new Republic hung victoriously from it. Then all the Volunteers in the vicinity briefly left their barricades to form up in a crude phalanx and fire a rifle salute into the air.

Section-Commander James Grace had been unable to eat any breakfast that morning. Yet he felt eager for the fight and was anything but nervous. In full Volunteer uniform, including the soft-brimmed hat which regulations laid down for field service, he was the first man, in fact, in "C" Company, Third Battalion, to turn up at his mobilization point. This was in Earlsfort Terrace, directly opposite Mr. Augustine Birrell's new National University, and here he waited for several minutes, a solitary if vivid figure armed with a long Lee-Enfield and fifty rounds of .303 ammunition, until the tall, fair-haired figure of Lieutenant Michael Malone hove in sight, riding his bicycle.

Aged twenty-eight, Malone was a good-looking, quietly-spoken, serious-minded soldier who knew how to handle a rifle well and was the best shot in the battalion. A bachelor ("the organization", as its members called the I.R.B., encouraged its recruits to keep clear of women), he also was wearing uniform and carried a Mauser rifle-pistol known as a "Peter the Painter". Grace felt sustained better when Malone revealed that he, too, had not been able to eat breakfast.

Not that Grace was a raw or callow recruit. On the contrary, during a visit to the United States in 1913, he had moved up into Canada to join a Territorial Regiment in order to learn how to use a rifle; three months later, on receiving a letter from home saying: "We are waiting for you," he had wrapped his long Lee-Enfield in a canvas bag and had caught the *Carthaginia* to Glasgow.

The rest of "C" Company gathered casually, almost as though they were meeting for a picnic. They were cheerful, but when Lieutenant Simon Donnelly turned up, he seemed haggard and worried. The reason became clear when he explained that the Company captain had refused to turn out and that Commandant de Valera had been forced to promote *him*. By 11.20, indeed, it had become clear that most of the Company were not going to turn out; altogether, only thirty-four were present. At 11.50, an anxious and deeply-disappointed Donnelly finally gave a reluctant order to march.

The Company moved off in two sections—Donnelly leading the way with a party of twenty men. Malone following with the full fifteen members of the Battalion's Cycle Corps. Both sections marched eastwards for about a mile until they reached Upper Mount Street. Here Dublin remains an oasis of quiet Georgian charm and genteel opulence, a part of the city preserved virtually intact in splendid eighteenth-century elegance. The streets are broad and empty, the squares treelined and gracious, and on this particular Easter Monday, hardly a human being stirred. In the distance a cab loped by, the jarvey's head jogging happily in rhythm with his nag's movements.

Donnelly and Malone briefly conferred, then resumed their march sepa-
rately. Donnelly cut down towards Boland's Bakery, de Valera's Battalion
headquarters, while Malone marched up through Mount Street Crescent
to the Canal, where he wheeled left towards Mount Street Bridge and then
halted his four unit-commanders—George Reynolds, James Grace, Denis
O'Donoghue and Patrick Doyle—to allocate them positions. Grace, with
two boys, Paddy Byrne and Michael Rowe, was told to march over the bridge
up Northumberland Road for about three hundred yards to the corner of
Haddington Road; two hundred yards east of this, towards the railway and
the sea, lay Beggar's Bush Military Barracks, and Grace's orders were to keep
the main gate under observation until the rest of Malone's party had had a
chance to take up their positions. Section-Commander Patrick Doyle and
three men were ordered to occupy St. Stephen's Parochial Hall, two hundred
yards up Northumberland Road on the right-hand side, and Company-
Adjutant O'Donoghue, the school on the left-hand side. Reynolds slipped
his blood-poisoned left hand from its surgical sling as Malone nodded to him
and indicated a big house standing on the corner of Clanwilliam Place.

From a military viewpoint, Clanwilliam House, a large three-storeyed,
stucco-fronted corner residence, could scarcely have been better sited. Here,
where the main Dublin-Kingstown road is carried along by Lower Mount
Street and Northumberland Road, the two long, almost straight avenues are
linked by Mount Street Bridge. Clanwilliam House dominated the Canal,
the school on the far side occupied by O'Donoghue, Northumberland Road
up as far as Haddington Road, and, most important of all, the bridge itself. It
was brilliantly positioned for an Irish Thermopylae.

Reynolds pushed his bicycle up the pathway and pressed the bell. A maid
opened the door.

"May we come in, please?" he asked politely.

The maid giggled.

"Bring in your bikes," ordered Reynolds stiffly and, before the girl could
prevent them, the five young men entered the hallway. James Doyle and
William Ronan were told to search the house. "And if you find anybody,
send them down," said Reynolds. On the first landing they found a middle-
aged lady—a Miss Wilson—whose mother owned the house.

"What's all this about?" asked Miss Wilson angrily.

"Will ye go downstairs, please, ma'am," said Ronan. "No harm'll come to
you if you do." Even as he spoke, old Mrs Wilson herself came out on to the
landing, and querulously demanded to know what all the fuss was about.

"If ye'll please go downstairs, ladies," insisted Ronan and ushered the two
women towards the head of the stairs. He and Doyle continued their search
of the house. When they had finished and had reported to Reynolds that the
house was empty, he called them into the front sitting-room. This was a large
bright room, with an oil-painting over the fireplace and a photograph of a
regular officer in full uniform on the mantlepiece.

"Now there's one thing I want you to remember," he told them. "From now on, remember that we're representatives of the Irish Republic, so I don't want you to behave like hooligans. For a start, be respectful to the residents of this house. And don't break any windows and do as little damage as you can." And to show them the way to conduct themselves, he crossed to the nearest window and carefully raised the lower sash. "Like this," he said. Then he gestured around the room. "Now, quick, get some of the furniture over here beside the windows, but don't make it too obvious that we've taken over the place."

While Reynolds was thus preparing Clanwilliam House for battle, Malone led Grace and the two boys into No. 25 Northumberland Road, a terraced mansion with stone steps leading up to the front door, situated on the corner of Haddington Road, and now empty. The owners, sympathetic to Sinn Fein and warned that the premises might be needed, had sent their servants away for the holidays and had then evacuated the place. Malone barricaded the front door with furniture, and loopholed the windows. He then filled several vessels with drinking water, ordering a few to be placed in each room.

In the street outside, twelve-year-old Gerald Morrissey and his friends, tired of waiting for something really exciting to happen, went back to their game of cowboys and Indians. The policeman who had been walking the beat in the area, sensing that this might prove to be a rather unhealthy district in the not-too-distant future, had already made himself scarce.

One hundred and fifty yards east of Clanwilliam House, Commandant Edward de Valera, a thirty-four-year-old New York-born Professor of Mathematics, had established himself in Boland's Bakery, a sprawling, low-lying building in Grand Canal Street. His command was hardly an enviable one. According to Plunkett's original plan, de Valera was supposed to occupy no less than sixteen outposts in the Ringsend area, including several Canal works, a railway station and a two-mile stretch of line, plus signalling cabins, gasworks, a granary, a railway loco-motive shop, dock-milling premises, several warehouses and mills, and the Bakery; a nightmarish task for an amateur commander, even with a battalion at full strength. As it was, he had only one hundred and twenty men.

De Valera's occupation of the Bakery and its environs had been effected with the minimum degree of force. He had chosen the Grand Canal Dispensary as his personal quarters; but when he and a party of his men climbed the wall separating the Dispensary garden from the Bakery, at about 12.10 p.m., the doctor's wife happened to be alone. In some terror she watched the men, led by the tall, swarthy-looking de Valera brandishing a sword, come running across her garden.

"You have five minutes in which to pack your valuables and leave the premises, ma'am," announced de Valera peremptorily. Mrs. Healy replied with a fit of hysteria and, for all his precise qualities of mind and learning, de Valera was hardly an expert on women. As Mrs. Healy ran screaming from the room, he turned in despair to an aide and said, "You'd better handle this," then hurriedly left and crossed back over the wall.

Mrs. Healy's hysterics continued until the return of her husband a short while later. Dr. Healy was admitted on the understanding that he would quit the premises again immediately, taking his wife with him. Reassured by his presence, Mrs. Healy quietened down, but Healy himself, sensing that he stood in little danger, decided to delay his departure as long as he could in the hope that help in some form or other might arrive.

"What'll happen if my property's destroyed or damaged?" he inquired of a rebel.

"The Irish Republic will recompense you," Lieutenant Joseph O'Byrne assured him.

"H'm," murmured the doctor doubtfully, and began writing an inventory of his possessions. When he had finished, he asked O'Byrne: "Can I have a receipt for these things?"

"You're not getting one from me, anyway," said O'Byrne, "because we're not going to steal anything."

When Healy and his wife eventually departed, O'Byrne and his men discovered six gold sovereigns scattered about loosely in the drawer of a desk. Determined to prove that they were honest men, and only fighting for their rights, O'Byrne locked the coins in the desk and scribbled a note to Healy telling him where to find them.

The seizure of the Bakery itself had also proved to be a comparatively simple matter, the only opposition springing from the bakers who, to begin with anyway, refused to take the whole thing seriously. Indeed, it was not until Donnelly threatened to shoot them, that they suddenly realized he was in earnest. Then they pointed out that they had more than a thousand loaves baking in the ovens, and that if these were allowed to spoil, the people in the district would go hungry.

"All right then," said Donnelly, "three or four of you can stay, but the rest must go." Even then the situation, for a moment, looked delicate enough. The angry bakers appeared determined to fight it out. But when a bayonet was shoved stiffly against one man's throat they decided to leave quietly.

From the beginning the great fear nagging de Valera and his officers was that the Bakery would be attacked in the first few minutes of the Rebellion from Beggar's Bush Barracks. Donnelly's immediate task, therefore, was to make emergency postings of four or five men at each corner of the Bakery, retaining a small mobile reserve in the centre. He then ordered several bread-vans to be pulled out on to Grand Canal Bridge where, stripped of their wheels, they made a formidable barricade facing up Clanwilliam Place towards Mount Street Bridge. His most important job, however, was the task of constructing a gangway leading from the Bakery up on to the main Dublin Kingstown railway line which sliced straight through their position. Here the railway tracks were elevated, banked to a height of sixteen feet. First, Donnelly had the brick wall separating the Bakery from the embankment breached; then he got the men to make a ramp by propping earth-filled flour bags under a causeway of planks. This gangway, when completed, gave de Valera quick and easy communication between his headquarters and his outposts along the railway line.

Within ten minutes of the rebels setting foot in the Bakery, the first shot was fired. Tom Walsh of "B" Company was unloading "stuff" from a donkey cart when a soldier returning to Beggar's Bush saw him and asked, "What are you up to?"

"Clear off!" shouted an insurgent sitting on top of the Bakery wall. The soldier ignored him and so the rifleman told him that a Republic had just been declared.

"You're nothing but bloody traitors then!" yelled the soldier.

"That fellow'll have to be shut up," murmured the rifleman and took aim. "Will you go away now?" he demanded.

"Traitors!" roared the soldier.

The rebel pulled the trigger and the soldier fell immediately. Walsh stared down at him and then back up at the smoking rifle. "Here, let's get on with it," remarked the rifleman coolly, and with a shrug Walsh handed him up a parcel of bombs. A big mill-worker, who had seen the shooting, now came over and demanded to know, "Why don't you put him in your cart and take him to Duns?" Walsh ignored him, but he persisted, "You can't leave him here!"

"I'm not taking him anywhere until I've finished this job," said Walsh emphatically. "In that case—" said the big mill-worker, then bent down and lifted up the wounded man. He started off up the street, staggering a little under the weight. At the corner, a crowd of spectators rushed forward to help him and Walsh heard them cheering.

Half a mile away, Volunteer George Lyons was trying to prevent the 12.15 to Kingstown from leaving Westland Row terminus. Like many another rebel that morning, he had discovered that the public were not yet ready to take the Rebellion seriously; not, that is, until they found themselves threatened with violence.

Lieutenant John Quinn, with the greater part of "B" Company, had seized the station a few minutes after noon, entering quietly from the rear and occupying the main incoming platform before either the staff or the public knew anything about it. Quinn continued down the line to put the signalling cabins out of action, while Lyons, his hand cupped, ordered the passengers to leave the train. "Go to the waiting rooms! Attention!—go to the waiting-rooms!" At once people poked their heads out of the carriages to stare at him, mystified. None, however, made a movement to obey. "I'll count ten," shouted Lyons, pointing his rifle at the near carriage. A trifle apprehensive, the passengers trooped out of the carriage and filed towards the waiting-rooms.

One man jumped down on to the rails and advanced towards Lyons shouting, "You're interfering with my business—do you know that?"

"Go back or I'll shoot!" warned Lyons, pointing his rifle towards him.

"What the hell do you mean threatening me with a gun!" shouted the man angrily. "I'm a better man than you any day of the week—and a better soldier if it comes to that." Lyons called out to two of his men, "Use your bayonets on that fellow!" Two youngsters leaped down on to the rails but advanced upon the man without much show of determination. "Ah, now, like a good man, can't you go back there and do as you're told!" they pleaded.

"Damned if I'll back an inch," insisted the man, stubbornly. For a moment they argued, then one of the rebels shouted, "He's a member of the Citizen Army!"

"Well, then, in the name of God, tell him to report to his officers!" said Lyons in exasperation. "He ought to be out with the rest of us."

Still muttering the man went away, but Lyons's problems were by no means finished. From the other platform the top-hatted stationmaster shouted across that he wished to talk. "Are you going to let this train leave?" he demanded.

"No," said Lyons abruptly.

"Are you going to let us do any business here today?"

"No."

"Are you going to let the public stay?"

"No—and you neither! You'd better go home now."

"Thank you," replied the stationmaster, sarcastically. "Thank you very much. But I'm in charge of this station and I intend to stay."

"We're relieving you of your responsibilities," said Lyons.

"There's money in this station, and I'm responsible for it," replied the stationmaster. "I'm not leaving, and that's that!"

Even Lyons was forced to admire the man's stubborn and admirable devotion to duty; but suddenly he faced a much more difficult problem.

As the public began leaving the station by the main door, a party of priests pushed through the crowd towards him.

"Reverend sirs, please turn round and leave the station," he shouted. But they still came on.

"Reverend sirs!" he repeated. "At any minute the military might rush the place. Every one of us here is in danger!"

Two priests began climbing the barrier.

"Retire!" shouted Lyons desperately. "Soldiers, prepare to fire!" Only two of his men, however, would raise their rifles.

"Can't I speak to you?" one of the priests asked quietly.

"You can give us your blessing, Father," said Lyons.

"What are you doing here anyway?" inquired the priest.

"Fighting for Ireland, Father. Ready to die for her." And Lyons banged his rifle-butt on the ground.

"But people will be slaughtered—innocent people. And the country ruined," objected the priest.

"We want to make Ireland independent, Father," said Lyons.

"Well, promise me this—will you stop fighting if you find out you can't win? You do realize that you're morally bound to yield to superior odds in order to prevent useless sacrifices?"

"If we can't hold our ground, then we'll give in!" promised Lyons. "But not before—I can tell you that."

Suddenly they were interrupted. Before Lyons could prevent him, one of his men dashed forward and knelt before the priest, asking, "Will you please hear my confession, Father?"

Glowering angrily at Lyons, the priest said, "We demand to be allowed to minister to the spiritual needs of these men!"

"Well, if you promise to confine your business to hearing confessions and don't try to give them any advice about what they're doing . . . " Lyons conceded.

"I agree," said the priest.

"All right, then," said Lyons, and opened the ticket barrier. The priests filed through and spread out along the platform. Slowly they moved down it, listening to the muted words of the confessing rebels who knelt before them, still gripping their rifles.

For over an hour out along the railway line Peter Nolan had been ripping up rails with a sledge-hammer while around him other rebels smashed signalling mechanism and closed level crossings. Sweating heavily, Nolan rested briefly before commencing to dig himself a shallow trench in the middle of the sleepers.

Volunteer Joseph Guilfoyle, on the other hand, had had it really easy. Ordered to guard a railway bridge, he had spent his time watching people walking on the roadway beneath, apparently utterly unconcerned by the presence of armed rebels immediately above them. Once, Commandant de Valera himself had come down the line, tall, foreign-looking, and tensed, and as he passed, he had called out curtly, "Remember, shoot anything you see in uniform!" As the lanky back vanished towards Lansdowne Road, Guilfoyle was left with an impulse to run after it and ask if the order included postmen but he decided that under the circumstances the Commandant was hardly likely to appreciate the joke.

Farther down the line, Guilfoyle's brother John, a lieutenant in "A" Company, started work on what was undoubtedly the most ambitious and back-breaking task of all. Ordered to invest Beggar's Bush, he had decided that the best way to do it was to occupy a shop opposite the main gates. There was only one way to do this, however, and Guilfoyle began boring his way through a row of cottages backing on to it. It would take him six hours to complete the job, but inside Beggar's Bush that evening the harassed military, watching rifle-fire spurt angrily from the little shop, would scratch their heads and wonder how the rebels had managed to get there.

7

JAMES JOYCE, a thirty-five-year-old private in the Citizen Army, had awakened that morning happy with the happy thought that on this day he was going to get some of his own back.

Twelve hours a day, seven days a week, Joyce, a bottle-washer by trade, worked in the cellar of a public house at Portobello Bridge. A menial job, it might just have been bearable if Davy, the "ould blackguard" who owned the pub, had only behaved "half dacently" with him; but, as it was, Davy would never allow him even a Sunday off to parade with the Citizen Army. And the Citizen Army meant a great deal to Joyce. Accustomed to the scorn and ill-disguised contempt of his fellows, Joyce had long ago discovered in the Army that degree of dignity and companionship for which his soul deeply longed. Boys like Paddy Buttner or Charlie D'Arcy would flock round him and listen to him wide-eyed as he vividly described how some day he would shoot "ould Davy". The man, after all, was beyond the pale; he had even warned Joyce that if he took another Sunday off he would be sacked with only a week's notice.

The previous Tuesday [of Holy Week], shortly after eight o'clock in the evening, Joyce had been one of a handful of men summoned to Mr. Connolly's room in Liberty Hall. This room was a bare place, sparsely furnished with a plain table, a few chairs and a cot in the corner where the Commandant-General often slept. Already in the room with Connolly were Captain Richard MacCormack, Captain John O'Neill (who had served with the British Army), Lieutenant Michael Kelly and two sergeants, Frank Robbins and Joseph Doyle. As usual, Connolly had wasted neither time nor breath. He explained that an insurrection would be launched in Dublin at half-past six on Easter Sunday evening. The main body of the Citizen Army would occupy St. Stephen's Green under Commandant Mallin and the Countess Markievicz, and as the first military threat to the Green would probably materialize from Portobello Barracks, he wanted Captain MacCormack to secure some outposts and hold on to them just long enough to allow Mallin and the Countess time to prepare their defences. Therefore, he was ordering Sergeant Doyle and sixteen men to occupy Davy's pub—"including you!" said Connolly, pointing at Joyce; Lieutenant Kelly would support them from the railway bridge overlooking the Canal, while MacCormack himself would seize Harcourt Street railway terminus to prevent the military rushing in forces by rail.

Connolly added an instruction to Doyle, "Don't fire on the military until you see the whites of their eyes!" Then he explained to Robbins, "I want you to prepare an escape route for these fellows when they are forced to fall back. Barricade Hatch Street at both ends. Find a way out for them into Stephen's Green through some of those big houses—I suggest Iveagh House." Finally, turning to Joyce, he said, "What would you do if a British soldier was chasing you, threatening to ram a bayonet up your backside? You'd take the shortest way out of that, wouldn't you? Well, that's what I want you to do for these fellows. Get them out of that pub the quickest and safest way you know."

And that was why, at 11.55 on Easter Monday morning, Joyce found himself marching briskly with Captain MacCormack's detachment up Grafton Street. Beside him trotted Paddy Buttner, aged fifteen.

All went well until the column debouched into St. Stephen's Green, where they suddenly sighted a young military officer on horseback, accompanied by an orderly, clopping down towards them.

"Lording it as usual!" murmured Joyce. "Keeping down the natives."

"What do you think we'll do?" asked Buttner, nervously.

"Just you wait and see," advised Joyce, darkly.

Tension grew in the rebel ranks as the gap between them and the two military horsemen narrowed. As the officer drew abreast, Captain MacCormack surprised everybody by saluting smartly. Instinctively, the British officer returned the salute—magnificently—and then he and his man had clattered past before they realized what had happened. At once they reined in their horses and Buttner, glancing back, saw them gazing after the column suspiciously.

The two horsemen, in fact, followed the column as it went up Harcourt Street. At the station MacCormack halted, and ordering Doyle to take eight men and two boys and march on to Davy's pub, he led his main body inside. By the time Doyle was ready to continue the march, the two cavalrymen had ridden past and stopped a short distance away. "We'll fix that fellow!" swore Doyle softly, hoping that he might get a chance at the next corner. Here, just before the main road turned left up towards Portobello Barracks, a narrow street offered a short cut. Everything depended upon the street chosen by the officer. If he decided to take the short cut, there was nothing they could do; but if he kept to the main road, they might just possibly nip through and head him off. Anxiously they watched as the horsemen rode towards the short cut, then sighed with relief as they rode past. "Right now, fellows, at the double!" shouted Doyle.

The rebel party dashed through the cut and reached the main road just ahead of the two cavalrymen. Doyle gave the order to fix bayonets and spread out across the road. Seeing the rebels attempt to form a barrier, the officer spurred his horse, but Private James Kelly lunged with his bayonet and shouted, "Begod, you won't," then fired. The shot missed, but the officer, reining in his mount, swung round sharply and galloped away, followed by his orderly.

"To Davy's—at the double," roared Doyle in triumph. Joyce led the way. Reaching Davy's, he kicked in the door and marched inside to find Davy himself standing behind the bar, serving a customer. Joyce strutted forward masterfully. "Ould Davy," putting down the pint, banged the counter with his fist and roared, "I'm giving you a week's notice, Joyce!"

"And I'm giving you five minutes, Mister Davy!" shouted Joyce, raising his rifle and opening fire at the bottles on the shelves. As Davy ducked in terror, glass showering round him, his customers ran for their lives.

The famous Long Bar of the Shelbourne was full; the atmosphere one of neat whiskies and gins, horses and military talk. Cavalry leggings, red tabs, and white whiskers mingled conspicuously with the heavy tweeds of the landed gentry up from the country for the Ballsbridge Show. Over-bred voices hummed loudly with pre-lunch chatter.

Through the tall, graceful windows the trees of St. Stephen's Green Park, new-leaved, stirred sweetly in the hazy sunlight. Green lawns glittered and heavy scents rose from the mingling rosebeds, high protecting shrubberies and the great shading elms, chestnuts and copper-beeches. White-bonneted babies crawled about on the grass or gurgled in their prams, watched over anxiously by uniformed nannies; old men reclined on the park benches and read their papers; Air Mechanic Pratt, R.F.C., and his young lady strolled arm-in-arm, then sat down on a seat to watch the antics of the ducks on the pond.

Commandant Mallin's men had filtered into the Green in twos and threes through eight different entrances. At the west entrance the park-keeper had stopped Mallin himself, saying "You can't come in here."

"I'm sorry—but we mean to," said Mallin.

"Well, at least wait until I get the women and children out," replied the park-keeper.

"Hurry up, then," said Mallin. "We'll help you."

Members of the public were quickly shepherded out and Mallin ordered the gates closed and barricaded with park benches. Then he put his men to work digging shallow trenches. Air Mechanic Pratt and his young lady sat on, watching it all with interest until, suddenly, they were spotted. A rebel was sent over to deal with them.

"I'm sorry, miss, but you'll have to go," he said. "And you, mister, I'm afraid you're a prisoner."

"But we're enjoying it all," protested the young lady. "Can't we stay and watch?"

"Look here!" said the young rebel. "We're fighting for Irish freedom!"

"But we won't get in the way," insisted the girl.

"Damn it all, miss, this is a Rebellion, don't you understand! *He's* a prisoner. *You* can go home."

"Aren't you simply carrying out manoeuvres?" asked Pratt as a look of astonishment crossed his face. In a daze he allowed himself to be escorted towards a summer-house, where he was told to sit down on some steps. Looking up, he found he was sitting under a statue of George II.

Countess Markievicz arrived in the Green, entering boldly by Traitors' Gate (the gate had been erected as a memorial to Irishmen who had lost their lives fighting for Britain against the Boers), almost as though she owned the entire Park. In that moment, she looked an unforgettable figure; tall and dark, hardly beautiful by modern standards perhaps, yet still the embodiment of that "wild Irish girl" the Anglo-Irish aristocracy once bred with a proliferating regularity. Behind her loomed a girlhood spent amid wealth and privilege; a girlhood of gay parties and the hunting field, of Lissadell, her father's great house in Sligo, where she used to entertain the poet Yeats. All of which she had forsaken to marry Casimir, Count Markievicz; but at least it had brought its compensations. She had entered upon the genteel world of Dublin's artistic salons and literary high teas and thence, through the ferment of emergent nationality, into the soup kitchens of Liberty Hall, where she had appeared like a flaming angel, ministering and exhorting during the worst moments of the 1913 transport strike. A grande dame, born in Carlton House Terrace, London, a girl who had once curtsied to Queen Victoria, she now marched into St. Stephen's Green at the head of her troops, dressed theatrically to adorn the occasion in a dark-green woollen blouse trimmed with brass buttons, dark-green tweed knee-breeches, black stockings and puttees, and round her waist a cartridge belt from which, on one side, dangled a small automatic pistol and, from the other, a convertible Mauser rifle-pistol; the whole topped by a black velour hat trimmed with a spray of cocque feathers. It hardly mattered that the troops she led in through the gate were merely Boy Scouts and women; she nevertheless marched them in with the imperious confidence of a woman whose ancestors had been conquerors.

The arrival of the Countess's contingent enabled a commissariat and a Red Cross post to be quickly established. Miss Margaret Ffrench-Mullen set up a Red Cross First Aid Post in the summer-house, while Miss Mary Hyland and Miss Kathleen Cleary commandeered the glass conservatory where they laid out sandwiches, cheeses, cakes, meats and hams. The Countess, naturally, ignored such purely feminine activities. Here, in these few acres of city park, in accordance with James Connolly's ideals, women were entitled to stand shoulder to shoulder with men; and if it came to it, she herself had no scruples about shooting the enemy. She even looked forward to it and as things turned out she would not have to wait long. Within five minutes Constable Michael Lahiff attempted to enter the Green at Traitors' Gate. He was told to go away, but obstinately, if courageously, refused. Informed of his attitude, the Countess rushed to the railings and took aim with her Mauser rifle-pistol. As she fired, two men beside her also shot. Lahiff slumped to the pavement, hit by three bullets. "I shot him!" shouted the Countess delightedly. "I shot him!"

Less than two hundred yards away, Miss Chris Caffrey stood at the door of the summer-house watching the men digging, the women laying out the first-aid equipment, the sunlight playing over the green lawns, and outside, people strolling past, stopping now and then to look in, and she found it hard to believe that this was the start of an insurrection. Near her, Commandant Mallin, a pale, slight figure with a tight, clean-cut walk (he had served with the Indian Army as an N.C.O.), strolled among his men, aiding and exhorting them and cracking quiet jokes. From his attitude she had no suspicion exactly how formidable a task faced him, complicated as it was by Connolly's directive that the position was to be regarded as of vital importance.

No fewer than ten streets led into St. Stephen's Green, three of them major routes to any penetration of the city from the south—Merrion Row, Leeson Street, and Harcourt Street. If the military, advancing from Kingstown, for example, were to meet stubborn resistance from de Valera and outflanked him by crossing the Canal by a higher bridge, then they must inevitably funnel down Merrion Row or Leeson Street on their way towards Sackville Street; troops from Portobello would probably work their way down Harcourt Street.

Mallin quickly realized that the Park was certain to prove an indefensible stretch of open ground, particularly if the military managed to seize the tall houses around its perimeter. He decided to forestall them. Aided by the Countess and a small party, he smashed the ground-floor windows of certain houses and placed men inside, telling the occupants that they could stay or leave as they wished. This done, he started blocking the streets. He halted traffic; and motorists, draymen, cabbies and tramwaymen were ordered to drive their vehicles into the four big piles of materials which rose rapidly in the roadway. The entire perimeter was soon blocked by barricades, with two derelict trams outside the Shelbourne also helping to impede movement.

Meanwhile inside the hotel itself there was consternation. Tweedy gentlemen, emerging after lunch, found themselves prisoners—although in most cases they were quickly set free again. Military men were treated more summarily. A khaki uniform appearing on the porch immediately drew a potshot. One or two of the more resolute spirits drew their revolvers and shot back, but in the end wiser counsels prevailed and it was decided to conserve ammunition in case the rebels rushed the hotel.

For all his reputed skill and experience, Mallin made no attempt to take the Shelbourne, although it was easily the most prominent building in the Green, and by virtue of its height, certainly the most commanding. Instead, his men continued to dig-in in the Green where, crouched in their shallow holes, they were able to gaze up at the brilliant façade, its stonework picked out in rich cream paint, and envy the wealthy who ate and slept there. He was to regret it, of course. For very soon now, and for all the hard days to come, it was to stand there and mock him.

Many were "out"; but even more were not. A few would join the fight later when they learned what was happening. But the truth was, that after all the years of waiting and planning, the insurrection had gone off at half-cock. In the end it had become a matter of haste and improvisation, of error mounted upon confusion. And ironically, after all their devious attempts to deceive MacNeill and the moderately-minded men who nominally controlled the Irish Volunteers, the Republican Brotherhood discovered themselves fighting the battle virtually alone.

For instance, only twenty-four out of the forty members of the Rathfarnham Company ("Pearse's Own") mobilized at Rathfarnham Church and Lieutenant Boland, Company C.O., declared that he saw no point in going into Dublin. "But we can't desert Pearse now!" exploded Lieutenant Edward Bulfin, furious that so many men who had known Pearse personally and upon whose loyalty he had counted had let him down. In the end, Boland agreed to march; but just as the Company was about to move off Professor MacNeill, accompanied by his son and a Volunteer officer, rode up on their bicycles.

"Where are you off to?" demanded the Chief of Staff, surprised at seeing them on parade.

"We've been called out by Pearse," explained Boland.

"But you can't go," said MacNeill. "You'll be marching into a death trap. You must disperse and go home." And it was only after another furious row between Boland and Bulfin that the Rathfarnham Company—or what was left of it—had marched to support their chief.

Even the plans to isolate Dublin, although originally drawn up with care, had been bungled.

For weeks before Easter, Captain Dermot Lynch, a Volunteer staff officer, had been collecting information about the telephone and telegraph lines in the city, helped by such men as Richard Mulcahy, an employee in the Post Office Engineering Department. On Holy Thursday a small group of Volunteers and Citizen Army men were detailed for various jobs. Mulcahy was ordered to cut the cable and telephone lines to Belfast and Great Britain at Raheny, outside Dublin; the brothers George and Sam King were told to blow up manholes in Lombard Street and Palace Street, thereby cutting the Castle's private wires to London and other parts of the country; Michael King was ordered to destroy the main Dublin telephone manhole outside the Telephone Exchange in Crown Alley, which would wreck most of the city's internal telephone system.

At 12.10 p.m. then, George and Sam King blew up the manholes as instructed, cutting Sir Matthew's direct circuit to Mr. Birrell in London and almost—but not quite—isolating the Castle. Mulcahy cut the cables and telephone wires at Raheny. But Michael King was unable to carry out his task, for the men who were to have assisted him failed to turn up. He reported this to Pearse and Connolly.

"In that case fall in with the other men," said Connolly. He and Pearse subsequently decided to send a small party to seize the Central Telephone Exchange itself.

The attempt ended ignominiously because of an old woman. As the party turned into Crown Alley, she rushed forward shouting, "Go back, boys, go back, the place is crammed with military!" Taking her at her word, the rebels fell back.

Five hours later the military occupied the Exchange which had stood undefended all day long.

Not that all the bungling was on the rebel side.

In the early hours of Easter Monday the District Inspector of the Royal Irish Constabulary at Tralee reported to Dublin Castle that the second of the three men who had landed from the German submarine had been captured and had turned out to be a Sergeant Daniel Bailey of Casement's Irish Brigade. After interrogation, he had talked freely, revealing that an insurrection was about to take place and that the Castle itself would be attacked. Wimborne urged Nathan to strengthen the guards both at the Castle and at Vice-Regal Lodge but, once again, the Under-Secretary demurred. When 10.30 a.m. passed and no incidents had occurred, Wimborne did not press the point. Revolutions, he believed, always occurred immediately after breakfast, and as nothing had happened so far, Bailey's warning appeared to have little value.

Even when, an hour later, reports began to flow in of damage to railway lines and other communications as far south as Kildare, neither Wimborne nor Nathan displayed any real sense of alarm. Their attitude was mirrored in the behaviour of Colonel Kennard, O.C. troops, Dublin, who was "absent from his office" when the insurrection began, and in that of his deputy, Colonel H. V. Cowan, Assistant Adjutant-General. Cowan believed that if the Sinn Feiners had been prepared to start any trouble, they would certainly have attempted to rescue Casement when he had passed through Dublin on Saturday night. No extra precautions, therefore, were taken. Only normal measures, which had been in force for some time, were in operation at noon that day—an inlying picquet of one hundred men from each regiment in Dublin was standing by, making a total of four hundred men altogether.

The military forces in Dublin that morning amounted to one hundred and twenty officers and 2,265 men—not all of them completely trained, but certainly all efficient enough to be turned out. These numbers were made up as follows:

At Marlborough Barracks, Phoenix Park: thirty-five officers and eight hundred and fifty-one other ranks of the 6th Cavalry Regiment.
At Richmond Barracks: eighteen officers and three hundred and eighty-five other ranks of the 3rd Royal Irish Regiment.
At Portobello Barracks: twenty-one officers and six hundred and fifty other ranks of the 3rd Royal Irish Rifles.

At the Royal Barracks: thirty-seven officers and four hundred and thirty other ranks of the 10th Royal Dublin Fusiliers.

By 12.10 the Dublin police, thanks to the failure of the rebels to seize the Central Telephone Exchange, had managed to telephone Military H.Q. at Parkgate with the news that the Castle was under attack. Colonel Cowan, advised by Major Owen Lewis of the General Staff, telephoned Marlborough Barracks and ordered a detachment of cavalry to proceed at once to Sackville Street. Then he ordered units from Richmond, Portobello and the Royal Barracks to march to the relief of the Castle. It was unfortunate, certainly, from a rebel point of view, that an attempt to destroy the telephone junction at Parkgate Street—through which all Irish Command telephone lines ran—had not been pressed home with resolution.

Nothing which resembled panic had as yet developed in either the Government itself or its organs, the military and police, although all, undoubtedly, were caught on the wrong foot. Adrenalin undoubtedly coursed more freely through a number of port-encrusted veins and there was a great deal of confusion. Wimborne, apprised that Nathan was besieged in the Castle and that an army of rebels was marching on Vice-Regal Lodge, called for military protection, then sent units from Marlborough Barracks to put out the fire in the Magazine Fort; active measures which gave him a chance to think. Yet he felt overwhelmed by the sheer responsibility of discovering exactly how many rebels were out, whether the country was going to rise in their support, or even whether the Irish regiments of the regular army were likely to go over to them. Above and beyond anything else, what of Germany?

According to insurgent calculations made on the actual morning of the insurrection (these have been amended over the years until they now amount to something like twice this number), there were just over seven hundred rebels out in Dublin altogether. Military forces, therefore, outnumbered the rebels right from the start by at least three and a half to one; by late afternoon the odds would have lengthened significantly, and within forty-eight hours would have risen to something like twenty to one. Yet the authorities made no real move to crush the rebels in a single quick devastating blow but, instead, cast about nervously for overwhelming reinforcements.

At 12.30 p.m. Colonel Cowan succeeded in getting through to the Curragh before his telephone lines were cut, and asked that the 1,600-strong Mobile Column in reserve there be dispatched immediately to the capital. He then attempted to call London, but was unable to get through. A junior officer offered a solution, volunteering to bicycle in civilian clothes through the insurgent lines to Kingstown, where there was a naval wireless transmitter. He reached Kingstown, seven miles from Dublin, shortly after one o'clock, and at 1.10 p.m. the news was flashed to London.

By then troops had already clashed with the rebels and the jittery Cowan had called urgently for further reinforcements. These would consist of a battery of 18-pounders brought up from Athlone; the 4th Battalion of the Dublin Fusiliers, from Templemore; a composite battalion (1,000 men) of New Army recruits, from Belfast; and an additional 1,000 men apart from the Mobile Column, from the Curragh. The rebels had asked for it. And now they were most certainly going to get it.

8

FROM A WINDOW of the Imperial Hotel in Sackville Street a young bride and her husband watched Pearse and Connolly emerge from the G.P.O. and halt inside the massive portico.

Mrs. Thomas Dillon had a special interest in the scene before her. Three of her brothers, the Plunkett boys, were inside that great grey building. Joseph, the eldest, had been closest to her. She had kept house for him, and they had planned to hold a double wedding—she marrying Tom Dillon, he the artist, Grace Gifford, whose enormous antique ring he wore on his finger and to whom the Will that lay next his heart bequeathed everything. A plan which had had to be cancelled because of the special circumstances.

The honeymooners could see little but a jostle of Volunteers and Citizen Army men inside the portico. They continued to watch as a crowd gathered, and a sudden hush fell over the street.

From the low step of the G.P.O. Patrick Pearse began reading the Proclamation of the Republic:

POBLACHT NA h-EIREANN
THE PROVISIONAL GOVERNMENT OF THE
IRISH REPUBLIC
TO THE PEOPLE OF IRELAND

IRISHMEN AND IRISHWOMEN: In the name of God and of the dead generations from which she receives her old tradition of nationhood, Ireland, through us, summons her children to her flag and strikes for her freedom.

Having organized and trained her manhood through her secret revolutionary organization, the Irish Republican Brotherhood, and through her open military organizations, the Irish Volunteers and the Irish Citizen Army, having patiently perfected her discipline, having resolutely waited for the right moment to reveal itself, she now seizes that moment, and, supported by her exiled children in America and by gallant allies in Europe, but relying in the first on her own strength, she strikes in full confidence of victory.

We declare the right of the people of Ireland to the ownership of Ireland, and to the unfettered control of Irish destinies, to be sovereign and indefeasible. The long usurpation of that right by a foreign people and government has not extinguished the right, nor can it ever be extinguished except by the destruction of the Irish people. In every generation the Irish people have asserted their right to national freedom and sovereignty; six times during the past three hundred years they have asserted it in arms. Standing on that fundamental right and again asserting it in arms in the face of the world, we hereby proclaim the Irish Republic as a Sovereign Independent State, and we pledge our lives and the lives of our comrades-in-arms to the cause of its freedom, of its welfare, and of its exaltation among the nations.

The Irish Republic is entitled to, and hereby claims, the allegiance of every Irishman and Irishwoman. The Republic guarantees religious and civil liberty, equal rights and equal opportunities to all its citizens, and declares its resolve to pursue the happiness and prosperity of the whole nation and of all its parts, cherishing all the children of the nation equally, and oblivious of the differences carefully fostered by an alien government, which have divided a minority from the majority in the past.

Until our arms have brought the opportune moment for the establishment of a permanent National Government, representative of the whole people of Ireland and elected by the suffrages of all her men and women, the Provisional Government, hereby constituted, will administer the civil and military affairs of the Republic in trust for the people.

We place the cause of the Irish Republic under the protection of the Most High God, Whose blessing we invoke upon our arms, and we pray that no one who serves that cause will dishonour it by cowardice, inhumanity, or rapine. In this supreme hour the Irish nation must, by its valour and discipline and by the readiness of its children to sacrifice themselves for the common good, prove itself worthy of the august destiny to which it is called.

Signed on behalf of the Provisional Government,

THOMAS J. CLARKE	SEAN MAC DIARMADA	THOMAS MACDONAGH
P. H. PEARSE	EAMONN CEANNT	JAMES CONNOLLY
JOSEPH PLUNKETT		

When Pearse had finished, the beaming Connolly took his hand and shook it vigorously, saying: "Thanks be to God, Pearse, that we've lived to see this day!" A few ragged cheers hung in the air, but the poet, Stephen MacKenna, who listened to Pearse read these words, recorded later that he felt sad for him, for the response from the crowd was chilling. There were no wild hurrahs, no scenes reminiscent of the excitement which had gripped the French mob before they stormed the Bastille. The Irish simply listened and shrugged their shoulders, or sniggered a little, and then glanced round to see if the police were coming.

But Connolly was delighted. Stepping out on to the pavement and looking up at the roof, where the two flags flew—the green flag on the left (at the corner of Princes Street); the Tricolour on the right (at the corner of Henry Street); he chuckled and called out to Miss Carney, his secretary, "Isn't it grand!" Nearby, young insurgents were posting up copies of the Proclamation, or handing them round among the crowd. One copy, weighed down with stones, was placed on the ground at the foot of Nelson Pillar so that everybody could read it.

Slowly the crowd broke up. Some strolled across to the Pillar, where they idly read the Proclamation; others just stood and stared up at the unfamiliar flags. Quite a few, bored with the whole affair, simply turned and wandered away.

Early in the afternoon, however, big crowds had gathered in Sackville Street. People sat on the parapets of O'Connell Bridge or collected on the far side of the river at the corner of D'Olier and Westmoreland Streets, waiting tensely for the military. People constantly flowed past the G.P.O. Boys and girls flirted as they walked under the walls, their laughter floating up to the rebels on the roof. Dublin, it was clear, was *en fête* and determined to enjoy herself. At intervals shrill cries of "Here's the military!" or "Here's the soldiers!" would sweep along the street, causing panic, but would prove to be false alarms.

Inside the G.P.O. itself the men were kept on edge by a succession of alerts. Each time, they would be forced to down tools, pick up their rifles or shotguns and run to the windows. In the scramble and confusion, weapons were continually going off, until Captain Brennan Whitmore believed it would be a great deal safer outside the building than in.

In the street the crowds thickened. Many of the people were "separation" women, drawn from the poorer class and clad in black shawls. First they abused the rebels, who answered them in kind; then they began squabbling among themselves. Inevitably they started fighting. Delightedly the rebels watched two shawlies hit out at each other. When they began dragging each other's hair out, cheers greeted their efforts.

All at once the crowd appeared to stagger. People pushed into each other as others pressed forward, and within seconds the squabbling shawlies had disappeared, carried roughly away. Brennan Whitmore saw a line of priests, their hands linked together, spreading themselves across Sackville Street and advancing steadily from the far side of the Pillar, driving the crowd back in disorder towards O'Connell Bridge. Like an encroaching wave, the priests surged forward. The crowd solidified into a black, bobbing mass of heads. Some broke away into the side streets and waited until the clergy passed before flowing back in again behind them, but most of them fell back until they were almost at O'Connell Bridge. The priests halted, turned and went back up Sackville Street again. Their faces stern and unyielding, they once more forced the crowd back.

From inside the G.P.O. the rebels could be heard singing:

"Soldiers are we,
 Whose lives are pledged to Ireland . . . "

Rifle-fire crackled from across the river, from the direction of Dublin Castle.

The priests pressed on. Suddenly they faced a different mob—a wilder, more ragged lot this time, a slum crowd; a mob at once excited and exhilarated by the knowledge that there had been a breakdown of law and order. For the first time they stood firm, while behind them more and more shawlies rolled up to chant ribald songs. At Nelson Pillar the thin line of priests was forced to divide. The mob surged forward, and within seconds, the priests went reeling back and were swept away like bubbles on the surf.

Suddenly there was a yell and the crowd scattered. Brennan Whitmore heard a shout:

"The Lancers! The Lancers!"

A sack of coal, intended to block a window, slipped from his hands, and he reached for his rifle. The G.P.O. became a confusion of movement. Men ran to their positions while officers bawled orders. Brennan Whitmore dropped flat on a table, poked his rifle through a loophole, and sighted along the barrel. His field of vision was narrow, barely stretching from Clery's, opposite, to the plinth of the Pillar on his left. The crowd were still scattering, most taking cover in doorways, but a handful, more daring, remained in the roadway, poised ready to run. Brennan Whitmore tongued the inside of his mouth and found it dry. It was his first time under fire, and like generations of men before him, he wondered how he would acquit himself.

He heard Connolly's voice rising above the noise: "Don't fire until I give the command! Don't fire! Let them gallop the full length of the building—is that clear? D'ye hear?—let them gallop the full length of the building! But whatever you do, don't fire until I tell you!"

9

ONE HUNDRED MEN of the 3rd Royal Irish Regiment halted approximately 200 yards from the place where Section-Commander John Joyce of the Irish Volunteers and his four comrades waited behind a low wall. While the Major in charge of the military forces cautiously scanned the rise of Mount Brown, Joyce began to experience a sense of pulsating excitement.

When the picquet halted at the crossroads, Lieutenant George Malone of the Royal Irish walked up from the rear to see why they had been halted. As yet he knew nothing of any Rebellion; all he knew was that shortly after noon, the picquet had been ordered to fall in, ball ammunition had been issued and they had been told to march to Dublin Castle. This kind of "parade" was hardly abnormal; several times over the past twelve months, the Battalion had been alerted in similar ways.

Now, as he reached the head of the column, he heard the Major in command (in peacetime, a District Inspector of the Royal Irish Constabulary) ask: "Which of you officers is senior?"

"I am," said Malone.

"Well, take a party of twenty men and march to the Castle. If you're fired on, take the appropriate action as laid down for street fighting. We'll give you support from here." Glancing up the hill to where the Sinn Feiners—one wearing a slouch hat with plumes—were leaning over the wall, rifles in hand, looking at them, Malone realised that clearly matters would be put to the test.

A word of advice from Company Sergeant Major Banks and Lieutenant Malone fell in his men. Then accompanied by a sergeant, a thickset man with a heavy moustache, he marched them off "at attention"—that is to say, in columns of four, rifles at the slope—in silence, slap down the middle of the tramlines. None of the rifles was loaded, as was proper for troops operating in a city. Later, Malone remembered the extraordinary silence and emptiness of that road—empty, that is, except for the Sinn Feiners still leaning over the wall. Then as they neared the spot, the silence was broken by a murmur from the men behind him. Some were veterans of Mons, with long service on the Western Front, others only partly trained lads from Tipperary and Waterford; the consensus of their opinion was that they were "marching into trouble." Malone turned his head and shouted "Silence!" Even as he did so, the Volunteers opened fire.

The range—and this is agreed by both Section-Commander John Joyce and Lieutenant (later Major) Malone—was no more than five yards. As an uneven fusillade rang out beside him, Joyce saw three of the soldiers drop; then the rest scattered and made for cover. "It was a pretty hot position" remembers Lieutenant Malone. For his part, Joyce was trying to focus his sights on one of the darting, running, crouching figures but they reached the far side of the street without additional loss and began breaking their way into the houses and other buildings there. Joyce was forced to admire the behaviour of the picquet sergeant. With his back to the rebels, he coolly stood his ground and directed his men as they attempted the flimsy doors of small houses. Several times Joyce tried to line him up in his sights, but the man kept shifting about so much that he became an almost impossible target. Finally Joyce fired, and watched his bullet kick into the brick wall just above his head. The sergeant gave no indication that he had been almost hit by the bullet. After that, Joyce shot rapidly, if wildly.

Almost opposite Joyce's position was a tan-yard. Now, the sergeant began battering on the door with his rifle-butt and it quickly gave way. The troops rushed inside. As Lieutenant Malone followed, he bent down to clutch the collar of a soldier who was lying face downwards in the doorway, dead. Suddenly he felt himself being hit but he staggered on down the yard where he stood for a moment, shouting orders and loading his revolver, before collapsing over a pile of sheep skins. As from a great distance he heard a voice announcing "the officer is hit." A long time later, or so it seemed, he found himself lying on a sofa in a kitchen, beside him, sitting in a chair, his jaw shattered, Private Moulton, and the body of a dead soldier lying on the floor. Two "kind and charitable young women" were bandaging his wound. Despite the casualties, the older hands who kept flitting about, seemed to be taking the matter lightly.

Meanwhile, Joyce and his comrades had come under fire from the remainder of the picquet, still some distance down the road. But once the advance party had gained cover, firing temporarily ceased.

For almost fifteen minutes there was an uneasy lull. Volunteer Lieutenant O'Brien and his party crouched behind their wall, quietly jubilant, pleased at the way in which they had surprised the military. They realised, however, that, as yet, they had not been exposed to anything like a full military onslaught. The lull, indeed, was ominous.

They had, in fact, every reason to feel apprehensive. Once the picquet had been fired on, there was nothing for it, so far as the 3rd Royal Irish were concerned, but to fall in the rest of the battalion and attack the South Dublin Union. Furious at the treatment handed out to his men, Lieutenant Colonel R. L. Owens, the C.O., assisted by the Adjutant, Captain Roche Kelly, a Boer War veteran, first dispatched a party to take up positions in the Royal Hospital, the official residence of the Commander-in-Chief and Dublin's oldest public building outside the Castle, which stood hardly three hundred yards from the rebel positions. From its roof and great dormer windows the rebel positions could be easily enfiladed. Then he sent his main party, led by Major Milner, Captain Edward Warmington and Lieutenant Alan Ramsay, to attack the Union from the rear. The party made their way down O'Connell Road which led to the Rialto Gate and into the South Circular Road. Here the men were divided into several small parties, which entered houses opposite the Gate. Fifteen men were ordered into the Rialto buildings on the far side of the Canal, while the remainder of the force knelt down behind garden walls and prepared for a quick dash across the road towards the Gate.

At almost exactly five minutes to one the assault opened. One second, there was only a brooding silence; the next, the air was filled with fury. To Joyce, under really severe fire for the first time in his life, the effect was shattering. To fight England, to do battle for Ireland, had seemed until this moment merely a simple, elemental matter of give and take; with success and survival depending largely upon rapidity of movement and accuracy of fire. There had been nothing in his experience to prepare him for the veritable wall of bullets which now swept over his head, not only from the front, but also from the rear and flanks. Were they encircled? In that instant, Joyce felt that he was utterly helpless; that there was nowhere he could hide.

"Get back, boys!" shouted Lieutenant O'Brien.

Time and place and their meaning had vanished. There was nothing, anyway, to fire at, for the military appeared to have vanished into thin air; yet from the bullets still spattering all about him Joyce knew they could see him. O'Brien, fortunately, kept cool and Joyce instinctively obeyed him as he shouted, "Spread out! Spread out!" He glanced behind him, seeking some kind of cover in the open field, but it seemed impossible that a man could survive out there. Yet there was no alternative. The only hope was the slight ridges and sudden dips in the ground and, rising, Joyce hurled himself towards a depression barely twenty yards away. He landed heavily, rolling over in the grass as he did so and firing wildly at the unseen enemy. Spread out across the field, his comrades were doing the same, then, pressed flat to the earth, firing as rapidly as their antiquated weapons would allow, before retreating again in short, sharp, running bursts. Under the wall from which they had just retreated lay the body of John Owens, aged twenty-four, fatally wounded, his plumed starch hat beside him. Rifle-fire crackled continuously. Then there was a new sound. A Lewis gun on the roof of the Royal Hospital opened up, sending bullets on every corner of the field. The rebel retreat towards the nearest Auxiliary hospital now became a series of belly wriggles; even then, men were hit. Joyce heard more than one cry of pain as bullets found a mark.

At the Rialto Gate itself, a ferocious military assault had been launched led by Lieutenant Alan Ramsay to coincide with the frontal attack. Here the rebels, under Irvine, holed up in the tin sheds near the Gate, soon found that they would have been as well off if they had stayed in the open; bullets cut through the corrugated iron as easily as through cheese, passed cleanly from one end of the long structure to the other. Within seconds, the thin sheeting looked like a sieve. Inside, the bullets ricocheted wildly, causing an outlandish racket as they struck against iron bedsteads. The ears of the rebels were singing. No place except the floor was safe. In addition, bullets fired by the military positioned on the far side of the Canal ripped through the gable end, catching them in a fierce cross-fire. One bullet pierced the Wardmaster's coat as he lay flat among his lunatics in No. 6 dormitory. Five minutes after the start of battle, seventeen-year-old John Traynor, the best shot in the Company, fell mortally wounded. Irvine went to help him as blood poured from his chest. As Traynor fought for breath, the other members of the party left their posts for a brief moment to kneel down beside him and pray. Even Irvine, a Protestant, joined them. Then Traynor, gasping, "May Jesus have mercy on my soul," died.

At this juncture Captain Warmington suddenly launched his attack. Backed up by strong rifle-fire from the men in the Rialto buildings and the machine-gunners on the roof of the Royal Hospital, he sent a party doubling across the road and along the Canal bank where, screened by the high stone wall of the Union grounds, they were able to dash towards a small rear entrance hardly two hundred yards away. Ramsay, a veteran of Gallipoli, personally led the assault on the main gate, eventually being backed up by a second wave led by Captain Warmington. The Rialto Gate was locked and barred and easily withstood the assault, but a small wooden door at the side was broken down, and Ramsay dashed through at the head of his men. He was met by a ragged fire from the sheds and from the lone insurgent dug-in opposite the gate, and fell, wounded through the head. Rebel fire directed at the narrow entrance proved too accurate at such close range and the military were forced back. In a lull which followed, the rebels permitted a stretcher party to enter the gate and take away Ramsay. Captain Warmington, informed that the wounded lieutenant had but a few minutes to live, swore vengeance. Infuriated, he lined up a party behind him and led a second charge through the door. He was killed at once, and his men broke and ran under heavy fire. Once again, the stretcher party was permitted inside the Gate and the Captain's body was carried out, to be laid down on the pavement beside that of his dead friend Ramsay.

Meanwhile, the troops attempting the break-in by the Canal wall had enjoyed only qualified success. As they smashed down the door, bullets kicked into the wall beside them or, falling short, sizzled into the Canal. This fire came from Captain James Murphy's men, holed up in Jameson's Distillery in Marrowbone Lane. The troops, caught without cover, flung themselves down on the grassy bank and returned the fire as best they could. A few tried scaling the ten-foot wall, but when astride it were raked by fire from the rebels inside the Union. One officer did manage to get his legs over but toppled back, shot through the head. A private climbed up a telegraph pole, bullets gouging out splinters of wood beside him, the rebels finding it difficult to hit him because of the way in which he screened himself behind the pole. Finally he was hit and fell in an awkward cartwheel, his body first bouncing off the edge of the bank before splashing into the water.

In the end, the door simply had to give way and the troops poured through, fanning out across the open field. Succeeding waves, however, met fierce opposition and had to wriggle in on their stomachs, but the six insurgents whom Ceannt had placed in the field opposite this Gate were soon forced to retreat. The difficulty lay in crossing the open ground to Hospital No. 2–3, the nearest of the outlying Union buildings. There was little cover and they could either make a dash for it or wriggle across. Either way they would be exposed to the direct fire of the fifteen-man military party holding the Rialto buildings. They chose to try it slowly, but as they emerged into the open from the shadow of the wall, crawling on their bellies, the earth spurted viciously all about them. The first man to be hit was Richard O'Reilly, who had a brother, John, in the Nurses' Home and two other brothers, then serving with the British Army in France. "Funny," said John later, "that day there were two of us fighting *for* England, two of us *against*." Volunteers Brendan Donelan and James Quinn were shot shortly afterwards, and their bodies lay where they had fallen for the remainder of the day. The troops, armed with superior fire-power, began to close in fast. At Rialto Gate, Irvine decided that his position had become hopeless and sent a messenger to Commandant Ceannt asking for instructions. Somehow or other the man got through; even managed to return, bringing an order that Irvine should retire. He was too late, however. The military, alert to the situation, increased their pressure. The most intense fire of the whole day now swept the ground over which the party would be forced to retreat. Rebel rifles grew so hot that the men had to take it in turns to stop firing to allow them to cool. When the volume of rebel fire dramatically lessened, the military at last mounted a final assault. The door of the hut, strongly barricaded inside, resisted them momentarily; in the end, three soldiers, carrying a heavy lawn mower as a ram, smashed it down. As the troops charged forward, they heard Irvine call out, "Don't shoot! Don't shoot! We surrender!"

Lucy Stokes, a blonde, attractive and long-limbed Trinity graduate, had risen at 8.15 that morning, eaten breakfast, dressed herself in a neat blue costume, put up her hair in a bun, pinned on her hat and had then caught a tram to the North Circular Road, arriving at the military hostel where she worked as a V.A.D. at exactly nine o'clock. At midday, feeling, as she put it, "like a dried hemlock from weariness," she decided to return home for lunch. She walked down to the Quays, where she waited an unusually long time for a tram. Eventually she asked some "excited-looking people" if something had gone wrong with the service.

"There's no thrams, miss," a man told her. "The Volunteers has the city; they have all the stations taken and the Bank of Ireland, the General Post Office, the Castle and the Green and they have killed two of the polis, blown up a train and all in it, and sure, isn't Sackville Street strewn with corpses.

Don't make any mistake and get on a thram! There now, did you hear them? The Volunteers in Guinness's Bathin' House, shootin' the soldiers—they're after shootin' two in a thram and the ladies in it with them." This was tremendous news; not that Miss Stokes believed a quarter of it. She had no alternative, however, but to walk home along the Quays. She stopped at the first bridge when she found men crowded around a pub. The pub was barricaded and from the inside rebels shouted to her to "hurry out of that" to safety. At that moment there was a crackle of rifle-fire and, looking across the river, she saw a large body of soldiers running out of the Royal Barracks and taking cover behind the opposite Quay wall. A few of them, more daring, came running across the bridge towards her, causing the crowd around her to shout, "The military's coming—their bayonets fixed! Lor', they'll take us for the Volunteers!" And in an effort to prove that they were not rebels, they broke into a cheer; even going so far, when the troops reached them, as to advise them to "Go around the back, ye'll catch them there. But kape to the wall, or ye'll be shot dead!" The soldiers hurried past without paying any attention, causing the crowd to change its attitude. "There now, d'ye see that!" said one man disgustedly. "Such muddling! Isn't it aisy to believe in all the muddlin' at the front!"

Miss Stokes decided her safest course would be to follow the soldiers, but two officers stopped her politely and suggested she would be better off taking a different route. So she crossed over the river and walked down along the north bank of the Liffey and past the Four Courts towards Sackville Street. Glancing across the river from time to time, she saw troops cautiously edging their way towards Dublin Castle.

These, in fact, were men of the 10th Royal Dublin Fusiliers. An advance party of them had succeeded in crossing the river, under fire from a token force of rebels in Guinness's Brewery, while the main body had continued on down along the northern Quays with the intention of crossing the river at a lower bridge and making a direct assault up Parliament Street to the gates of the Castle. They were surprised, however, by fire from the Mendicity Institution, held by John Heuston and his small party of youthful rebels.

Still ignorant of rebel strength, the military did not know that when they emerged from their barracks two hundred strong they had appeared an overwhelming force to the dozen youths barricaded inside the old building. At this juncture a resolute charge might well have carried the place but as Heuston's men opened up with a wild and inaccurate fire, the troops scattered for cover. Some found refuge in deserted tramcars, but most crouched down behind the river walls or took cover in doorways or side streets. The exchanges were ragged, and in a short while, leaving a strong party to cover them from behind the low river wall, the main force recommenced filtering along the Quays towards Queen Street bridge. They crossed this under severe fire, but when they succeeded in reaching the far side without incurring really serious casualties, it had become clear that the relief of Dublin Castle could hardly be long delayed.

Professor Liam O'Briain, lecturer in Romance languages at National University, unexpectedly bumped into his friend Harry Nicholls, one of the few Protestant members of the Irish Volunteers, just off St. Stephen's Green.

"What the hell's going on?" demanded Nicholls, who was not wearing uniform. "I wasn't mobilized. Why the devil wasn't I? If I could get my hands on him, I'd give hell to the fellow that should have mobilized me!"

Nicholls, a graduate of Trinity College employed by the Dublin Corporation, and Captain of Engineering in the 4th Battalion, Irish Volunteers, was an adviser to the Volunteer Executive on problems concerned with barricades, water supplies and sewage; too useful a man, reflected O'Briain, to be over-looked in a scrap.

"I was just going to get my own sword and equipment," explained O'Briain. Ignorant himself of the I.R.B.'s decision to go ahead with the Rebellion, he had only begun to suspect that "there might be trouble," when he had seen MacDonagh's detachment parading in St. Stephen's Green, shortly before mid-day. One of the group of Volunteer officers who had met MacNeill at Dr. O'Kelly's house on Saturday night, he had spent the week-end carrying the countermanding order out into the countryside around Dublin. As a result, he believed that Pearse's plans had been well and truly scotched. He had not slept at home on Easter Sunday night and had, therefore, missed his own mobiliza-tion call. On Monday morning, on his way to see the Chief of Staff and report on his mission into the country, he had seen MacDonagh's men parading and, a few minutes later, had fortuitously run into the agitated MacNeill who was even then cycling into the city to find out what was happening. He had remained with the Volunteer Chief while John Fitzgibbon, a Volunteer Staff Officer, toured the centre of the city and returned with confirmation that the Volunteers—or some of them, anyway—were in rebellion. MacNeill, deeply distressed at this fresh evidence of Pearse's double-dealing, bravely declared that he would go home and put on his uniform and join his men. (He did not, in fact, take any active part in the Rebellion.) O'Briain and he had then parted.

Attempting to reach his home on the north side of the city, to pick up his sword and equipment, O'Briain had stumbled into fierce fighting at Portobello Bridge, where troops from the nearby barracks, attempting to march to the relief of Dublin Castle, were held up by the rebels under Doyle in Davy's pub. O'Briain saw the soldiers pull a Maxim gun up to the bridge, on a wheeled bogey, and open fire on the pub. He saw riflemen, lining the whole southern bank of the Canal, firing with a careful parade-ground precision, the first line lying flat on their stomachs, the second kneeling, and behind them an officer, his coat ripped to shreds by bullets but still scornful of the rebel marksmanship, directing their fire. To O'Briain it had all looked an extraordinarily *formal* way of fighting.

He had tried to filter to the right along the Canal bank, hoping to cross at another bridge, but the officer had spotted him and, with a smoking revolver pointed at his heart, O'Briain had been ordered to turn back.

While working his way around to avoid this fighting, he ran into Nicholls. They decided to walk along Earlsfort Terrace and into St. Stephen's Green and join the rebels there. Already—and it was just 12.45 p.m.—the normal life of Dublin had come to a halt. A line of deserted tramcars stretched back up Leeson Street. The gates of the Park itself were barricaded with benches (and, in one place, an up-ended wheel-barrow) while, behind the railings, men in Citizen Army uniform prowled busily about. One was hectoring the people strolling by, "If you're any bloody good, why don't you come in here and fight for Ireland?"

The two men crossed the road and O'Briain said, "So the fight's on, then?"

"Yes!"

"Is everybody out?"

"They are that! All over the city. And we're holding it! If you're any good at all, can't you come on in here?"

"But we're Irish Volunteers and would prefer to join our own Company," O'Briain pointed out.

"Arrah, won't this place do you as well as any other? That is, if you want to fight at all!"

The sudden sound of shots coming from the west end of the Green, from the direction of Jacob's biscuit factory, interrupted them. "Well, I'm with you boys!" Nicholls shouted, and using his bicycle as a prop, began climbing over the railings.

"Begod, in that case!" said O'Briain, and threw away his stick. Even as he climbed upon Nicholls's bicycle he could not help thinking what the young ladies of his French class would say if they caught sight of him then; but all misgivings vanished in a sudden flood of exhilaration as his feet touched the grass and he realized that he stood "in a different world to the ordinary, everyday, shabbily-genteel existence of dear old Dublin." He was in the fresh-born Irish Republic, and could now drink deep of the heady wine of freedom.

The shots which O'Briain and Nicholls heard were part of a sharp exchange then taking place between Commandant MacDonagh's men and the troops from Portobello Barracks who, having dislodged the rebels from Davy's public house, had begun a careful advance down Camden Street to the relief of Dublin Castle.

MacDonagh and one hundred and fifty men occupying Jacob's giant biscuit factory, however, stood directly in their way. A great, solid, triangular affair, bounded on each side by a labyrinth of narrow streets and small houses, Jacob's seemed almost impregnable. Its two immense towers, too, provided the rebels with a magnificent bird's-eye view of the city and, with the aid of field-glasses, enabled them to pick off men inside Portobello Barracks or, in the opposite direction, inside the Castle itself. Its strength promised to pose a formidable problem for the military, for it seemed that unless they were prepared to raze all the small dwellings in the vicinity, they would be unable to bring up artillery against it. And rifle-fire alone would be useless.

It was almost one o'clock when a picquet of ten men whom MacDonagh had stationed in Camden Street signalled that the military were approaching. Besides the main body inside the factory, MacDonagh had scattered men in Camden Street and in side streets turning off it. The military, trailing a Maxim gun, advanced with a small party out ahead, and MacDonagh warned that no one was to fire until the main party was in sight. Bishop Street (in which Jacob's lay) was itself only a turning off Camden Street, so that the military would find themselves enfiladed. MacDonagh's plan was frustrated when some of his men prematurely opened fire on the small advance party. An officer and six men were knocked over, but the main military party hurriedly retreated and decided to find an easier way of reaching the Castle. And thus an opportunity to inflict massive casualties on the military at the very outset of the Rebellion was carelessly cast away.

The 12.20 train from Kingstown to Westland Row jolted to a halt at the disused Sandymount Station just inside the city limits and John J. O'Leary, a newspaper reporter, deciding that it was probably only a ticket check, fumbled in his pocket. When a few minutes had passed, however, and the collector had not appeared, he put his head out of the window. He saw that some passengers had already alighted, and decided to join them. Together they stood around wondering what was happening, until the guard stumbled along the line towards them.

"What's going on?" asked O'Leary, his professional curiosity aroused.

"We're not going any further, that's all I know," replied the guard, and strode on.

Sensing a story, O'Leary decided to walk along the line and find out for himself what was wrong. At the next station he found another train stopped, and here a porter told him, "The Sinn Feiners have taken the city and occupied Westland Row." Pointing to the nearby rugby grounds—headquarters of the Irish Rugby Union—he said, "Look, you can see them ripping up the rails." O'Leary saw a bunch of shirt-sleeved men hard at work with picks and shovels. He decided to leave the railway line and walk along the main road into the city. As he neared the centre, he began to see "extraordinary scenes." Knots of people were standing about everywhere, talking excitedly; near Mount Street Bridge he saw a line of deserted trams; a little further on he heard his first shot.

A short distance away, in the suburb of Donnybrook, a region of well-kept lawns and solid Victorian houses, Mrs. Margaret Taaffe put down the telephone and, turning to her son Michael, said, "Avice says Stephen's Green and the G.P.O. are full of rebels. You know how your aunt exaggerates but, all the same, I'm going down to Northumberland Road to see if Mother is all right."

"Rebels?" said Michael, astonished.

"Yes, Sinn Feiners, I suppose. Please get me my bicycle."

She rode off on her wooden-rimmed bicycle, and after a while Michael decided to follow her. Half-way down Leeson Street (which leads into

St. Stephen's Green) he heard a shot, and he ducked right towards Merrion Square, deciding to make for Trinity College where he was a student. At the Lincoln Gate, Massey, the porter, dressed in the traditional peaked velvet cap and brass-buttoned coat, let him in.

"What's going on inside?" asked Taaffe.

"Ah, they're all up at the Front Gate, arranging what I heard tell was a plan of campaign," said Massey. "'Tis quiet here, anyway," he added. Taaffe hurried across College Park to the Front Gate and found it shut and locked. A khaki figure, complete with a short leather cane and a Military Cross gleaming on his tunic, bounded out of the Porter's Lodge.

"Well, thank God for that!" grinned the apparition. "Another medical student's turned up! Jolly good! Come to win the war?"

From somewhere outside Trinity there was the sound of shots, and Taaffe jerked nervously. "Can't have too many men," barked the figure in khaki. "Got to defend the library at all costs, y'see." This remark caused Taaffe to envisage a desperate last stand at the library windows, ammunition spent, while a horde of rebels with fixed bayonets swept across the Fellows' Garden. "What can I do to help?" he asked, uncertainly.

"Well, you'd better come up to the Regent House and see Lawford," said the khaki figure.

Upstairs, in the magnificent room over the Front Gate, Taaffe found an ancient Fellow sunk in a chair, fast asleep, a rifle between his knees. At a table under the high windows Tom Lawford, a brewer, wearing his captain's uniform, sat writing. He too was wearing the M.C. He looked up.

"Are you in the O.T.C.?" he asked.

"I'm afraid not."

"Oh, well. Anyway, you'll want to see what's going on above. You can get to the roof if you go out that way. But watch yourself." He pointed and Taaffe climbed up through a trapdoor on to the leads. Keeping his head well down for fear of snipers, he crawled forward until, suddenly, the dirty face of a divinity student known to him as Pinky Wilson confronted him.

"Thank God you've come!" said Wilson. "Another five minutes an' I'd have given in."

"Why, what's wrong?"

"If I don't get to the lavatory this minute, I'll not be responsible for what happens, I tell you! You'll find the gun an' all up there in front. Orders are to treat everyone you see who isn't in khaki as a rebel."

"You mean—*shoot* at them?"

"Of course, that's what you're here for!"

"Have you been shooting at everyone?"

"'Course I haven't, but those are the orders. I think it's that bloodthirsty little sod with the M.C."

Wilson left and Taaffe inched forward to the parapet, where he found a .303 rifle, several clips of ammunition and some cigarettes and matches.

Sixty feet below lay Dame Street, leading up towards Dublin Castle. Taaffe scanned the roofs but they seemed deserted enough. Gingerly he examined the rifle, checked that there was a bullet in it, then put it down and lit a cigarette. After a while he picked up the rifle again and sighted along the barrel at the Bank of Ireland opposite, pretending that he was focusing a rebel in his sights. Suddenly the rifle jumped, and on the other side of the street, high up on the stone façade of the Bank, a little cloud of dust appeared.

"What the hell do you think you're shooting at?" hissed Wilson, emerging from the trapdoor. . . .

About this time James Stephens, poet and novelist, was on his way home to lunch. He noticed an unusually large number of people standing about in small groups and gazing rather apprehensively towards St. Stephen's Green, but thought they were trying to enjoy the holiday in their own peculiar way. It was not until he was returning to the library where he worked and saw that the crowds were still congregated near the Green, that it occurred to him that there must be something really important happening. He asked a man, "Has there been an accident?"

"Don't you know?" said the man. "The Sinn Feiners have seized the city."

"Oh!" said Stephens.

"The Green is full of them!" said the man.

"My God!" said Stephens. Courageously he turned and made for the Green despite a sudden crackle of rifle-fire. He arrived in front of the Shelbourne to find the whole area in a state of siege—barricades of motor-cars and carts thrown across the streets and empty tramcars lying derelict all round the perimeter. Opposite the hotel he saw three rebels dash from the Green and call upon a chauffeur-driven car to halt. He heard the rebels apologizing to the occupants of the car, a man and a woman, and courteously asking them to alight. Then they ordered the chauffeur to lodge the car in the barricade.

"What's the meaning of all this?" Stephens asked a rebel, a young man of about twenty.

"We're expecting a military attack at any moment," explained the rebel. Then, pointing to the crowd standing at the far gate of the park, he said, "And imagine!—those people won't go home for me!"

Miss Stokes, still trying to reach home, arrived at the same barricade a few minutes later, in time to see another "splendid motor-car" held up and "a dignitary of the Catholic church" forced to step down after a rebel had saluted him and explained, "I beg your pardon, my lord, but it's my orders." By then the barricade consisted of a big dray, with the horse lying dead beside it, a side-car, two motor-cars and a laundry van, with the laundry baskets and their contents strewn all over the road. She had half-expected to see some Germans lurking about, for on her way up Grafton Street an army recruiting sergeant had warned her, "The Germans have the Green, ma'am, and are after sendin' off a volley." The incredible truth was that many people in Dublin that afternoon were convinced that the Germans *had* landed. Richard

Humphreys, for instance, wandering down Westmoreland Street a short time later on his way to the G.P.O., heard an old woman call out, "A corpse of Germans has landed on the Green!"

While Miss Stokes was still at the barricade, yet another car came whirling down the side of the Green. Trapped, the driver slammed on his brakes.

"Drive to the barricade!" shouted a rebel as the driver struggled to turn his steering-wheel and drive away. The rebel shot at his tyres and burst one open.

"Now, drive it on the rim!" he shouted, and the infuriated driver, left with no alternative, drove slowly forward and lodged his car with the others. At Miss Stokes's side an elderly gentleman said, "If those ruffians had shot him, I'd have shot them," and he showed her a small revolver up his sleeve.

A half-mile away in yet another part of Dublin, Patrick Doyle was working in his greengrocer's shop at the corner of North King Street and Church Street, when he heard galloping hooves and looked up to see a riderless horse flash past his front door. A moment later, a neighbour put his head in and shouted that a Lancer had been shot dead. Doyle went to the door and saw armed men busy up Church Street dragging cabs, milk floats and lorries into the street from Moore's the coachbuilders. He saw them enter Murphy's, the chemists in North King Street, and roll out empty oil drums and wooden barrels, then take chairs, tables, and beds from some houses and pile them all up together in the street to make two barricades—one across Church Street at No. 77, and another across North King Street at No. 159. A little later, rebels entered his shop and said they wanted to commandeer a bed. Doyle did not argue with them, and watched them silently as they carried out the bed in sections and took it across to the Father Mathew Hall, where they set up a Red Cross post. Some then returned and ordered him to get into the back of the house.

"But I haven't any back rooms," protested Doyle, pointing out that his premises were on the corner and all windows faced the street. "And I've two sick children upstairs," he added, explaining that his wife had gone off with his mother-in-law to Fairyhouse and had left him to take care of young Jimmy and Margaret, who were upstairs in bed with measles.

"Well, get back as far as you can," they told him. "There's going to be trouble." He watched them smash his windows in order to leave themselves a clear field of fire. Then they brought up sacks of flour commandeered from Monk's Bakery nearby and loopholed the windows. Finally they flung themselves face downwards and poked their rifles out. And there they waited.

10

THE TROOP OF Lancers halted at the top of Sackville Street beside the smooth obelisk commemorating Parnell, while Colonel Hammond, their officer-in-command, cautiously surveyed the potential battlefield. He watched the crowds scattering into the doorways and side streets, and saw a solid mass of people surge back towards O'Connell Bridge, where some seated themselves on the parapets, or even scaled lamp-posts, to get a better view. High over the Post Office flaunted two strange and incongruous flags. Having satisfied himself as to the situation, he trotted forward, obediently followed by his troopers.

The Lancers looked a stern and quite superbly martial sight indeed. Their horses, high-spirited, silken-coated, magnificently groomed, trotted forward in an even line, their hooves striking sharply against the flinty square setts. The troopers themselves sat their mounts like ramrods, their tall, slim, pennanted lances emphasizing their superb posture. With each movement of the horses, carbines jerked menacingly in their holsters. Harness jingled pleasantly; bits and spurs glittered. Colonel Hammond himself looked almost as self-possessed and as arrogant as if he were on the parade ground. The very perfection of the ensemble ought, of itself, to have been sufficient to shatter the morale of the insurgents; as, indeed, it was obviously intended to.

Inside the G.P.O. there was a rush of rebels to the windows and to the parapet around the roof. On the other side of Henry Street (which constitutes the northern boundary of the building), Volunteer Captain James O'Brennan flattened himself on the roof of the corner building and poked forward his single-bore shotgun. In the Imperial Hotel, Mrs. Dillon almost fell out of the window in an effort to obtain a better view, but was held by the protecting arm of her bridegroom. Back in the G.P.O. Connolly's orders, taken up by his officers and sent echoing throughout the building, helped to build up an almost unbearable atmosphere of excitement; an atmosphere strangely welcomed, for up until now, rebellion had meant nothing more than lugging about sacks of coal to block up the windows; or pushing chairs and desks and tables into position—tasks carried out to the accompaniment of a chorus of accidental rifle-shots which threatened to leave the British Army with nothing to do.

It was at this moment that the Rathfarnham Company of Volunteers, late arrivals on the scene, decided to cross Sackville Street and enter the G.P.O.

While the Lancers sat their impatient steeds beside the Parnell Monument, they had waited in Lower Abbey Street, trying to make up their minds whether it was safe to cross. Cheered on by several youngsters—and one tough-looking Dubliner who encouraged them with the slogan "Up the Volunteers! Hammer the sh— out of the f—s!"—they finally decided to risk it and began running across the street just as the Lancers broke into a trot. Most of them succeeded in reaching the side entrance of the G.P.O. in Princes Street before the troopers actually charged. Shouts of "Who are you?", from inside, however, greeted the desperate men.

"We're from Rathfarnham!" shouted Lieutenant Bulfin. "For God's sake open up." But the door remained closed as somebody yelled, "Mind yourselves! The Lancers!"

"Line up! Line up!" bawled Captain Boland, getting ready to fight in the street.

"To hell with that!" replied one man. "Break the blasted windows and inside with you, you bloody fools!" At once a rebel smashed the nearest window with the butt of his rifle and the Company began scrambling in.

Even as they did so, the Lancers approached the Pillar at a sharp gallop. They were still twenty or thirty yards from it when the inexperienced and excited rebels lost their heads and, despite Connolly's emphatic orders, opened fire with a ragged volley. Had they been seasoned troops, and waited, Colonel Hammond and his troopers must surely have been decimated. As it was, four Lancers toppled from their saddles, three dying before they hit the squaresetts, the other falling with fatal wounds. A second volley caused them no casualties and, indeed, so wild and inaccurate was the rebel fire, that the Lancers were nearly as safe in the middle of Sackville Street as the rebels behind their bricks and barricades. A bullet fired by a Volunteer posted on the other side of Sackville Street entered the telephone booth where Lieutenant Chalmers lay trussed, and buried itself in the woodwork above his head. Another bullet killed a rebel firing from a second-floor window. Yet another caught a sixteen-year-old member of the Rathfarnham Company as he waited his turn to climb in through the shattered ground-floor window—this window was towards the rear of the G.P.O. and one the defenders, up until then, had apparently not had time to smash and barricade—and this led to another rebel casualty when, in the ensuing scramble, Volunteer John Keeley accidentally shot himself in the stomach. While this was happening, a Lancer, madly spurring his mount, dashed past Nelson Pillar. Captain Brennan Whitmore, peering through his loophole, tried to catch him in his sights, but the horse, hit by someone else's bullet, stumbled and fell, flinging its rider over its head. Shaken but otherwise unhurt, the man picked himself up and staggered towards the pavement. His hand to his head, he reeled drunkenly along the far side of the street and disappeared down North Earl Street. Brennan Whitmore, with a spurt of compassion, had made no attempt to shoot him.

Meanwhile Colonel Hammond, his sword cutting the air helplessly, yelled, "Get back! Get back!" and the troopers wheeled and, with all their splendid order gone, galloped back towards the top of Sackville Street, leaving their casualties lying behind them. A newsboy nipped across to where a trooper's carbine lay just below the Pillar and Brennan Whitmore saw him pick it up and come running towards the G.P.O. He had almost reached the pavement when a shawlie stepped forward and tried to grab it from him. All she got for her trouble was a clout on the head. She collapsed, screaming, and the boy ran up to the G.P.O shouting, "Here yez are! Here yez are!" and flung the carbine through a window.

Casualties among the insurgents had been negligible. The worst incident was when a home-made bomb blew up in Lieutenant Liam Clarke's face just as he was about to throw it, mashing his face into a bloody pulp. When it became clear that he was going to survive this misfortune, a rebel commented wryly, "So much for those bloody canisters! If poor Clarke's head wasn't blown off, the divil little else use they'll be—except perhaps for moral effect."

Reporters Maurice Linnane and Michael Knightley, eagerly pursuing incidents, raced up Sackville Street in the wake of the retreating Lancers. At the Parnell Monument they watched Colonel Hammond re-form his men and, for a moment, Linnane even thought he was going to attempt another charge. The Colonel evidently thought better of it, for with a crisp, angry shout, he wheeled his own mount towards Great Britain Street and, followed by his troop, clattered away crestfallenly amid the jeers of the crowd. To the citizens of Dublin who saw it, their retreat seemed significant; proof, if that were still needed, that the rebels were determined men and that no mere display of martial strength was likely to shift them.

Outside the G.P.O., ambulances made their first appearance of the Rebellion, picking up the dead and wounded without interference from the rebels.

Hampered by their long skirts, the women of the Citizen Army found it no easy matter to get into the City Hall, for an iron-trellis gate barred the way up the steps to the main door. Casting modesty to the winds they hoisted up their skirts and scrambled over in what was unquestionably a quite unmaidenly fashion. Emily Norgrove, for one, split her skirt.

Once inside, Helena Moloney set up commissariat and Red Cross quarters in the caretaker's kitchen and allocated duties. Some women were told to fill buckets with water, others to prepare bandages, others to see to the cooking. Emily Norgrove was ordered to do sentry duty in the main entrance hall. She found it a lonely post, for there was little to do but listen to the sounds of firing by the men up on the roof and answering shots from the military across Castle Yard.

To those besieged inside the Castle, the racket was such that it seemed as though half Ireland had risen in Rebellion and had seized the surrounding roofs. If the volume of fire was not heavy, it was continual. Distressingly, too, hard upon the death of Constable O'Brien, had come the shooting of Sergeant-Major Brosnan. Brosnan, wearing mufti, was mistaken for a rebel and shot by a soldier. His death seemed the more poignant, perhaps, because he should not have been in the Castle at all. A musketry instructor stationed at Buncrana, Co. Donegal, he was visiting the Castle, where his wife and children lived in quarters, for the holidays, and was about to leave for the station when the attack on the Castle opened. He had at once gallantly offered his services.

At 1.40 p.m., the first military relief arrived at the Ship Street entrance—one hundred and eighty men of the Royal Irish Rifles and the Dublin Fusiliers, thereby destroying any hope John Connolly and his men ever had of taking the Castle or at least neutralizing it.

A V.A.D. who served in the Castle during the siege has left a vivid account of these moments:

"I ran into the Sterilizing Room to see what was happening at the back. A troop of soldiers had arrived and were drawn up in Barrack Yard. The heavy solid gates were closed and also shut across, with a sentry at each peep-hole. Outside, instead of men with bayonets, were small children, staring with open mouths at the massive gates. Rifle shots were heard at intervals but we could not see where they came from. At First Dinner there was a general atmosphere of unrest. Conversation flagged, although a few people kept up constant questions—chiefly asking if we had seen the policeman's helmet in the hall, and the holes made by the bullet. There was a noise of people rushing down the corridor and the sisters ran out to see if they were needed. Several times during the meal stretchers passed up and down the corridor outside and each time we asked the same question: 'Killed or wounded?' and someone came in and said, 'Dead,' or 'Very bad.'

"My only conscious sensation at the moment was of a burning desire to go out and have a shot at the rebels myself. Instead I remarked prosaically to one of the V.A.D.s: 'It doesn't look much like the theatre tonight?' 'Hush,' she said. 'Don't suggest to anyone that it would not be safe; it'll be all right by then and we must go.' We could not cross the Yard to our rooms after dinner, so I took a tour through the Picture Gallery and Throne Room, where all the windows were thronged with spectators. The Throne Room faces the Front Gate and from there I could see that the Gate was locked and guarded by rebels. Otherwise things looked much as usual; only rifle-shots rang out at intervals. 'Look! You can see the sniper; watch the roof of that house,' said one of the men next to me. Presently something popped up on the roof—a puff of smoke—bang! When I came back to the Supper Room I found a nurse in great agitation. 'I was nearly killed!' she exclaimed. As there did not seem any immediate danger, I asked how. 'I was leaning out of the window, and a bullet whizzed right past me—look at the mark on my apron!' She pointed to a rent, which I was convinced had been there all morning, and tactlessly said so. 'Well, it passed very near me, anyway,' she protested, 'and I got such a fright.'"

It was just after two o'clock when the rebels investing the Castle lost their leader, John Connolly, a small lean man, who had been an Abbey actor of great promise.

Helena Moloney, Jenny Shanahan and Bridget Davis were up on the roof at the time. Anxious to see something of the battle and to take food to the men, they had daringly climbed up on to the balustraded balcony rimming the great dome. Here, high and remote, Helena Moloney remembers, she felt quite safe so long as she crouched down behind the dome. Connolly was only three or four yards away from her, leaning against the dome and cautiously peering round now and then to take a shot.

As she turned to speak to Bridget Davis she saw Connolly slump sideways. "Oh! Oh!" she gasped, and crept along the rim towards him. She spoke, but he made no answer. "I think he's bad," said Jenny Shanahan and loosened his tunic. "Go and get Dr. Lynn," said Helena Moloney (Dr. Kathleen Lynn, a member of the Citizen Army, was with Mallin's forces in St. Stephen's Green). As the girl left, Miss Moloney breathed an Act of Contrition into Connolly's ear, cradling his head on her lap. He was still alive, moaning faintly, when Bridget Davis returned with Dr. Lynn. The two women began crawling on their knees across the bullet-swept roof. Before they could negotiate the passage, Connolly was dead. "I'm afraid he's gone," said Dr. Lynn gently. A few yards away, on his hands and knees, crouched the dead man's brother, fourteen-year-old Matthew Connolly, fighting back his tears.

At 2.30 fifty soldiers dashed through the door of the Canal wall at the South Dublin Union, to be met by a hot fire as they fought their way across open ground towards Hospital No. 2–3.

Section-Commander John Joyce and his surviving comrades, trying to reach the security of the permanent buildings, were unable to raise their heads because of the machine-gun and rifle-fire. They could only edge their way slowly back to the Convent, which lay fifty yards from Hospital No. 2–3. It took them an hour and a half to reach it and establish themselves temporarily in the Women's Hospital near it.

The military found the going no easier. Fire from the upper windows of Hospital No. 2–3 was furious. In a series of short rushes, however, they succeeded in closing up to the hospital walls. They broke into the central courtyard, only to be fired on by two rebels posted on the ground floor. They smashed the windows and began chasing the rebels through the building where a strange battle developed in the cold, echoing passage-ways. At the end of each corridor the rebels halted briefly to fire upon their pursuers, then bolted immediately. At the front of the hospital, they flung themselves through the ground-floor windows, and tumbled out on to the lawn amid a shower of shattered glass. Pursuing them hotly, the military shot at a rebel who shouted to his companion as he fell, "Run on! I'm hit!" The second man sprinted across to the main buildings, only to find his retreat cut off by a second military party. Diving round a corner of the building, even as bullets thudded viciously into the brickwork, he ran into Commandant Ceannt, who was kneeling tending a wounded comrade. Both men prepared to make a stand but, astonishingly, the military failed to appear.

They had stopped, in fact, to clear out six Volunteers who fired on them from the upper floor of Hospital No. 2–3. The rebels were quickly forced back into the west wing. While the military made their preparations for a final attack, there was a lull. In the west wing, a young nurse, Sister Keogh, remarked to a colleague, "Thank God, the military aren't attacking this building any more— I hope there'll be no bloodshed here." She had scarcely finished speaking when there was rifle-fire downstairs. "The patients, the patients!" cried Nurse Keogh, and ran towards the stairs. "Wait!" shouted her companion. But the pretty nurse had already disappeared down the dark stone stairway.

At the bottom, where a porch and door opened to the left into a long corridor, two soldiers had taken up position. As Nurse Keogh appeared in the opening she was met by the fire of two rifles and killed instantly. Her friend, rushing down after her, cried out, but the military officer asked her roughly, "Are there any Sinn Feiners upstairs?"

The grief-stricken girl shook her head, then begged the two soldiers to help her lift the corpse of her friend up on to a table.

"All right," said the officer impatiently. "But hurry."

The two men lifted the dead nurse on to the table. As her weeping friend began fussing over the body, a Union inmate staggered in from the other end of the corridor carrying the young rebel who had been shot on the lawn. The boy was still alive, but one look at the waxen face and the bloody wound in his chest satisfied the officer. He signalled his men towards the stairway.

The appearance of the military in the ward caused several patients to become hysterical. Already the walls and ceiling bore testimony to the ferocity of their first onslaught. The military stopped at a partition separating the east wing from the rest of the hospital. The officer called for a pass-key and, while this was being obtained, caught noises from the other side. "Come out with your hands up when we open this door!" he shouted.

The key found, a soldier advanced and opened the door. There was a fierce hand-to-hand struggle before the rebels surrendered.

By mid-afternoon, both sides had suffered heavy losses. Ceannt had come off the worst, for most of his outposts had been driven in. Yet he had done all that could have been expected of him. The Royal Irish Regiment were still held up and, although the danger to the Castle had been removed, Sir Matthew Nathan was still, in fact, a prisoner.

Half-a-mile away, Lord Wimborne, snatching a moment from his other duties, wrote to Mr. Birrell:

"The worst has happened, just when we thought it averted. If we only had acted last night with decision and arrested the leaders as I wanted, it might have been averted. The Post Office is seized—Nathan is still besieged in the Castle but I hope he will be out soon. Almost all wires are cut. Everybody away on holiday. Bridges blown up. Fortunately we got the Curragh before interruption and about 2,000 are arriving. The situation is not yet in hand, but if we get through the night, I hope we shall settle them tomorrow. No news from the provinces, but there is sure to have been trouble. I fear, too, a raid [*from Germany*]. This is too audacious to have been undertaken without hope of support. We must have troops. At least a brigade. I should prefer a division. I am attempting to form a Privy Council quorum to proclaim Martial Law or whatever now corresponds to it. I shall take the most energetic and sternest measures consistent with my resources. The situation is very serious and we need energetic help. So far, no general rising or sympathy with the Sinn Fein, so far as I can hear, but one never knows what may be developed."

There was, indeed, something not far from panic at times among the highest military quarters in the capital. No one knew just how many rebels were out— or how many might yet come out; the situation in the country remained obscure because of the breakdown in communications. Worst of all, news of an invasion was awaited hourly, for no one believed that the rebels would be mad enough to attempt a Rising without guarantees from Germany. This foreboding that they would be overwhelmed transmitted itself to the various barracks. The extreme audacity of the rebel moves and the skilful way in which they had seized the most important strategic points in the city, together with the nature of the fight they had already put up wherever the military had so far encountered them, led everyone to believe that their actions were based on careful plans and calculations made somewhere in Germany. When Major Sir Francis Vane hurried back from lunch at Bray to help organize the defence of Portobello Barracks, he found the place in a state of dire confusion, caused principally by the rumours that the Germans had landed on the west coast, had been joined by huge insurgent armies and were even now marching on Dublin. The confusion and the panic were further compounded by the presence of innumerable refugees, both military and civilian, and the fact that the total force in the barracks was just under six hundred men, compared with a normal peace-time establishment of two battalions.

Luck, however, had not entirely deserted the authorities. Pearse and Connolly, handicapped by their shortage of men, blundered on from one mistake to another. Their most serious error was their failure to appreciate the importance of Trinity College as a strategical position, despite the fact that it sat astride their communications with St. Stephen's Green. Here the authorities were to gain a gratuitous lodgment in central Dublin.

Trinity was put into a state of siege by the University O.T.C. within an hour of the Rebellion starting. Early in the afternoon, a handful of Canadian and Anzac soldiers, in Ireland for a brief furlough, made their way into the university when they learned it was being held for the Government. Several more were recruited by Trinity students who paraded the streets in mufti, looking for anyone who would help. Young Ernest O'Malley was stopped by three students he knew.

"What do you think of these damned Sinn Feiners?" one asked him.

"Well, I don't know," replied O'Malley, "but I suppose they'll soon be chased out of the place."

"Well, we're collecting people to defend Trinity. Will you come along? We'll give you a rifle—we've plenty belonging to the O.T.C."

O'Malley, however, had not made up his mind. "Oh, I'm on my way home now," he said to put them off. "But look—perhaps I'll come back later."

11

PROFESSOR O'BRIAIN found Commandant Michael Mallin a small, quiet man who impressed him as being both efficient and possessed of a deep and thoughtful judgment. Mallin welcomed O'Briain and Harry Nicholls warmly, then ordered a rifle to be given O'Briain, who had not got one, and the two of them to be allocated positions. Nicholls was told to dig a trench at the corner of the Green opposite Cuffe Street, and O'Briain to report to Lieutenant Bob de Coeur, who immediately handed him a pick and ordered him to get busy. It was the first time in his life, as O'Briain himself puts it, that he had ever done "a decent day's work," and it irked him "to see Citizen Army fellows, most of whom were accustomed to using their hands and muscles in their various trades," always more eager to give up the back-breaking stuff and do sentry duty than he, a soft-palmed, unmuscled linguist.

"I'll go sentry-go now, Bob," he heard them volunteer time and again, while he struggled with some recalcitrant piece of mud. He consoled himself with the thought that the ache in his back was the least he could suffer for Ireland.

Passers-by continued to stroll by and look in through the railings all afternoon. They stared at the rebels curiously, almost as though they expected them to turn and bite. There was always the odd fellow, too, who fancied himself a comedian.

"Ah, when Ireland calls you must obey!" shouted one man, sarcastically.

"Get in or get out!" growled de Coeur, angrily.

Once O'Briain lifted his head, to find a slender girl regarding him with interest. He grinned up at her and was rewarded with a smile.

"Do you need any food?" the goddess asked him.

"Well, we can do with all we can get," replied O'Briain.

"In that case I'll bring you some," she said. Watching her as she walked away, O'Briain thought, "Trinity College, that one. She has the look of Trinity College, that beautiful, deep, Protestant look about her." He was rudely jerked back to reality by a shout from de Coeur, "Get back to your digging, man—that trench needs to be wider. Sure yer giving yourself no arse room!"

It did not take O'Briain long to find out that his fellow-rebels were far more eager to discuss politics than they were to dig trenches. Few Irish Volunteers had thought deeply about the kind of Ireland they wanted to see if the Rebellion succeeded; all that mattered to them was that the shackles should be flung off and that, once again, Irishmen should be able to walk freely with their heads held as high as anyone else's. The Citizen Army men, on the other hand, seemed to be more concerned about the economic and social consequences of the battle.

"I thought this military revolution was to be followed by the industrial revolution," said a man called O'Leary.

"Indeed!" replied O'Briain, flabbergasted. "The industrial revolution!— what industrial revolution?"

"A general strike," explained O'Leary.

O'Briain had never even heard the expression before and, when O'Leary explained what it meant, O'Briain thought it an ingenious idea; it would certainly shake the Castle up a considerable degree more than a bomb or two.

The shadows lengthened. A tall old man, very straight, with a moustache and side whiskers *à la* Franz Josef, came to the railing and shouted, "Can anybody join in or is this a private fight?"

"You can come in," replied O'Briain, "if you know anything at all about it."

"I was seven years in the American artillery," said the old man proudly.

"Begod, in that case come right in!" replied O'Briain warmly, and went over to help him—a move he was to regret later when he discovered that the man, a returned Yank called Sullivan, was almost crazy.

In the late afternoon, Mallin, justifying O'Briain's good opinion of him, wakened up at last to the weakness of his position. He ordered Sergeant Frank Robbins to seize the Royal College of Surgeons, a well-proportioned building with a fine classical façade dominating the west side of the Green.

By the late afternoon, the military began advancing into the city through the northern suburbs, forces under Major Somerville, commander of the School of Musketry at Dollymount, eventually managing to seize the vital North Wall railway station, main terminus for dock traffic. A second party, filtering down the Great Northern Railway line in an effort to seize Amiens Street Station, ran into one hundred rebels at Clark's Bridge over the Royal Canal, and were sharply engaged. The rebels, commanded by Captain Tom Weafer of the Second Battalion, were escorting a convoy of military and medical supplies to the G.P.O. and were taken by surprise. Weafer, a sensible and level-headed fellow, kept his wits. He ordered one party to engage the military; a second party to scatter and seize defensive positions near Ballybough Bridge—which would enable them not only to control the road and rail approaches but also to protect their battalion headquarters—while with the rest of his forces he gathered the remnants of his scattered convoy together and pushed on rapidly to the G.P.O. The forces left to engage the military retreated, taking up new positions commanding Annesley railway bridge. They occupied corner houses in North Strand, Spring Garden Street, Annesley Place and Leinster Avenue, and when an advance party of military, flushed with their initial success, reached the bridge, opened fire. Caught in the open on the railway line, the military tried desperately to get their machine-gun mounted, but quick and accurate rifle-fire knocked it out before they could begin firing. Driven down from the railway line, the military sought cover in the side streets while, some two hundred yards further back, just north of the bridge, their main body dug in and prepared to repel an attack. .

Taking advantage of their lack of aggressiveness, the rebels slipped away, and by late afternoon had arrived safely at their destination, the G.P.O.

Ten minutes before the gala matinée performance of Yeats's poetic play, *Cathleen ni Houlihan,* was due to begin at the Abbey Theatre, a stage-hand rushed into the office of St. John Ervine, the manager, and declared excitedly, "I don't think we'll be able to hold a performance, sir."

"Why not?" asked Ervine.

"I think there's a rebellion or something on, sir—anyway the Sinn Feiners are out."

Ervine laughed.

"Listen," said the man. There was the sound of rifle-fire.

"Oh, that's only someone skylarking," said Ervine and went on writing. A little later, he went down to the front of the theatre to see how the house was filling up and noticed small knots of people standing about in the street. "This is damned funny!" he decided, and walked to the corner of a nearby lane.

He heard a rumble of carts and saw an extraordinary convoy approaching; two cars piled high with vegetables, mostly cauliflowers, escorted by a body of armed youths. The idea of the rebels stuffing themselves with interminable cauliflower seemed to him irresistibly funny, and he burst out laughing.

For the rebels inside the G.P.O. time hung heavily. Winifred Carney, taking a brief respite from typing Connolly's orders, wandered over to the telephone booth where Lieutenant Chalmers lay tied up.

"Here, have a bit of chocolate," she said impulsively, and shoved a piece into his mouth.

Volunteers Jack Plunkett, Joseph Reilly and the brothers Ernest and John Nunan, who had started boring a tunnel at the back of the G.P.O. to give a line of retreat, broke into the Dublin waxworks in Henry Street. They found effigies of His Majesty King George V and Lord Kitchener and, declaring them "prisoners of war", carried them back into the G.P.O., where "His Majesty" was used to reinforce a barricade. Jack Plunkett placed his cigarette case on the top of Kitchener's head as a cockshy and soon, after a hail of bottles of ink and other objects had been hurled at them, the stern features of the old martinet looked like those of a punch-drunk pug.

Captain Brennan Whitmore, having worked out the position of each rebel unit in the city with the aid of a bundle of dispatches and a large street map, sat back and observed the contrasting behaviour of Pearse and Connolly.

Connolly seemed to him much the more positive character. Forever on the prowl, he was a restless, energetic figure, continually seeking out weaknesses in the defences, continually demanding more effort from his men. Pearse, on the other hand, appeared to be "lost somewhere in the clouds"; at times "even looked supremely futile." Yet Brennan Whitmore felt that by his very presence alone, he added an untold value. There was an ambience about him which spread calm confidence. Noticing that, wherever he went, the eyes of the garrison followed, Brennan Whitmore thought, "If that man had lived in the Middle Ages, he would have been a saint."

On the first floor, a bored Volunteer took a pot-shot at Nelson, but only chipped his nose. Connolly, annoyed at this indiscipline, sternly ordered, "Tell them to stop that firing up there!"

The Commandant-General had, in fact, suffered a great deal from over-zealous officers who insisted on showering him with relatively unimportant dispatches. Handed one such message, Connolly declared in despair, "If that man was standing on his right foot, he would send me a dispatch saying he was shortly going to put down his left foot!"

Somebody asked Tom Clarke how he felt. He replied, "I've lived to see the greatest hour in Irish history."

Pearse glanced at his watch and commented, "We've already put Emmet's revolt in the shade." (Robert Emmet's rebellion in 1803 lasted approximately two hours.)

At the main door, Volunteer James Kenny, on sentry duty, barred the way of two foreign sailors who wanted to enter the building.

"Ye can't," said Kenny.

"But we would like to," said one, and explained that he was a Pole and his friend a Finn.

"I still can't let you in," said Kenny.

"But we come from small nations," persisted the sailor, "and we wish to fight on the side of a small nation. Also we understand guns."

Kenny was impressed. "Well, hold on," he said, "and I'll ask Mr. Connolly."

Connolly's answer was brief. "Tell them they're welcome!"

Kenny led them inside and handed them two shotguns. He had hardly done so when one of the guns went off. The shot ricocheted off the wall and blew the heel off his foot. Kenny looked down in astonishment as a pool of his blood spread over the marble floor.

By late afternoon, Lord Wimborne had recovered his grip on the situation to such an extent that he felt bold enough to issue the following Proclamation:

"Whereas, an attempt, instigated and designated by the foreign enemies of our King and Country to incite rebellion in Ireland and thus endanger the safety of the United Kingdom, has been made by a reckless, though small, body of men, who have been guilty of insurrectionary acts in the City of Dublin:

Now, we, Ivor Churchill, Baron Wimborne, Lord Lieutenant-General and Governor-General of Ireland, do hereby warn all His Majesty's subjects that the sternest measures are being, and will be, taken for the prompt suppression of the existing disturbances, and the restoration of order:

And we do hereby enjoin all loyal and law-abiding citizens to abstain from any acts of conduct which might interfere with the action of the Executive Government, and in particular we warn all citizens of the danger of unnecessarily frequenting the streets or public places, and of assembling in crowds:

Given under our seal, this 24th day of April, 1916.

WIMBORNE."

From the roof of the G.P.O. the contents of this Proclamation were shouted across to O'Brennan and McGahan manning the roof of the building on Henry Street corner.

"Ah, the ould cod!" yelled back O'Brennan defiantly. "Will ye send us over more bombs!"

The rebels knew it was essential that if the Rising were to achieve its full impact abroad, other countries—and especially the United States—would have to be speedily told about it. Joseph Plunkett, therefore, had made elaborate arrangements for broadcasting the news to the outside world. Originally he had enlisted the services of three men—Fergus O'Kelly, David Bourke and Con Keating—to set up a pirate transmitting and receiving station at his father's Kimmage farmhouse. O'Kelly had served with the Army Signalling Corps and the other two were trained Marconi operators. They had found it impossible to construct a transmitting set, but they had managed to build a crude receiving apparatus by using a gramophone motor. This, unfortunately, had refused to work. Plunkett's intention had been to use this pirate radio to pick up any messages broadcast by the Germans concerning the *Aud*. When the set would not work, he sent Keating and Bourke to Kerry to seize the Government's apparatus. On their way down Keating lost his life when his car took a wrong turning and plunged into the sea, Bourke luckily escaping.

Late in the afternoon, then, when it had become clear that the authorities lacked either the will or the strength to crush the insurrection promptly, Plunkett told O'Kelly to occupy the Dublin Wireless School of Telegraphy on the other side of Sackville Street. This had been closed by the authorities at the beginning of the war; most of the apparatus had been dismantled and the doors were sealed. O'Kelly took six men, among them a cockney, Lieutenant John O'Connor (known as "Blimey"), and Arthur Shields, the Abbey Theatre actor (and brother of Barry Fitzgerald, who became a Hollywood film star), and climbed the stairs to the school, which was on the top floor of a building known as Reis's, in the block between Lower Abbey Street and the river. They broke the seals, entered the place and Bourke set to work to reconnect the apparatus. It was to prove a long and tedious task. O'Kelly walked out onto the roof, and found that the aerial had been taken down. The two poles, however, still lay on the roof, and a Volunteer was sent to search electrical shops in the neighbourhood for the right kind of wire. O'Kelly, studying the position from a military point of view, thought it too exposed for comfort; it was completely dominated by the pagoda-like dome of the Dublin Bread Company's restaurant two doors away, which, if seized by the military, would make the School untenable. He sent a man back to tell Connolly this; the Commandant's reaction was to order Captain Tom Weafer to occupy the entire block.

The principal threat to G.H.Q., as it appeared to Connolly, was that the military might attack up Lower Abbey Street from Amiens Street railway terminus (which he had not been able to occupy). Accordingly he told Weafer to barricade the mouth of Lower Abbey Street, blocking access to Sackville Street. Two hundred yards down Abbey Street, Weafer discovered several large reels of newsprint in a warehouse owned by the *Irish Times*, and his men pushed these on to the street. Next he "commandeered" £5,000 worth of brand-new motor-cycles and piled them up beside the newsprint. While they were at work an anti-rebel mob jeered and catcalled them. Volunteer John Reid remembered how angry this made the rebels; yet, unless the mob physically attacked them or tried to pull down the barricade, what could they do? They could not fire on their own countrymen.

12

EIGHTEEN-YEAR-OLD Volunteer James Doyle, crouching in the back bedroom of Clanwilliam House and staring intently down Lower Mount Street, idly wondered if he would soon die. In the distance, at intervals, he could hear rifle-fire; suddenly, he jerked into life as shots sounded nearby.

Seconds later, Volunteer Willie Ronan, his bald pate shining pinkly, put his head round the door and said, "You're to go into George in the front room." Doyle went in and found Reynolds kneeling at the middle window, studying Northumberland Road through field-glasses. Following his gaze, Doyle saw a number of khaki-clad figures lying, apparently dead, on the pavement near Haddington Road. "Don't fire, anybody!" Reynolds warned.

The figures, in fact, were members of a Home Defence Force known as the Georgius Rex (irreverently christened by Dubliners "The Gorgeous Wrecks"), most of them elderly men—many of them British Army veterans—drawn from "respectable" business and professional circles in the city. That morning they had taken part in sham exercises near Kingstown, using rifles *but no ammunition*. When news reached them that the Sinn Feiners had risen in the city, they had at once marched on Dublin.

Nearing Beggar's Bush Barracks about 4 p.m., they had split into two columns. The main party, led by Major Harris of Trinity College O.T.C., forked right and marched along Shelbourne Road (which borders the railway line and runs parallel to Northumberland Road), where they came under fire from rebels up on the railway embankment. Major Harris and some of his men managed to reach the main gate of the barracks while the rest, retiring up Lansdowne Lane, succeeding in climbing in over the barracks wall. Altogether, eighty-one men and nine officers survived the ambush. They found Beggar's Bush in a state of near-panic; between them the garrison possessed only seventeen Lee-Enfields and were glad of the extra six carried by the G.R.s; the G.R.s themselves were advised to use their old Italian rifles *as clubs* if the rebels attacked.

The second party, under the command of Mr. F. H. Browning, amounting to forty men all told, marched straight into real trouble. Forking *left* as they neared the barracks, they marched along Northumberland Road and what happened then has been described by a woman resident of the district, who contemporaneously wrote:

"As I stand at the drawing-room window, I see a small detachment of G.R. veterans. The afternoon has been warm, they look hot and tired. A sharp report rings out, and the man in the foremost rank falls forward, apparently dead, a ghastly stream of blood flowing from his head. His comrades make for cover—the shelter of the trees, the side of a flight of steps. Bullet follows bullet with lightning rapidity. The road is unusually deserted until one of the veterans dashes across the road, falls at the feet of a woman who sets up a wail of terror. I cannot bear to look and yet I feel impelled to do so. Of six men by the tree only one is now standing—they must have lain down—but no, they have fallen on their backs, one over another—they are all wounded! Oh, the horror of it all—what does it mean? A wounded man is being borne in the direction of our house—we rush to open the door and offer assistance but they take him next door. I cannot watch any longer—I must go back to my mother, who is sitting quietly by the fire. She is very old and frail and must not know of what is passing so I try to appear as usual. After chatting to her for a short time, I return again to the window just in time to see a bare-headed white-coated doctor drive up in a motor-car. He disappears into one of the houses where he tends the wounded, some of whom are carried off to the hospital; the crowd which had gathered at the cross-roads gradually melts away."

It was an unfortunate incident; Malone and Grace held their fire immediately when they realized that the G.R.s carried no ammunition. But when news spread throughout the city that a body of unarmed and elderly men had been attacked by the rebels, it produced a violent public reaction. That night Pearse tried to rectify the damage by issuing an order expressly forbidding his men to fire on anyone who was unarmed—whether they were in uniform or not.

The G.R.s did not stand around long mourning their losses. Aided by a garrison in Beggar's Bush, they climbed up on to the barracks roof and, from several vantage points, opened a hot fire on the rebels on the railway line. One man, indeed, daringly worked his way over the barracks walls and through back-gardens until he reached the rear of No. 28 Northumberland Road, almost directly opposite No. 25. Malone and Grace, disturbed to find bullets kicking through *their* windows, took some time to locate him. Then Grace heard Malone's "Peter the Painter" tearing out shots and jerked his head up just in time to see the sniper, inside a room of the house opposite, snatch at the window blind and pull the curtains down around him even as he crashed to the floor.

Thereafter, Northumberland Road quickly returned to normal. In a little while, Gerald Morrissey and his friends scampered up to the corner of Haddington Road and picked up the rifles dropped by the G.R.s, which they handed over to the Volunteers in the Parochial Hall. A little later, George Reynolds ventured out the back of Clanwilliam House, dropping over the garden rail on to the pavement so as not to disturb the barricaded front door.

On his way to see Malone, he stopped to ask Company-Adjutant O'Donoghue if he had received any orders about firing on unarmed men.

"My orders are only to attack armed men trying to force their way into the city," said O'Donoghue.

"That's my view, too," said Reynolds. "And I'm going to take no notice of men, even if they are in khaki, who are not prepared for war."

Inside the school the time passed slowly. In the early evening excursionists began to pass in towards the city on the way home after their day out. Long shadows fell across the Canal, and O'Donoghue decided to eat. Food was scarce because the boys who made up half his garrison had not thought to provide themselves even with sandwiches, so he handed over his revolver to one youngster and told him to keep watch while he ate. The youngster interrupted him every few minutes, however, shouting, "There's a car coming, what'll I do?" In disgust, O'Donoghue roared at him, "Don't fire at all—at anything. If you see the whole British Army coming down the road, don't *fire!*"

Inside Clanwilliam House Reynolds knocked on the dining-room door and told Miss Wilson that she might feel happier if she gathered all her valuables together and put them in a suitcase, which could then be locked up in a room.

"That's certainly very kind of you," said Miss Wilson.

With the assistance of her maids, she collected silver and other objects, filling *two* suitcases, which young Doyle carried to a rear bedroom at the top of the house. Reynolds then locked the door in Miss Wilson's presence and handed her the key.

Not long after this, Reynolds had to face his first crisis; the youngest member of the party, a lad of seventeen, began to show signs of nerves. He sat shivering on his hunkers at the back of the room, his face pale and glistening with sweat.

Casually Reynolds said to him, "Would you like to go home for a while. Then, when you're feeling better, you can always come back."

The boy nodded.

"All right, then," said Reynolds, "you can get out the back way." Without a word the boy hurried away.

"We're better without that fellow," explained Reynolds when he had left, and young Doyle glanced around. Only four of them were left now and he himself had never fired a rifle in anger before—in fact, the only rifle practice he had ever had was on a miniature range.

He thought rather enviously of the lad who left.

Little Willie Nolan hoisted his red-painted, official Post Office bicycle on to the parapet of the Halfpenny Bridge, and then let it drop down into the Liffey with a loud splash. Relieved, he watched it disappear instantly. All that remained to do now, he happily realized, was to get rid of his uniform.

Little Willie—and he was little, only 4ft. 8in.—had spent most of the morning riding around the suburbs delivering telegrams. On the way back, he had taken a short cut which brought him out at the rear of the G.P.O. In Princes Street two armed men in trench coats and soft black hats stopped him.

"What do *you* want?" growled one.

"I work here," explained young Willie.

"Well, you don't any more now," said the man, "don't you know we've declared a Republic?"

Willie, with no idea of what the man was talking about, shook his head.

"Well, you know now," said the man. "Now, get to hell out of here at once—and take that British uniform off if you don't want to be shot!"

Willie had bolted back sharply into the alleyway. When half-way along it, he heard shooting. "My God! They're after me," he thought, not knowing whether to ride his bicycle or wheel it. He had soon realized, however, that so long as he had it in his possession, he was in danger of "being identified as a British official and shot." So he had decided to drop it in the Liffey. After that, he felt a great deal better. Still, he hurried home, anxious to get rid of his incriminating uniform. He found his mother distracted, for all sorts of wild rumours were sweeping the neighbourhood. He told her what he had done with the bicycle.

"My God!" she said. "You'll get five years for that—destroying Government property. We can thank the bloody Sinn Feiners for this."

When she went out to discover from the neighbours what was happening, he took off his uniform and burned it. Better to go to jail, he thought as he watched the flames devour it, than be shot by men in soft black hats.

At 4 p.m. the first reinforcements from the Curragh drew into Kingsbridge station, and were met by rebel rifle-fire. Aboard the train was a first draft of a thousand troops of the Mobile Column, among them Captain Carl Elliotson of the 3rd Reserve Cavalry Regiment.

The column had been forced to entrain without horses or limbers because of the hurry, and Elliotson's first task was to secure trolleys to handle the equipment and ammunition. The station staff lent him three luggage-trolleys and at 5.30 p.m. the column advanced towards Dublin Castle. A fan of scouts ahead, they moved carefully down the south bank of the Liffey and past Guinness's Brewery without opposition then, by making a detour through the side streets, arrived safely at the Ship Street entrance to the Castle inside half an hour.

This meant that Colonel Cowan had the rebels now outnumbered by at least five to one—although he did not know it and his problem remained: exactly how many rebels were there, and would the country rise? Even more important, when and where in Ireland would Germany strike?

Meanwhile, denied a respite, Ceannt's forces continued to defend the South Dublin Union with stubborn gallantry. All that hard day—that long and brilliantly-sunlit, death-hunting day—hunger and thirst had waxed among them and a terrible weariness, even a despair, had begun to replace their earlier sense of exhilaration and achievement. By tea-time, too, the fighting had deteriorated into a game of cat and mouse; a nerve-racking, heart-stopping battle of unexpected death, with rarely a let-up. A sense of purpose, a flame of patriotism, still flickered strongly, but by now abstract conceptions had given way to realities and battle had been pared down to its true components. The pressure, in short, had begun to tell.

It was just past five o'clock when the military launched their last assault of the day; a move intended to clear Section-Commander Joyce and perhaps a half-dozen men from the Women's Infirmary. It was an extraordinarily incongruous battlefield. Although the Union authorities had evacuated most of the patients, some women still remained when Joyce and his comrades flung themselves down on the floor at the intersection of Wards 16 and 17 and got ready to pick off the military whom they could hear breaking their way in below. It was a desperate plan; their only chance of success—and that a remote one—was that the military, caught in the narrow entrance to Ward 16, might suffer such heavy casualties that they would be forced to retire.

The smell of wax polish stroked Joyce's nostrils as he lay there, hardly conscious of the patients who, after the first hysterical hubbub, had now crowded into a corner and surrounded themselves with beds. Suddenly the military stood in the doorway. For a second they halted, like tiny, brown gnomes. Joyce fired and, as women screamed, the crack of rifles opened up all around him. Then he scrambled back with his comrades and slammed the ward door shut. The military rushed to it, banging loudly, and demanding, "Surrender! In the name of the King!"

Joyce flung himself down again as bullets crashed through the door. Only a thin partition divided the antagonists, and the rebels lay pinned to the floor. Joyce hardly knew what he was doing but he was certain of one thing; he was not going to surrender.

Then the firing ceased and an educated English voice shouted, "I'll count five. Either surrender or we're coming in."

Joyce listened to the count: "One . . . two . . . three . . . "

A comrade shouted, "Quick! This way!" and Joyce got to his feet and ran. At the end of the ward a locked door barred their way, but they shot the lock off and ran on. At the far end of the next ward once again they flung themselves down and turned on their pursuers. There was a wild mêlée, with both sides grovelling about on the floor, trying desperately to take an accurate aim. Joyce took cover behind a bed as bits of plaster showered over him like hailstones.

In the end the rebels successfully retreated. Joyce's memory of what happened next became vague in later years. He remembered racing into an empty part of the building, running along bare corridors, and finally finding himself outside in the grounds, with the sounds of pursuit dying away. He made a last dash across an open courtyard and got safely inside the Nurses' Home.

Here he and his comrades collapsed, exhausted. Their spirits rose, however, after they had eaten their first meal that day; corned beef, followed by reviving draughts of hot tea. They cheered up even further when Ceannt announced that the Rising was going well everywhere, and that the military had been successfully held at all points. Then the whole garrison knelt down and recited the Rosary.

By early evening, if they had been determined enough, Pearse and Connolly could still have taken Trinity. Professor John Joly, F.R.S., arriving there at about 4 p.m., found the College almost defenceless. Major Tate, O.C. of the O.T.C., was not to be found, and Captain Alton and Lieutenant Waterhouse were doing their best to cope without him. Lieutenant Luce, R.I.R., home on sick leave from France, was also proving a tower of strength, but a determined rebel assault could certainly have taken the place. Joly, indeed, could not understand why it had not been taken already, for apart from its obvious strategical importance, several hundred rifles and thousands of rounds of ammunition lay in the O.T.C. stores.

Sir John Mahaffy, great and famous Provost of Trinity, was barricaded inside his house and even Joly found it difficult to talk to him. In the end he succeeded and then went back to his home to tell his family that he was going to help defend Trinity. On his return, the number of defenders had increased to forty-four—including eight Anzacs.

"The Shinners" found themselves vastly unpopular with the returning holiday crowds, especially with the fathers of families who, finding trains and trams stopped, in some cases had to walk five miles in the waning heat, dragging their weeping offspring behind them.

The Fairyhouse crowd, bathed in euphoria, arrived back in the city in a state of happy insensibility. A judge, driving his car along Sackville Street, was highly indignant when halted and, with his two lady passengers, forced to get out at gunpoint. On the other hand, a military officer, when held up by a youngster, simply got out of his car, knocked the rebel down and drove off, his two lady friends laughing uproariously—something he may not have attempted if sober. Stopped by rebels at a canal bridge, a motorist asserted that he was as good an Irishman as they were, had no connection with British officialdom, and anyhow, wasn't he only coming from Fairyhouse? "Here, tell us," said an insurgent, "who won the last race?"

Even "Madame" was not above the infection. When her men held up two cars and escorted the occupants before her, she recognized one as an old neighbour from the west of Ireland.

"I've no wish to detain you or your friends," she apologized, "but I'll have to keep the cars. *For military purposes,*" she added. Then, turning on her charm, she said, "Now, I know you and the ladies would like some tea!"

As the cups were handed round, the Countess presided over it all as though at a garden party.

And yet the shadow of tragedy was never far away. James Stephens saw a man stride over to a barricade and begin tugging a cart from it. "Put down that cart.

Let out and go away. Let out at once!" yelled a voice from the Green and three shots rang out. They flew harmlessly past. But they incensed the cart-owner even more and he marched towards the railings, wagging his finger at the rebels.

"Go back," shouted a rifleman. "Go back and put that cart back where you found it—or you're a dead man. Go on before I count to four. One, two, three, four. . . ."

He fired and the man sagged to the ground in two slow, twisting movements. Women screamed. Stephens ran to help the shot man. He was bleeding from the head and Stephens and some bystanders carried him on to the pavement. "At that moment," Stephens later wrote, "the Volunteers were hated."

A man who assisted to carry the shot man away turned and shouted at the rebels, "We'll be coming back for you, damn you!"

13

"HOOROOSH! HOOROOSH!" shouted the drunken old woman. "They're raiding Noblett's." And her shawl-covered arms flapped excitedly like two great black wings.

Up out of the slums, the worst in Europe at that time outside the stews of Naples, from the tenements of Gardiner Street and Marlborough Street, from the back streets behind Moore Street and Great Britain Street, swarmed the underprivileged—or as 1916 knew them, the poor. The women outnumbered the men by at least four to one. There were old crones in their black shawls and young girls in their bare feet. The men wore mufflers round their throats and even their caps were ragged and dirty. The backsides of urchins showed bare through their ragged pants and the little girls had grubby pinafores.

Suddenly, with a tremendous crash, the plate-glass front of Noblett's, a confectioner's on the corner of Sackville Street and North Earl Street, crashed on to the pavement.

Sweets spilled out in a cascade; and men, women and children dived to the ground to scoop up handfuls of chocolates, Turkish delight, glacier mints and fruit bon-bons. Glass jars stuffed with sweetmeats were smashed and boxes ripped open and the contents strewn over the street. The mob grew wild with excitement and, as news of the spoils available spread, swelled in size. Then in the middle of all the looting, somebody shouted. "The soldiers are coming!"

There was a swift scattering. Women and children knocked and trampled each other down as they surged towards O'Connell Bridge. But when the military failed to appear, they crowded back to Noblett's again.

Once one shop had gone there was no halting the destruction. Quickly two others were broken into, the noise of their crashing plate glass sounding all the louder because of the new and awful stillness that had fallen over the city. Guttersnipes ran out of Dunn's, the hatters, decked out in silk hats, straw hats and bowlers. One urchin danced to the edge of the pavement with the three different varieties perched perilously on his head, on top of each other. A second made a swipe at him and knocked the lot over. As the hats landed in the gutter, his friends began to kick them about like footballs. Drunken women reeled from the Saxone shoe shop, brandishing satin slippers and knee-high Russian boots. It was like a gigantic lucky dip; but by the hazard of chance, too, some got too much of one article and not enough of another. Women, clasping boxes of shoes to their breasts, fought their way out of the shops, only to find that they had grabbed a whole series of left-foots. A barter system was soon established. "A lady's No. 4 black Russian boot with fur lining—left foot only," shouted a woman, hoping to find its companion.

Sean O'Casey watched a slum crowd fling clothing all over Sackville Street and try on brand-new garments over their rags; one woman got into the wrecked tram at the corner of North Earl Street and stripped naked to try on camisoles. A man ran past him carrying a jar of whiskey in one hand and a pair of looted boots in the other, and O'Casey saw a bullet hit the jar and smash it. "Jasus!" said the man disgustedly. "The wasteful bastards!"

Pubs, of course, were obvious targets. In Henry Street, women dragged a case of champagne into the street and danced around it, only desisting from time to time to drink the contents.

For James Connolly the looting posed an agonizing dilemma. The people committing it were the poor, the down-trodden and the ignorant—the very people to whom he had dedicated his life; the people who stood to benefit most if he won what he had set himself out to win. Yet they were not only disgracing the insurrection; they were hindering it. Sadly Connolly ordered, "Fire a volley over their heads."

The first volley scattered the looters, but they quickly gathered again and a second volley had to be fired.

"Ah, they're only blanks!" shouted a man and led the way into another shop.

The first serious attempt to stop it all was made by Francis Sheehy-Skeffington. A stocky, red-bearded, knicker-bockered figure, Sheehy-Skeffington was probably Dublin's greatest eccentric. Most Sunday afternoons he could be heard near the Custom House expatiating to amused crowds on any subject involving Justice and Fair Play. He was for Votes for Women and Socialism; he was against War. Most people regarded him as a crackpot. Both Pearse and Connolly, however, considered him a man of high principle and intelligence, though he had often argued with them that they could achieve their ends more easily by civil disobedience than by rebellion.

Earlier in the day, during the assault on Dublin Castle, he had demonstrated the quixotic streak in his character by rushing forward amid a hail of bullets to help Second Lieutenant Guy Pinfield of the 8th Hussars, lying shot in Upper Castle Yard. Unable to staunch the wound himself, Skeffington dodged through the rifle-fire to get aid from a nearby chemist. Remonstrated with later by his friends for risking his life for an "enemy", Sheehy-Skeffington answered, "What else could I do—I couldn't let the man bleed to death."

Now he mounted the steps of Nelson Pillar and appealed to the mob to go home. They hooted him. Angrily Sheehy-Skeffington strode across to the G.P.O., demanded to see Connolly, and urged him to take sterner measures. As a result, MacDermott, with a small escort, hobbled out of the building and, climbing up on to the wrecked tramcar, called upon the mob "not to disgrace the battle for freedom." Even his words and personal prestige failed

Landing guns for the Irish Volunteers at Howth, July, 1914

Patrick Pearse with parents and teachers at St. Enda's. Pearse sits in the centre, looking at the camera, with his left hand resting on his knee.

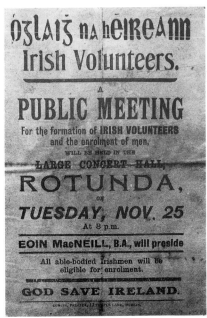

Handbill announcing the meeting for the Rotunda, November 25th, 1913, at which the Irish Volunteers were founded

A formal portrait of Patrick Pearse

Barricades in the streets during Easter Week

Irish Rebellion. May 1916.
Soldiers holding a Dublin Street.

James Connolly

IRISH VOLUNTEERS.
DUBLIN BRIGADE.

COMPANY MOBILISATION ORDER.

on Sunday 23

The ....8....... Coy., ...4th....... Batt., will mobilise ~~to-day~~ at the hour
of....4..... *P* m. Point of Mobilisation.... *Emerald Square*.................

Full Service Equipment to be worn, including overcoat, haversack, water-
bottle, canteen.

Rations for........8..............hours to be carried.

ARMS AND FULL SUPPLY OF AMMUNITION TO BE CARRIED.

Cycle Scouts to be mounted, and ALL men having cycles or motor cycles to
bring them.

P. Ryan

....
Captain or Officer Commanding.

Dated this....23....day of......4 month......................, 191.6.

An Irish Volunteers mobilization order for the abortive Sunday rebellion. It was orders
like this which were countermanded by Eoin MacNeill.

Tom Clarke

Front page of the *Daily Express* for Wednesday, April 26th, 1916

Detail of the photograph below, showing James Connolly (centre, in civilian clothes and Homburg hat)

Liberty Hall before the Rising, showing members of the Irish Citizen Army drawn up outside

Liberty Hall after the Rising

Destruction in Earl Street following the artillery barrage

to produce any effect. Connolly finally called Sean T. O'Kelly and told him, "I want you to take a dozen armed men and go over there and stop that."

O'Kelly led a small armed party across Sackville Street, even as a shawlie shouted, "Isn't Clery's broken into yet?" By the time O'Kelly reached the pavement, Clery's—the principal department store in Sackville Street—had been "broken". But when the mob saw him and his men bearing down on them, rifles at the ready, they fled.

O'Kelly placed a guard on the premises, then moved to a tobacconist's next door which had also been broken into, and cleared this. Meantime, the mob were busy smashing their way into McDowell's, the jewellers. In despair, O'Kelly decided to obtain fresh orders from Connolly.

"Have you shot anybody?" demanded Connolly brusquely, when he reported back.

"No—but we've shot over their heads," said O'Kelly.

"Shooting over their heads is useless," said Connolly. "Unless you shoot a few of them you won't stop them. I'll have to send somebody else over there who'll deal with them."

"Am I released then?" asked O'Kelly, hopefully.

"Yes," said Connolly, "you are."

O'Kelly took himself upstairs to the commissariat to get something to eat. Plunkett was lying on a mattress on the floor, looking very pale and ill.

"Is he not well?" asked O'Kelly.

Tom Clarke shook his head gravely.

Inside St. Stephen's Green, the sight of several attractive young female rebels helped to take Air Mechanic Pratt's mind off his plight.

"It's no use moaning, old man," he remarked to a fellow-prisoner, "they're going to shoot us, whatever we do, so we might as well enjoy ourselves while we can." So he began chaffing some girls who were preparing a meal nearby. In a short time, he had so advanced matters that he had succeeded in kissing one. In fact, he had his arm around the girl's waist when Countess Markievicz, attracted by the sounds of laughter coming from the summer-house, rushed across. When she saw what was happening, she lost her temper.

"Get out of here at once, you hussy!" she stormed at the girl, who ran off in tears. "Now, get back to your duties at once, the lot of you," she shouted, rounding on the rest of the girls. "Is this what you call fighting for Ahland!"

Later, when the Countess's back was turned, Pratt's girl sneaked back to the summer-house, carrying a plate of ham and several custard pies. As he ate, Pratt decided that he had nothing against revolutions, provided they were all conducted in the sensible way this was.

Lieutenant Bob de Coeur marched over to the trench where Professor Liam O'Briain was arguing with two Citizen Army men and bawled, "Fall in!"

O'Briain and the two Citizen Army men stepped from their shallow trench, presented arms and waited at attention as Commandant Mallin came up, followed by Countess Markievicz. De Coeur seemed pleased about something; what it was became clear in a moment.

The news was exciting, Mallin declared. The whole country was up. The West was up; Kerry was up; Limerick was up; so was Cork. The Boys of Wexford were on the march again—one hundred and eighteen years after their epic stand at Vinegar Hill. O'Briain murmured to the man beside him, "Begod, this is the biggest thing since 1690." Then Mallin, having stirred their blood and sent their spirits leaping, smiled at them pleasantly and walked back with the Countess to the headquarters hut. Behind them they left an excited buzz of speculation. Ireland, indeed, had seen nothing like this for centuries. Could it be really happening? Was the apparently impossible actually on the verge of being achieved? Excitement reached new heights when somebody announced as pure gospel that the Germans would be sailing up the Liffey at 3 a.m.

With this exhilarating news clanging about his ears, O'Briain was picked out with twenty men and ordered to march to the top of Leeson Street and occupy houses commanding the bridge over the Canal. They were supplied with home-made bombs and told to toss them down from the roof-tops if the enemy attempted to storm the bridge. As they filed out by the west gate, they were saluted by an old gentleman, who leaped to attention, doffed his hat and held it solemnly across his breast. It was a simple gesture which somehow made O'Briain realize for the first time the solemnity and importance of what they were doing.

Led by de Coeur, the party advanced cautiously up Leeson Street, splitting into two files of ten men each on opposite sides of the street. At the top they paired off and began knocking on doors. O'Briain and de Coeur knocked at the last house and when they got no reply, de Coeur lifted his pickaxe and hacked it into the door, a fine piece of eighteenth-century wood, exquisitely fashioned. Although ruined within seconds, the door still refused to give. Annoyed, the two men turned round as the door of the next house opened and a maid came out. Before she could run in again, they had whipped round and shoved past her. They went up through the house and got out through a skylight on to the roof and climbed along it until they reached the first house. They found this empty and began preparing for a siege.

"What you need in a revolution is furniture removers," remarked O'Briain, as he pushed a heavy wardrobe. When they had finished barricading the place, O'Briain wrote a note to the owner, apologizing for what they had done. "Sorry for any damage to the furniture. Hope you approve of the cause," he scribbled.

It was a beautiful night, and later, on the roof, O'Briain watched his comrades squatting cheerfully on the roofs of other houses. Parapets two feet high protected them against falling into the street. Shortly after they had taken up positions, one of the men, Jem Little, shouted from the next roof, "Hey, Bob—there's an ould fellow down here, a judge or lord or something—anyhow the maids kept calling him 'me Lord'—and he's annoying us."

"What's he done to you, Jem?" asked de Coeur.

"He's telling us we should go home," said Little, indignantly. "Telling us we've no right to be in his house, d'ye ever hear the like of that?"

"Oh, we'll soon put a stop to that," said de Coeur, determinedly. "William," he said to O'Briain (who had never been called anything but Liam), "William, you know how to talk to these people—go down and tell that ould fellow what this is all about."

"Take me to him, Jem," said O'Briain, and skirting the parapet, he climbed over the intersecting wall and dropped down through the skylight behind Little. Downstairs in the drawing-room he found a portly, highly-dignified old gentleman, white-haired and bearded and dressed in a frock coat, standing in front of a big fire blazing in the hearth. Beside him stood his wife and three terrified maids.

"I understand you've been telling these men to go home?" began O'Briain, with as much authority as he could muster.

"Yes, that is so. They've absolutely no right to be here. And you've no right to be here either. The whole thing is entirely illegal. I protest against your presence in my house."

"You don't think we're just burglars, do you? You realize that this is an insurrection, and that we're acting under orders?"

"Yes, that's right," chipped in Little, "and you know, we must obey orders!"

"I'm sorry," continued O'Briain, "But you'll have to make the best of it. We'll do as little damage as we can to your house. If there should be any fighting, I advise you to go downstairs and go to the back of the house. By the way, some of the other houses are giving the men tea."

Judge Drennan Andrews (one of whose ancestors had helped to found the United Irishmen of 1798) drew himself up with great dignity. "I am an old man [he was eighty-three] and I am ill. I cannot prevent you taking anything you want from my house, but if I offered hospitality to these men then it would mean that I should be giving them permission to be here—and that I shall not do."

"Well, all right, sir," said O'Briain. "In that case we won't disturb you." And followed by the incongruous proletarian figure of Jem Little, he withdrew.

Up on the roof again, he settled down as snugly as he could to stare down into the dark and silent street and to listen to the odd crack of a military rifle or the reverberating boom of a Howth Mauser somewhere away in the distance. After a while it grew colder, so he and de Coeur came down off the roof and went into a bedroom, which they found a great deal warmer. Neither attempted to sleep. Just before midnight, a side-car came trotting along, the voices of the jarvey and his customer floating up to them quite clearly. The jarvey declared portentously, "I tell you, sir, there's something behind all this."

Shortly after midnight, O'Briain jerked alert. He heard, from the far side of the Canal bridge, the measured tramp of an approaching column. He grabbed a bomb and scrambled out on to the roof. He saw shadowy figures stealthily taking up positions along other roofs. He crouched close to the parapet, the nose of his rifle just topping it, the bomb immediately beside his hand. Then, as the approaching column reached the bridge, de Coeur shouted, "Fire!"

There was an ear-splitting uproar as twenty antiquated weapons spewed lead on to the bridge below. O'Briain swung his arm in a quick, jerking arc and there was a stunning noise from below as the bomb exploded. Shouts and cries floated up from the bridge. Then somebody shouted, "Stop shooting, we're Volunteers! Stop shooting!"

"Cease fire!" bawled de Coeur.

The firing stopped. From below they heard shouts and cries as the scattered column reassembled. Along the roofs the men crouched down, softly cursing into the night at their mistake.

At Dublin Castle, late in the evening, the situation had begun to resolve itself a little.

Inside the Castle, Captain Carl Elliotson had carried out a careful reconnaissance of the position. Huddling close to the buildings, he had edged towards the main gates, stopping now and then to examine the lines of fire which would enable him to dominate the City Hall and the Rates Office opposite it. In double-quick time he had his Vickers gun set up in a concealed position and opened fire. A jet of bullets streamed out towards the City Hall. Inside, Helena Moloney and Dr. Kathleen Lynn, happening to look out, thought the weather had changed; it appeared to be hailing. Then they realized "the hail" was simply bullets. As military marksmanship grew more accurate, the effect became nerve-racking; bullets sizzled through the windows, banging and ricocheting around the walls like stones in a bucket. Plaster crashed from the ceiling; sections of cornice and wall rumbled down in clouds of dust that soon made the place as dark as midnight.

Young Annie Norgrove, aged sixteen, whose father George was fighting on the roof, had spent most of her day running back and forwards from the kitchen to the roof, carrying food and water to the men, risking death each time she emerged on to the perilous rim of the dome. Here bullets had hopped about her, smashing chimney pots nearby, kicking up small clouds of brick-dust. As the fight wore on, she had seen the lips of the men puff with thirst, and their faces blacken from gunpowder. Some of them tied handkerchiefs round their hands to protect them from their overheated rifles. During one machine-gun burst she was almost hit. "Down Annie—down for God's sake!" shouted one of the men, and she ground herself into the roof as the bullets kicked and ripped around her. A few inches above her head a chimney pot showered into pieces and, after that, she was no longer asked to go up on the roof.

Downstairs, Dr. Lynn spent much of her time trying to assist eighteen-year-old John Coyle, one of the severely wounded. As bursts of fire intensified and the whole City Hall seemed to be coming down around their ears, he began trembling violently. "Oh, don't leave me!" he kept moaning. To give him a feeling of protection she and Helena Moloney tied him up in a high wooden-backed chair, which they moved up against a pillar, placing it so that he was shielded by the pillar in front and the high back in the rear.

The Castle defenders had already mentally prepared themselves for a long siege. A great cheer went up, therefore, when a milkman rolled a big can with the evening's milk supplies into Upper Castle Yard; nobody had expected him to get through. Morale rose immediately, except possibly among some badly wounded cases in the Red Cross Hospital. One soldier declared. "We might as well go back to France!" Another said, "I'm getting out of here tomorrow and going home!" Eventually, towards dusk, an order was given to pull down all blinds and dowse the lights, and it was explained that the troops were going to launch a counter-attack. "After a while," wrote the V.A.D., "I peeked out and saw an officer and some men congregated near the main Gate. I heard the officer giving orders and then saw two or three men dash towards the Gate and disappear, followed an instant later by two or three more."

All in all, the military were to employ two hundred troops in the assault on the City Hall, almost seven times the total number of insurgents facing them. One hundred men took part in the first frontal assault. They succeeded in taking the Provost-Marshal's house, which was found to be empty, but failed in an attempt to recapture the Guardroom because of rebel barricades.

Captain Elliotson and his machine-gun crew kept up a continuous fire on the City Hall from the roof above Mr. Birrell's office as the second military assault party raced out on to the Cork Hill and around to the front entrance. But a concentrated fire, poured down on them from the roofs of the *Mail & Express* office and Henry & James's shop opposite, caught them and several men, including the officer-in-charge, fell. Command was taken over by the troop sergeant, who ordered a retirement, and the military left twenty khaki-clad figures in the roadway, most of them dead.

Because of the increasing danger, the doctors and nurses in the Red Cross Hospital decided that the patients should be moved from the Picture Gallery and the Throne Room to the relative safety of St. Patrick's Hall. Into the great room where Queen Victoria, and afterwards her son King Edward VII, had received the homage of their Irish subjects, the wounded were brought, twitching unhappily as the sounds of battle recalled memories of the Western Front. Soon the corridors were also packed with fresh casualties. "I'd like to get every one of those Sinn Feiners and torture them, and then turn machine-guns on them," one man told a V.A.D.

As it was, the rebels inside the City Hall were undoubtedly suffering enough even to satisfy him. Conditions on the ground floor, where most of the women and the wounded lay huddled behind the pillars, had become simply appalling. Above the noise of machine-gun fire arose new sounds—of exploding hand grenades, thrown by troops who, attacking the rear of the City Hall, had outwitted the rebels by advancing unseen through the Castle cellars and emerging through a small area opening right under the windows. After an initial "softening-up" with bombs, the troops rushed the windows. It was the first chance the rebels on the roof had to fire on them, and they seized it. In moving out from cover, they exposed themselves to Captain Elliotson's machine-gun; the gallant Captain did not fail to take the opportunity. Among the first rebels to be mown down was big Jack O'Reilly, 6ft. 6in. in height, who had succeeded to command after John Connolly's death.

On the ground floor, the din was so great that Emily Norgrove (no less than five members of whose family were "out") thought the great dome was about to come down. The noise became fantastic, for as the military stormed the rear windows, they were met by a devastating fire from rebels who came down the stairs to repel them. The first wave was decimated but a second followed, forcing back the defenders. They retreated to the first landing as the soldiers crashed through the dust and rubble searching for them. Then a concentrated volley sent the military reeling back down the stairs.

Falling back in confusion, they collided in the dark with another wave of their own forces. Mistaking each other for rebels, the two parties opened fire at close quarters and slashed out wildly with their bayonets. The rebels poured volley after volley into them from the landing above. For a moment it looked to the rebels as though they had been saved by a miracle, but somehow, above the shouts and the screams and deafening noise of exploding firearms, the military found out their mistake. They retreated to reorganize themselves. Then, courageously, they came forward yet again, this time in a determined and purposeful assault which swiftly overwhelmed the tiny rebel party on the landing. An abrupt silence descended upon the City Hall.

Up on the roof, the rest of the rebels, thoroughly exhausted by now, their rifles so hot that they could no longer fire them, welcomed the respite. Downstairs, as some of the confusion died away, an officer's voice rang out through the darkness demanding, "Surrender in the name of the King!" A torch shone through the choking dust, swept round the battered interior of the City Hall and picked out the handful of terrified women and wounded men crouching behind the pillars.

"Hands up or we'll fire!" shouted the officer.

Dr. Kathleen Lynn advanced into the circle of light, the rest following behind her, their hands raised. "We surrender!" she called. "We surrender!"

The torch beamed fixedly on her; she was harshly ordered to step forward. Soldiers approached her, bayonets at the ready, suspicious of a trap. One party searched behind the pillars, then reported that there was no one there.

"Is this really all there is?" asked the officer in surprise.

"I'm afraid that's all, sir," replied the soldier.

"Oh, well then, line them up!" said the officer resignedly.

While stretcher parties carried away the wounded, the women were escorted through one of the great broken windows at the rear; they had to scramble over rubble and debris, and without assistance from the military. They were led into Upper Castle Yard and thence to Ship Street Barracks, where they were lodged in a vermin-ridden wing unoccupied for years; they were expected, apparently, to lie upon a few filthy cushions. Two soldiers brought them tea and hard tack biscuits, and now, for the first time, they began to sense the enormity—in their captors' eyes—of what they had done. Lewd suggestions and coarse remarks added to their realization that they had sacrificed the privileges of citizenship, that even their lives might now be forfeit.

While Dr. Lynn and her party were being led away, a military detail advanced up through the different floors. In a small upper room, they discovered Jenny Shanahan, a Citizen Army girl who had taken refuge there. Jenny was not in uniform and the officer-in-charge, assuming that she had been held prisoner, asked her gently, "Are there many of them here?" adding, "Have they treated you badly?"

"Oh, no, sir—they treated me well enough," answered Jenny, "but there must be hundreds of them still up there on the roof."

"H'm," murmured the officer thoughtfully. He hesitated, then gave the order to retire; nobody, after all that had already happened, relished a night-battle among the rooftops. The final clearance of the City Hall would have to await the coming of daylight.

Unfortunately for Miss Shanahan, her new status did not last long. She was politely escorted to Ship Street Barracks, where it was intended that she should identify some of the women rebels. Shouts of recognition greeted her appearance.

"Oh, so you're *one* of them!" shouted her escort angrily, and she found herself suddenly propelled forward by a shove in the back.

Two hours after they had first attempted to storm the barricaded Castle Guardroom, the military succeeded in forcing the door. They found the guard still trussed up, their rifles and ammunition gone—but no sign of the rebels. There was no need to wonder how they had got away. A press was pulled back from the wall to disclose a small iron grating. The rebels had removed this and crept down the piping. At that moment, in fact, Tom Kain was encamped with his men less than twenty yards away. His party had emerged from the pipe into Castle Street and, sneaking along the side of the wall, entered the first premises they came to, a plumber's called Lahiff's. They made their way down into the cellar and decided to stay there until things quietened down. They had plenty of water, for a drinking pipe ran through the cellar, and Kain made a small hole in it with a pin. When the hole was not in use he plugged it with a match.

Above them, in Castle Yard, the military built two large watchfires about fifteen yards apart. Here, as the night grew cold, the soldiers stamped on the ground and warmed their hands at the blaze.

On the roof of the City Hall, the tired rebels crouched together and shivered. They were still determined to fight on, although they knew, as they gazed over the dark tiles, waiting for a sniper's flash to show from the high Bermingham Tower, that on the morrow almost certainly they would die.

14

TO OBTAIN A better view of what was happening in Sackville Street and particularly in the G.P.O., William Redmond-Howard, nephew of John Redmond, decided to move from the Metropole Hotel, where he had been staying, to the Imperial Hotel opposite. Here he found a similar state of confusion but, amusingly, a different collection of rumours. First, he was told that his uncle had been taken prisoner and shot; then, that the Castle was in flames; and finally, that Father O'Doherty, one of the priests from the Pro-Cathedral, had been shot dead when he dared to venture forth, fully vestmented and with a cross in his hand, to remonstrate with the rebels. Redmond-Howard hurried upstairs to his room with the intention of noting down as many incidents as he could.

Shortly after 9.30 p.m. he saw the first flicker of fire briefly reflected in the windows of the Metropole. Leaning out of the window, he saw that the Cable shoe shop next door had caught fire. He ran downstairs and out into the street, where he joined a crowd of some two hundred people watching the place burn down. High up in the face of the building, a chink of light shining from a curtained window showed that there were people living upstairs. The blaze was crackling merrily through the lower floors, belching out black and blinding smoke. Realizing that the people above were as yet unaware of their peril, Redmond-Howard raced round to a side door. He found it locked, and pounded on it without avail. He called out for assistance. Even so, the door still resisted the combined weight of three men. At last the kicks and hammering had an effect; a window snapped up and a man popped his head out.

"The place is on fire!" yelled Redmond-Howard.

"My God!" shouted the man. "There are women and children sleeping in this place!"

At 10.06 the Dublin Fire Brigade under Captain Purcell reached the scene. By this time the side door was open and Redmond-Howard was helping the trapped women into the street, but he was disconcerted when an expectant mother, already in labour, refused to leave her bed. Even Captain Purcell had never before been confronted with such a problem, but he firmly ordered his men to remove the woman whether she liked it or not, and she was carried down screaming through the smoke and flames. Part of the staircase had caught alight and the whole place was being consumed so rapidly that two more sections of the brigade were called out. By 10.50 the fire was under control, but the firemen had hardly finished their task when the looters set fire to a second shoe shop and, wearily, they had to start all over again.

Redmond-Howard returned to the Imperial Hotel, where the manager had offered rooms to the evacuated families, but unable to sleep sat down at his bedroom window to watch the scenes below.

The hungry crowds had grown even more turbulent. First a tobacco shop went; then a jeweller's. Within seconds, urchins were diving in among the ruck of legs and flying elbows and reappearing with watches and rings which they bargained off at ludicrous prices. Towards midnight, a new sound rose above the noise of the looters gathered outside the burning shoe shop. Craning out, Redmond-Howard saw that furniture was being tossed into the street from premises at the corner of the block.

These new disturbances were caused, not by the looters, but by a rebel party under Captain Brennan Whitmore. Connolly had told him to build a barricade across North Earl Street to prevent a British attack from Amiens Street station. He had also ordered him to occupy and fortify, as part of this defence position, all the buildings from the corner of North Earl Street down to the Imperial Hotel.

Breaking into the corner shop, Brennan Whitmore's men hurried upstairs to the Pillar Café on the first floor, and rapidly began to put it into a state of defence. Then they tossed tables and chairs into the street to make the barricade. As the furniture poured out of the windows, a buxom young shawlie shouted, "God! They're giving away all the lovely furniture. Mary! Come on!" and she grabbed a chair as it hit the pavement. She was carting it away when Brennan Whitmore ran after her.

"Put that back where you got it!" he ordered sternly.

The woman was tipsy, and began to argue. So he gave the chair a push and she dropped it. For a moment, he believed she was going to ask the mob to help her. Instead, she flung out her arms and attempted to embrace him, while the crowd howled derisively. Brennan Whitmore turned and shouted, "Look! We've risen to free our country, and we expect the help and goodwill of every true Irishman and woman."

The plea partly succeeded, and a few men came forward to help build the barricade. This left Brennan Whitmore free to attend to the tunnelling of the walls from the Pillar Café to the Imperial Hotel. This turned out to be such a formidable task that he had to send a second party down to the Imperial Hotel to work through from that side. By the early hours of the morning the job was accomplished; but to Brennan Whitmore's consternation, the tunnellers had not allowed for the fact that the floor of the Imperial was on a different level and the hole came through the wall only a foot or so below the ceiling. At first he was annoyed; then he saw the funny side of it and began to laugh heartily.

Down in Boland's Bakery and out along the railway line—as far out as Sandymount and as far in towards the City as Westland Row station—it had been a hard and wearing day. Commandant de Valera, already strained and haggard-looking from lack of sleep for the past two nights, had roamed about ceaselessly, shotgun in hand, a restless, continually dissatisfied, strangely-odd exotic figure.

For the men themselves the problem in the first few hours of the Rebellion was to work up a real sense of bloodthirstiness. Ripping up rails, digging trenches, building ramps and ordering bakers about hardly helped to create a real hatred for the enemy. It was almost with relief that they watched a small party of military from Beggar's Bush Barracks emerge on the railway line; but a few shots, delivered at random, quickly put them to flight.

Just before midnight, however, panic swept some of the positions. The men had bedded themselves down in shallow foxholes dug between the railway sleepers, and Volunteer Peter Nolan was cat-napping when he was suddenly shaken awake and a voice roared in his ear, "The enemy's coming." He stared hard into the night, then began firing away at the shadows. There were a few answering flashes before the enemy retreated; after this things quietened down for a while. During the lull a rather strange instruction was passed along the line; if an aeroplane flew overhead during the night, nobody was to fire on it—it would be German. At midnight, de Valera issued orders for the first of the on-again, off-again projects which were to distinguish his leadership throughout the insurrection. He told Donnelly to take four or five men and scout towards Kingstown to find if there was any sign of reinforcements coming in from England. Donnelly picked four men, made sure that they had full equipment (rations, full water-bottles, rifles) and, as a precaution against his raw, rather jittery troops losing each other in the dark, made each man rub flour on the back of the man in front of him. Just before they were due to move out, however, de Valera changed his mind and ordered the expedition cancelled. During the week his officers were to get used to preparing for brilliant improvisations which subsequently had to be called off.

In Clanwilliam House young Doyle, guarding the back scullery, jumped up nervously when "some bloody cats started fighting outside." His nerves were so ragged that he was forced to light a candle. Soon afterwards, Reynolds came down to see how he was faring. "Good God! Surely you're not afraid of the dark, Jimmy!" he said, and blew out the candle. Later, he relented and came back. "I've been thinking it over, Jimmy," he said. "It must be lonely all right, down here by yourself. I'll tell you what, let's barricade this place and then you can come upstairs with the rest of us."

On the far side of Mount Street Bridge, Mick Malone left No. 25 and scaled a telegraph pole to tap the wires to Portobello Barracks. He said he was calling from the Curragh and cautiously asked questions about garrison strength. The barracks grew suspicious, however, and refused to give any information.

In the Church Street-North King Street area, the rebels had spent a weary day erecting barricades, arguing with inhabitants, and coping with drunks lumbering home from Fairyhouse who simply wanted to fight anybody who stopped them at the barricades. Commandant Daly had set up his headquarters in a small room set aside for his use by the French Sisters of Charity in St. John's Convent, Church Street; his own day had been a tiring if profitable one, spent touring his scattered outposts, making sure that the barricades were in the right positions, and that his men were strategically placed to withstand attack. He had decided that the main military threat would come from the Broadstone Station to the north and from the Royal Barracks, Kingsbridge railway station (where troops from the Curragh would arrive), and Marlborough Barracks (in Phoenix Park) to the west. So he posted a dozen men in a high building known as Clarke's Dairy, in the narrowest stretch of Church Street, commanding the rise known as Constitution Hill (which led up to the Broadstone), and scattered snipers in houses nearby. His heaviest concentration of posts was at the North King Street-Church Street intersection, where he had three barricades. He had another one farther down North King Street, opposite Coleraine Street. He had also seized the tall, tower-like building known as Jameson's Malt Granary, and this was now occupied by Volunteer Frank Shouldice and five men, who found themselves wallowing in grain four feet deep. On the outside wall of the Granary an iron staircase led to a metal, hook-shaped grain elevator on the roof, and from a platform on top of this, Shouldice had a commanding view of Beresford Street and North King Street, as well as the roof of the Jervis Street Hospital and the Bolton Street Technical Schools. Just under him, in Beresford Street (a turning off North King Street), there was yet another barricade, unmanned, its defence depending on men posted farther back across waste ground, in a number of workmen's cottages.

In the early hours of the morning, and while it was still pitch-dark, Daly's men briefly skirmished with the enemy. The action took place at Church Street Bridge, when a party of military escorting six transport wagons along the south bank of the Liffey, and apparently making their way to Dublin Castle, were fired on by Lieutenant Peter Clancy's men. Several saddles were emptied and the military galloped back up the Quays; next morning Daly's men crossed the bridge and picked up five rifles and 1,000 rounds of ammunition.

With the onset of night, a brooding quietness fell upon the South Dublin Union; but it was quietness a little too tense for men whose nerves had already been stretched beyond normal limits. Sentries were inclined to imagine they could see *things* out there in the dark. Lieutenant Cosgrave, after finally dozing off, was awakened by a sentry who whispered, "They're out there digging a trench," pointing vaguely towards MacCaffrey's Estate.

Wearily Cosgrave arose and went over to the window.

"Where?" he asked.

"There, just in front. Don't you see it?"

Cosgrave looked again; sure enough, there *did* seem to be a trench out there. Revolver in hand, he stole quietly from the Nurses' Home and crept over the grass with all the stealth of a Red Indian scout. Then he realized that the "trench" was a macadamed path.

"It's only an ould path," he reassured the sentry when he returned to the Nurses' Home.

"What about the noise?" insisted the man. "I heard them digging. Listen!"

Cosgrave listened; someone was digging. Or were they? Once again he investigated and upstairs found the answer; a loose window blind flapping in the wind.

Captain Brennan Whitmore, seated uncomfortably on the roof of the Pillar Café, gazed down pensively upon an oddly silent Sackville Street. The last drunks had gone reeling off into the night although, even now, a lone voice could still be heard at times caterwauling up near the Parnell Monument. The street lamps still shone and, seen from behind his parapet, they radiated a garish red glow, strangely reflected in a misty vapour hanging high and motionless in the sky; a weird picture which was to etch itself for ever into Brennan Whitmore's memory.

Across the street the G.P.O. lay dark and heavy; the lights inside had been cut off and the garrison were using candles. Sentries were visible at the windows and now and then shadowy figures could be seen passing to and fro. Brennan Whitmore felt an unfamiliar sense of isolation creep slowly over him.

A few yards away Redmond-Howard still kept vigil by his window. He and Mr. Marsh, manager of the Coliseum Theatre, had been asked to share a room, and they had agreed to take turns watching and sleeping. Fifty yards away the G.P.O. lay etched by the street lamps in pale blues and greens, looking for all the world like the backcloth in a theatre; Redmond-Howard had the impression of sitting in the dress circle of some gigantic opera house. Now and then a rattle of rifle-fire broke the eerie stillness.

Inside the G.P.O. itself, a Volunteer asked Connolly how he thought the fight was going.

"They're beaten," said Connolly, as always superbly terse and confident.

Shortly after midnight, Captain Carl Elliotson was ordered to take one hundred men and his machine-gun crew, occupy the Shelbourne Hotel and "have a go" at the rebels.

At 1.45 a.m. his column loaded up—a thousand-round box of ammunition to each two men, gunners carrying spare parts and other equipment—and at 2.15 a.m. moved out of Lower Gate to begin a stealthy march along Dame Street. It was no easy matter for one hundred and twenty men, clad in iron-shod boots and carrying weights up to thirty pounds each, to tip-toe quietly along the pavements, and Elliotson felt sure that their presence would be detected. They reached Kildare Street without incident, however, and occupied the Shelbourne, and the United Services Club a little way along the Green, in a surprisingly easy manner. It was just 3.20 a.m. when guards were placed on the hotel entrances and all windows were double-manned. The machine-guns were placed in position on the fourth floor, and shortly before four o'clock were ready to fire.

Below in the Green, swept by a cold wind, women lay huddled together for warmth on the seats in the summer-house; others lay on the ground. Countess Markievicz curled up comfortably in Dr. Lynn's car, an act of thoughtlessness for which she apologized in the morning when she learned how the other girls had suffered.

In a shallow trench at the corner of the Green, immediately under the Shelbourne Hotel, little Paddy Buttner closed his eyes and slept an untroubled sleep.

At 3.45 a.m. Brigadier General W. H. M. Lowe, commanding the Reserve Cavalry Brigade at the Curragh, arrived at Kingsbridge station with leading troops of the 25th Irish Reserve Infantry Brigade, and assumed command of all forces in the Dublin area. In Cork, General Stafford assumed direction of operations throughout the south of Ireland, while in Belfast, Brigadier Hackett-Paine took over responsibility for Ulster. Lowe's reinforcements brought the total of military forces in the capital to 4,650 men—which meant that the rebels were now outnumbered by almost five to one.

Some three hundred and fifty miles away in Whitehall, Field-Marshal Lord French, Commander-in-Chief Home Forces, was once again delightedly sniffing battle. For six weary months he had languished at a desk in Horse Guards Parade, busying himself, rather drearily, with the hypothetical defence of Britain, working out measures to stop this damned Zeppelin nuisance and training raw battalions for Kitchener's New Armies in support of his successor, Sir Douglas Haig. For the former British Commander-in-Chief in France, the arrival then, late on Monday afternoon, of a wireless message stating that rebellion had broken out in Ireland, was almost welcome.

Like an old warhorse, French had at once leaped into action. From a chat with the Irish C.-in-C., General Friend who had been in to see him on Saturday, he had already gathered that things were rather tricky in Ireland, on top of which, over the week-end, there had been this business of Casement. A rebellion at any time in Ireland, of course, was a serious matter for the British Army; in wartime it was unthinkable. Behind this latest calamity, French had no difficulty detecting the withered hand of Kaiser Wilhelm.

His first action was to dispatch an alert to the 59th (North Midland) Division which, under Major-General A. E. Sandbach, C.B., D.S.O., was then encamped in billets round Watford, St. Albans, Hemel Hempstead, Luton, Wheathampstead, and other towns and hamlets in Hertfordshire. The 59th was a mobile division (nicknamed "The Lost Division" by those serving in it because they had long ago lost any hope of getting to France) made up of three Brigades; the 176th (2/5th, 2/6th South Staffs. Regiment, 2/5th, 2/6th North Staffs.); the 177th (2/4th and 2/5th Lincolnshire Regiment, 2/4th, 2/5th Leicestershire Regiment); and the 178th Infantry Division (2/5th, 2/6th, 2/7th, 2/8th Sherwood Foresters). Convinced that the Germans were eventually bound to try something on the east coast of

England, Kitchener as War Minister had placed the 59th astride two railway systems, later known as the L.M.S. and the L. & N. W., so that it could be shunted north at an instant's notice; trains were held in a state of constant readiness at Watford and other stations in the vicinity. The division was a second-line one and had lost substantial drafts to the first-line regiments in France. As a result it was now made up of a medley of old hands, who had had plenty of practice digging trenches and firing obsolete Japanese rifles, and of recruits under the Derby scheme, whose only musketry drill so far had been in miniature ranges, and whose average length of service was less than three months.

Shortly after French had alerted General Sandbach, General Friend entered his office. Completely unaware of events in Dublin, he had been enjoying a stroll in the St. James's Park sunshine. For Friend it was possibly the worst moment in his whole lifetime. The interview with the Commander-in-Chief was both sharp and brisk, and he left hurriedly for Ireland, aware that his career there had very likely been blasted for good. When he was gone, French confirmed orders that two of the Brigades were to move as quickly as their transport could be arranged. In doing so, he noted: "I was aware that I was acting beyond the powers which were delegated to me but I considered the situation to be so critical that it was necessary to act at once without reference to the Army Council."

The 59th Division, extraordinarily enough, was hardly prepared for such an order. To the normal English passion for an extended week-end had been added the complication of the Easter holidays. Shown the message by the Battalion Adjutant, Captain G. J. Edmunds, O.C. "A" Company, 2/6th Sherwood Foresters, could only comment bitterly, "The damn fools would have to go and have an entraining at this particular time." He and the Adjutant, in fact, were the only two Battalion Officers left in the camp at the time. Even the Brigadier, Colonel E. W. S. K. Maconchy, was absent. Practically everybody was on leave, which was not due to expire until midnight. Most officers and men had gone up to London. Hundreds more had gone home for the week-end. Men like Reginald Hutchinson and Wilfred Tunley of Field Ambulance or Edgar Hill of 2/5th Sherwoods were still on the train travelling back from the dales of Derbyshire or from Nottingham after visiting parents and girl-friends. Some had remained in billets, enjoying the glum pleasures of wartime existence in towns which were more than fed-up with men in khaki by now. Bernard Boram of the 2/6th Sherwoods and Robert Bury, 2/5th Sherwoods, were watching a Charlie Chaplin film at the cinema; Captain John Oates, 2/8th Sherwoods, was enjoying a meal of plum and apple jam and bully beef in billets with his two friends, Lieutenants Daffen and Elliot; Harold Browne, 2/6th Sherwoods, was drinking with the R.S.M. in a pub at Kings Langley; Albert Slack, 2/6th Sherwoods, was cycling back from Harrow after "dodging off" for the afternoon; Captain Frank Pragnell, 2/7th Sherwoods, was in billets with his wife at Watford. And then there was the unfortunate attached to Brigade H.Q. who had just been married and had to be roused from his hotel at Watford on his wedding night.

Messages were hurriedly flashed on screens in canteens and cinemas: "All 178th Brigade men return to billets immediately." Redcaps and patrols scoured pubs and clubs in the area; soldiers with their girls in Cassiobury Park, Watford, suddenly heard the tramp of iron-shod feet and the barked order, "Back to camp, you! At the double!"

Amid uproar and confusion, the 59th Division gradually sorted itself out. There were Lewis guns, Vickers tripods, iron rations, blankets, ammunition, limbers and mules for heavy guns, officers' valises, company books to be dealt with and billets to be paid up before the 178th, the first Brigade due to leave, was ready to go at 4 a.m. In the middle of preparations there was a Zeppelin alert, and all lights had to be dowsed and air-raid patrols sent out. Staff-Captain Godfrey Tallents swore like a trooper as he endeavoured to get heavy wagons, regimental cookers and water carts lifted sideways on to railway trucks. He called for the station master.

"Look," he said. "Put these bloody lights on."

"I can't, sir," said the man. "There's an air raid on London."

The first train, carrying the 2/6th Sherwoods, left Watford at 4 a.m. The rest of the Brigade followed on trains at 8.30 a.m. and 10 a.m. It was a strangely sober crowd of young men who departed for God knows where. There was the inevitable attempt to be cheerful; choruses of "Who's your lady friend?" and "Tipperary" were sung, but on the whole there was little horseplay. Few of the officers and none of the men knew they were on their way to Ireland; all took it for granted that they were going to France. When it was discovered that the trains were travelling north, there was renewed speculation. In Captain Oates's carriage, everybody plumped for Russia. When the train stopped at Crewe there was some enlightenment. Some men, going forward to get their tea "mashed", found out from the engine driver that their destination was Liverpool. Harold Garbett asked a porter, "Any idea where we're bound for?"

"Ten to one it's Ireland," said the man. "They're fighting like hell over there—the streets are running with blood."

Bernard Boram bought a paper carrying an Admiralty announcement saying: "During the period between April 20th and April 21st an attempt to land arms and ammunition in Ireland was made by a vessel under the guise of a neutral merchant ship but in reality a German auxiliary in conjunction with a German submarine. The auxiliary was sunk, and a number of prisoners were made, amongst whom was Sir Roger Casement."

At 10 a.m. when the first train reached Liverpool, the dock authorities reported heavy fighting in Dublin. Two ships and a destroyer escort were waiting and both the 2/5th and 2/6th Battalions were embarked. In the haste and confusion most of the officers' kit, as well as Lewis guns, were left behind.

As the Brigadier took stock at the quayside, he found he was short of everything except men. He had perhaps fifty rounds of ammunition per man and absolutely no bombs. And he had no maps. He lost no time in ringing the Director of Operations at the War Office to explain his position.

"Good God!" said an agitated voice. "How much do you want then?"

"Four hundred bombs and ten thousand rounds of ammunition. To be at Kingstown tomorrow morning!"

But maps? Where was he to get *them*? It struck him that hotels were likely to have them, so he sent a party to scour the city for maps of Dublin. They returned with only a few and even these had had to be torn from hotel guidebooks.

At 3.30 p.m. the Brigadier and his staff, accompanying one and a half battalions, embarked on the *Ulster*, a fast mail boat temporarily diverted from the Holyhead run. During the crossing, the escort commander boarded the ship to inform Colonel Maconchy that he had news by wireless that the rebels had taken Kingstown and that the landing was certain to be opposed.

The air raid on London, which had so annoyingly interfered with the 59th Division's departure for Ireland, had been a part-payment by Germany of her obligation to render assistance to the Irish rebels. At 9.15 p.m. on Monday, Lord French, dining quietly with General Sir Ian Hamilton (who had been the British Commander at Gallipoli), was informed that six Zeppelins had been sighted forty miles north-east of Cromer, making for London. Four hours after the bombing of the capital, Germany further backed up her promise to the rebels by staging the desired "naval demonstration" in the North Sea as a support operation to the Zeppelin attack. At exactly 4.10 a.m. four battle-cruisers, with attendant light cruisers and destroyers from Admiral Scheer's High Seas Fleet, opened a general bombardment on the east coast port of Lowestoft. Half-an-hour later a local coast patrol courageously engaged the enemy, who at once turned away, apparently in the hope that they might draw major units of the Grand Fleet out to do battle, an invitation which was not accepted on this occasion. Later the Admiralty listed the damage to the town as follows: "Despite the heavy guns employed by the enemy, the damage was relatively slight. A convalescent home, a swimming bath, the pier and 40 dwelling houses were extensively damaged and some 200 houses were slightly damaged. Two men, one woman and one child were killed, three persons seriously wounded and nine slightly wounded. Most of the damage was to houses on or adjoining the sea front. The roof and front was partially smashed and interiors were exposed amid wreckage of beams, timbers and plaster. In others, a table was knocked away and copings dislodged. Big holes were made through the walls in cases where shells passed through one or more of the houses in a row. A number of enemy shells, however, were aimed wildly; some went right over the town and fell into Oulton Broad, two miles away."

In short, it was hardly the kind of operation which would do much to help the rebels in their travail.

15

FROM HIS POSITION on the roof of the General Post Office, Volunteer Richard Humphreys watched a summer-like dawn rise over a quiet and apparently peaceful Dublin. Yet there were signs that all was not normal. Up near the Parnell Monument the roadway was white as though there had been a fall of snow. Cardboard boxes and sheets of paper, debris of the previous night's looting, lay piled up in drifts, tossed there by the night wind. Sackville Street itself lay empty and apparently undisturbed; yet, on the far side, high above the Wireless School, the silver-like thread of an aerial, which had not been there the day before, now stretched between two chimney pots. Distantly a clock boomed four. Its notes had scarcely died when there was a sharp volley somewhere away up near the Green; firing which lasted for ten minutes, then stopped abruptly.

The shots jerked St. John Ervine awake from an uneasy doze. He rose and, crossing to the window, peered out. It was still not bright enough to see properly, but he made out a huddled heap where an insurgent sentry had been standing guard the night before, near it a horse he had thought shot dead struggling to rise to its feet. Even as he watched, the animal fell back again in exhaustion, and he muttered peevishly, "Why the devil don't they kill it?"

Young Paddy Buttner, asleep in his shallow trench inside the Park, awoke to an even greater shock—the surprise of machine-gun bullets spurting angrily into the earth beside him. At first he was not able to grasp what was happening: then he realized that the angry buzzing noises around him were flying bullets. He started to rise.

"Get down!—do you want to be killed?" hissed Sergeant James O'Shea, catching him by the back of the neck. Buttner flopped on to his belly again, terrified. He squinted up at O'Shea and found comfort in the sight of that strong, hard face. A moment later he even poked his rifle forward and tried to pick a target; but he was too close to the Shelbourne to get the right elevation—and besides, of the sixty-two windows winking out of the façade, which one did you fire at? As the machine-guns belted their racket of sound over the Park, the bullets caught some youngsters whom Mallin had sent out during the night to work on a barricade. Volunteer Philip Clarke died immediately. Another boy fell wounded, and Mallin rose from the trench where he had been observing the military fire and ran to his assistance.

Buttner watched the Commandant pick him up and drag him in under sustained fire.

For almost three hours the vicious battle continued. Twice the Countess, lying in a shallow trench with Mallin near the Shelbourne Gate, temporarily silenced one of the machine-guns with her Mauser rifle-pistol. At about 6.30 a.m. she crawled over to O'Shea and Buttner and said hoarsely, "Commandant Mallin's orders are to withdraw to the Cuffe Street (south-west) corner."

By then Mallin had come to realize that he could no longer hold his exposed positions. The south-west corner afforded good "natural" defences— trees, shrubberies, and above all, a mound of earth. Yet even as young Buttner and the two men with him prepared to scramble from their trench, young James Fox, having apparently lost his nerve, dashed for the railings on the north side. Shouts of, "Don't do it, Jemmy, you fool!" ripped over the lawns after him, but the boy, crazed with fear, ran on heedlessly. He was almost over the railings when the machine-gun, scything round in a wide sweep which scattered every duck on the ornamental pond, caught him. Hit several times, he fell back, arms spread out, yelling. O'Shea held Buttner firmly by the arm as bullets kicked the ground all round Fox and his agonized screams filled the air. Then, abruptly, he stopped yelling. He still lived, however, for Buttner saw him crawl a few inches; a movement which brought the wrath of the military down on him again. A second swathe of bullets cut across him and he stopped moving. But each time the machine-gun swept the green lawns bullets struck the body, making it twitch and jerk for a moment as though it were still alive. Another stream of bullets would immediately be directed at the body, each new bullet that hit creating a fresh illusion that the boy still lived. The dead, it seemed, would not be allowed to die.

All over the Green, now, the insurgents were crouching and huddling into the earth, completely pinned down. On the roof of the College of Surgeons, Frank Robbins ate his bread and bully beef, the last of his rations, and in between bites fired a hopeful shot towards the Shelbourne Hotel. St. John Ervine heard a sudden *boom, boom*, and someone under his windows cry out "Oh," four times. Pulling back the curtain, he saw an old labourer lying dead outside his door. Someone, it seemed, who had decided to go to work as usual, unaware or heedless of how serious this Rebellion was. Opposite the Shelbourne, young Buttner slithered out of his trench, following O'Shea, who warned him, "Keep close to me—and keep your head down." He was so scared that he could hardly move; nevertheless, somehow he edged after O'Shea, his face so close to the earth that the blades of grass looked like giant stalks of corn. Together they crawled to some shrubberies. Sheltered by these, they were able to make better progress, and they reached the mount safely.

Clusters of tall elms protected the area. Women and boys squatted on the ground, taking advantage of the luxuriant cover. The Countess, scorning to take cover, defiantly stood her ground even as bullets smacked into the trees and clipped branches above her head. A line of men lay behind the mound, returning the fire from the Shelbourne and the United Services Club. Mallin, however, was soon forced to give the order to retreat to the College of Surgeons and the small force assembled near the west gate. If Mallin felt any misgivings about his handling of the situation, no sign of it showed in his quiet, good-humoured face. He had decided that the move would be made in small parties of two and three, and despite the screen of trees and shrubberies, he expected it to prove a perilous business, especially for the women, handicapped by their hobble-skirts.

The first party crossed the road safely enough but when the Red Cross nurses made their dash, they came under heavy fire, their white skirts and bright-red badges proving an easy target. One girl had her skirt torn by a bullet; another had the heel of her boot ripped off. Young Buttner, waiting his turn to go, hardly gave a thought to the danger; a long night under the open skies had given him a tremendous appetite, and all he could think of were the cooked hams and custard pies that were being left behind in the greenhouse. He even considered going back for some, until he saw a man cut down by machine-gun fire on the roof of the College of Surgeons. Hit by several bullets, Private Michael Doherty slumped forward over the parapet. For a moment he teetered and Buttner believed he was going to fall into the street. Instead he hung there, head and arms dangling, his blood staining the face of the building. The machine-gun again raked the parapet and, unable to stand the sight of Doherty being cut to pieces, Captain Joseph Connolly (brother of John Connolly who had led the attack on the Castle) dashed across the road and, entering the College of Surgeons, rapidly mounted the roof. Within a minute, he appeared at the bullet-swept parapet and, amid cheers from the rebels still in the Park, dragged Doherty back below the parapet to safety. Angrily, as though annoyed at being cheated of a victim, another burst of machine-gun fire whipped tiny puffs of grey dust from the stonework.

Doherty was found to have fifteen bullets in him when Connolly brought him down to the ground floor and Frank Robbins, gazing down at the bloody face of his friend, said, "I'm afraid you're a gonner, Mick—may the Lord have mercy on your soul." It proved to be a premature judgment for Doherty lived to become a victim of the 'flu epidemic in 1918. There was little time for the wounded or even the dying, however. Once again bullets chipped splinters out of the roadway as the retreat from the Green continued. Robbins did what he could to give covering fire, but suddenly there was an uproar behind him. Turning, he saw three Citizen Army men running towards him, closely pursued by a mob of civilians hurling rotten vegetables. He recognized Captain MacCormack, Lieutenant Kelly and a Volunteer named Donnelly, who had been occupying houses farther up the Green. Leading the mob was a young woman who had spent most of her time the previous evening hurling insults at him through the Park railings. On an impulse, Robbins knelt down, raised his rifle, and shouted at MacCormack, "Out of the way, Mac!" He had the woman in his sights and was about to shoot when Lieutenant Kelly jerked his arm up, shouting, "For God's sake, don't shoot, Frank!" Robbins, incensed, tugged his arm free, and again took aim. Kelly bawled angrily, "That's an order!" Discipline, if somewhat loose in the Citizen Army, was not so loose that Robbins could ignore a direct order. The young woman, who had stopped in fear when she saw herself a target, took to her heels when Robbins lowered his rifle, but continued to jeer at him from the safety of the mob.

By 7 a.m. the evacuation of the Green was complete. Five bodies lay behind on the greensward, victims of a grave rebel misjudgment. Yet few who survived welcomed the change from the bright sunlight and surging green of the Park to the grim, shadowed interior of the College of Surgeons. Mary Donnelly wrote later: "The classrooms of the College seemed huge and draughty. Everywhere were huge glass cases filled with objects for students, pebbles and specimens. In an adjoining room the jars had parts of human bodies preserved in liquid." Into this uninviting place then, with its smells of formaldehyde, over one hundred men, women and boys now withdrew. Weary, glad to be out of immediate danger, some ripped up carpets and, wrapping themselves around like mummies, flopped down on the floor of the large lecture room and were soon fast asleep.

With the first flush of daylight, the military began creeping stealthily up the cold stone stairway towards the roof of the City Hall. Here, fewer than a dozen insurgents, their faces blackened, their tongues swollen, their hands raw and scorched by powder, their eyes red-rimmed through lack of sleep, squatted in considerable disarray after a night spent in cold and jangling tension. From the roof of the Castle buildings, from the high Bermingham Tower, just as soon as it was light enough to pick out a target, machine-gun fire sent them rapidly scurrying for cover. Minutes later, the troops scrambled through the skylight and fanned out over the roof. In less than half-an-hour it was all over. Outnumbered, and outgunned, their successive leaders, John Connolly and big Jack O'Reilly, both dead, the rebels gave in; one man escaped by climbing inside a chimney and holding on by his fingertips. Others, of course, still held out in the *Mail & Express* offices, and in Henry & James opposite, and although the military repeatedly called on them to surrender there were only defiant shots in reply.

At dawn, too, from their window in the Imperial Hotel, Redmond-Howard and Mr. Marsh watched a party of insurgents emerge from the G.P.O. and begin stretching wire across the street. Some minutes later, James Connolly himself walked out of the building, first to sniff at the morning air, then to issue orders in a "clear and resonant" voice. For an hour or so afterwards, nothing much happened but eventually there was a stir up near Nelson Pillar.

At all entrances to Sackville Street rebels were stopping people and warning them to stand back and "get out of the firing line." Up at the Parnell Monument a rebel explained to some people, "The Pillar is about to be blown up." At exactly 7.10 a.m. Redmond-Howard heard a loud explosion and watched a cloud of smoke billow upwards from the base of Nelson Pillar. The great column never even quivered. Three more explosions followed within less than ten minutes—all equally abortive. Above the smoke and noise proud Nelson still stood steadfast, ignoring those who sought to pull him from his perch. In later years, rebel apologists maintained that there was never any attempt to bring down the Pillar; all they had been trying to do was to blow down tram standards to get more wire.

Work had continued throughout the night in the Wireless School, and by dawn, Fergus Kelly and his comrades had got the dismantled government transmitter going again. Told the good news, Connolly ordered that the following message should be transmitted: "An Irish Republic has been proclaimed. Dublin is firmly held and all British attacks have been repulsed." David Bourke, an experienced Marconi operator, dispatched the message on the ordinary commercial wavelength, hoping that it might be picked up by ships at sea. Unable to get the receiving set to work, Bourke had no way of knowing whether the message was picked up or not. Nevertheless, he kept repeating it at intervals.

Brennan Whitmore awoke refreshed and rather pleased with himself; only one man had deserted during the night, the barricade across North Earl Street had been completed, and his men had succeeded in tunnelling through to the Imperial Hotel. In addition, four *Cumann na mBan* girls had come across from the G.P.O. late the previous night and he and his men could now look forward to a sensible breakfast.

He was only half-way through his bacon and eggs when a messenger arrived from the G.P.O. to announce that General Pearse was on his way over to see him. Brennan Whitmore rose and went downstairs. Pearse was just crossing the street, and Brennan Whitmore advanced to meet him, saluting smartly and falling in behind the Commander-in-Chief as he marched over to inspect the barricade.

"H'm, it looks frail," said Pearse doubtfully.

"Try pulling it apart, sir," said Brennan Whitmore, respectfully. Pearse tugged at a chair but it held firm; wire which Brennan Whitmore had intertwined among its components had given it a deceptive strength. Satisfied, Pearse turned on his heel and, without a further word, walked back to the G.P.O. Fifteen minutes later, when Brennan Whitmore had just finished his cold breakfast, he heard a rousing cheer from the street, and, glancing out, saw James Connolly striding across. Resignedly, he went downstairs again. Like Pearse, Connolly wanted to inspect the barricade. He was more critical than Pearse had been.

"This is far too small and frail to stop a charge," he insisted.

"Why don't you try and knock it down then, sir?" suggested Brennan Whitmore.

Connolly seized the leg of a table and pulled at it vigorously. It refused to budge.

"You can see how I've interlaced it," pointed out Brennan Whitmore. Connolly smiled and nodded, seemingly satisfied. Then his eye, roaming around, alighted on a shoe shop on the opposite corner. Baulked by the excellence of the barricade, he asked sharply, "Have you occupied that building yet?"

"No, as a matter of fact, I haven't tried to," said Brennan Whitmore. "I haven't enough men. I didn't think it would be any good putting two or three men in it."

Connolly puckered his face for a moment; then nodded his agreement and stuck out his hand.

"Good luck," he said and they shook. He walked slowly back across Sackville Street and Brennan Whitmore never saw him again.

The city itself woke to a morning of irritating inconveniences and the most incredible of wild rumours. Only one newspaper was published, the pro-Government *Irish Times*, which had its own separate power supply (de Valera having thoughtfully deprived the city of its normal gas supplies first thing on Monday by dismantling most of the Gas Works). No letters were delivered or collected, and all shops in the centre of the city remained closed. There was no traffic. In such conditions and in a city boasting perhaps the most loquacious population in the world, it is hardly surprising that rumour abounded. The whole country had risen, it was said; all the cities of Ireland were in the hands of the rebels; Cork Barracks had fallen; the Germans had landed in force at Queenstown and thousands of Irish-Americans, led by German officers, had also invaded. In addition, the Lord Lieutenant was being held prisoner in Liberty Hall, and the Pope and the Archbishop of Dublin had committed suicide. Worst of all, the Orangemen were marching on Dublin. The tales grew taller and spread rapidly.

The *Irish Times* was of little help. The paper consisted of only six pages and most of these were made up of advertisements and "stock" matter. There was a detailed account of the Fairyhouse races; reports of a meeting of the Irish Traders' Assistants' Association; an article on the D'Oyly Carte Company and a short leader on the Spring Show. The only references to the Rebellion were two boldly displayed items on the editorial page; one the Lord Lieutenant's Proclamation, the other a short report which said:

SINN FEIN RISING IN DUBLIN

Yesterday morning an insurrectionary rising took place in the city of Dublin. The authorities have taken active and energetic measures to cope with the situation. These measures are proceeding favourably. In accordance with this official statement early and prompt action is anticipated.

Worse than the absence of reliable information, however, was the growing shortage of food. By now the supplies laid in to last over the Easter holidays had begun to run out. In the Church Street and Boland's Bakery area the rebels distributed bread, but in most central areas of the city there were no bread vans, no milk deliveries and no butchers. Milkmen who ventured out into the streets near St. Stephen's Green were stopped at revolver point by Lily Kempson and Mary Hyland, two young Citizen Army women, and had their supplies commandeered. Thus, to the growing list of grievances against the rebels, was now added the threat of partial starvation.

Dublin, in fact, had already had enough of its glorious insurrection, and was impatiently waiting for the military to do something about it.

For the rebels garrisoning Clanwilliam House, morning produced a disagreeable surprise. Sent across to the school to pick up extra ammunition, Doyle returned to report that during the night the men there had cleared off. When Malone arrived for a brief conference shortly after dawn, Reynolds pointed out how this had weakened their position around Mount Street Bridge. Malone agreed it needed strengthening and suggested Reynolds should ask Captain Connolly for reinforcements. Reynolds sent young Daniel Byrne across to Boland's Bakery with a request for more men and food. Byrne returned with pieces of *fruit cake* and Reynolds had to send him back again to emphasize that the urgent need was for *men*, and that, so far as food was concerned, they would appreciate something a little more substantial than fruit cake.

Just after seven o'clock reinforcements arrived in the persons of Volunteer Patrick Doyle and Volunteer Richard Murphy. Doyle was a married man with several small children, Murphy a young tailor who had just become engaged. A little later, the Walsh boys, James and Thomas, arrived. This brought the garrison strength up to an uninspiring total of seven, young Byrne having, in the meantime, been sent home. Among them, the seven men had four Lee-Enfields, two Martini rifles, two Howth guns, two .38 revolvers, two .45 revolvers, one .38 automatic and an ammunition reserve of 2,000 rounds.

Malone paid another visit to see how they were faring, and Doyle heard him remark to Reynolds that it would be a pity if the owners of the house were killed or injured in any way. Subsequently, Reynolds prevailed upon the Wilsons to leave the house and go to friends nearby. Barricades on the ground floor were then strengthened, and two heavy wardrobes placed at the top of the stairs so that a push would send them toppling and block the stairway. Sheets were torn to make bandages and soda-water syphons filled with water and placed at each window.

In de Valera's headquarters in the nearby Bakery, spirits could scarcely have been better; the rumour that the Germans had reached the Naas Road and were advancing to their aid was accepted without question; the air, after all, seemed pregnant with possibility. Had they not held out now for twenty-four hours? And had not the British Army proved powerless? To the rank and file anything seemed possible. They had strong British forces cooped up in Beggar's Bush Barracks and their efforts to break out had been surprisingly easily brushed aside. There had been casualties—but not anything like so many as they had anticipated.

Commandant de Valera, however, shared none of this optimism. His long, austere countenance still bore a perpetually-anxious look. Shortly after daybreak he called a parade and announced that all boys under the age of eighteen were to go home. To soften the blow, he explained to the youngsters that they were no longer involved in peaceful manoeuvres but in a real act of war. If they went home now, he said, they would have performed their duty and would be rewarded eventually by the new Republic. It took some time to persuade the boys to leave. Two adamantly refused to go. Willie Fitzgerald, aged fifteen, was "hunted" away time and again, and in the end won the right to stay. Richard Perle, aged sixteen, told his mother when she called at the gate in response to the pleas of officers, "Go home, Mother, this is no place for a woman."

At 9.30 a.m. Pearse issued his first communiqué:

"The Irish Republic was proclaimed in Dublin on Easter Monday 24th April at 12 noon. Simultaneously with the issue of the Proclamation of the Provisional Government the Dublin Division of the Army of the Republic, including the Irish Volunteers, Citizen Army, Hibernian Rifles and other bodies, occupied dominating points in the city. The G.P.O. was seized at 12 noon, the Castle was attacked at the same moment, and shortly afterwards the Four Courts were occupied. The Irish troops hold the City Hall and dominate the Castle. Attacks were immediately commenced by the British forces and were everywhere repulsed. At the moment of writing this report the Republican forces hold all their positions and the British forces have nowhere broken through. There has been heavy and continuous fighting for nearly 24 hours, the casualties of the enemy being much more numerous than those on the Republican side. The Republican forces everywhere are fighting with splendid gallantry. The populace of Dublin are plainly with the Republic, and the officers and men are everywhere cheered as they march through the streets. The whole centre of the city is in the hands of the Republic, whose flag flies from the G.P.O.

Commandant-General P. H. Pearse is Commander-in-Chief of the Army of the Republic and is President of the Provisional Government. Commandant-General James Connolly is commanding the Dublin districts. Communication with the country is largely cut, but reports to hand show that the country is rising, and bodies of men from Kildare and Fingall have already reported in Dublin."

Printed under the heading:

STOP PRESS!
The Irish Republic

in *Irish War News*, a four-page quarto-sized sheet issued from the Post Office, the communiqué contained several deliberate inaccuracies. (The first issue of *Irish War News* numbered Vol. 1, No. 1 turned out to be the only one ever to appear.) Perhaps the most outrageous invention—although it might be pleaded that its inclusion was necessary for morale—was that the country was rising. The truth was that outside the capital there was almost complete lack of action.

In Galway, late on Monday, the small towns of Athenry and Craughwell were seized and the police barracks in both places surrounded. The railway lines to Limerick and Athlone were cut, and a contingent of rebels marched west to capture Oranmore and then to take Galway City. This attempt was crushed when British destroyers shelled the road and scattered the insurgent column. A hot reception awaited them, anyhow, in Galway city, for the police had armed themselves and Redmond's National Volunteers had declared for the Crown.

North of Dublin, there were a few isolated skirmishes. At Donabate, the rebels tried to blow up a railway bridge, but succeeded only in disturbing the rails. At Skerries, their activities prevented Mr. John Clancy, M.P., from opening a local fête. On the other hand they managed to seize Castle Bellingham, Co. Louth, and make its three constables prisoner.

In the north of Ireland, Brigadier-General Hackett-Pain crushed any hopes the rebels had of seizing the County Tyrone by sending in a flying column of three hundred troops from Belfast.

In the south, Limerick and Clare were both quiet; Cork and Kerry fairly so. At Castlegregory, thirty insurgents turned out on Monday afternoon, but after wandering about disconsolately and seeing no overt signs of an Irish Republic or perceiving any way they could help to establish one, they went home. In Cork city, by the time local Volunteers finally moved, the military had seized the city.

In the County Wexford, historically the most rebel of all the counties, Pearse's forces enjoyed more success, despite a declaration by the Mayor of Wexford and other public bodies for the Crown. Both Ferns and Enniscorthy were captured and the police besieged in their barracks. Stores and other war materials were commandeered, railway lines cut, communications destroyed, trees felled and roads blocked.

But it was in the immediate environs of Dublin itself that the rebels could lay claim to their only convincing successes. Here some fifty Volunteers conducted operations under the command of Commandant Thomas Ashe. Before the week ended they were to chalk up several minor victories (defeating a column of fifty armed policemen in a brilliantly-handled engagement at Ashbourne), but the fact was that when Pearse wrote his communiqué they had as yet done nothing.

16

WHILE SERVING IN North-West India in 1914, an outbreak of cholera forced Captain George Mahony of the Indian Medical Service to go higher into the hills. Negotiating a narrow path in the Himalayas with Captain Baldwin of the First Gurkha Regiment, they were forced to dismount to allow their Sikh bearers to lead the ponies. They had hardly got down when Baldwin's pony shied and sent Mahony hurtling over the precipice. Forty feet below he crashed into a boulder and managed to hold on. After a two-hour struggle, his friends succeeded in tying a rope round him and pulling him up. Nursed by missionary girls at Dharmsala, he was sent home to Ireland to convalesce.

At 10.30 on Tuesday morning, he stepped off the train in Harcourt Street station after a week-end spent with friends in Wicklow and, finding no cabs or taxis waiting, decided to walk towards St. Stephen's Green. He was wearing full uniform, a light-coloured gabardine suit with black I.M.S. gorget patches. He had not gone far when a man stopped him and said, "Don't you know the Shinners are out?" Mahony had no idea what Shinners meant, but thanked him anyway and continued walking. Taking the man's advice though, he skirted the Green, and was crossing Dame Street towards the Quays when someone shouted, "Not that way—the Shinners are there!" He stopped, uncertain where to go next. At once a crowd gathered round and began to give him advice. "Report to Portobello," said one man. "Go up to the Castle," said another. While he was trying to make up his mind, a clergyman came by, trundling his bicycle. He introduced himself: "My name is Canon Hemphill. You know, of course, you're in grave danger, walking around in that uniform."

"What can I do?" Mahony asked helplessly.

The canon thought for a moment. Then he said, "H'm, I think you'd better come home with me."

Mahony thanked him and they started off together. Canon Hemphill led him through back streets, detouring rebel positions, but in Upper Leeson Street a woman standing at her door warned, "Don't go that way—an officer has just been shot up there." She added, "And get out of that uniform at once, for God's sake!"

"That's all very well, ma'am," said Mahony, "but what am I to put on instead?"

"Wait a moment," she said. "Better still, come inside."

Mahony followed the woman and she gave him a macintosh, a cap and a pair of blue serge trousers, into which he changed. He kept on his khaki jacket, however. "Be sure and keep that mac well buttoned up," the woman warned.

It was only a short walk to Ailesbury Avenue, where the Canon lived. Mahony was introduced to the Canon's wife and daughter, and was invited to lunch.

"Would you mind if I used your telephone to let my sister know I'm all right?" he asked.

Mrs. Hemphill smiled. "I'm afraid there's no telephone. The wires have been cut."

After lunch Mahony remarked, "I think I'll take a chance now and go."

"Well, if you must, you must," said Mrs. Hemphill. "But if I were you, I'd take off that tunic. I could let you have one of the Canon's."

"That's very kind of you. But the trousers should be a good enough disguise—along with the mac."

"Well, I still think you're very foolish," said Mrs. Hemphill, doubtfully. "You know, you could easily stay with us until all the trouble is over."

"I would, if I weren't so anxious about my sister," explained Mahony. He thanked the Hemphills again, then left and walked down to Ballsbridge, where he found a garage.

"I'd like a taxi," he told the garage owner.

"Well," said the man, "it's not but that I've got plenty of cars, but I've nobody to drive you, you see. Sure, haven't they all gone down into the city to see the fun."

"It's very important I get across to Drumcondra," explained Mahony, taking a pound note from his wallet.

"Oh, if it's *that* important," said the man, "then I'll drive you myself."

They crossed the Liffey at Butt Bridge and drove past Amiens Street station. A moment later, Mahony spied his first rebels, squatting on the roofs of houses along the main road. Approaching the first Canal bridge, the car slowed down, and peering through the front window, Mahony saw three or four young men signalling them to stop. The driver pulled up and the men surrounded the car. "We're searching this car for munitions," one explained.

Mahony sat quietly while they poked around the interior. Suddenly one barked at him, "Open that coat!" He had no choice but to pull it open, showing the khaki underneath. The cab driver, raising his eyes to heaven, protested, "Honest to God, boys, I didn't know anything about this!" Mahony, at gunpoint, got out of the car, and the taxi man immediately swung the car around and drove off. Left alone with what appeared to him three extremely villainous-looking rebels, Mahony hardly knew what to expect. They marched him to the offices of the Dublin and Wicklow Manure Company, and led him before an officer. Recognizing the black gorget patches, the rebel officer said, "Oh, so you're in the Indian Medical Service."

"I am," said Mahony.

"Well, in that case I'm sorry about this," the rebel apologized, "but you're wearing khaki, you see, and I'm afraid I've no option but to take you prisoner. Incidentally, I was once stationed in Secunderabad myself."

Following a brief interrogation, Mahony was led into a small lavatory, where the door was locked behind him and a guard placed on it. A little later a rebel came in and asked, "Would you like some tea?" Mahony nodded and the rebel went away and returned shortly with a cup. Soon afterwards, the same man came back and asked, "Would you like to go in with the boys?" Mahony had no idea who "the boys" might be, but anything was preferable to his present prison. "Yes," he said, and was led into a big, comfortably furnished office, where several rebels were squatting on a Turkish carpet, their rifles across their knees. Leaning against a wall were three British soldiers, and Mahony was allowed to talk to them. One was a Royal Irish Fusilier who had been taken prisoner while enjoying a drink; his chief grievance was not so much that he had been taken prisoner but that they had not given him time to finish it.

Inside the G.P.O. hardly a minute passed without someone accidentally discharging his rifle. The rank and file, their appetites whetted by the action against the Lancers, longed to be under fire again, and Mary Ryan, who was there, remembers that the men on the roof were at this time shooting at almost anything. On one occasion, when a burst of firing shattered the morning calm, Connolly shouted out in exasperation, "Would you tell those fellows once and for all that unless they're firing at something useful, they're not to fire at all."

He was driven to the extreme limits of his patience when some men of the Citizen Army approached and asked permission to leave the building. "Why?" asked Connolly, genuinely surprised. "Where do you want to go?"

"To work, Mister Connolly," said their spokesman. "Now that the holidays are over," he explained.

Most Dubliners, in fact, still failed to appreciate exactly what was happening. How else explain the carelessness of Lord Dunsany and a friend, who bowled along in their motor-car straight into the rebel barricade at Church Street Bridge shortly before noon. Not until a bullet grazed his cheek did Dunsany realize that these disturbances were something more than a mere riot.

In the Pillar Café, a man asked Brennan Whitmore for a few hours off. "Why, in the name of God?" he demanded angrily.

"I've got the keys of my work," explained the man, "and the boss won't be able to get in."

"I should think there'll be a lot of bosses this morning who won't be able to get in," said Brennan Whitmore.

Ordered back into the College of Surgeons from his outpost at Leeson Street, Professor Liam O'Briain found himself on duty in an upstairs room. On the

wall, surrounded by portraits of former Presidents of the College was a magnificent portrait of Queen Victoria.

As O'Briain stared through a loopholed window, hoping to glimpse one of
the machine-gunners in the Shelbourne, out of the corner of his eye he
noticed a young "chisellur" enter the room and stand in front of the Queen's
portrait. O'Briain believed he was admiring it and was delighted that
Dublin's "lower classes" were at last beginning to appreciate art. Suddenly the
boy stepped forward and ripped the painting from its frame with a knife.
"This'll do for leggings," he explained.

Shortly afterwards, Mallin entered the room and stopped short at the sight
of the slashed portrait. Frowning, he demanded of O'Briain, "What was
that—who did it?" All in a single sentence.

"*That*," said O'Briain, "was a portrait of Queen Victoria."

"What in the name of God has happened to it?"

"A youngster slashed it."

"Slashed it!" shouted Mallin. "If we find the man who did that I'll shoot
him!"

"It's only Queen Victoria," pointed out O'Briain.

"That doesn't matter a damn," said Mallin. "I'll shoot the man who did
that."

Hearing part of the discussion, the young fellow who had ripped the
painting came over eagerly.

"Is it Queen Victoria you're talking about, sir. Here's a bit of her if you
want it." He tugged a piece of canvas from his leg and offered it to the
Commandant.

Mallin stared at him speechlessly. Then he found his voice. "So it was you,
you scamp!" he roared. And he clipped the lad on the ear.

Almost at once, the entire medical and nursing services of the city, both professional and voluntary, had swung into action.

First to offer their services to the authorities were the Dublin Red Cross
Society and the St. John Ambulance Brigade. Everywhere, however, men and
women of good will rushed forward to help, irrespective of whether those
whom they tended were members of the military forces, or civilians, or even
rebels. All eighteen metropolitan hospitals made preparations to handle casualties, and doctors and surgeons and nursing staffs discarded normal working
schedules to be on call at all hours. The Irish Automobile Club offered a complete motor ambulance service. Dr. Ella Webb, Lady District Superintendent
of the Red Cross, supervised the transforming of a supply depot into a temporary hospital which provided an operating theatre and thirty beds. Large
private houses—those of Miss Fletcher at 35 Fitzwilliam Square, Mrs. Jackson
at 11 Bushy Park Road, Rathgar and Miss Meade at 32 Fitzwilliam Square, for
example—were also turned into auxiliary hospitals. Some one hundred and
eighty-four male ambulance workers and two hundred and thirty-nine vol-

untary nurses offered to look after refugee women and children, help prepare surgical dressings, and carry stretchers through the firing line, and even ride in ambulances amid a hail of flying bullets.

In the South Dublin Union, Ceannt's men improvised a flag, painting an emerald harp upon a yellow window blind and nailing it to a long pole. Solemnly, this emblem was raised from an upper window of the Nurses' Home, while the garrison stood to attention and sang "A Nation Once Again."

The military reacted at once. From their hard-won positions within the Union, and from the roof of the Royal Hospital on the far side of the valley of the Camac, they opened heavy fire. The flag was not damaged. But a woman sitting reading a book in her home in James's Street, and a holidaymaker from Belfast, walking along the South Circular Road, were both shot dead.

Shortly before noon, Major Sir Francis Fletcher Vane, acting second-in-command of Portobello Barracks, sauntered into the mess looking for something to eat. He found the place empty, save for a single officer who sat slumped over a table, his head cupped between his hands. Vane recognized him as Captain J. Bowen-Colthurst, a member of the well-known Ascendancy family who owned Blarney Castle. A veteran of the Boer War, Bowen-Colthurst had also been at the retreat from Mons. When Vane approached Bowen-Colthurst raised his head. Then he said, "Isn't it dreadful, Sir Francis, to have to shoot Irishmen?"

"Indeed," replied Sir Francis, perceiving no special significance in the words. Indeed, he forgot all about the remark until next day events rather forcibly reminded him of it.

Despite a dark, lowering sky, the mobs again crowded Sackville Street. With most offices, shops and factories still unable to open, young men and women flocked into the city centre. As early as ten o'clock, Messrs. Frewen and Ryan's Emporium was broken into by looters. Women and children, the chief perpetrators, dived into the shop in a yelling, squabbling mob, emerging with bundles of collars, hats and caps. Tall silk hats and bowlers arced out into the roadway, to be kicked about like footballs in a glorious orgy of destruction. Crowds of "better class people" stood around watching them, loth to join in themselves, but nevertheless enjoying the fun.

Towards one o'clock, Sheehy-Skeffington emerged from the General Post Office and walked rapidly towards O'Connell Bridge, carrying under his arm a bundle of posters, a paste-brush and several walking sticks. Earlier, he had climbed on to the wrecked tramcar at the corner of North Earl Street and harangued the mob. The looting had ceased for a while, but he had hardly got down when it began again. He stopped at Smith-O'Brien's monument to paste up a poster and a crowd gathered round. They read:

"When there are no regular police in the streets, it becomes the duty of citizens to police the streets themselves and to prevent such spasmodic looting as has been taking place in a few streets. Civilians (men and women) who are willing to co-operate to this end are asked to attend at Westmoreland Chambers (over Eden Bros.) at five o'clock this (Tues.) afternoon."

Then he moved on, stopping only to chat with St. John Ervine on O'Connell Bridge. He offered Ervine a walking stick, explaining his idea about forming a civilian constabulary. Ervine thought it characteristic of the man to submerge his scruples about violence in order to safeguard his country's honour. But regretfully, he refused the walking stick.

So far, the behaviour of the military had been a mystery to both rebels and civilians alike. To the ordinary Dubliner the idea that a handful of Volunteers and Citizen Army boys could take over his city and *apparently* scare off the British Army was a matter for sheer wonder. There were few, however, who imagined that, by nightfall, there would be any other outcome than that, between them, the Army and the police would have chased all the rebels home. Meanwhile, exactly where *was* the Army?

Certainly the military could not be accused of acting with brilliance or audacity. Their movements, so far, had been marked with a perhaps commendable caution and method. They had ignored the rebels where possible, and had slipped into useful positions from which they would eventually be able to exert a stranglehold. Most of the South Dublin Union had already been cleared, if only as part of the overall operations to relieve Dublin Castle. The City Hall had been retaken because it was intolerable that rebels should squat on the Castle's doorstep. And, during the night, forces under the command of Major H. F. Somerville of the School of Musketry, Dollymount, had seized the Custom House and the North Wall railway terminus, so securing the vital dock area. Trinity College had been held by the O.T.C. and soldiers from the Empire. But the operations in the Shelbourne Hotel and the United Services Club, although so far producing surprisingly good results, could scarcely be regarded as a really offensive operation. Neither Colonels Kennard and Cowan—nor even Brigadier-General Lowe when he assumed command—were prepared to risk their reputations by precipitate action which, while their uncertainty lasted as to the exact number of rebels fighting and the chances of the Germans landing, might have recoiled upon them disastrously.

With approximately 5,000 troops under his immediate command in Dublin, General Lowe, in fact, had the rebels outnumbered by the kind of superior odds, which if they could have been brought to bear on the Western Front, would have ended that war inside a week. But instead of risking a series of frontal attacks, Lowe sensibly decided to throw a cordon round the centre of the city. He ordered Colonel Portal, commanding the Curragh

Mobile Column, to establish a line of posts from Kingsbridge station to Trinity College via the Castle. With this line, running west to east along the line of the Liffey, he would effectively drive a great arrow-wedge through rebel positions. When more reinforcements arrived that afternoon—the 4th Royal Dublin Fusiliers from Templemore, the composite Ulster Battalion of Belfast, and a battery of four 18-pounders from Reserve Artillery Brigade at Athlone—he commenced operations in the northern suburbs to establish a second line which, when joined with the first, would create a tight cordon round the G.P.O. and the Four Courts and cut off the rebels in G.H.Q. from their outposts.

The insurgent commanders, utterly in the dark as to these intentions, did nothing to hamper Lowe's ambitions. Driven back into his "fort" in the Nurses' Home, Commander Ceannt had already lost touch with his three main outposts at Jameson's Distillery, Watkin's Brewery and Roe's Malt House and even when the military pressure against him eased, he made no attempt to re-establish contact. Captain Cornelius Colbert in Watkin's Brewery, tired of being cooped up with his twenty men in a narrow street, joined Captain James Murphy and his larger forces in Jameson's Distillery; here nearly one hundred and twenty men, well-armed and supplied, and with women to cook and provide first-aid for them, squatted down and waited unimaginatively for military attacks which were never to develop. Unaware that they had been by-passed, they were content to take pot-shots whenever the military were careless enough to show themselves. The C.O. in Roe's Malt House behaved with an even greater pusillanimity. Cut off, like the others, from Ceannt, and short of both inspiration and determination, he abandoned his post and sent his men home. Under such circumstances it was an easy task for Portal to establish his posts from Kingsbridge station to the Castle.

At the Castle itself, of course, Lowe's situation was less satisfying. James Connolly, delighted at the fight put up by the men in the City Hall and the buildings surrounding it, had twice sent reinforcements from headquarters. A dozen men, led by Sergeant George Norgrove of the Citizen Army, had arrived the previous evening, in time to take part in the City Hall fight. Early on Tuesday, Connolly dispatched additional reinforcements to occupy the roofs and windows of hotels and houses immediately behind the *Mail & Express* offices and Henry & James, the two chief positions still held by the rebels. An ominous silence preceded the attack. Occasionally a bullet cracked down towards Trinity College; now and then a military sniper on the roof of the City Hall shot at a rebel shadow on the *Mail & Express* roof. Civilians, sensing an entertainment, huddled close to the walls in Dame Street, or crouched in shop doorways. Suddenly, a withering shower of bullets from Upper Castle Yard poured into the newspaper offices. It brought an immediate reply, so intense that it was clear the rebels had been simply waiting for this moment. The effect on the crowd was comical. Men darted away like rabbits, women fainted. Some people in their panic ran straight into the firing line, causing a sudden cease-fire, and the combatants shouted at them angrily from the roof-tops. But at ten minutes past two, when the streets had been cleared, operations were recommenced, machine guns chattering above everything else.

A large crowd gathered at the top of Lord Edward Street, some reckless individuals making furtive dashes up Dame Street as far as Eustace Street and Crampton Court, while the military on the roof of the City Hall shouted at them angrily, "Keep back!" A thick cloud of brick-dust rose over the street, as bullets spattered into walls. The fire was intense, bullets booming, echoing and crackling in the narrow canyon of the street in a persistent, relentless barrage. After fifteen minutes of this unremitting onslaught, a score of soldiers with fixed bayonets made a rush from Upper Castle Gate. Several were knocked over and the rest scrambled back. Three minutes later, a second wave of khaki hurled itself across the street. Over the soldiers' heads, solid sheets of lead poured in a covering fire on to the roof of the newspaper office in an effort to pin down the defenders. Spectators heard exultant cries as the military gained the protection of the *Mail* wall and forced open the door. Certain individuals, anxious to glimpse the struggle taking place inside the doorway, stepped out into the roadway, only to be driven back by ricocheting bullets.

"It makes me fidgety to know what they do be doing inside," yelled a young woman in explanation, as she dashed back into safety.

"Begob, ma'am, and if ye had one of them things in you, ye'd have the fidgets, sure enough," remarked a man.

Twenty minutes after the second assault wave had launched itself at the *Mail* office, a third wave, twice as heavy, went in. Although the distance they had to cover was not much more than thirty yards, they moved forward with great deliberation, ducking, weaving, crouching, advancing now a step or two, then retreating a step, making themselves almost impossible to hit. The tactic was effective and casualties were fewer than with earlier waves. When they reached the far side of the street, however, they were forced to fan out along the wall of the newspaper building and wait, because those who had got across earlier were still held up just inside the doorway. In the confined space the military were unable to make full use of their superior numbers, and already the doorway was blocked with their casualties. Some had tried rushing the stairs, only to be sent sprawling back by volleys from the upper landings. But one by one the reinforcing troops managed to duck in, to find themselves enveloped in an inferno of smoke and noise.

Fifteen minutes after the third wave had crossed the street, the issue was still undecided. Yet another wave of military—about thirty this time—led by two officers, made the deadly crossing. Noise rose to a new intensity. Stretcher parties hurried back and forward with casualties. One badly wounded soldier who could still walk was helped by a comrade. Finally, ten minutes after the preceding assault, twenty more soldiers dashed across the street. This time, as the ground floor had been cleared, they had no difficulty in getting inside. A shock awaited one Dublin Fusilier. As he worked his way round to the rear, he came face to face with his younger brother. Lowering his bayonet, he hissed, "Run, you young fool, run!"

By this time the battle had shifted to the stairs. Almost out of ammunition, their rifles so hot they could no longer fire them, the rebels fought the troops with the butts. These moments were perhaps the most savage and brutal of the whole battle—a period of crude, primitive slugging and killing. On the roof-tops, firing continued for some four or five minutes more, but with lessening intensity. Then, at precisely one minute to three, all firing ceased. The crowd, its attention fixed on the doorway, waited to see the captured garrison led into the street. But the minutes ticked by and—ominously—none appeared. After five minutes, a labourer remarked to his friend, "Jim, I'm going home for me dinner, the fun's over," and started off down Crane Lane. Some of the crowd, idly following him, saw seven insurgents leap from the side windows of houses at the rear of Henry & James and run towards the river, where they were quickly lost to view. Behind them, they left twenty-two dead comrades, token of the bitterness of their fight.

"Have a look at our corpse!" said Boyd-O'Kelly gleefully, throwing open a door next to the porter's lodge in Trinity College. Although, as a medical student, Michael Taaffe was hardened to the sight of dead bodies, he found this one, lying on the floor of a stone-walled niche, somehow different. It was that of a young man, so new to death that he looked as though he might get up any moment and walk away. There was a small black hole through his temple.

"They came through on bikes, heading towards the G.P.O. during the night," explained Boyd-O'Kelly. "Didn't expect anyone to be here, I dare say. We got this chap and winged another, I think, but he kept on going."

Taaffe, wishing that wars—especially of this kind—could be fought without casualties, returned to his eyrie on the roof of Regent House. Sixty feet below lay deserted Dame Street. He scanned the roofs, which as far as he could see were as deserted as the streets. As he sat there, hunched down, his rifle at the ready, a party of khaki-clad soldiers approached, filtering slowly from the direction of Grafton Street, hugging the walls, their bayonets flashing. He watched an officer with drawn sword dash into the cobbled yard below, signalling his men to follow. The College gates must have been opened to them because the whole party disappeared below.

Taaffe had no way of knowing it but he had just seen the completion of the first arm of General Lowe's cordon. From now on the rebels scattered in the South Dublin Union, Jameson's Distillery, Jacob's Biscuit factory, the College of Surgeons and Boland's Bakery were to find themselves cut off from headquarters in Sackville Street.

With the capture of the last rebel positions around Dublin Castle and the completion of the southern arm of his cordon, Lowe began pushing forward units to establish his northern arm.

The rebel command had made no attempt to create a series of strongpoints or "forts" in the northern suburbs of the city, but had been content to establish barricades along the North Circular Road and its vicinity at specific points where there were road and railway bridges. In no place had they dug themselves in strongly as compared with their positions south of the Liffey. The role of the northern suburbs, as Plunkett had envisaged it, was simply to protect the rear of the main rebel army and to keep the way open for a retreat towards Ulster, if such a course became necessary.

Two battles developed among these northern outposts during the afternoon. A party of Volunteer Second Battalion men had tried to blow up the Great Northern railway line across the Tolka River just after dawn, and when the explosives had failed to do enough damage, had ripped up tracks further north. This was like shutting the gate after the horse had bolted, for the military, under Major Somerville, had moved in along this line during Monday night and had already occupied Amiens Street and North Wall termini. At 2 p.m. a strong military detachment in an armoured train pushed out from Amiens Street to repair the ripped up tracks, only to be met by rebels ensconced at Annesley Road bridge. For two hours the outnumbered military fought courageously, at one stage even taking the offensive and working their way in among the streets and avenues in the vicinity in an effort to surround the rebels. But in the end, they were forced to retreat, leaving several prisoners behind.

The second engagement proved far more significant. This time there were ominous signs of the enormous strength the military were capable of exerting. Despite the views of his colleagues, James Connolly had always argued that the Government would never employ artillery in Dublin. "A capitalist Government will never destroy property," he insisted. But at precisely three o'clock that afternoon he was to learn that any Government, whether capitalist or otherwise, threatened from within and possibly from without, would not hesitate to utilize every weapon at its command, property or no property.

At that moment, an 18-pounder brought up from Athlone opened fire from the gate of the Medical Officer's Residency at Grangegorman Asylum, near the Broadstone station. Shrapnel burst over the heads of rebels defending a barricade on the North Circular Road at the intersection of the northward-running Phibsborough Road. Simultaneously they found themselves under machine-gun fire from the Broadstone station. The rebels could probably have silenced the machine-guns, for their position looked down on the Broadstone and they had an excellent field of fire. But sighting women on the platform, they withheld their fire. Then the 18-pounder belched again. It carried away most of the barricade and, in some disorder, the fifteen men guarding it fell back on a second barricade at Cabra Road Bridge. Warned that the military were now using artillery, the men defending this barricade sent out a six-man scouting party who advanced along the Cabra Road until they ran into strong military reinforcements moving out from Phoenix Park.

The rain poured down as the scouts, crouching in shop doorways or lying on the glistening pavements, opened fire on the military, who reacted sharply and, advancing at a rush, forced them to flee. Behind the Cabra Road barricade, some thirty men shivered in the drenching downpour and waited for the first glint of British bayonets. Volunteer Joseph Canny, a twenty-six-year-old barman, braced himself to meet a bayonet charge. But all the rebels saw or heard of the enemy was a tremendous volley of bullets, which struck like hail against their barricade. The rebels replied as best they could through the curtain of heavy rain. Then the military fire suddenly ceased and the rebels thought they had beaten off the attack. At 3.45 p.m. a burst of shrapnel crackled over their heads, and for the next three-quarters of an hour the rebels defended their position desperately. Within minutes their barricade was carried away by shellfire and they were exposed to machine-gun and rifle-fire. Then they broke and ran; the affair had become a rout. They fled across fields and railway tracks, or tried to lose the soldiers in a maze of back streets or along the Canal banks. A few made their way to the G.P.O. Others joined up with Commandant Ashe and his 5th Battalion, operating in County Dublin; but most of them, drenched to the skin and with an understanding, perhaps for the first time, of the weight of men and material they were up against, simply went home and stayed there.

By nightfall, the whole rebel position in the northern suburbs had disintegrated as, threatened by encirclement, the remaining forces holding positions in Fairview and at Annesley Bridge, retired upon Headquarters.

De Valera, still tense, still sleepless, still burning up energy as though he had an inexhaustible supply, now produced yet another offensive idea.

Sitting at a table which had been brought out on to the railway embankment, and surrounded by his officers, he pored over a street map, trying to work out a plan to relieve Mallin's hard-pressed men in the Royal College of Surgeons. In the end, he decided to lead a party through the back streets and lanes behind the Shelbourne Hotel and take the enemy in the rear.

News of the projected sally caused excitement in the Boland's garrison. Action would be a welcome change from sitting cooped up in the Bakery or huddled together in the rain in a shallow trench dug between railway sleepers. Waiting had by now become the most intolerable part of the Rising; for a man's imagination worked overtime when he had not enough to do.

De Valera picked twelve men to accompany him, and as a morale-builder handed each man a cigar. Then, after issuing instructions that each was to be provided with a modern rifle, fifty rounds of ammunition and a day's rations, he went off by himself. The party set out along the railway line towards Westland Row station. They had reached the first signal cabin when the Commandant, tall and commanding, came striding to meet them with disappointing news.

"Men," he announced hurriedly, "I'm sorry but it's all off. The fact is I don't feel justified in leading an attack with only twelve men. With twenty-four I could afford to lose half of you perhaps, and know that the safety of our main position would not be seriously affected. But with our numbers so few I can't take such a risk—especially as our chances of succeeding are slight. The whole position could be too easily ruined and no good result come from such a wastage of men. In God's name therefore, we'll go back and stand by our own area."

Disappointed, the men turned away. Even as they did so, a sentry posted on the bridge over Great Brunswick Street shouted that a party of mounted police was approaching. De Valera's first thought was for the civilians on the roadway below, who might be caught in the line of fire. A gaunt skyscraper of a figure, he must have looked like a lunatic to the people below when they looked up and saw him gesticulating wildly and heard him roaring at them to get off the street. They paid no attention to him, of course; Dubliners, even in normal times, were used to all sorts of queer fellows, and another one, especially in the middle of a rebellion, was certainly hardly worth bothering about. Fortunately, de Valera's dilemma was resolved for him. A civilian warned the police, "The Shinners are up on the railway bridge," and they bolted back up the street.

De Valera's humanitarianism brought a welcome warmth to the curious regard in which he was held by many of his men. He was inclined to be aloof and reserved even with his officers. In another man, in the circumstances, this might have been a fault. De Valera, however, had earned the natural admiration of his rank and file by virtue of his academic prowess and his reserve could be construed as another mark of his undoubted abilities. His tendency to prepare what appeared to be telling and effective operations and then suddenly cancel them, hardly appealed to some of them, however, buoyed up as they were with an offensive spirit and almost completely igno-rant of the terrible task which, in common with his fellow-Commandants, de Valera faced. A few, as with soldiers all over the world, grumbled. But even these gave full marks to their Commandant for his humanitarianism, and especially for his willingness to take great personal risks. It was his humani-tarianism, his desire to avoid injuring the innocent or causing any unneces-sary damage to property, that had caused him to dismantle vital parts of the Gasworks late on Monday evening, plunging half the city into darkness. He feared that the gas mains might explode during the fighting and cause a dis-aster to the civilian population. Early that day he had ordered Captain Simon Donnelly to make certain that the forty horses belonging to the Bakery were fed and looked after. He had personally released the animals at the Dogs and Cats pound in Grand Canal Street, knowing that they would face starvation and thirst if the Rebellion continued much longer.

He certainly had plenty of good military ideas which under different cir-cumstances might well have paid off handsomely. In the afternoon he asked Company Adjutant Denis O'Donoghue: "Do you know anybody who could drive a train?" (O'Donoghue was a railway worker.)

"Yes, sir, my brother-in-law," replied O'Donoghue.

"If we could get steam up in an engine," remarked de Valera, thoughtfully, "we could move it up and down the line with an armed party aboard."

O'Donoghue saw his point. Rapid hit-and-run raids could be launched against Beggar's Bush Barracks; more importantly, if the military broke in anywhere along the line (and this was so thinly held that it was likely), it would give de Valera a mobility which might enable him to fling back the soldiery.

"Right, sir," said O'Donoghue, "I'll see what I can do, sir."

17

FOR THE SLUM population the Rebellion still meant no more than a great and glorious spree. Having extracted what fun and monetary advantage they could from Frewin's Emporium, the mob drifted into Upper Sackville Street, seeking fresh excitement. Like wild children they fell upon Lawrence's toy-shop.

Redmond-Howard could not help seeing Sackville Street as with two faces, one of tragedy, the other of "infantile comedy." South of the Pillar, where the rebels were fortifying the whole of the east side of the street from Captain Brennan Whitmore's position on the corner of North Earl Street down to Hopkins & Hopkins, the jewellers, on the corner of O'Connell Bridge, the great street by now had the arid, deserted look of a battlefield, with war-like wire stretched out in front of the Post Office to hold back the crowds. North of the Pillar it looked a veritable nursery-land. As the mob triumphantly smashed its way into Lawrence's, mothers squatted on the dead horse and watched their grubby children emerge carrying bundles of Union Jacks, which they dumped into the road. Then a flame leaped up and, in an instant, a giant bonfire was burning between Nelson Pillar and the Parnell Monument. Wilder and wilder grew the mood of the mob as they danced around the bonfire while the children, revelling in a paradise of toys, ran in and out of the toy-shop, carrying away one prize after another. An airgun battalion, led by an eight-year-old "officer" wearing a grey silk hat, marched to the G.P.O., where they first saluted and then impertinently fired off their pellets at the rebels. They ran away, then reformed and began singing:

"We are the Volunteers, Volunteers, Volunteers,
  We are the Volunteers
  And we'll whack the British Army!"

In the midst of the junketing, a burst of heavy firing sounded from the Quays; the military were beginning yet another attack on Heuston and his men in the Mendicity. Red Cross ambulances raced down Sackville Street and the sight of the mob dancing and singing and building their bonfire ever higher, against a backdrop of speeding ambulances, while the guns thundered and crackled along the river, struck Redmond-Howard as "the most extraordinary example of pathos and humour" he had ever encountered.

The beautiful Miss Stokes, pausing in Sackville Street on her way to the Broadstone station, felt "stunned by the spectacle of one of the greatest streets in Europe as it looked under the control of the rebels and the mob." From an upper floor of Lawrence's, women and children were flinging down cameras, pictures, and gilt frames to their friends below, while other youngsters let off squibs.

From the barricade at North Earl Street Brennan Whitmore watched the scenes at Lawrence's grow wilder. He was astonished that even now, twenty-four hours after the flags of the Republic had been run up over the Post Office, half of Dublin still did not seem to know that they were in the middle of a rebellion. The mob still appeared to regard the whole affair as simply a magnificent excuse for letting off steam.

"What's it all about?" a young woman asked him. "Why don't you all pack up and go home before the military get you?"

Brennan Whitmore attempted to explain. While they talked, a bearded man staggered towards them, wearing a silk hat and clutching a walking stick, with a lady's feather boa round his shoulders and a lady's undergarment on his arm.

"Would you look at that ould reprobate!" demanded the young woman. Then, as the old fellow, his face grave and dignified, came abreast of them, she called out, "It's at home saying your prayers you should be instead of stealing other people's property, you old fool!"

Without a word or even a change of expression, the old man took off the feather boa and handed it to a youngster, who snatched at it angrily then kicked it into the gutter, shouting, "You want to be ashamed of yourself." The old man stalked off with what dignity he could muster, still holding the lady's undergarment.

The mob continued rapaciously. Two more shops in Upper Sackville Street were broken into, and young Ernest O'Malley saw shawlie women auctioning off diamond rings and gold watches for as little as sixpence. One shawlie woman, clad in smart Russian leather boots, sailed past him with rings glittering on all ten fingers. Several overblown women wandered about crammed into evening dresses several sizes too small for them. One young woman wore a sable coat over her shawl. From its pockets dangled a pair of pale pink drawers; from her wide black hat streamed ribbons of blue silk. She strutted about, calling out to her friends, "How do yez like me now? Any chanst of yer washing, ma'am?" A boy offered a look through prismatic glasses at the British snipers on the roof of the Trinity College. "Only tuppence a look," said he coaxingly.

Rebels on the roof of the Arch bar in Henry Street found themselves faced with the task of ejecting drunken rioters from the premises. Short of shooting them, they could think of no way to get rid of them until Volunteer Barney Friel had an idea. He ordered buckets of water carried to the edge of the roof, then shouted, "Ready!" and fired a shot through the skylight. The shot scattered the mob, and as they charged out into the street, Volunteer Paddy Bracken tipped over the buckets drenching them and driving them away.

From his Imperial Hotel window, Redmond-Howard watched a great black cloud of smoke rise into the sky above Lawrence's. The mob had set the shop on fire, and soon the roar of the flames could be heard more than one hundred yards away. Ten minutes later the flames reached the fireworks. Roman candles, Chinese crackers, high-flying rockets fizzled up into the sky or shot wildly out on to the street in a holocaust itself as crazy as the mob. Finally, a big yellow, blue and green bouquet shot into the air, falling back into the street in a shower of sizzling sparks, scattering the crowd in all directions.

Sick at heart, Redmond-Howard and Marsh finally withdrew from their window, having watched for four solid hours. Outside, the mob still rampaged and looted and cheered the flames rising above Lawrence's. Marsh suggested a game of chess but Redmond-Howard declined. Chess, in the middle of a revolution, seemed too incongruous.

Shortly afterwards they went down to the dining-room to have a meal. They had hardly sat down when they noticed two rebels crossing the street from the G.P.O. Redmond-Howard, conscious of the time he and Marsh had spent at their window, decided that the rebels were coming to arrest them, and would probably shoot them as spies. He was wondering whether to make a dash for it when Mr. Woods, the manager, sensing their predicament, crossed to the table and reassured them, "There is nothing to worry about, gentlemen, the rebels tell me that they are simply taking over the hotel."

He had hardly spoken when the dining-room was invaded by a party of rebels. Their officer said courteously, "Finish your meal, gentlemen. There is no need to hurry. But I must ask you to leave." Then he ordered his men, "Now, two men to every window. Take furniture, tables, chairs, anything you can find—and barricade them. We may have to stand a siege."

"Is there any immediate danger?" asked Redmond-Howard.

"None, sir, save from your own resistance. Civilians are perfectly safe as far as we're concerned; we're only fighting the troops of England. You may find our men firing over your heads as you pass in the streets, but take no notice; these are partly our own signals to give us warning and, of course, they're also intended to clear the streets of looters. If you want, you can have a safe conduct out of the city to the north, where our guards have orders to allow all civilians to pass. You see, it's possible our positions may be shelled; we might even be gassed."

It was raining heavily when Redmond-Howard and Marsh set off to walk to the latter's home at Howth, nine miles away. As they passed the Pillar, the Fire Brigade was arriving to tackle the fire at Lawrence's. Two long ladders were edged into the air, in an effort to reach a woman and child who could be seen clinging to the roof, but they proved too short. And already the side wall of the flaming building had begun to totter. Too sick to watch any more, the two men hurried on. Behind them the sound of shots cut across the screams of the trapped woman, as the rebels fired over the heads of the mob to scatter them and give the Brigade a chance to do its work. As Redmond-Howard and Marsh turned into Lower Great Britain Street, they were caught

in a stream of refugees which vividly reminded them of newspaper photographs they had seen of French refugees streaming away from Ypres. As the
rain continued to fall heavily they were glad to accept a lift in a coal cart.

To the rebels incarcerated in the great grey building beside the Pillar, there
seemed nothing particularly ominous in the flames licking high above
Sackville Street or the intermittent rattle of muskets and maxims along the
river. Neither by word nor gesture had Pearse or Connolly hinted that the situation was anything but good and constantly getting better. Connolly, beaming confidently, ceaselessly roamed the building, keeping up the spirits of the
garrison. Despite the discomfort and lack of sleep, the continual alarms and
the sheer boredom, the men still retained much of the original feeling of high
adventure. On the roof Fintan Murphy lay against the tiles and yawned.
Joseph Sweeny turned his face to the dripping sky and thought what an
unfortunate country Ireland was in which to try anything; you were sure to
get wet. But the news was good and the scent of victory was in the air.

The whole building buzzed with rumours, all of them good. MacDonagh
had forced his way into Lower Castle Yard, although now driven out temporarily by machine-gun fire. Cork, Kerry and Limerick were ablaze with
revolt. Irish regiments of the British Army were defecting everywhere and
declaring for the Republic. Jim Larkin, Connolly's old boss, had landed in
Sligo from America, and was fighting his way across Ireland with 50,000
men. The Turks had landed at Waterford. U-boats had sunk a British transport in the Irish Sea. And the Germans had landed in force; their scouts had
been seen on the Naas Road. It was all completely splendid.

Down in the street, urchins still marched through the rain, singing,

"We are the Volunteers and we'll whack the British Army!"

In the College of Surgeons, Professor O'Briain peered through his loophole. Behind him, men lay on the floor, wrapped in bits of carpet, singing
softly and with great emotion the old rebel song, "Wrap the Green Flag
round me." O'Briain caught himself flicking a tear from his eye.

Twelve-year-old Tommy Keenan returned in triumph after escaping from his
family. A Citizen Army woman had insisted that he return home to tell his
parents where he was and what he had been doing. Tommy's father had
locked him in his room, but the boy had climbed out of the window and
scrambled down a drainpipe.

Frank Robbins with a company of men began tunnelling from the Turkish
Baths, which lay about half-way along the Green towards Grafton Street,
through houses to South King Street at the top of Grafton Street. This was
part of a bold plan by Mallin aimed at burning out the military in the
United Services Club. Once a tunnel had been cut through to South King
Street, his men could emerge in the dark of night, run across Grafton Street,
and set fire to the corner houses on the north side of the Green. With luck,

the whole block might go up, including the United Services Club. It was not too fantastic to hope that the flames, once they had got going, might jump the intervening gaps of Dawson Street and Kildare Street and burn down the Shelbourne also. In excellent spirits, Robbins handed seven-pound hammers to his men, commenting, "Right, boys, we only need a hole in every wall big enough for a man to crawl through on his hands and knees."

Towards dusk the backbreaking job was completed.

At 5.30 p.m. Francis Sheehy-Skeffington, having arranged for a meeting that evening to discuss his civilian police idea, met his wife Hanna, and had tea with her in one of the tea-shops still open. Then, anxious about their young son, she left him and went home.

Some time between six and seven, "Skeffy"—as he was known to his intimates—decided to visit home first before going to his meeting. As he neared Portobello Bridge, he saw that it was guarded by a picquet of Royal Irish Rifles. These men, in common with their comrades cooped up in Portobello, had undergone a morale-sapping experience. Following a brief action at Davy's public house early on Easter Monday, they had come under fire again in Camden Street from MacDonagh's men and had been harassed by them, night and day, from the roof and towers of Jacob's, which loomed over their position. Rumours of continuing catastrophe to British arms constantly flooded the barracks. Most believed they would eventually have their throats cut. Under such circumstances, judgments could scarcely be expected to be at their soundest.

As Skeffington approached the bridge he kept to the middle of the road, now without traffic, so that he could be seen clearly. The military did not attempt to stop him and he crossed the bridge. It was not until a man standing on the footpath called out his name that Lieutenant Morris of the 11th East Surrey Regiment, in command of the picquet, called on him to stop and sent two soldiers to arrest him. Skeffington was hauled into Portobello Barracks, where he was searched and questioned. Then he was taken in front of the Adjutant, Lieutenant Samuel Morgan.

"Are you in sympathy with the Sinn Feiners?" asked Morgan directly.

"Yes, but I am not in favour of militarism."

At a loss what to do with him, Morgan reported to Irish Command H.Q. that he had questioned Skeffington, known to be a friend of the rebel leaders, but had been unable to find grounds on which to formulate a charge. Was it in order to release him? The answer was a curt and categoric "no". Morgan therefore ordered Skeffington to be detained but entered no charge upon the charge sheet.

It was midnight when Captain Bowen-Colthurst approached Lieutenant Dobbyn, captain of the guard, and formally ordered him to hand over the prisoner. This, in itself, was an illegal act, because no officer could demand the custody of a prisoner without a written order from his commanding officer. Skeffington was hauled out of the guard room and ordered to say his prayers. Bowen-Colthurst himself prayed: "O Lord God, if it should please Thee to take away the life of this man, forgive him for Our Lord Jesus Christ's sake." Skeffington's time, however, had not yet come. All Bowen-Colthurst wanted with the unfortunate pacifist at this stage was his presence as a hostage while he and a small party of soldiers carried out a raid. Bowen-Colthurst led them to Portobello Bridge, then ordered his deputy, Lieutenant Leslie Wilson, to hold Skeffington, adding that he was to be shot immediately if the Sinn Feiners fired on Bowen-Colthurst or his party. The captain then headed up the Rathmines Road, firing his revolver wildly into the air. At Rathmines Church he spied two boys—one a seventeen-year-old youth called Coade— who had just left the church and were on their way home. Some hours earlier, Lord Wimborne had proclaimed Martial Law; now Bowen-Colthurst roared at the two terrified youngsters, "Don't you know Martial Law has been proclaimed and that I could shoot you like dogs?"

Anxious to avoid trouble, young Coade turned away. At once Bowen-Colthurst screamed, "Bash him!" and a soldier, lifting the butt of his rifle, slashed it across the boy's face, breaking his jaw-bone. As the youngster fell senseless to the ground, Bowen-Colthurst whipped out his revolver and shot him dead.

Rampaging on, Bowen-Colthurst led his men to the licensed premises of Alderman James Kelly, under the impression that they belonged to a Sinn Fein alderman of the same name. He began by bombing the place, then he entered the wrecked premises and seized four men who were still alive. Two were barmen, the others magazine editors named Dickson and MacIntyre, who had taken refuge there. Dickson, a cripple, edited *The Eye-Opener*, MacIntyre, *The Searchlight*, both violently Loyalist papers which had strongly supported John Redmond's recruiting campaign. Despite protests, Bowen-Colthurst took them back to Portobello, and locked them up. Then, satisfied with his evening's work, he retired to his quarters where, for the rest of the night he sat without sleeping, praying continuously. In the small hours, he came across a text in the Bible which seemed apposite to him. It was from St. Luke: "But those mine enemies, which would not that I should reign over them, bring hither and slay them before me."

By the time dawn arrived, he felt he had the sanction of religion to do what he intended to do.

Towards evening, Captain Mahony was told to line up with the other prisoners, three privates and a civilian, and then under escort, was marched to the G.P.O. Hustled in through the side door, he was brought before an officer who asked him his name and sneered, "A nice name that to be wearing khaki!" His watch and money were taken from him (they were returned next morning), then he was led up to the second floor and ushered into a room where Lieutenant Chalmers was held prisoner. He found Chalmers in a "bit of a funk" about "these wild Irishmen"; apparently he was expecting to be shot at any moment. One of the Sinn Fein women, Miss Louise Gavan Duffy, came in and asked if they would like some tea. Mahony asked if a message could be sent to his sister in Drumcondra, telling her that he was safe.

"If you like to write it, I'll show it to the Provisional Government," promised Miss Gavan Duffy.

When he had finished this, at Chalmers's suggestion they both settled down for the night under a table for protection. Chalmers had an idea that the military were sure to attack during the night and that, if they did, the roof of the G.P.O. might be blown in.

Pearse, seated on a high clerk's stool at the counter just inside the main doorway, had spent most of the afternoon drawing up a manifesto to the citizens of Dublin. When the downpour which had cleared the mob off the streets had eased a little, and the crowds were able to emerge from shelter, he strode out into Sackville Street and, with a small escort, walked over to Nelson Pillar. There was an immediate rush in his direction and several hundred people milled round him as he began reading:

"The Provisional Government to the Citizens of Dublin:

The Provisional Government of the Irish Republic salutes the Citizens of Dublin on the momentous occasion of the proclamation of a SOVEREIGN INDEPENDENT IRISH STATE now in the course of being established by Irishmen in arms.

The Republican forces hold the lines taken up at Twelve noon on Easter Monday, and nowhere, despite fierce and almost continuous attacks of the British troops have the lines been broken through. The country is rising in answer to Dublin's call, and the final achievement of Ireland's freedom is now, with God's help, only a matter of days. The valour, self-sacrifice and discipline of Irish men and women are about to win for our country a glorious place among the nations.

Ireland's honour has already been redeemed; it remains to vindicate her wisdom and her self-control.

All citizens of Dublin who believe in the right of their Country to be free will give their allegiance and their loyal help to the Irish Republic. There is work for everyone; for the men in the fighting line, and for the women in the provision of food and first aid. Every Irishman and Irishwoman worthy of the name will come forward to help their common country in this her supreme hour.

Able-bodied citizens can help by building barricades in the streets to oppose the advance of the British troops. The British troops have been firing on our women and on our Red Cross. On the other hand, Irish regiments in the British Army have refused to act against their fellow countrymen.

The Provisional Government hopes that its supporters—which means the vast bulk of the people of Dublin—will preserve order and self-restraint. Such looting as has already occurred has been done by the hangers-on of the British Army. Ireland must keep her new honour unsmirched.

We have lived to see an Irish Republic proclaimed. May we live to establish it firmly, and may our children and our children's children enjoy the happiness and prosperity which freedom will bring.

Signed on behalf of the Provisional Government.

P. H. Pearse

Commanding in Chief of the Forces of the Irish Republic and President of the Provisional Government."

There were some cheers, but long before he had finished speaking, the restless crowds, bored with words and longing for action, had begun to drift away. Some of them, tired of watching the Fire Brigade's efforts to rescue Lawrence's, crowded over to one of the few unlooted shops left in the street. Not long afterwards this shop, too, burst into flames. With a small escort, Brennan Whitmore threatened to open fire on the mob if they did not clear off. Two men were particularly obstinate so he sent a messenger to Connolly asking permission to arrest and shoot both as an example. Despite the jeers of the crowd, he held on firmly to them until Connolly's reply came, expressly forbidding him to harm them and reluctantly he let them go.

Thwarted, the mob went rampaging away up Sackville Street and Connolly ordered a few warning volleys loosed over their heads. He was really not prepared to waste time on them, for although the military had not attempted to repeat the Lancers' reconnaissance, they had opened up intermittent sniping on the Sackville Street positions from three different places: the roof of Trinity College, where the Canadians and Anzacs, aided by the O.T.C. and units of the Leinster Regiment, were heavily entrenched; from a shop called McBirneys, a little way along the Quays on the far side of the river; and from the tower of Amiens Street railway station. In spite of specific orders not to fire back, for Pearse and Connolly still hoped that Irish regiments could be induced to defect, a Volunteer named Gallagher silenced a sniper on the roof of Trinity, and some of the men took an odd pot-shot at Amiens Street station. The occasional crack of a bullet no longer scared the looters, possibly because they guessed that the rebels were trying only to frighten them. But bullets are wild and uncontrollable things, especially in the hands of inexperienced marksmen. A man and a woman were shot dead while standing beside a fire engine at the corner of Henry Street, and another man, brother of one of the Brigade turncocks, was killed while standing beside the engine driver in Cathedral Place. Not that all the civilian casualties were caused by the rebels. The military sniper in McBirney's, trying to knock over one of the three-man rebel garrison in Hopkins & Hopkins, the jewellers at the corner of Sackville Street and Eden Quay, missed him and killed a young woman instead.

But the crowd did not seem to care very much. A stray bullet was a small price to pay for a front seat at an entertainment which would almost certainly never be repeated.

On the whole, the rebels' behaviour had been exemplary so far as looting or drunkenness—the latter the traditional curse of Ireland—were concerned. Although most of the men were accustomed to the borderline of poverty, it is not recorded that any rebel took or "commandeered" anything other than what was essential for operations. The absence of drunkenness, too, among men supposedly wedded to the enjoyment of a "pint", was striking. Colonel Brereton, a prisoner in the Four Courts, afterwards paid tribute to the self-control of men who, although exposed to the temptation of one of the finest cellars in Ireland, resolutely refused to touch liquor. In one instance, while breaking their way through shops towards South King Street, Sergeant Frank Robbins's men entered a brandy store; but not a drop was sampled, and the only bottles taken were sent back to the Red Cross post in the College of Surgeons. In the General Post Office, some men were offered bottles of stout by grateful publicans whose premises they had saved from the looters; most refused them. One man, as he raised a bottle to his lips, had it dashed to the floor by an officer, who fiercely reprimanded him for forgetting that his country's honour was at stake.

Shortly after dusk, when Commander Daly learned that the military had carried away his barricades in the North Circular and Cabra Roads, he attempted to impede their progress by occupying the Broadstone station. Daly had intended originally to make this station one of the focal points of the area under his command and, indeed, Captain Denis O'Callaghan and a small party had been sent to seize it at noon on Monday. O'Callaghan, however, acting on his own initiative, had decided to go no further than North Brunswick Street, believing that he had not enough men to carry out the order. Now, with twelve men, including young Garry Holohan, he set out to take it if the military had not forestalled him.

The mission proved abortive. When within fifty yards of the main station entrance, Holohan saw a khaki figure flit across the carriage entrance. Almost immediately his friend Edward Martin flung up his hands and screamed, "Garry, I'm shot!" After a brisk exchange, the insurgents fell back, leaving the Broadstone in the hands of the military.

Daly's men were again repulsed a few hours later, when they made a determined attempt to burn out the Lancers, under Lieutenant Hunter, from the Medical Mission in Charles Street. A party firing from the Chancery Lane gate of the Four Courts peppered the Mission, while two Volunteers, carrying rags and paper soaked in oil, flung their incendiary bundle through a window. The "bomb" proved ineffective, however, being easily dowsed by the military and as the two Volunteers scrambled back to their base, one of them, Paddy Daly, was badly wounded.

At 10 p.m. precisely Mallin's men in the College of Surgeons began an intensive fire on the Shelbourne Hotel and the United Services Club, the military replying with heavy machine-gun fire. Meanwhile, a small rebel party waited for the signal to dash across the top of Grafton Street and set fire to the houses on the north side of the Green. But even while the firing was at its height, the Countess Markievicz struggled down through the tunnels and ordered a cease fire, explaining, "The idea has been abandoned."

When the din had subsided, Robbins heard someone shouting loudly in a high-pitched voice, and found that Private Patrick Poole of the Citizen Army, deafened by the firing, thought he was talking in conversational tones.

Strain and effort, indeed, were now beginning to take their toll. Sergeant Joseph Doyle fainted—not surprisingly, as he had been three days without rest or proper food. A little later Robbins himself, having slept for only two hours out of the past sixty, fell asleep with his rifle pointing towards the Shelbourne.

In the G.P.O., Joseph Sweeny remembers, some of the men began to imagine things, to think that they could see queer faces in the sky. Hunger and weariness were exacting a price with no help from the forces of Government.

Brennan Whitmore first caught sight of the woman when she was half-way across Sackville Street, walking as if to say, "Take this nonsensical Rebellion out of my way." She teetered right past him, without even looking at him, and marched straight towards his barricade. In astonishment, he let her pass, then went after her and stopped her.

"I'm sorry, but I'm afraid you can't go this way," he said, as politely as he could. "The street is blocked."

"And what right have you to block up the street and prevent decent people going home?"

"Sure, haven't you only got to walk a few yards further down the street and then you can get round easily enough. Is that too much to ask under the circumstances?"

"I've gone home this way all my life and I'm going home this way tonight, and I'd like to see anyone try and stop me."

"You might break your neck," he said, as she advanced towards the barricade.

"It's my neck," she retorted. "But if I do break it, it's your fault." And, with that, she began to climb the barricade while the crowd cheered. A shout of encouragement, unfortunately, led to her undoing. Angrily she turned to answer the man and her foot slipped. Down she came in a tangle of petticoats and underwear, and the crowd roared hilariously. Furious, she got to her feet, and with arms akimbo, lashed them with her tongue. Then, to renewed cheering, she returned to the barricade. After slipping once or twice, she reached the crest. On the way down the far side, however, a chair collapsed under her and again she lost her balance. For a second time the predominantly male crowd was entertained by the sight of her pretty underwear; then she rose and roundly abused the "awful Shinners" before disappearing down the street.

Towards midnight the crowds began to thin out. But outside the G.P.O. a cornet player still earned himself a few coppers by playing national airs. As the sad music of a conquered race sighed in through the windows where the weary rebels crouched, voices inside the great building began to take up the song:

"Then here's to their memory—may it be
  For us a guiding light,
  To cheer our strife for liberty,
  And teach us to unite!
  Through good and ill, be Ireland's still,
  Though sad as theirs, your fate;
  And true men, be you, men
  Like those of Ninety-eight."

And thus the Rebellion entered upon its third day.

At midnight Northumberland Road lay quiet and deserted. In No. 25 Lieutenant Michael Malone called James Grace downstairs and said, "Look here, Jimmy, you know we haven't a chance. The odds against us are overwhelming and the Germans haven't arrived at all. So I'd like to send young Rowe and Byrne away. They're not even sixteen yet, and the chances are they'll lose their lives if they stay on in this house."

"I agree with that," said Grace. "It's all right with me."

Malone called the two boys and explained the position. They accepted his advice and, creeping through the skylight, slipped quietly away over the roofs. When they had gone, Grace suddenly realized just how desperate their position was; and how grey and haggard Malone looked, partly because of strain and tension, partly because he had not slept now for almost four nights.

"Why don't you go to bed for a while?" he suggested.

Malone, almost too tired to answer him, simply nodded his head.

Left to himself, Grace set several booby traps in the hall and on the stairs, and then placed himself in the drawing-room window, his rifle resting across his knees. Shortly afterwards he dozed off and remembered no more until he found himself blinking in the dawn light.

A little after midnight, sixty-six rebels who had controlled the suburb at Fairview since noon on Monday, joined the G.H.Q. garrison inside the G.P.O. Their arrival was the first evidence that the slowly-constricting military pressure was at last beginning to become effective.

One man, Volunteer Charles Saurin, missed Pearse's welcoming address with its declaration that Dublin had redeemed her honour because he had slipped and cut his hand on glass littering the pavement. Later, when his wound had been dressed, he rejoined his party, and was served with a large slab of cake, hardly the most nourishing food for a half-famished man. But he was not given time to mull over his woes; a section of his party was instructed to occupy the buildings lying between the G.P.O. and Middle Abbey Street, and Saurin was among twenty-two men who were lined up in Sackville Street and briefly addressed by James Connolly. He listened to Lieutenant Oscar Traynor protest that he felt unfitted to command a whole block, and to Connolly reply brusquely, "Isn't it enough for you that I tell you?"

When they entered the Metropole, two waiters escorted the party to Mr. Oliver, the manager, who was in the foyer with his wife. Traynor explained his mission and Mr. Oliver simply shrugged and stood aside. Mrs. Oliver asked Saurin if he could find her a taxi to take her to Westland Row station. He said he was sorry, but that it was not possible. When she asked him if he could provide an escort of Volunteers to see that she and her husband could walk safely through the streets, Saurin pointed out that this was certain to get them fired on by the military.

"What about my personal property?" she asked next. "My dresses, my coats?"

"They'll be perfectly safe," he assured her.

"Well, thank you very much for being so nice when you might easily have been otherwise," she said.

In the smokeroom, a Volunteer prodded a harassed-looking individual in front of Lieutenant Traynor. "This man's a spy, a British spy in mufti," he declared.

The prisoner seemed a mild-looking individual. "How do you know he's a spy?" Traynor asked.

"Ah," said the Volunteer, "when I said 'Quick march', he stepped off with the left foot."

Traynor looked up at the ceiling in despair. "Who are you?" he asked the prisoner.

"I'm a master at Portora Royal School, and I've never been so outraged in my life!"

Traynor patted the Volunteer on the shoulder. "Like a good man, will you let him go?" he said.

Meanwhile, across the street, unseen by the rebels, a military sergeant and four privates crept up to the door of the Gresham Hotel and were admitted by the porter.

Half an hour after midnight, some sympathetic civilians arrived at the G.P.O. and informed James Connolly that strong military forces were advancing from Phoenix Park and had been spotted near Parnell Square.

The information was accurate enough, but Connolly misinterpreted it. He thought it meant a major night attack. Like everyone else in Dublin, both he and Pearse believed that the military would inevitably charge the G.P.O. He sounded the alert, ordered all lights extinguished and every point manned from which a rifle could be fired or a hand-grenade flung. For the men it meant an end of the weariness and increasing boredom of the past thirty-six hours. Possibly the most excited rebel of all was old Tom Clarke. Grabbing a rifle, he took up position at one of the windows, and no one could remember him looking happier. He seemed in his element, laughing, joking, peering out into the black night, praying to God every now and then that He would let the English come so that at last he could have a crack at them.

All over Dublin it was a long sleepless night. Even James Stephens, safe in his bed, could not sleep. There was an edge to the air, a tension, as though everyone sensed that this great act of defiance would not be allowed to continue much longer; as though every minute that passed only stored up greater retribution for the rebels.

In Boland's Bakery, O'Donoghue, fagged out beyond anything he had ever experienced, tried to snatch some sleep. About 1 a.m. he lay down, but sleep eluded him. Then someone kicked the soles of his boots. "Get up," said Lieutenant John Guilfoyle. "I want you to relieve an outpost down near Beggar's Bush."

O'Donoghue, his eyelids heavy as stones, scrambled leadenly along the railway line. Guilfoyle had told him to occupy a small white house on the right-hand side of the track. Nearing it, he discovered some Volunteers lying between the sleepers. "Get down, you fool!" they hissed. He flopped on his stomach and then, crawling over those in front, he slipped through a network of wire. He was about to fling himself over a low railway wall when he heard a revolver click and somebody ask, "Who goes there?"

"Volunteer," he answered quickly.

"You're lucky I didn't shoot you," said de Valera. "What are you doing here anyway?"

"Relieving outposts, sir."

"Get back at once!" declared de Valera angrily. "Don't you know you should never advance when a retirement has just been ordered?"

"I was only obeying orders, sir."

"Well, get back."

It was 4 a.m. when O'Donoghue got another opportunity to try to sleep. He had hardly laid his ear against his knapsack when Simon Donnelly kicked his boots. "I want men to dig trenches up towards Westland Row," said Donnelly. O'Donoghue suggested he could find fresher men, and stubbornly refused to budge. Donnelly again kicked his boots. O'Donoghue let him go on doing so, until finally he got fed up and went away. For a whole blissful hour he enjoyed a state of unconsciousness. Then the cold awakened him and, shivering like a man with ague, he got up and went looking for something with which to cover himself. He had scarcely risen to his feet when Donnelly again pounced on him. "The very man I want. I've got a job for you."

"My God!" said O'Donoghue. "What is it this time?"

"I want you to go to Robert's Yard, next to Clanwilliam House. Take three men and enough provisions. Hold on a minute and I'll go across and show you the position. You'll be under Mick Malone. You mightn't get a chance to get back here, but even if you don't—even if we retire—hold on there. Fight to the end."

"H'm," said O'Donoghue doubtfully, and looked up at the sky. The first streaks of dawn were appearing and, from the looks of it, it was going to be a glorious day. Then, having considered what Donnelly had said, he remarked, "Aye, indeed—well that's certainly a handy one all right!"

18

A FEW MINUTES before eight o'clock on Wednesday morning a low, grey shape nudged its way up the Liffey and dropped anchor opposite the Custom House. This was the *Helga*, a small fisheries patrol boat acting under Admiralty orders. At exactly eight o'clock she opened fire on Liberty Hall. Her aim was ill-judged, and instead of bringing the Citizen Army's deserted headquarters tumbling down around the ears of its only occupant, the caretaker, Mr. Peter Ennis, the shell hit the Loop Line railway bridge with a resounding clang.

Embarrassing as this was for the red-faced crew of the *Helga*, the sound echoed over Dublin like the crack of doom. Father John Flanagan, priest of the Pro-Cathedral, halted the Latin Introit for a brief moment to glance round his meagre congregation of less than a dozen women (and one server), and then, somewhat perturbed, continued with his Mass. On the roof of Trinity College, Professor John Joly, who had been amused watching the antics of an urchin driving his looted toy motor-car round Grattan's Monument, laid down his rifle for a moment and made a mental note that this was the end for the Sinn Feiners. In the Pillar Café, Brennan Whitmore and his men rushed to take up their positions, leaving their breakfasts of bacon and egg uneaten. In the G.P.O. James Connolly smacked his fist into his palm and said, "By God, they're beaten!" In the suburb of Glasnevin people rushed out of their houses to watch the destruction, as they thought, of their city. In Hopkins & Hopkins the garrison of three Volunteers, afraid to go near the windows because of the sniper in McBirneys, rigged up a periscope to enjoy the fun.

The operation to root out the rebels who were supposedly still holding Liberty Hall had been mounted with care and preparation. At first it had been hoped to employ two 9-pounder field guns. As it transpired, it was not found possible to set them up in time. However, in addition to the big gun of the *Helga*, nests of machine-gunners were placed on the roof of the Custom House, in the tower of the Fire Station nearby, and on the roof of Trinity College, ready to slaughter the Sinn Feiners as they were driven out by the bombardment. Troops of the Royal Irish Regiment and the Ulster Composite Battalion waited in the Custom House with fixed bayonets to follow up the onslaught with a gallant charge across Beresford Place. It was by far the biggest military operation yet mounted against the rebels. No one, apparently, realized that Liberty Hall was empty.

Aboard the *Helga* the gunners fiddled with their sights. Two things prevented them getting a direct bang at the building, that infernal Loop Line railway bridge, and a cargo boat belonging to Messrs. Guinness which lay anchored alongside the quay. The alternative was to try and lob the shells over both, the way a player would lob a tennis ball. Sights, therefore, were raised, trajectories checked and, finally, a second shot was fired. This time the result was better and the crew raised a resounding cheer; the shell landed squarely on top of Liberty Hall, wrecking the interior but leaving the outer walls intact. The dose was quickly repeated.

Reporter John O'Leary, sitting at a window across the river, saw the side door of Liberty Hall open as immense clouds of dust and debris spurted into the air. A figure darted out on to the street, that of Peter Ennis, the caretaker. Immediately, two machine-guns opened up and this—in O'Leary's own words—is what then happened.

"A machine-gun is turned on him. Bullets hit the pavement in front of him and behind him, they strike the roadway and the walls of the building along his route and still he runs on and on. I hold my breath in awe as I watch his mad career. Will he escape? He will . . . he won't. 'My God!' I exclaim as a bullet raises a spark from the pavement right at his toe. A hundred yards in nine seconds—a record! Nonsense, this man does the distance in five and disappears, his breath in his fist, his heart in his mouth but—safe!"

For an hour the *Helga* pounded and shook the area, sometimes hitting Liberty Hall, more often missing. A steady stream of rifle- and machine-gun fire was poured into the empty building under the impression that terrified rebels were still cowering there, although not a single shot was ever fired in reply. All that happened was that hundreds of poor people living in the tenements and small houses in the vicinity ran out into the streets, and a few got hit. At the end of an hour, the *Helga* smugly withdrew, leaving a cloud of dust hanging hazily in the air. Liberty Hall still stood, although little more than a shell. Northumberland House next door had taken a worse battering. As the haze settled, O'Leary saw twenty soldiers emerge from the Custom House and, advancing cautiously across the open square, set the seal on their victory by climbing over the rubble into the ruined building.

The bombardment, if it had done little else, had at least succeeded in damaging rebel morale. For the first time in their lives, the young rebels began to understand the meaning of the words "greatly superior odds." Until then, most of them had simply envisaged enormous numbers of khaki-clad men advancing in a swollen, easy-to-hit mass. The shock of artillery fire robbed them of this idea of a man-to-man fight. To die for Ireland was glorious. But not to be able to hit back . . . !

James Connolly, listening to the boom of the *Helga's* guns, tried to be reassuring. "Don't be alarmed," he told his men in the G.P.O. "When the British

Government uses artillery in the city of Dublin, it shows they must be in a hurry to finish the job—but there are probably some forces coming to help us." To Willie Pearse, indeed, he passed on the good news "that the Germans are about to land." A little later, up in the Instrument Room, he repeated this story to Michael Collins. The time for fine words and promises, however, was nearly past. Sackville Street was beginning to know the steady clip of machine-gun bullets as the gunners on the roof of Trinity College belted away fiercely at the two buildings on the opposite corners of O'Connell Bridge, Hopkins & Hopkins on Eden Quay, and Messrs. Kelly, fishing tackle and gunsmiths, on Bachelor's Walk. The fire scattered the crowd which had gathered daily on the corner of D'Olier and Westmoreland Streets, south of the river, since Monday afternoon. When they had been chased into the side streets, the Anzacs on the roof of Trinity and the sniper in McBirneys, on Aston Quay, began a persistent rifle-fire. Bullets zipped into rebel-held buildings all the way along Lower Sackville Street. They tore holes in the proud Starry Plough which Connolly had raised over the Imperial Hotel at seven o'clock that morning. They spattered against the leaden roof of the cupola of the Dublin Bread Company's Restaurant, from which a small nest of rebel snipers intermittently replied; whizzed into the Wireless School and made it impossible to continue working the transmitter; spat along the roadway, kicking up tracer-like sparks. Sackville Street became a battleground. The quiet ebb and flow of the first two days of the Rebellion suddenly vanished, an indication of the frightening coils which the military, like some giant boa-constrictor, had flung around the city.

The previous evening, secure in the knowledge that a whole British division was already on its way from England, General Lowe had decided to waste no more time and to set about liquidating the rebels at once. He decided to leave outposts such as the South Dublin Union, Jameson's Distillery, Boland's Bakery, St. Stephen's Green and the impregnable-looking Jacob's alone, and to concentrate upon the reduction of the two most important rebel positions in the city, the G.P.O. and the Four Courts. His grand strategy was first to draw a single wide cordon round both these places, then to draw separate smaller cordons round each of them. The first of the small cordons was to run from the Castle along Dame Street to Trinity College, thence across Butt Bridge to the Custom House, and on to Amiens Street station; then up Gardiner Street into Lower Great Britain Street, across the top of Sackville Street at the Parnell Monument, thence to Capel Street where it would swing back towards the river, and across it to the Castle again. The second noose, also starting from the Castle, was to run northwards directly over the river, up Capel Street, then swing west along North King Street as far as Blackhall Place where it was to make a right-angled turn back towards the river, crossing it high up, and then by way of Watling and James's Streets, terminate at the Castle.

But before either noose could be tightened, two obstacles had to be swept away; first, Liberty Hall, which would supposedly obstruct the projected noose round the G.P.O.; second, the Mendicity Institution, which would interfere with the noose around the Four Courts. Late on Tuesday, therefore, when he had already received artillery reinforcements and knew that advance units of the 59th Division had sailed from Liverpool, General Lowe decided to attack these two positions early on Wednesday morning. As a result, even while the *Helga* was lobbing her shells into Liberty Hall, Dublin Fusiliers were knocking quietly on doors near the Mendicity Institution, asking the occupants to leave, as operations would be shortly commencing in the area. Further down the river, a position was being prepared for the two 9-pound field guns. In reaching his decision to use them, Lowe, however, had entirely overlooked the problem of recoil. Under normal circumstances a field gun when fired drove a spade-shaped plate of iron into the ground, "fixing" itself. The stone squaresetts of Dublin did not permit this. Holes would have to be dug, but with the rebels entrenched across the river, digging them presented difficulties. Some time before the *Helga* opened fire, therefore, six volunteers from Trinity O.T.C., dressed as navvies, sallied forth with picks, crowbars, and spades. To the curious Dubliners who watched them commence work, they explained: "Something has gone wrong with the gas main to Trinity College and we've come to put it right." Oddly enough, the sight of "navvies" labouring away on the far side of the river aroused no curiosity among the rebels in Hopkins & Hopkins or in Kelly's. Possibly they were too busy boring through walls, or in trying to pick off the sniper in McBirney's. Even so, the Trinity men found it hard to make headway. The squaresetts, six inches long by four wide, were so closely set together in tar that there was no room for the pick to enter between them. A crowbar was broken and the men had to send for further tools.

Meanwhile, up the river, Dublin Fusiliers filtered into the streets and lanes at the rear of the Mendicity, or took up facing positions behind the wall on the far side of the river while assault parties prepared to attack across the bridge.

In the G.P.O., young Richard Humphreys watched the bullets kicking into the walls of the D.B.C. Restaurant and the Reis building across the street, until an officer roared at him to get back to work and make his window absolutely bullet-proof. Soon he had a wall of ledgers seven feet deep in front of him.

In the small room which was their prison, Captain Mahony played three-handed bridge with Chalmers and Lieutenant King of the Royal Irish Fusiliers who had been taken prisoner outside the G.P.O. while spying. Mahony soon tired of this, however, and settled down to read *The Hunchback of Notre Dame*, which The O'Rahilly had sent in to him. So far their treatment had been exemplary. After an excellent breakfast, The O'Rahilly and the rebel Quarter-master, Desmond Fitzgerald, had interrogated them. Mahony had asked, "Are you going to shoot us?" Both had looked at him in horror.

"Good God, no—you're prisoners of war!" burst out The O'Rahilly angrily. To which Mahony replied, "You know I'm a doctor—you shouldn't keep me a prisoner."

"If you're a doctor," said Fitzgerald, "then we've something else for you to do."

Across the street, Brennan Whitmore warned his men to keep their heads down and to fire only when they sighted a definite target. Not that it was easy to locate the enemy, for by now the volume of fire was really heavy and increasing steadily. He stopped at a window for a moment to watch a burst of machine-gun bullets spatter against Kelly's corner, then had to duck as a stream of bullets cut through the window right above his head.

Over the river, reporter O'Leary also ducked as rebel counterfire, most of it coming from the snipers in the D.B.C. cupola, battered the front of buildings along Aston Quay. Deciding that it had become too dangerous to look out, he rigged up a crude periscope, using two mirrors. Through this, at approximately 11.50 a.m., he saw three young women emerge cautiously from the G.P.O. under a Red Cross flag, then move out into the middle of the street. All firing died away and for two minutes not a shot broke the silence as the women crossed to the Hibernian Bank. The moment they disappeared, the rifles and machine-guns opened up with renewed fury.

While all this was happening at Sackville Street, James Stephens, less than half-a-mile away, was able to walk through the streets and enjoy the sun, stop to read Wimborne's Proclamation of Martial Law, which had been posted everywhere except in rebel-held positions, and to chat with friends or acquaintances. He found most people smiling and gay. Few of his men friends had any sympathy for the rebels, but the women were more decided in their views. "I hope every man will be shot," one woman told him. Yet he discovered that most felt an odd sense of gratitude towards the rebels, almost as though they were grateful to them, as representatives of Dublin, for not allowing themselves to be humiliated by a quick defeat.

"Of course they'll be beaten—but at least they're putting up a decent fight," explained one man, and this seemed to epitomize the city's attitude towards the Rising.

Passing through St. Stephen's Green, he saw small boys darting in and out of the Park gates, trying to pick up rifles and bandoliers abandoned by the rebels, then skipping out again as bursts of fire broke over their heads. But all firing ceased when Mr. James Kearney, the park-keeper, entered the Green to feed the ducks; twice daily both sides observed a truce to allow him to perform this duty.

In Portobello Barracks, after a night of prayer, Captain Bowen-Colthurst rose with his mind made up. At five minutes past ten he entered the guardroom and told Sergeant William Aldridge of the Dublin Fusiliers that he wanted to bring the prisoners, Sheehy-Skeffington, Dickson and MacIntyre into the yard behind the guardroom and have them shot. He ordered seven men to accompany him as an escort for the prisoners. As they moved out of the guardroom, he bumped into Lieutenant William Dobbyn of the Royal Irish Fusiliers. Quickly he explained, "I'm taking these men out of the guardroom and I'm going to shoot them, as I think it's the right thing to do."

He marched the three unfortunates into the yard, then ordered them to walk by themselves to the far wall. As they obeyed, he ordered the escort party to present arms, then gave the command, "Fire!"

Lieutenant Dobbyn, on hearing the shots, hurried towards the yard and was in time to meet Bowen-Colthurst coming away. The captain seemed calm and not excited. While Dobbyn was examining the three bodies, he noticed a movement in one of Sheehy-Skeffington's legs and sent Lieutenant Tooley to the orderly room to report this to Bowen-Colthurst and to ask what was to be done. Bowen-Colthurst's reply was that they were to "Shoot again." Reluctantly, Dobbyn stood by while four soldiers complied with the order.

Fifteen minutes later, Bowen-Colthurst reported the shooting to Lieutenant Morgan, explaining that he feared an armed attempt might be made to rescue the men. He then mumbled something about having "lost a brother in this way" and that "I'm as good an Irishman as they are." As he crossed the barrack square on the way to the mess, he ran into Major James Rossborough, in temporary command of the barracks, and reported that he had shot three prisoners, adding, "I suppose I'll get into trouble for it." Rossborough, staggered by the callousness of the offence, could only stare at him in astonishment.

Although the military had drawn a tight ring round the Mendicity, Volunteer John MacLoughlin found it an easy matter to sneak in and out whenever he wished. By this time the youthful garrison were both hungry and short of ammunition, for Connolly had never intended that young Heuston, promoted Commandant on Easter Monday morning owing to the shortage of officers, should occupy the place for more than a few hours. Consequently no stocks of food and ammunition had been laid in. Heuston's role, as envisaged by Connolly, had been simply to harry any military advancing from Richmond or Royal Barracks and prevent them attacking the Four Courts before the rebels there could entrench themselves. In pursuance of these orders, Heuston had opened fire on the Dublin Fusiliers on Monday, as they marched to the relief of Dublin Castle, and since then he had been under continuous siege.

A tall, lanky lad, hardly sixteen, MacLoughlin had found it easy to move in and out because he was no different from a hundred other youngsters, who, drawn by curiosity, wandered at will about the area. He had managed to obtain small supplies of food and extra ammunition for the hard-pressed garrison, and to fetch and carry dispatches between Heuston and G.H.Q. Heuston himself, and almost his entire garrison, could probably have sneaked out of the institution almost any time without the military being any the wiser, but Heuston, encouraged by his success in keeping the military at bay, gallantly never thought of this alternative. By midday on Wednesday, however, there was no longer any question of anybody getting out.

MacLoughlin had sneaked through early that morning with a dispatch for Commandant Connolly. Towards noon, when he was returning via Queen Street Bridge, he heard the attack beginning on the Mendicity. At the bridge itself, large forces of troops were moving across under heavy fire. Despite the bullets, a crowd had collected at the north end of the bridge, enjoying the operation as though it were a football match. As MacLoughlin edged forward he was recognized by a woman, who shouted, "There's another of them!" MacLoughlin turned and ran until he reached the safety of Commandant Daly's headquarters in Church Street.

Meanwhile, the military pressed home their attack. One party, creeping stealthily under cover along the wall fronting the Mendicity, leaped up suddenly, to toss bomb after bomb through the windows, creating pandemonium inside. Quickly recovering, the young rebels courageously grabbed the bombs as they dropped on to the floor and hurled them back, a brave and desperate effort which cost them four men. After a ferocious and sustained attack lasting fifteen minutes, Heuston hung out a white flag, and thus, within an hour of the commencement of the operation, twenty young rebels were marched out to a rough reception from the infuriated Dublin Fusiliers.

This left General Lowe in a position now to draw the noose tight around the Four Courts.

Inside the noose, Daly had been struggling to maintain the brave spirit of the early hours of the insurrection. A hundred yards to the north of North King Street lay Linenhall Barracks, one of the oldest military establishments in Dublin. By 1916 the barracks were no longer used to house fighting troops, but had been turned over to the Army Pay Corps, forty of whose members had been cooped up inside it since the start of the Rebellion. Daly decided to attack it. Towards noon, a rebel party under Captain Denis O'Callaghan, marched up to the main gates and demanded the garrison's surrender. Courageously the half-trained soldiers refused to give in, and O'Callaghan was forced to blow a hole in the barracks wall. Once the rebels began to pour in, the garrison raised the white flag and were marched under escort to the Father Mathew Hall, where their services were requisitioned to help bake bread and fill sandbags.

Although aware that this was hardly tit-for-tat, Daly was satisfied; for the operation had achieved its primary aim, which was to make his men feel that all was not yet lost.

Towards midday the weight of military fire directed against the east side of Lower Sackville Street had finally begun to tell. Volunteer Lieutenant "Blimey" O'Connor (he had a cockney accent) and Volunteers O'Kelly and Bourke, finding they could no longer operate the wireless transmitter, obtained Connolly's permission to transfer vital parts to the G.P.O. with the intention of setting it up there again. During a lull, the party hurried across Sackville Street, carrying a few pieces of apparatus in an upturned table. When it became clear, however, that it would take at least half-a-dozen trips to transport all the material, Connolly called the plan off.

By 12.30 firing had become so desultory after the morning's fierce activity that a crowd ventured again to gather beside the grandiose monument to the great Emancipator, Daniel O'Connell, immediately to the north of the bridge. This appeared to irk the sniper in McBirney's, who opened fire on them, apparently with the idea of driving them away. At once a machine-gun started up in sympathy, and bullets danced off the O'Connell Monument, sending sparks in all directions. The crowd scattered across the bridge to the comparative shelter of D'Olier Street corner.

From the G.P.O. meanwhile, Connolly had been carefully observing the effect of the sustained fire on the D.B.C. cupola. He was worried that bullets from the machine guns might penetrate the fragile lead covering and wipe out the handful of men he had placed there. It was far more important to him that they stayed there and carried out observation than that they should attempt to use the cupola as a snipers' post. He had to know what each military move was, and from what direction and in what strength they were closing in upon him. For he felt certain that a direct assault on the Post Office could not be long delayed. Accordingly, he sent a messenger ordering these men to stop firing and give the military the impression that the place had been evacuated. Delivered orally, the message was misinterpreted and the tower *was* actually evacuated. Shortly before one o'clock, reporter O'Leary watched its garrison run across Sackville Street in single file, bullets kicking all around them. The last man across had wrapped a mattress around himself for protection, but half-way across, a bullet nipped through and it flopped to the ground. The man stumbled and fell, then picked himself up and raced to the Post Office as military snipers tried to pick him off.

Five minutes later, O'Leary saw a door open along Eden Quay and a blind man emerge. He puttered his way up to the corner, his white stick probing out in front. After a moment's hesitation he stepped down from the footpath and crossed towards the O'Connell Monument. Perhaps the McBirney sniper failed to realize that the man was blind; whatever his reason, he fired on him and the old man "fell wriggling to the ground." From the south end of the bridge, Mr. Henry Olds of St. John Ambulance Brigade ran to his aid. O'Leary saw Olds kneel down, take off the blind man's coat and bandage his wound. Then he helped the man to his feet and led him across the bridge. Ruthlessly, the McBirney sniper fired twice again, both shots finding their mark. The two men lay prone. Later, an ambulance drove on to the bridge, picked up the two bodies and drove away. . . .

A hush fell over the battlefield and O'Leary thought it an ominous prelude.

19

FROM TEN O'CLOCK onwards on Tuesday night, units of the 178th Brigade had been arriving at Kingstown. They consisted, for the most part, of a bewildered and seasick bunch of English Midlanders. Half of them still had the impression that they had landed in France, and even next morning a soldier greeted a girl, "Bonjour, ma'moiselle."

Food was short because kitchens and transport had not yet arrived. Most of the men had only their iron rations to munch on, supplemented by tuppenny sandwiches from stalls quickly set up by local entrepreneurs. Men of the 2/5th and 2/6th were luckier; for them there was crisp bacon and eggs under the pinetrees in school grounds about a mile outside the town.

For the officers there was a civilized breakfast at the Yacht Club and animated conversation with the members, who had information about the fighting. At 8.30 a.m. the Brigadier, Colonel Maconchy, called a conference of officers and issued these verbal instructions:

"(1) The rebels are known to be preparing to oppose the movement of troops from Kingstown to Dublin.
(2) Troops will therefore advance in two parallel columns; the left, consisting of the 2/5th and 2/6th Sherwood Foresters (Derbyshire troops) will advance by the inland Stillorgan-Donnybrook route; the right, comprising 2/7th and 2/8th (Notts. troops) will follow the coast road through Ballsbridge. Destination in both cases—the Royal Hospital, Kilmainham. Starting point: Kingstown Harbour 10.30 a.m.
(3) The right column will be led by the Robin Hoods (the 2/7th). Order of Companies: first 'C' Company (Captain F. Pragnell), second 'A' (Captain H. C. Wright), three 'B' (Major H. Hanson), four 'D' (Captain L. L. Cooper). O.C. Advance Guard will dispose his platoons as follows: one in advance, one to clear houses overlooking the road, one to deal with side roads, one in support. Every house and side road will be searched and cleared.
(4) Fall in: 10.15 a.m."

At 10 a.m. the troops charged magazines. Lieutenant-Colonel W. Coape Oates, an old Munster Fusilier who commanded the 2/8th, conscious that most of his men had seen less than three months' service, ordered them down to the quayside to carry out this dangerous operation "so that," as he put it later, "apart from the limited amount of danger to fishing smacks, little risk was run." Even so, shots peppered the clear Irish sky and Colonel Oates rode down on horseback and angrily warned, "Any man in any platoon who lets off a shot will be considered to have disgraced the whole platoon and will be sent back to England." Aboard a transport approaching the harbour was Wilfred Tunley of Field Ambulance, who remembered that they were ordered to "Keep your heads down, the rebels are sniping."

In fresh, glorious sunshine the 2/5th and 2/6th Sherwoods moved off. The Irish countryside was so quiet and peaceful that Colonel Oates found it quite impossible to imagine that less than six miles away "bloody murder" was taking place in the streets of Dublin. Fifteen minutes later the right column followed, with the 2/7th in the van, and the C.O., Lieutenant-Colonel Cecil Fane, C.M.G., D.S.O., an experienced cavalry officer and Mons veteran, leading the advance guard. Major F. Rayner headed the main body. The 2/8th followed at an interval of four hundred yards, contact between the two Battalions being maintained by Lieutenant W. Hewitt, commanding a party of Battalion scouts. Their minds filled with bloody details supplied in embellished form by a newspaper seller on Kingstown Pier, the men were hardly prepared for the welcome they received. As they reached the outer, well-to-do suburbs, hot and laden down with full marching equipment, doors opened and maids came down the steps with steaming pots of tea, followed by their mistresses bringing trays with cups. Chocolates, oranges, bananas, sandwiches, sweets were pressed on the men. "Thank God you've come," a woman told eighteen-year-old George Reynolds of "C" Company, as she pushed a bunch of grapes into his hand.

The officers welcomed the break. Expecting to be ambushed at any moment, they were grateful for the scraps of information eagerly offered. Some residents brought maps and field-glasses. Fortified, the right column resumed its march towards Ballsbridge. The left, after experiencing similar hospitable treatment, pressed on warily. But lacking anyone with the Irish experience of Colonel Oates, officers of the 2/5th and 2/6th suspected all hospitality and word was passed down the line that the troops were not to accept any gifts, especially of food and drink. Word filtered among the troops that the Sinn Feiners were trying to poison them, and by the time the column reached Donnybrook, men were swearing blindly that they had personally seen chaps keel over, foaming at the mouth and gripping their bellies.

For Captain F. C. Dietrichsen, in private life a Nottingham barrister, then Adjutant of the 2/7th, the march brought a pleasant surprise. Unknown to Dietrichsen, his wife, fearing Zeppelin raids, had sent their children from England to stay with her parents outside Dublin. The children happened to be standing on the pavement waving to the troops, when their father suddenly marched by. His fellow-officers saw Dietrichsen drop out of the column and fling his arms around the children. It was a joyful scene, carrying no hint of tragedy to come.

By midday, the right wing had reached Ballsbridge Showgrounds, where they glimpsed a mêlée of prize bulls, heifers, fine hunters and innumerable agricultural implements before Brigadier-General L. B. Carleton of the 177th Brigade and Colonel Maconchy set up temporary headquarters in Pembroke Town Hall. (Pembroke was one of Dublin's "independent" suburban townships, with its own local administration.) Useful, if mostly inaccurate, intelligence was gathered by staff, and Colonels Fane and Oates were told to expect strong opposition at Mount Street Bridge *where the rebels were known to be holding a school* on the right-hand side of the road. Fane was ordered to take this position and then push on into the city. After a short halt, the column resumed its march, moving more warily than ever. At approximately 12.15 p.m. it rested again, not far from an imposing residence known as Carrisbrooke House. People seemed friendly and gathered round to talk. Suddenly, several shots rang out.

Under fire for the first time in their lives, the young soldiers reacted with admirable coolness, and dispersed rapidly. The shots appeared to have come from Carrisbrooke House, so from the cover of walls and shop doorways, the troops answered back fiercely and smashed all the front windows. Rapid fire was kept both on the house, which in fact, was empty, and its gardens, where a few members of the Blackrock Company of Volunteers lurked, and then a small party advanced to seize the place. By then the rebels had decamped and Fane ordered the march to be resumed. Flankers were sent out in Indian file. Behind them the main body advanced slowly, at short intervals dropping flat on the roadway. Fane led the van along with Nottingham accountant Captain Frank Pragnell of "C" Company, Captain Dietrichsen, and a party of stretcher-bearers under Captain E. P. Stachell, R.A.M.C. Anxious about his right flank where the rebels were known to be entrenched on the railway line, he detached a platoon under twenty-year-old Lieutenant William Foster of Southwell, Nottinghamshire, to make a reconnaissance. Then, while still roughly a quarter of a mile from Mount Street Bridge, he halted his men. They were now into Northumberland Road itself and expected action at any moment. Ordering the main body under Major Rayner to wait in reserve in St. Mary's Road, Fane went ahead, accompanied by Captain Pragnell and his Company.

The school still lay out of sight round a slight bend in the road. On each side were substantial middle-class houses, with trim front lawns, and tiled passages leading up to the front steps. Northumberland Road seemed quiet and as well-ordered as Kensington. Bloodshed and violence seemed far away and quite unreal.

Meanwhile in the drawing-room of Clanwilliam House, seven young rebels squatted round an ornate occasional table, munching steak sandwiches. Beside them lay their rifles, sights set at three hundred yards. All morning they had listened to the far-off boom of a field gun and the crackle of steady rifle-fire. Time had dragged slowly. Young Tom Walsh, moving around the house, picked up a magazine or newspaper, glanced at it, put it down again; then returned to the window to gaze out at a vista which had become irksomely familiar.

Tom and his brother had spent the night in the back drawing-room, crouching in a red plush settee and two arm-chairs which they had pulled over to the windows, watching the sinister shadows in Lower Mount Street and fighting off a desire to sleep. Their Howth Mausers had rested in front of them, lying on folded rugs spread over a blanketful of coal—brought up from the cellar despite the objections of Reynolds, who kept reminding everyone of his promise to the owners to do as little damage to the house as possible. Beside them, also, lay a box of Mauser ammunition, the seals unbroken, bearing the label HAMBURG. Tom had two hundred rounds of ammunition for his rifle and a .45 revolver with sixty rounds, Jim a .32 with fifty. At eleven that morning, as Tom, using a piece of string, was pulling up a parcel of food brought to the house by his young brother, a man cycled past and shouted, "The British have landed in Kingstown and are marching on the city—yez'd better watch out!"

Reynolds at once ordered everyone to fix sights at three hundred yards. All knelt and prayed, then rose and went to their posts. There were three windows in the room. Patrick Doyle and Dick Murphy occupied the window on the right, Reynolds took the one in the centre and young Jimmy Doyle and Willie Ronan the one on the left. The two Walshs went back to their windows at the side and rear. Scared though he was, Tom Walsh opened his food parcel and realizing that this could well be their last meal on earth, he decided to share it.

"Here," he said, walking into the drawing-room and placing the parcel on the table, "help yourselves."

They were sitting there, munching quietly, glancing now and then out of the window up the Northumberland Road, when suddenly they heard a volley of shots.

Towards noon Jimmy Grace had noticed his sister Bridget and a Miss May Cullen of the Cumann na mBan coming along the Northumberland Road from Mount Street Bridge, carrying what appeared to be a bundle of food. They entered the gate of No. 25 and hammered on the front door. Cautiously, Grace leaned out and explained that he could not let them in— the door was barricaded.

"But we've got a dispatch for you," shouted his sister.

"In that case you'd better put it through the letter box," he said.

"What about the food?"

"Thanks all the same—but I'm afraid we'll have to do without it."

The dispatch was from Connolly, warning Malone that British troops had arrived at Kingstown during the night and were marching on Dublin. If they decided to enter the city along Northumberland Road, every effort was to be made to stop them.

"Well," said Malone, handing the slip of typed paper to Grace, "this is it, then!"

Grace read the message and murmured, "Yes, this is it."

Malone said, "I wonder should we move into Carrisbrooke House?" Situated half-a-mile further out towards Kingstown, the house should have been occupied by fourteen Volunteers from the Blackrock Company but Malone, while reconnoitering during the night, discovered that they had left it, and taken up isolated positions in the grounds and nearby fields. Carrisbrooke House was originally intended to be an important outpost of the Mount Street position. It stood at the fork of Pembroke and Northumberland Roads—Pembroke Road continuing left towards Baggot Street Bridge, Northumberland Road right towards Mount Street Bridge. If the English troops elected to fork left, they would outflank de Valera's whole position round Mount Street Bridge, and there would be nothing to stop them until they reached St. Stephen's Green. Malone had decided to move up to Carrisbrooke House when he glanced out of the bathroom window, which gave a view up the Northumberland Road towards Ballsbridge. Grace heard him call out and joined him.

"Look, Seamus!" said Malone.

Through the field-glasses which Malone handed him, Grace could see, near St. Mary's Road, several military officers, backed by a large body of troops, poring over maps. Swinging the glasses slightly, he focused them upon the quarter-mile of Northumberland Road which lay between him and the officers. Into his sights jumped the tight, strained faces of young English soldiers advancing towards them with fixed bayonets.

The first volley from No. 25 Northumberland Road, recalls Captain Frank Pragnell, claimed ten Sherwood Foresters—all of them youngsters who, but a few months earlier, had been clerks and shop assistants or workers in the leather, lace and tobacco industries; lads who had hardly learned how to fire a rifle.

A little surprised, because neither he nor Fane had expected to meet opposition until they were nearer the school, Pragnell yelled, "Drop!" and hit the ground. In that first terrible second it was impossible to tell where the shots had come from, except that they had come from close by. A second fusillade resolved some doubts. "There!" shouted Pragnell, pointing. "That house there. Prepare to fire!" And the youngsters, taking aim, fired a volley. Suddenly a young soldier dropped his rifle, clutching at his shoulder and crying out, "Oh God, I've been shot!" Pragnell wriggled over to help him. Then he bawled angrily, "Good God, man! You're not hurt—it's only the recoil. Pick up that rifle!"

For several minutes the troops remained pinned. Near Pragnell a young soldier screamed in agony as a bullet tore away a piece of his backside. Then, as Malone and Grace drew breath, Fane and Pragnell rose to their feet, and brandishing their swords bravely, shouted "Charge!"

In Clanwilliam House, Patrick Doyle, the oldest man there, shouted hoarsely, "For God's sake, keep steady!" Reynolds quite coolly gave the order,

"Remove safety catches." Then away up at Haddington Road, James Doyle saw a mass of khaki uniforms charging towards No. 25. Some dropped on one knee in the roadway to fire up at the windows while others charged courageously into the short passageway and up the stone steps to the hall doorway.

"Fire!" yelled Reynolds and the crash of the Howths in the confined space sounded as terrible as artillery. Seven soldiers fell and the rest scattered. Young Doyle saw flashes of fire spurt from No. 25 and Reynolds shouted "Good old Mick!" Doyle was so pleased with himself after his first taste of action that he felt capable of stopping the whole British Army if it came down the Northumberland Road.

To Malone and Grace, firing bullets into the Robin Hoods at point-blank range, the Tommies seemed utterly lost. On the other hand, Captain Pragnell remembers how, crouched in the lee of railings with Colonel Fane, they found it impossible to pinpoint the exact spot where the main fire was coming from; it appeared to come from half-a-dozen directions at the same time. In the end, Fane decided to lay down a heavy curtain of fire along both sides of the road, with special emphasis on No. 25, from which firing was certainly coming, and the school at the bridge, where, according to Intelligence, they would meet the main opposition. As yet, recalls Pragnell, they had no idea that they were being fired on from Clanwilliam House on the far side of the bridge, or from the Parochial Hall, a few doors down from No. 25. Fane also decided to outflank and then encircle No. 25 by sending Major Hanson and "B" Company up Haddington Road to secure Baggot Street Bridge and then filter back down along the Canal bank to Mount Street Bridge. For the tall, good-looking Fane it was to prove a costly decision.

As Hanson led his men towards the corner of Haddington Road the other companies sprayed the area indiscriminately in heavy support. "We listen to the sound of the battle," wrote a lady living nearby. "There seem to be many men engaged: we think there are some in our garden or on the steps. The soldiers are attacking the two corner houses—No. 25 opposite and No. 26 and 28 on our side of Northumberland Road."

As Hanson led his men into Haddington Road, Malone, crouched at the bathroom window with his high-powered "Peter the Painter", almost decimated the whole of the first wave. "We fear they are wavering," wrote the lady, "for I hear a voice shouting: 'You won't give way now, boys!'"

Despite his losses, Hanson pressed on. Once through the gauntlet he found himself in an oasis of peace, yet he advanced cautiously towards Baggot Street Bridge, having learned that appearances in this weird kind of fighting could be deceptive. Far cry, indeed, from the type of warfare for which he and the regiment had been trained—the trench warfare of France.

In Northumberland Road, the ramrod figure of Colonel Fane buckled as a bullet did terrible havoc to his left arm. Stretcher-bearers rushed forward but he waved them away and, calling on Major Rayner to take command, he staggered to the lee of houses on the same side of the road as No. 25, and had his wound treated. When Lieutenant Foster returned from his reconnaissance towards Beggar's Bush Barracks, he found Major Rayner, scorning cover, directing the battle from the centre of the road. His jacket had been cut to ribbons and a pocket flapped down where a bullet had torn it. It was an inspiring display of calm leadership, only equalled by the Colonel's own example when he returned, with his arm in a sling, and clearly in pain, to resume command.

The young recruits, undergoing their baptism of fire, bewildered by their inability to find or hit back at the lurking enemy, were steadied by the example of their two senior officers. Foster took cover in the garden of a house opposite No. 25, directing the fire of his men through the iron railings. Other companies occupied the windows of the houses beside him and kept up furious fire on the beleaguered rebels while their comrades attempted to advance towards Mount Street Bridge. But before they reached Haddington Road, concentrated fire from Malone and Grace claimed heavy casualties.

Inside No. 25, the two rebels found themselves in a strong position. Grace, firing from a top window, found enemy bullets either ploughing into the ceiling or striking the sill in front of him in a continuous patter. The enemy at this time appeared to be directing their main fire at the ground- and first-floor windows. Malone, from the bathroom window at the side of the house, found he could enfilade and cut to ribbons every attempt to advance past Haddington Road.

From Clanwilliam House, young Jimmy Doyle watched stretcher-bearers carrying the British wounded back to Ballsbridge. Now and then firing would cease altogether to allow ambulance men to pick up the dead and wounded. So far the military had not actually fired on Clanwilliam House, apparently still unaware that it was occupied. Presently the first chatter of machine-gun fire was heard, and George Reynolds asked if anyone could locate it. "It seems to be in the Baggot Street direction," he suggested. "By the way, be careful if you see anybody on the roofs over there—it could be Mick or Jimmy Grace trying to get away."

Doyle nodded and turned his attention back to Haddington Road. He watched as the military again attempted to storm Malone's post. There were brief flashes of fire from the house and again Reynolds roared, "Good old Mick—that's the stuff!"

At Baggot Street Bridge, Major Hanson, satisfied that the area was free of rebels, posted a platoon to guard the bridge and started doubling back along the Canal bank into Percy Place. He saw the low, huddled clump of buildings which was the school, the windows bright with the reflection of sunlight. He advanced cautiously.

The battle had been raging for almost an hour now. As yet, neither Tom Walsh nor his brother had been in action. Suddenly Tom, his ears cocking to the crackle of rifle-fire from beyond the bridge, saw a khaki figure dart out of

Percy Lane and run up the steps of a house four doors from the bridge. As the man hammered on the door, Tom had an easy target. He fired—for the first time in his life—and he paid for his inexperience and his neglect of company lectures; he felt a stunning blow and knew no more. His brother, who had been sent upstairs a short while before, watched a second soldier join the first at the door of the house, and fired. He saw one man drop and the other dive from the door and start running. Jim feverishly reloaded. His next shot hit the second man, and he, too, tumbled over.

To Hanson and his men, crouching under the Canal railings, it looked as though the two soldiers had been shot down from the house they had been attempting to enter. Immediately they opened fire on it. A lady in the house next door, who had been watching from her window through field-glasses, screamed and tumbled back into the room as a stray bullet hit her. Within seconds no less than fifty bullets had embedded themselves in the bedroom ceiling of the house under attack. Yelling fiercely to give themselves courage, the men charged forward under a screen of fire, and began battering on the front door. When they got inside, they found a terrified lady, Miss Scully, and her maid cowering behind a settee, and promptly arrested them.

Tom Walsh regained consciousness to find that a chunk of the window-sill in front of him—which was made of granite—had been blown away, and that he had been knocked out by the recoil of his own rifle. It took him several minutes to recover and he still felt shaky when he picked up the Howth again and peered out cautiously to see where the enemy were now. A number of them were trying to make their way down Percy Place, crouching and kneeling, then running in short dashes, before making for cover.

Under attack from the other men in the front drawing-room, they were dropping all over the place. It seemed as good a moment as any to join in. He cuddled the butt of the Howth tight against his shoulder and, swiftly running over in his mind all he could remember of the lectures on how to fire a rifle correctly, he squeezed the trigger. This time he did it right. The bullet crossed the bright Canal and struck somewhere among the crouching, darting soldiers, but Tom was unable to tell whether he had hit anyone.

20

AT TWO O'CLOCK that afternoon the military began occupying build-ings along Aston Quay, where reporter John O'Leary sat watching Sackville Street through his twin-mirrored periscope. Quickly they posi-tioned themselves at windows or swarmed out on to the roofs, placing a machine-gun behind the parapet of Purcell's, which stood on the apex of the triangular block dividing Westmoreland and D'Olier Streets. From across the river the rebels in Kelly's observed this movement, and bullets began to pep-per O'Leary's window. Two carried away the upper mirror of his periscope, showering glass over him and toppling him from his comfortable seat. He picked himself up, discovered he was unhurt and, quickly regaining courage, crouched down below the level of the window-sill and peered out.

The two 9-pounders from Trinity College opened fire almost simultaneous-ly. At their first report every pane of glass in the vicinity shattered; in Trinity itself the solid buildings quaked. In the G.P.O., the boom shook the walls, and the rebels looked at each other in consternation. No one quite knew what had happened and somebody shouted that the bombs downstairs must have blown up, but a second great boom resolved all doubts. It was artillery.

The shells cleaved the river and tore two fairly large holes in the façade of Kelly's. Simultaneously machine-guns on the tower of the Fire Station, the roof of the Custom House, the Tivoli Theatre, and Purcell's corner added to the battle noise. When James Stephens arrived at O'Connell Bridge a few minutes later, he counted six machine-guns in action. Rifles were also potting at Kelly's from every conceivable angle and, at regular intervals of half a minute, the 9-pounders would lob a shell through its windows.

The guns had been manhandled into position under the very noses of the rebels, who put up no opposition. After fruitless hours had been spent trying to dig holes for the recoil, Colonel Portal impatiently ordered that the guns were to be trundled into position, with or without holes, and brought into action at once. The Brunswick Street gate of Trinity was swung open shortly afterwards and horses were driven out, trailing the guns on limbers. The horses drew them into side streets where they were unlimbered and then manhandled on to the Quay by a party of O.T.C. and civilians. Under bom-bardment, clouds of red dust and smoke soon rose over Kelly's.

"Not even a fly can be alive in that house," said an awe-struck man beside Stephens, who already sensed that Sackville Street was doomed.

"What chance have they in the Post Office?" someone asked.

A tough-looking labourer answered fiercely, "None! And they never had, or never thought they would have." He nodded towards Kelly's. "That'll root them out quick enough."

A dozen or so men were clustered in a nearby lane, and suddenly Stephens heard a terrible flow of language coming from their direction. He turned. A young girl, no more than nineteen, was hurling the obscenities at them.

"Cowards—that's what you are! Why don't you march out into the streets like men? And them dying for you in Kelly's!" And then a stream of oaths.

Half-way up Sackville Street, Brennan Whitmore watched British bullets ricochet off the tramlines and hit the G.P.O. His own men, face down at the open windows, were doing their best to reply to the fire, especially from the military on the roof of Trinity College and on the D'Olier Street triangle. Suddenly he saw a small man in moleskin trousers, blue reefer coat, and peaked cap stagger out of Henry Street and sprawl flat on his face in the gutter. Behind him a woman screamed and then flung herself on top of him. Brennan Whitmore thought that she had also been shot, but a second later she got up and started calling out. Three men dashed out from the G.P.O. and carried the body into the shelter of Henry Street, the woman following, loudly lamenting.

Brennan Whitmore had been so engrossed that he had failed to notice a tall, lanky man in a bowler hat, carrying a light shower coat over his shoulder, careering down the middle of the tramlines amid a torrent of rifle and machine-gun bullets. Gloriously, ecstatically drunk, he was singing and waving his hands wildly as he zigzagged along in a series of fits and starts, which probably saved his life. One second he lurched forward, in a kind of jog trot; the next he wavered to a dead halt, blissfully unaware of danger.

From both sides of the street rebels bawled fierce warnings, but he stood there in the middle of the road, pivoting first on one heel and owlishly glaring about him at an extraordinarily noisy world that was entirely unfamiliar to him, then twisting back on the other. In the end he went careering away towards O'Connell Bridge, still somehow miraculously preserved, until at last he disappeared from sight.

When Brennan Whitmore was able to turn his attention to more important matters, he found that his telephone link to the G.P.O. had been wrecked. He therefore wrote out a message for Connolly and called for someone to volunteer to take it across the street. The senior Cumann na mBan woman stepped forward. "I need bandages, lint, and anaesthetics, anyway," she explained. "We're not likely to escape casualties."

"I'm sorry," said Brennan Whitmore shortly. "Obviously you can't go, but the man who goes across can bring those things back for you."

"But he wouldn't know where to look for them in the G.P.O.," she insisted with courageous obstinacy. In the end, despite misgivings about allowing a woman to carry out such a dangerous mission, Brennan Whitmore gave in.

The woman was not in uniform and her skirt swept the ground fashionably. It had to be slit down one side from just above the knee so that she could run. From the relative safety of his position in North Earl Street, Brennan Whitmore watched her race across Sackville Street, the slit skirt flapping wildly. Bullets flew at her, but she reached the far side safely.

Fifteen minutes later he saw her reappear in the doorway of the G.P.O. She put her head down and, with her arms full of medical supplies, commenced her return dash. Even while she was in the roadway another shell hit Kelly's, sending up a choking cloud of dust, and the machine-guns opened up again. Sparks flew off the street near her, but somehow or other nothing hit her and, panting fiercely, she reached North Earl Street where she collapsed in Brennan Whitmore's arms.

On the G.P.O. roof, Desmond Ryan was making the discovery that he possessed a stoic quality. Perhaps it was because he was weary and desperately needed sleep; perhaps it was because he was hungry, or possibly it was only because of the incessant noise. Whatever the cause, he began to lose the feeling that things were happening. Noise, shells, rifle-shots, machine-guns, even visual experiences such as the vast traceries of dust appearing along the façades of the buildings down near the river, all ceased to have meaning or reality.

Quartermaster Fitzgerald asked Captain Mahony to accompany him to the ground floor. "I want to show you our hospital," he said.

He led Mahony through a maze of men, sweaty, begrimed and somewhat apprehensive-looking, to a corner of the great public office where a number of wounded men lay on mattresses. Mahony ran an expert eye over the equipment arranged neatly on a counter. There were sterilizing needles, forceps, and surgical knives. At the other end of the counter, chucked down in a higgledy-piggledy fashion was a collection of stuff obviously commandeered from various chemists' shops by somebody who had no idea of medical needs. Among them was a veterinary thermometer for registering the temperature of cows.

A man lying on a mattress had been shot through the lung so Mahony gave him an injection of morphia. While he was engaged in this, a young man came up and introduced himself as McLoughlin of Derry. He was a "chronic", he said; for ten years he had been trying to qualify as a doctor and still could not get his degree.

"And then I was simply walking down Sackville Street when some of the boys saw me and shouted out 'Come in and help us.' Anyway, in I came—like a mug, I suppose. Now I don't see any way of getting out." And he grinned.

Up on the roof, Richard Humphreys lay flat and watched the machine-gun bullets ripping clouds of mortar from the D.B.C.'s Restaurant and peppering the Imperial Hotel. When the stream swept against the G.P.O., the men around him replied with an indiscriminate volley from their Howths. Pearse, accompanied, as usual, by his brother Willie, came up on the roof to observe the fighting and encourage his men. He looked calm and still gave an impression of great confidence although rumours had been heard all morning that a military assault was imminent. Throughout the great building, indeed, men crouched anxiously by bowls containing their shotgun ammunition, with stacks of reserve pikes and revolvers close at hand.

As each man steeled himself for the big attack, a venerable white-haired priest stumbled out on to the roof and, crouching down as far as he could, made his way towards the front where the defenders lay. Behind him crawled a young Dublin urchin, hardly twelve years old, who had managed to sneak into the building because the guards on the door thought he was with the priest. The priest gathered the men around him and explained that, as an attack was imminent, he intended to give them all conditional absolution. As the men lowered their heads reverentially a sudden flow of obscenities interrupted the solemn moment. The urchin was standing at the parapet, his face transfigured with a look of sheer exaltation.

"Janey, what don't I wish the fuggers!" he yelled at the top of his voice. "They're all s— and wind. Listen!" His face blazed excitedly as a shell thumped against Kelly's, followed by the low roar of Howth guns in reply. "D'ye hear that now! Ye'll wipe them out before you're done with them!"

"Clear out of here!" shouted a rebel. "What the hell are you doing here anyhow? . . . Pardon me, Father."

The priest smiled understandingly. Then he addressed the boy. "Listen, my son, this is no place for a lad like you. Go home now and leave the fighting to those whose business it is."

"But, Father . . ." protested the boy. He left the sentence unfinished as another shell boomed out across the city. "Janey," he said excitedly, "there goes another one! By God, I'd see them all in hell!"

The priest shrugged in mild despair and returned to the business of absolution.

"You understand what I mean by conditional absolution, men, don't you?" he asked, taking up where he had left off. "I shall ask each of you in turn if he is sorry, then pronounce absolution." The men remained kneeling, heads bowed, their hands clasping the long rifle-barrels, as the priest pronounced the Latin words.

He had scarcely left the roof, taking the urchin with him, when the men on the roof had to listen to a fresh hurricane of oaths and obscenities. Jack White, a Citizen Army officer, was a picturesque ex-sailor who had picked up an extraordinary vocabulary of scabrous words in seaports all over the world. The imminence of eternity had not diminished his gusto for life, and as he handed out canister bombs from a bundle that he was carrying, oaths poured from him in a wild and eloquent cascade. The contrast between the preceding quiet moment of reflection and exhortation and this terrible flow of language proved too much for most of the men. Surrounded by the habiliments of death and violence as they were, White brought a breath of familiar life to them. They roared with helpless laughter.

White left the roof in a final blaze of sulphurous language to which he was still giving vent when he reached the ground floor.

"Heaven help us all!" protested an extremely religious Volunteer. "Do you want the ground to open under us?"

"To hell with you and the ground both!" said White pleasantly, and strode on.

The outraged Volunteer was not prepared to leave it at that. He collected some friends, and they went after White to insist that he attend Confession.

"But I haven't been for fifteen years," spat the ex-sailor. "Why the hell should I go now?" and to emphasize his point, he let loose a string of blasphemies.

Father John Flanagan, unofficial chaplain to the garrison, intervened. Gently he explained to White that time was not necessarily an obstacle to making a good confession. The blaze died out of White's eyes and his face grew almost pensive. To everybody's relief, he finally agreed to make his peace with God.

There was little the rebels could now do but sit and wait. Sometimes they said the Rosary. A few more fervent than the rest, fingered Rosary beads or the holy scapulars around their necks. The waiting was worst for the men on the ground floor, as yet they had no targets—only empty streets to look at. For those on the upper floors or on the roof, there was at least the occasional flash of khaki as a soldier ran across a street opening. It had become obvious to everyone, of course, that they were hemmed in on at least three sides. Southward, the military held Dame Street, Trinity College, D'Olier Street corner and the Quays on the college side of the river as far as Butt Bridge. Eastward, they held the Custom House, Liberty Hall (or what was left of it), and Amiens Street railway station as well as numerous positions in Lower Abbey, Gardiner, and Talbot Streets. Here they were reported to have adopted rebel tactics and to have built barricades. Westward, they had been spotted moving now and then across the head of Upper Sackville Street, and they had a machine-gun on the roof of the Rotunda Hospital.

The insurgents—their senses and nerves increasingly under assault by the incessant chatter of Lewis and Vickers guns, and the intermittent noise of the artillery still attacking Kelly's—sought to hit back at their largely unseen enemy. From the roof of the Hibernian Bank, little John Reid, armed with a Howth Mauser almost as big as himself, attempted to pick off the khaki specks as they dashed briefly across Butt Bridge. Finally, however, the tremendous volume of machine-gun and small-arms fire, and the loss of Captain Tom Weafer, drove him and his comrades below.

From the Henry Street corner of the G.P.O., Volunteer Joseph Sweeny tried equally hard to knock over some of the khaki blurs dodging across Upper Sackville Street at the Parnell Monument. Once it seemed as if the big attack had really begun when an extraordinary contraption lurched into view. Sweeny blinked in astonishment; nothing like it had ever been seen in Dublin. Two months before Sir Douglas Haig would surprise the Germans by throwing thirty-six newly invented tanks into the Battle of the Somme,

General Lowe and Colonel Portal were trying out their own improvised armoured vehicles. They were Portal's idea. First he secured two big iron boilers from Guinness's Brewery and the Inchicore Railway Works. He asked the railway people to mount these on two motor lorries and in the sides had holes and slits bored through which troops could fire. Dummy holes were painted beside the real ones to confuse the rebels. Each boiler accommodated eighteen soldiers in some discomfort, but certainly offered comparative safety.

Sweeny watched the first of these iron-clad nightmares lumber down Sackville Street until it got as far as the Gresham Hotel, where it halted momentarily. Beside him Volunteer Sammy Reilly and several other men were blazing away at it, despite a terrible feeling of helplessness. No one was sure whether it had advanced merely on reconnaissance or whether it was the spearhead of an attack. Sweeny's weapon was a modern Lee-Enfield and he was a good shot; taking careful aim, he fired at the narrow slit in the front, hoping to hit the driver. His first three or four shots bounced off the armour, but one must have gone home because, after a jerky attempt to restart, the iron-clad stopped dead. For the remainder of the afternoon it lay immobilized, a stuffed prehistoric monster which belonged in a museum.

From the roof of the Metropole Hotel in the next block, Volunteer Charles Saurin enjoyed a superb panorama of the battle. Dublin, had it not been for the noise which never let up, seemed an almost-deserted city. The military hardly ever showed themselves. Saurin could see his comrades on the far side of the street, a few floors below him, lying flat at the windows, firing away, but he saw no targets. The most incongruous sight was of men and women sitting in the windows of Wynn's Hotel in Lower Abbey Street, watching the battle as from a theatre seat.

Pearse did little during this waiting phase except speak a quiet word or two now and then to some of his more intimate friends. Members of the Provisional Government had congregated on the ground floor, where they sat on some upturned barrels and talked. Pearse's favourite perch was a high stool near the main entrance. Beside the barrels were mattresses on which the leaders slept. Plunkett, now very ill, rarely rose from his. Connolly still moved among the men like a relentless machine, ticking them off for sloppy work, making them strengthen their defences, constantly finding them new tasks. He had already begun preliminary work towards securing an escape route, ordering the erection of barricades in Henry Street and Moore Street on the north side of the Post Office.

Clarke and MacDermott, neither of them military men, interfered as little as possible with Connolly's direction of the battle. Both still remained cheerful, Clarke especially so. Miss Mary Ryan, a member of Cumann na mBan, remembers him beaming every time another shell burst. "I have never seen him look happier—he was like a bride at a wedding," she recalls. And this despite the knowledge that time was running out; that their lives would soon be forfeit. Neither man had any illusions about the position. The population

of Dublin had not risen to join them. Not a single trade, political, or munic-
ipal society anywhere in Ireland had declared for the Republic. There had
never been any chance of a German landing or a massive Irish-American
invasion. The British had them surrounded and were bombarding Sackville
Street. Yet what did it matter? Every hour they held out, every shell that
destroyed yet another brick of Dublin, was a victory.

Feeling restless, Pearse, accompanied, of course, by his brother Willie,
climbed out on to the roof again just as a tremendous cross-fire of bullets
drenched Sackville Street. As Pearse and his brother, bending low, moved
towards the front of the roof, Lieutenant Michael Boland, O.C., out of sheer
habit, rapped out an order to keep under cover. Suddenly realizing that he
was talking to Pearse, he hastily apologized.

Pearse smiled. "Thank you, Lieutenant Boland," he said gently. Then,
looking around at the exhausted men, some of whom had been continuously
on duty on the roof since Monday afternoon, he promised, "I'll try to see to
it that you are relieved shortly."

The brothers stood for a while looking out over the roofs of the city. "A
curious business," remarked Willie at last, in his slow, lisping way. "I wonder
how it will all end." Pearse, absorbed in the scene below, did not reply. . . .

"What do you think of it all?" one of the men asked Lieutenant Boland
(a Boer War veteran) after Pearse had left the roof.

Boland shook his head. "It's a mad, bloody business," he said. "Here we
are, shut in, with all our leaders and the flags flying over our heads to let the
enemy know exactly where we are. Why didn't we take to the hills—and
fight like Boers? But I suppose all we can do now is stick it out!"

Brennan Whitmore, having moved into the Imperial Hotel, now faced the
problem of keeping in touch with Headquarters, since dispatches could no
longer be carried across the street through the bullets. If he could rig up a
line, he decided, messages could be passed back and forth. A search yielded
several balls of twine and some quarter-pound weights. One man flung a ball
of twine from the window, hoping it would land near the G.P.O. It barely
cleared the pavement. A second reached the middle of the road. A third rolled
into the gutter, and someone dashed out and pitched it up to the men in the
first-floor windows of the Post Office. A message attached to the twine asked
the men in the G.P.O. to run the line around a post and then fling it back.
This would make a two-way cable. It was soon done, but the first attempt to
send a message failed. When the canister holding the message was hauled in,
there was a neat bullet hole in it. Half an inch higher and the string cable
would have been snapped.

"For God's sake, simply tie the message on by itself," ordered Brennan
Whitmore. "They'll never see a bit of paper."

This was tried and it worked. But even as Brennan Whitmore stood at the
hotel window studying the progress of a message through field-glasses, he

heard a sudden whistling sound nearby and instinctively ducked. A tongue of smoke, flame and debris belched into the air beside the Post Office and a loud detonation followed. For a moment he thought the G.H.Q. had been hit. Then, as the smoke and dust cleared, he saw that the shell had struck the offices of the *Freeman's Journal*, organ of Redmond's Parliamentary Party. His men cheered loudly, and an answering shout floated back from the G.P.O.

Then suddenly, away to the right, a long way off, probably up near the Broadstone station, a great cloud of black smoke ascended into the air. Brennan Whitmore learned later that this was the work of Commandant Daly's men. Pressure in the Four Courts area had also been increasing steadily, although not with the intensity of that building up against the Post Office. The men guarding Daly's northern outposts, holding the high buildings beside Moore's Coach Factory, and in Clarke's Dairy at the corner of North Brunswick Street were constantly duelling with military snipers in the Broadstone station and houses in that area. The whole of Church Street was under long-range fire from across the Liffey—especially from a military sniper in the Bermingham Tower (who had chalked up fifty-three rebel casualties before he himself was killed on Saturday morning) and from the bell tower of Christ Church Cathedral. A machine-gun on the roof of Jervis Street Hospital constantly sprayed the area, but accurate sniping, with the aid of powerful field-glasses, by Volunteer Frank Shouldice, high up in Jameson's Malthouse off North King Street, drove them down.

With the steadily increasing military activity in the area, the beleaguered Lancers, holed up in the Medical Mission in Charles Street since Monday, grew bolder. Their snipers began to make it hot for the rebels inside the Four Courts. A carpenter called Murphy finally hit on the idea of burning the Lancers out by shooting a crude flaming arrow (made from a stick tied with rags soaked in petrol) through one of the Mission windows, but when it fell on the floor inside, the Lancers quickly put it out.

Daly's men—on the whole, probably as tough and as able as any of the rebel commandos—still retained most of their early buoyancy and confidence. They launched a sudden raid on the Bridewell Police Station and made prisoners of twenty-four policemen they found hiding in the cells. The D.M.P. had been there since the beginning of the Rebellion, subsisting on the skillet they normally served to their prisoners.

Captain Denis O'Callaghan and young Garry Holohan went back to the Linenhall Barracks, which they had captured earlier that morning. Daly, because of a shortage of men, had been unable to garrison it, yet somehow he had to deny it to the military who, if they recaptured it, would place themselves in the heart of his position. He therefore decided it should be set on fire. O'Callaghan and Holohan carted several drums of oil and paints from a nearby chemist's shop, sloshed them around the large room on the first floor, then set the place alight. O'Callaghan flung open the windows to feed the flames. These flared so rapidly and so fiercely that the two men found themselves almost trapped, and Holohan still recalls the terrible heat as they ran towards the door. Behind them smoke and flame ascended into the clear air. For a moment they lingered to look at the blaze, almost appalled at what they had done.

From the rebel positions in Lower Sackville Street, that smoky cloud looked ominous. All day long, nerves had been racked by the military onslaught. None had slept properly or eaten well since the Rebellion began; early feelings of triumph had given way first to boredom, then sheer weariness, and now fear. Under the circumstances, Connolly's order to the men in the D.B.C. cupola to cease firing—misinterpreted as an order to leave the whole building—was easily translatable into further sanction for a general evacuation of all the Lower Sackville positions. By late afternoon every building up to the Imperial Hotel had been left empty. First, under a Red Cross flag, a party of women and nurses had scrambled across Sackville Street from the Hibernian Bank, where a large Red Cross flag had been flying all day, the military holding their fire to allow them to cross. Then the men of different garrisons crossed singly. Something like panic had gripped them. Small in numbers, robbed of the steadying influence of their captain, Tom Weafer, who had died an agonizing death after being shot through the lung, they were scared by their first military attack.

Brennan Whitmore, watching the military close in, suddenly realized that by allowing themselves to be trapped inside the city instead of fighting from open country, they had lost the battle. A man beside him summed it up: "Another Irish Rebellion ending in blood and tears."

To Brennan Whitmore it seemed hopeless to continue fighting. The Howth rifle, which had to be reloaded after every bullet, was no match for artillery and machine-guns. Surrender was unthinkable. There was one alternative—to break out through the military cordon and escape into the countryside. There they might regroup and start the guerrilla warfare which Professor MacNeill had envisaged if ever the Irish Volunteers were forced to fight. Brennan Whitmore gently hinted at the idea to a couple of his senior men, asking them what the chances were of breaking northward through the military cordon. One thought it could be managed; he knew several back streets and alleyways through which he thought they might filter without being detected. Brennan Whitmore suggested that they sit down and work out a plan.

In the G.P.O., James Connolly lost his temper for the first and last time that week. He had a shrewd idea that the hurried evacuation of the D.B.C. cupola had been due less to a genuine misinterpretation of an order than to simple panic. The pattern of modern warfare, he knew, was to soften up the enemy by artillery fire before launching an infantry attack; and it seemed obvious that, once the guns had ceased firing, the military would advance at the charge across O'Connell Bridge. He intended to make that move as costly for them as he could. He asked for thirteen volunteers to reoccupy the buildings along Lower Sackville Street. Gallantly thirteen men, including most of the original garrison, recrossed the fire-swept street, utilizing the cover of Nelson Pillar. They gained North Earl Street without loss. From there they infiltrated along Marlborough Street and thence into Lower Abbey Street, where they had to run a gauntlet of fierce fire, so fierce that only eight men managed to reoccupy the D.B.C. block.

At five o'clock to the minute, following three hours of intermittent bombardment, the military fire ceased. Damage caused was slight despite the uproar. Kelly's looked much as it always had. Far from reducing it to rubble, the shrapnel shells had caused only slight damage. Five shells, piercing the brickwork, had left distinct holes not much larger than a man's hand. Not one window remained whole, but single panes of glass were left here and there. The interior, however, had been wrecked, and if the few rebels who had initially occupied the place had stood their ground, they must certainly have all been killed. As it was, once they had found themselves under fire, they had hurried back through the holes they had bored in the walls.

One thing was clear. At this rate of progress, it would take several weeks of intensive bombardment to drive the rebels out of Sackville Street.

Meanwhile Captain Bowen-Colthurst continued his personal campaign of extermination. While searching suspected premises in Camden Street, not far from Portobello Barracks, his men flushed out Volunteer Richard O'Carroll, a Dublin city councillor. Bowen-Colthurst marched O'Carroll into the backyard at the point of a revolver, remarking, "So you're a Sinn Feiner?"

"From the backbone out!" said O'Carroll defiantly.

Bowen-Colthurst hardly hesitated. He fired a bullet through O'Carroll's lung, and the rebel collapsed. As he lay writhing in pain, a soldier said, "Sir, he's not dead yet."

Bowen-Colthurst, who was striding away, glanced back.

"Never mind, he'll die later. Take him into the street." Two soldiers dragged O'Carroll outside, where he lay in the gutter until a passing bread van eventually picked him up. After living for ten days in agony, he died, exactly a fortnight before his wife gave birth to a baby.

Still on the rampage, Bowen-Colthurst claimed yet another victim. This time it was a youngster in his early teens, from whom the crazy captain demanded information. When the boy refused to speak, Bowen-Colthurst ordered him to kneel in the street and summarily shot him in the back of the head as he raised his hand to cross himself.

An hour later, Captain Edward Kelly of the Royal Irish Rifles walked into the mess at Portobello and found Bowen-Colthurst lying half across a table, his head resting on his arm. Kelly took a seat and watched him for a while. Occasionally Bowen-Colthurst would look up and stare across the room, then fall forward again. After a while Kelly went to Captain James MacTurk of the Royal Army Medical Corps. "For goodness' sake, keep an eye on Colthurst," Kelly warned. "I think he's off his head."

MacTurk decided to see Colthurst. He found him apparently rational enough, though obsessed by his behaviour that morning. "It's a terrible thing to shoot one's own countrymen, isn't it?" said Bowen-Colthurst.

By this time his maniacal activities—he had disposed of at least half-a-dozen persons in cold blood and with some degree of cruelty—had become known both to Dublin Castle and Irish Command H.Q. Neither evinced any interest in his behaviour or did anything about the murders. Bowen-Colthurst, after all, had considerable "pull" at the Castle; he had been A.D.C. to the former Viceroy, Lord Aberdeen, Wimborne's immediate predecessor. Major Rossborough, who was temporarily in command of Portobello, was a kindly man, but even when he learned of the cold-blooded shootings, felt inclined to leave well alone.

Bowen-Colthurst might well have continued his insane career until the Rebellion ended had it not been for Major Sir Francis Vane. No longer a young man, Vane had spent the greater part of the war travelling up and down Ireland addressing recruiting meetings, doing what he could to arouse the conscience of young Irish farmers to their duty as citizens of the Empire. On the outbreak of insurrection, he had hurried back from Bray, where he had been lunching with friends, to help organize the defences of Portobello under Major Rossborough. On his way back from posting snipers in Rathfarnham Town Hall early on Wednesday, he was disturbed to hear a crowd near the barracks shout at him, "Murderer, murderer!" Once inside he asked if anything had been happening, and was told about Bowen-Colthurst. Indignant—from what he already knew of Bowen-Colthurst he thought him a hysterical fanatic—he stormed in to see Rossborough, demanding Bowen-Colthurst's arrest. Rossborough pointed out that apparently neither the Castle nor Irish Command to whom the matter had been reported, wanted him to take action with regard to the captain, and that he was not prepared to defy his superiors. There was the feeling in the regiment, too, to be considered; there was hardly an officer in the place who favoured anything but the harshest penalties against the rebels.

"But think of the effect these murders will have on the reputation of the Army!" expostulated Vane. "Worse still, think of the effect they will have on America and on the Colonies where there are large numbers of Irish people."

In the end Vane persuaded Rossborough to confine Bowen-Colthurst to barracks, at least until the insurrection was over. Then he summoned a meeting of all officers under his command and read them a severe lecture on their duties and responsibilities under Martial Law. "If there are any other shootings like this," he warned them, "I will see to it that the perpetrators are held responsible for murder under Common Law, as soon as Martial Law has ceased."

Late that afternoon, General Lowe was able to issue a communiqué stating: "There is now a complete cordon of troops round the centre of the town on the north side of the river."

In Westminster, the Prime Minister, Mr. Asquith, reassuringly announced: "Steps have been taken to give full and accurate information to our friends abroad as to the real significance of this most recent German campaign."

Mr. Augustine Birrell, in turn, added: "We were anxious, indeed, during these last few days that news should not reach the neutral countries and particularly our friends in America, which would be calculated to give them an entirely false impression as to the importance of what has taken place. Therefore during the short period there has been a censorship—that, I hope, will be taken off almost at once."

21

SOMEWHERE UP Northumberland Road a piercing whistle sounded. Young Jimmy Doyle, kneeling at the left-hand window of the drawing-room in Clanwilliam House, saw an almost solid mass of English troops charging straight towards him. It was such a foolhardy thing to do that at first he was almost too astonished to fire. He saw some of them charge up the steps of No. 25 but the main force came on, led by their officers, easily identifiable by their Sam Browne belts and revolvers. Then suddenly the whole drawing-room erupted with explosive noise and he was firing as rapidly as his Italian Martini would allow.

It was sickening slaughter. Even as Doyle picked out two men and, one after the other, knocked them over, he could see that the soldiers who had charged No. 25 were being cut to ribbons. Fierce rifle-fire had burst from the Parochial Hall, too, as the main body got abreast of it—apparently they did not know that this also was held by the rebels. Of the sixty young Englishmen who had commenced the brave charge, less than a dozen got further than the Parochial Hall. Doyle saw with surprise that they were nearly all as young as he was. Somehow, it shocked him; he had never dreamed that the British Army could be simply young boys. But youngsters or not, as they funnelled up to the bridge, George Reynolds yelled, "Pick up your revolvers and let them have it!" A sheet of bullets flailed into them, knocking them over like nine-pins, and the survivors halted in their tracks, bewildered. They appeared to be confused as to their real objective and apparently had no idea from where exactly they were being hit. So they flattened on the roadway.

Their confusion was understandable. For most of the battle Colonel Fane and his officers were to maintain the fixed idea that their principal objective was the school. The hail of fire which caught them obliquely as they tried to charge No. 25 was thought to be coming not from Clanwilliam House but from the school buildings on the near side of the bridge. This fallacy and confusion persisted until late afternoon. It compounded the difficulties which were certainly not all of Fane's making.

The truth was that the 2/7th and 2/8th Sherwood Foresters had set off to march into Dublin, through territory known to be held by rebels, without a single bomb (hand grenade) or machine-gun—all of which had been left behind on the docksides at Liverpool. There the disorganization had been so complete that a whole company ("D" Company) of the 2/8th had been left behind when the rest of the Battalion had sailed. A little later, an entire battery of heavy guns was dropped into the River Mersey during loading operations. In addition both Irish Command and Brigade had erred in giving Fane incomplete and therefore inaccurate information about the strength of the rebel forces at Mount Street Bridge. And finally they had erred in ordering Fane to advance into the city by Northumberland Road and Lower Mount Street when there was at least one safer route open. Although badly wounded and suffering agonizing pain, Fane's personal bravery and coolness under fire did much to steady his bewildered young soldiers.

In Clanwilliam House, George Reynolds told his men: "If they charge again, the two men in the right window fire to the left: the two in the left fire to the right footpath and road, I'll take the middle of the road."

Below, on the far side of the bridge, the wounded were trying to slip off their heavy equipment, manoeuvre water bottles to their parched lips. In Percy Place, the heavy fire coming unexpectedly from the side of Clanwilliam House picked off Major Hanson's "B" Company men in devastating fashion. Hanson himself took cover behind the coping stones along the Canal bank and motioned his men to do likewise. To Tom Walsh, huddled in the back drawing-room of Clanwilliam House, a dry, cokey feeling filling his mouth, there was little to fire at but the slight humps of khaki haversacks on the far side of the silent Canal. He blazed away at these, though he had no way of telling whether his bullets were hitting the mark or not. Then he noticed that there was a small gate roughly opposite the fourth house up Percy Place and that inevitably, the khaki humps would have to negotiate this. He held his fire and waited for them to show.

Suddenly there was a khaki blur there. The Howth roared in his ears as he fired, but he could not tell whether he had hit anything or not. Again a blur showed and again he fired. From the room above he could hear the roar of his brother's Mauser as he joined in. Yet their fierce fire appeared to be having little or no effect: on came the camel humps. Then something astounding happened. Suddenly several doors opened along Percy Place and the residents came to their doorways holding aloft white sheets. Before Tom Walsh grasped their intentions, they had dashed down the steps. He saw them—men and women both— lifting khaki figures into the sheets, then staggering with them back up the steps and into the houses. He made no attempt to fire on them, nor did his brother.

Hanson's Company had suffered severely. Hanson himself, Second Lieutenant Lamb, and Second Lieutenant Hartshorn were early casualties. The officers gone, it had been left to Company Sergeant-Major Towlson to drive the men forward. But as he led them out on to the bridge, Company-Adjutant O'Donoghue and the three men with him in Robert's Yard for the first time opened fire. With only seven or eight men to back him up, Towlson could get no farther. Tom Walsh, in a frenzy, was pouring bullets on to the bridge. The big Howth bullets lay on a chair just beside his knee. He had to keep stooping, picking up a bullet and inserting it, firing, then ejecting the spent cartridge and firing again. The Mauser grew so hot in a short while that he had to stop firing altogether to allow it to cool. While waiting, he decided to go up and see how his brother was faring. He took a ramrod with him, for if Jim kept on firing as frantically as he had, his rifle would burst eventually. The din in the upstairs room was so intense that Jim did not hear him enter.

Tom moved carefully and tapped him on the shoulder. "For God's sake, mind yourself!" he warned, handing him the ramrod. "You'd better clean your rifle, the way you're firing it. Is it hot?"

Jim, his face blackened with powder, stroked the metal and grinned. "It isn't exactly cool."

When Tom got back to the room below, he found three holes neatly drilled through the wooden shutter, near where his head would have been had he not gone upstairs. What was particularly interesting was their angle of penetration. He glanced around the room. Near the wainscoting behind him were three scorched marks where the bullets had ploughed their way through the carpet. He crawled over, put his head down, and squinted back at the holes in the shutter. In the far distance rose the spire of St. Mary's Church, Haddington Road. They had evidently come from there. So he called Reynolds, and showed him the shutter holes and the burns in the carpet.

"H'm!" said Reynolds. For devout Catholics this posed a difficulty: could they fire on the house of God?

Meanwhile, Colonel Fane had decided to turn the right flank of the school. He had ordered Captain H. C. Wright and "A" Company to work their way around by Beggar's Bush Barracks (where the C.O., Colonel Frederick Shaw, unfortunately nabbed a platoon from him to help defend the place) and the first the rebels knew of this outflanking attempt was when Company-Adjutant O'Donoghue spied a single figure darting out of Grand Canal Street, furtively trying to pull aside one of the bread vans Simon Donnelly had put there as part of the barricade. O'Donoghue opened fire and the soldier "leaped into the air as though stung," and abruptly vanished.

Wright, of course, had almost blundered into de Valera's main position, and his men, circling cautiously around an enormous turf stack in Grand Canal Street, came under fire from Volunteer Joseph Guilfoyle, perched on a narrow platform high up in a railway tower between two giant water tanks. Guilfoyle's field of fire was almost blocked by one of the tanks, and he had to lean out to shoot around it. His attack on Wright's men, therefore, was hardly distinguished marksmanship, but at least it scattered them. Wright managed to regroup them and sent back for further instructions, the men meanwhile washing and shaving in the streets while they waited out of line of rebel fire.

At 2.45 p.m. Colonel Fane finally informed Brigade that, although he had taken Baggot Street Bridge, he was held up at Northumberland Road and urgently needed bombs and machine guns if he were to make progress. Irish

Command suggested that, as the Sherwoods' own supplies were still in Liverpool, Fane could try Captain Jeffares of the Elm Park Bombing School of Instruction, near Ballsbridge. Jeffares was contacted and agreed to help. Yes, he could let them have plenty of bombs. Better still, he would come along himself and throw a few.

As the long, golden afternoon advanced, Colonel Fane's efforts became increasingly desperate. The failure of Hanson to distract the rebel fire from the frontal attacks, and of Wright to outflank the bridge, left him with little alternative but to proceed more forcefully with his frontal attack. After an interval, he launched another determined charge. This met with exactly the same fate as the one which had preceded it. "D" Company, under Captain L. L. Cooper, which until then had been kept in reserve back in St. Mary's Road where the whole 2/8th Battalion waited for the Robin Hoods to clear a way for them, was hurriedly called up and told to occupy what windows and roofs they could around No. 25. Captain Pragnell was ordered to take "C" Company and reinforce Hanson, with the object of breaking through to Mount Street Bridge.

As Pragnell led his men round Haddington corner under covering fire from Cooper's men, Malone again brought his "Peter the Painter" into action with devastating effect. In the space of twenty yards, Pragnell lost at least ten men, including Lieutenant Hawken, but he had won through the gauntlet and was in the clear. Behind him Cooper's men opened what was perhaps the heaviest and most sustained assault yet on Malone's position. James Grace, inside No. 25, began, for the first time, to know the desperate feeling of being trapped, of experiencing the shattering effect of bullets zipping and zinging into the room he occupied. All he could do was to keep his head down and "tremble from head to foot in a panic of fear." The trembling disappeared only in the brief intervals when he was able to fire back.

There had been no movement for some time in Percy Place. Tom Walsh, crouching on his little settee, could hear the continuous crackle of rifle-fire from the front of the house, but he could see little or nothing himself. At the beginning of the fight George Reynolds had come in now and then to drop him a word of encouragement but for some time now, he had apparently been far too busy. Walsh decided to go upstairs again and see his brother.

Jim Walsh knelt quietly on an easy chair, waiting patiently for the military to show themselves again in Percy Place. For almost an hour there had not been a single movement along the far side of the Canal. The tree shadows had grown perceptibly longer on the still waters, broken now and then by a slight ripple as a gentle breeze stroked across them. With a jerk of his head Tom indicated that Jim should follow him. Together they padded down the stairs and crawled into the drawing-room on their hands and knees. Reynolds motioned them to the middle window. Jimmy Doyle and Willie Ronan were on their left, Richard Murphy and Patrick Doyle on their right. (James and Patrick were not related.)

In front of them stretched an unforgettable sight. There were khaki troops everywhere—crouched behind flights of front steps, behind the garden hedges, behind the trees lining Northumberland Road. And lying in the road; especially lying in the road. Four great khaki caterpillars pulsated towards them like obscene monsters. Two lines had stretched themselves in the gutters and two more crawled along on their bellies, jammed against the coping stones. It was not like killing men; it was more like trying to slaughter a great insect or animal. Tom Walsh at once opened fire and just kept on firing—at the men in the gutters. As one man was killed another crawled up and over him. When he, too, reached the head of the line, he was either killed or wounded. Sometimes, as the caterpillar tried to move forward—it could never advance beyond the group of dead and wounded at the entrance to the bridge—it appeared to be weaving from side to side as men elected to move around a dead or wounded body rather than risk crawling over it. Sometimes a few men at the head of the line would rise up and attempt to charge the bridge, generally led by an officer with drawn revolver. None ever got beyond the half-way mark.

Tom Walsh had forgotten all fear; he never, despite his intense religious emotions, dreamed of praying. No one talked. Every now and then, when a terrific spurt of fire flashed out from No. 25, George Reynolds would bellow, "Good old Mick!"—but that was all. Tom sometimes glanced quickly at Jim to make sure that he was all right, and they would exchange grins. Then suddenly Tom saw a clergyman dart forward from Lower Mount Street, coming from their rear, and run out on to the bridge, followed by two young girls. In sheer surprise he stopped firing and watched them kneel down among the bodies.

"Hold it, boys!" roared Reynolds, and then, leaning forward slightly, he shouted out of the window, "Get back, you women!" and ducked in again. Neither the girls nor the clergyman paid any attention, however, and other people also began to run forward. In a moment all firing died away and the battle stood, quite incredibly, suspended.

Redmond-Howard had never envisaged a battlefield as strange as this; as different from the trench warfare of the Western Front as chalk from cheese. On the city side of the bridge, continually edging closer to Clanwilliam House, was a massed crowd of civilians; the whole neighbourhood, it was clear, had turned out to watch the Thermopylae so improbably taking place on their doorsteps. "The soldiers were crouched along the roads and hedges like a great khaki caterpillar," he wrote later. "They were in the most exposed order so that if a rebel shot missed the first, it was bound to hit the second. For the most part the soldiers were boys, ignorant of the town. There was not an enemy in sight, only a mass of civilians up to within fifty yards in front of them and blocking the street. I saw them writhing in the roadway, struck by the terrible leaden bullets of the Sinn Feiners. I wanted to rush over and help."

Somebody warned him, however, that the rebels would open fire on him. "They'd fire on anybody, the blackguards," said the man.

"I don't believe that," said Redmond-Howard.

"Nor do I," said the Reverend Mr. Hall, a local Methodist minister. Together they walked down a laneway in the rear of Clanwilliam House, which took them to Sir Patrick Dun's Hospital on Grand Canal Street, directly facing Boland's Bakery. Here a number of doctors, surgeons, and nurses stood in the doorway trying to decide what they could do to help. Among them were two well-known medical men—Dr. Myles Keogh and Dr. C. B. O'Brien. All of them felt desperately that the wounded Tommies could not be left to die out there on the bridge. At Redmond-Howard's suggestion, they finally decided to advance under cover of the Red Cross and put the matter to the test. Redmond-Howard rigged himself out in a white coat and the small party, holding a Red Cross flag aloft, walked around to Mount Street Bridge.

The crowd opened a path for them and as they came into the clear space just before the bridge, Redmond-Howard saw bodies lying on the bridge itself in prodigal confusion, and on the far side, two great caterpillars still pulsing forward irresistibly. As they reached the side of Clanwilliam House, two young girls—sixteen-year-old Kathleen Pierce and seventeen-year-old Lou Nolan—came out, from among the crowd, carrying two big white jugs of water. Impatiently the girls ran ahead of Mr. Hall, and the clergyman, anxious for their safety, also broke into a run. A great shout went up from the crowd as the girls rushed into the firing zone and knelt to give water to the wounded and dying. The military fire died away and the battlefield grew silent save for the moanings of the wounded and the faint shouts of "Water, water!" Meanwhile Dr. Keogh and Dr. O'Brien marched to the front of Clanwilliam House, their hands raised above their heads, and shouted up that they wanted rebel permission to remove the wounded.

George Reynolds briefly raised his head and looked down at them. "Go ahead!" he shouted.

On to the bridge ran fourteen nurses and several young doctors and civilians. There were not enough stretchers, so the wounded had to be hoisted on to the backs of the doctors, or carried away one at a time by two or three nurses.

The lull was brief. Young Jimmy Doyle saw the military begin edging up, taking advantage of the ceasefire to work themselves into more favourable positions. Suddenly from the direction of Haddington Road there sounded a whistle blast, and down the road came the Robin Hoods, shouting, "Good old Notts!"

"Fire!" shouted Reynolds. "But for God's sake be careful of the nurses!"

Spurts of flame broke from the Parochial Hall, and from O'Donoghue and his men in Robert's yard. Once again only a handful of the brave youngsters reached the bridge. Their bodies fell in heaps at its approach, and the aprons of the nurses, who darted to their succour in the brief interludes between firing, grew more and more bloodstained.

As progress continued slow and casualties mounted, the Brigadier, Colonel Maconchy, ordered Colonel Oates, whose Battalion, the 2/8th, had so far taken no direct part in the battle, to detach a company on the right flank and try and turn the position at the bridge. Oates at once ordered Captain Quibell to take "A" Company and work his way round Beggar's Bush Barracks along the same route taken earlier by Wright. The men had scarcely moved off, however, when a countermanding order arrived from General Lowe. He wanted no diversionary tactics; the Sherwoods must press the matter frontally. The order was delivered in a peremptory, impatient manner; clearly Lowe had the impression that the Sherwoods were making surprisingly heavy weather of what was only a relatively simple job. Maconchy decided to move up to Northumberland Road and see for himself what was wrong. He rode on horseback through the township of Ballsbridge, where the Spring Show still carried on as though nothing untoward were happening less than a mile away. Nearing Mount Street Bridge, he saw crowds gathered in the roadway and white-aproned maids out on the doorsteps or leaning out of upstairs windows. Some people cheered him and it was clear that most of the inhabitants, at least, were friendly towards his troops.

Fane made no attempt to belittle the serious nature of the position. "The second-seventh can't take it alone," he said firmly. "If it has to be taken—and I don't see why—then it will take the second-eighth as well to do it."

Maconchy nodded grimly and rode back towards Ballsbridge where he got through by telephone to General Lowe personally. Quickly he sketched in the difficulties of the situation emphasizing that the 2/7th Battalion had been badly cut up.

"The bridge *can* be taken," said Maconchy, "but I'll have to throw in the second-eighth as well, and there'll be heavy casualties. Is the situation sufficiently serious to demand the taking of this position at all costs?"

"I think it is," replied General Lowe, shortly.

At 4.40 Maconchy sent for Oates, who at once rode back on his horse to Ballsbridge.

"The second-seventh have suffered terribly, as you know," began Maconchy. "Fane is wounded and so are most of his officers. I've just heard that Captain Dietrichsen has died. I don't think it's fair to expect them to take the school; their casualties have been heavy and they've been under fire all afternoon. I want you to come through with the second-eighth and get on with the job. I want your battalion to storm the Mount Street Schools—at all costs, *at all costs*, mind you, and penetrate further if you can."

"Very good, sir," said Oates and saluted.

Captain Pragnell, nearing the school, paused to admire the courage of the nurses, who were still working on the bridge despite the heavy rifle-fire. Then he led the way out of Percy Lane, where he and his men had taken shelter as they filtered down Percy Place, and dashed across the road towards the Canal, only to be caught in a tremendous cross-fire from the other side of the water.

In Clanwilliam House, George Reynolds had watched him coming and had warned his men: "That lane must be kept open—it's the line of retreat for Mick and Grace." Every rifle in the drawing-room was therefore focused on Pragnell's Company.

In Robert's Yard, Company-Adjutant O'Donoghue placed his rifle in a fixed position so that it covered the gap in the railings noticed earlier by Tom Walsh; now he lay flat on the roof of a small shed and, protected by a low wall, fired blindly as one of his men, "spotting" for him, cried excitedly, "You're on target; one has just rolled down the grassy bank."

Pragnell reached the bridge with fewer than half-a-dozen men, bullets zipping about them like angry insects. He flung himself to the roadway at the entrance to the bridge and started to crawl, shouting at his men to follow. Abruptly he gave an agonized cry as an excruciating pain shot up his left arm. His revolver clattered to the ground and, as he twisted around trying to escape the pain, a terrible thump hit one shoulder, and blackness descended on him.

Still the Sherwoods continued to attack. At twenty-minute intervals the whistle would blow and yet another wave would make a frontal charge on the bridge. When this, too, had been mown down, the doctors and nurses from Sir Patrick Dun's would rush out and rescue as many of the wounded as they could before the whistle blew again and the tactics were repeated. In Robert's Yard, O'Donoghue wondered why the English did not advance in more rapid waves—if they had, he believed, he and his comrades must inevitably have been quickly overwhelmed.

Once, indeed, the Sherwoods actually got across the bridge. Lacking officers or even N.C.O.s, however, the young soldiers, by the time they had got this far, were in disarray. They leaped over the Canal wall, taking cover on the Clanwilliam side of the bridge, right under the rebel guns, unable even to raise their heads. From their shouts of distress, O'Donoghue realized that many of them were wounded and ordered his men to hold their fire, which gave some of them a chance to crawl to safety under the bridge.

Physically his own men had begun to suffer from the continuous action and the strong sun. The heat, bouncing back off the tar and sanded roof of the shed on which they were lying, caused discomfort little short of real torture. They were behaving well, however, remaining calm and saving precious ammunition by firing only when they had chosen a precise target. Midway through the afternoon O'Donoghue sent a man back to Boland's to ask when they could expect relief.

He returned with the discouraging order, "There are no reliefs. Hang on."

Failure to reinforce or relieve the hard-pressed garrison at the bridge remains one of the most extraordinary aspects of the battle of Mount Street. Seventeen men had kept a whole English battalion at bay for almost five hours of bloody and continuous fighting, yet de Valera never made any serious attempt to help them. Some six hundred yards up Northumberland Road, the 2/8th Sherwoods had lain inactive for most of the afternoon in St. Mary's Road. Although his men held the nearby railway line and could have sallied forth along a number of avenues to sow chaos and panic in the enemy's rear, de Valera did nothing towards relieving the pressure being inexorably exerted against the Mount Street Bridge position. All afternoon his Battalion H.Q. staff lay doggo, apparently waiting for their outposts to give way—as they inevitably must—and the military to switch their main attack to Boland's. It is true, of course, that the main position was being constantly sniped at from Beggar's Bush Barracks and that Wright's outflanking attempt had been sufficiently harried to deter it. But as the afternoon wore on and it became clear that the great weight was against the bridge itself a less anxious attitude might have been expected even only as a diversion.

At 5 p.m. a dramatic change came over the situation. Captain Jeffares arrived with bomb and machine-gun reinforcements and inside half an hour no less than three separate bombing attacks were launched against Malone's position. One bomb, landing on five hundred rounds of Howth ammunition, left lying on a bed, almost wrecked the room. But both Malone and Grace kept up a ferocious fire, darting from the front to the side of the house and back again, changing weapons when those they were using grew overheated. Somehow or other they repulsed the early charges. But at the end of the third charge, a squad of Captain Jeffares's men was ready to blow in the door. Corporal H. Hutchinson and Private J. E. Booth, of the 2/7th Battalion bombing section, crawled forward on their stomachs under heavy covering fire and attached slabs of guncotton to the door handle. Then they retreated and the door, or most of it, disappeared in an explosive cloud. The men of "B" Company charged inside as the defenders pumped lead into them at point-blank range, but for some time they made no attempt to penetrate the stairs which were booby-trapped.

At 5.50 p.m. Colonel Oates called a conference of his officers and senior N.C.O.s in St. Mary's Road and explained that the 2/8th were about to enter the fight.

"Round the bend of the road, on the right, is the School and several houses strongly held. These must be taken tonight at all costs. 'B' Company will lead, 'A' will be in close support to press the attack home and 'C' Company will remain in reserve. Start in three minutes. Once under fire, move quickly." And the old Boer War veteran gave his venerable white moustache a business-like twirl.

With Colonel Maconchy, the Brigadier, accompanying him, Oates led the way down Northumberland Road. By that time No. 25 had been silenced and the old Colonel, with the Brigadier watching, stood on the west side of the road just beyond the intersection of Haddington Road and pointed out the school. At 6 p.m. precisely, "B" Company, led by Lieutenant Daffen, began moving along the west side of the road, losing men right from the start and being finally checked just opposite the school. Captain Quibell, leading

"A" Company and realizing that the hottest fire was being directed to the west side of the road, moved over to the right.

Lieutenant Foster led his men after Quibell's. Directing withering fire both on the school and on Clanwilliam House up ahead, they succeeded in climbing the railings and breaking into the school-yard. Foster himself rushed a window, broke it, and flung himself in, expecting to be blasted at point-blank range by the Sinn Feiners. Incredibly, he found the place empty and a hurried search disclosed only the dead bodies of the caretaker and his wife, lying in the grounds. With a platoon, Foster edged out of the school and darted towards the low parapet wall immediately facing Clanwilliam Terrace.

His men began firing over this wall and the Canal, raking Clanwilliam House and the house next to it. Foster was delighted to find himself so cool and unflustered under fire (it was his first time in action) and he was almost enjoying himself. He ordered his men to distribute their fire carefully, each picking a window. To his annoyance their first efforts were amateurish; not a single man managed even to hit Clanwilliam House. In disgust, he roared at Corporal Warren, "How is it that normally this platoon has plenty of excellent marksmen and first-class shots and yet now you can't hit a whole terrace at fifty yards' range?" As the fight continued, however, their marksmanship improved.

Meantime Lieutenant Daffen led yet another charge across Mount Street Bridge. Backed up by Lieutenant Browne, he almost succeeded in reaching Clanwilliam House, but just beyond the north-west corner of the bridge, he was killed outright and Browne fatally wounded. The 2/8th, like the 2/7th, were finding it no easier to shift the rebels.

22

FROM THE BELL tower of St. Mary's Church, Haddington Road, three sharpshooters plugged away steadily at No. 25 Northumberland Road, at intervals varying the target to back up the troops charging Clanwilliam House. From five o'clock on they were reinforced by a machine-gun.

In No. 26 Northumberland Road, where Captain Dietrichsen had died, and the wounded lay stretched on the dining-room floor, the lady resident and her mother narrowly escaped death as a bullet crashed through a window, shattering the mirror over the mantlepiece. Upstairs was no safer.

They had hardly taken shelter there when a window was blown out. On the far side of the Canal a bullet entered No. 20 Delahunty's Buildings, passed through Mrs. Elizabeth Kane, killing her and wounding her daughter Nan, standing immediately behind her. Miss Henrietta Mitchell, a rheumatic invalid, forgetting her illness for a moment, ran out of her house into Mount Street to watch the Sherwoods attack and found herself—as though by a miracle—permanently cured. Miss Ethel Walsh, looking from her window, saw little Mr. Hayter, a local grocer, foolishly dart into the road and get himself killed; then twelve bullets shattered the window where she was standing, showering her with glass. Emily and Gertrude Byrne, aged seventeen and nineteen respectively, sent to get milk, crawled on their stomachs across the garden and, in Warrington Place, saw a man just in front of them shot dead. Little Mary Brady excitedly tugged at her mother's hand demanding, "What are all the bangs about, Mummy?" "Hush," soothed her mother. "They're only firecrackers."

By this time both Malone and Grace had undergone almost every emotion it is possible to experience so near the edge of death; they had, in turn, felt both exhilarated and panic-stricken; yet at no time had they considered surrender or its alternative—escape. As their ordeal grew worse, as hopes of relief or even reinforcement vanished, they resigned themselves to the inevitable. But while they had a bullet left to fire, they were determined to fire it.

According to Grace's own account written afterwards, it was almost 8.30 in the evening (the military say it was shortly after 6 p.m.) when, after a particularly heavy bombing attack—probably when the door was blown in—Malone ordered him to the ground floor. He got downstairs safely and was standing in the hall, waiting for Malone to join him, when he heard movements in one of the rooms off it and saw a door handle turning. He opened fire through the door and heard a sudden rush of feet scuffling away in the opposing direction. Seconds later there was a crash of glass, the back door was burst open, and troops rushed in. Grace, emptying a fresh clip at them, dived for the stairs to the basement even as he heard Malone shout down, "All right, Seamus, I'm coming."

There was another rush of feet, several soldiers appeared at the head of the basement stairs, and he fired on them. There was a lot of scuffling above, shouts of "Get him! Get him!" and then a volley of shots in which Malone must have died as he came down the stairs.

Grace rushed to a small cellar window and saw an officer leading men up the steps of the front entrance. He opened fire, dropping the officer and scattering the men. Then his automatic jammed. Desperately he ran into the basement scullery and held the barrel under the water tap to cool it, quickly dried it, and loaded a fresh clip. As he prepared to fire again through chinks in the kitchen window shutters, two bombs were flung into the basement— one exploding at the kitchen door to his right, the other beside the window of a small cellar opening off the kitchen—driving him to take shelter behind the gas cooker. It had grown dark now, so that when the military came to search for him, they passed within a few feet without seeing him. And there he remained until the noise of the search died away and the sounds of battle grew less.

Sheer weight of numbers and weapons had begun to tell. With No. 25 Northumberland Road gone, the four insurgents holding the Parochial Hall attempted to escape by the back, but were caught in Percy Lane. By 7 p.m. only Clanwilliam House itself and the men in Robert's Yard barred the way to Trinity College.

Suddenly, the machine-gun positioned in the belfry of Haddington Road Church began chattering furiously and within seconds every window sash in Clanwilliam House had been cut to pieces. Through field-glasses Reynolds tried to fix the gun's position accurately. He had again spotted soldiers filtering out of Percy Lane on to the side of the Canal, and repeated fiercely, "That lane must be kept open. It's the only line of retreat Mick and Grace have." Moments later he had muttered something about Patrick Doyle and himself going across into Warrington Place to take up a position at the Canal wall opposite the lane, so as to give the two men cover if they should make a break for it. The machine-gun opened up again as he spoke and he quickly abandoned the idea as impracticable.

On came the 2/8th again in a really determined advance. Jimmy Doyle's Martini jammed and Reynolds scrambled into a corner and asked the men to pass their rifles to him for quick cleaning. Doyle watched horrified as the military rushed the bridge and some half-dozen soldiers actually reached the railings right below him. He saw one soldier fling back his arm and throw something. This was followed by an immediate explosion downstairs. But

Reynolds continued calmly to clean the rifles, even as there were further explosions below. Second by second it was becoming more and more difficult to return the heavy fire and to hold back the soldiers. Several gained the cover of an advertisement hoarding directly opposite and, although Doyle and his comrades plastered it until it looked like a sieve, they were unable to drive back the English.

The drawing-room was thoroughly wrecked by now, but somehow or other the crystal chandelier had not been destroyed. The bullets, however, were beginning to carry away bits of it, adding a curious tinkling harmony to the odd orchestration caused by pieces of plaster crashing down on to the grand piano and bullets pinging against the wires. Fire became so intense that Reynolds, hoping to draw some of it off, ordered Jimmy Doyle and Willie Ronan to go to the windows upstairs. They crawled out of the room on their hands and knees and then discovered that the stairs were almost unusable. Two steps had been practically obliterated and the remains were hanging together tenuously. Walls had been completely stripped of plaster and a water pipe sliced into, so that a great jet of water was springing out. By flattening themselves against a wall and sidling up an inch at a time they were able to get upstairs. Ronan took over the room directly facing Mount Street Bridge, Doyle the one at the side of the house overlooking Lower Mount Street, Warrington Place, the Canal itself, and on the other side of it, Percy Place.

Downstairs in the drawing-room, the bullets continued to jangle into the piano wires as though a mad musician were playing. The great chandelier disgorged its last shower of crystal and parts of the room were already smouldering. Unpleasant-smelling smoke curled up from the upholstery, chairs, settees, carpets, and curtains.

Still Patrick Doyle was enjoying himself. Even as the military pressed forward with new energy and the rate of fire reached a new intensity, he kept roaring, "Boys, isn't this a great day for Ireland?"

"Isn't it that!" said Tom Walsh, between bullets.

"Did I ever think I'd live to see a day like this!" bellowed Doyle happily. "Shouldn't we all be grateful to the good God that He's allowed us to take part in a fight like this?" Then suddenly he was no longer saying anything.

"What's wrong with him?" Tom asked his brother. Jim spoke to Doyle, but got no reply, so he tugged his coat. Doyle fell over into his arms—shot through the head. Jim laid him gently down and, together with Dick Murphy, the brothers said a short prayer.

To make up for Doyle's loss, Tom Walsh decided to rig up a dressmaker's dummy he had discovered downstairs the previous night and had brought up to play a joke on the lads. He had placed it on the landing with a hat on its head, and in the dark it had been easy to mistake it for a human figure. There had been a few moments of panic when it was first seen. Now he dragged the dummy in, placed Doyle's hat and his own jacket on it, and set it near the window. Within seconds it had been riddled. Then the small red settee he and his brother were kneeling on caught fire. Jim picked up the siphon bottle with which they had been cooling their rifles, squirted a jet of water on the fire, and put it out. He turned the nozzle towards his own parched mouth and prepared to drink. Just then the bottle shattered in his hand.

A few minutes later Dick Murphy went quiet. Jim touched him gently and found he was dead. By now the room was in a frightful condition. Bullets still shattered into the walls and ceilings, cut the chopped-up window frames into slivers; pictures and bric-à-brac littered the floor while plaster dropped from the ceiling in a continual rain. The piano still jangled out its crazy tunes, and choking smoke filled the room as more pieces of carpet and upholstery burst into flame. Outside whistles were sounding all along the Canal bank. Someone bawled "Surrender!"—and Reynolds replied by emptying his revolver. Then he left the room to see how the men upstairs were faring.

By themselves now, the Walshs found it no longer possible to keep firing from their positions. They decided that they were next for it, so they crawled out onto the landing and began negotiating the wrecked stairs. In the upper back bedroom, Jimmy Doyle climbed on to a table he had pushed over to the window and had begun firing on troops moving from Percy Lane towards the bridge when there was an explosion near him. . . . He regained consciousness to find himself lying on the floor with George Reynolds bending over him, wiping blood from his face.

"You're all right, Jimmy," said Reynolds, "but I'm afraid the rifle is finished." Doyle saw his Martini lying on the floor, its stock split. Reynolds said, "Here, take mine—there's a spare one downstairs." As he spoke, there was a series of explosions below and, satisfied that Doyle was all right again, Reynolds left the room. He had hardly done so when there was a terrific explosion on the roof. A shower of plaster clonked down on Doyle's head and Ronan called out from the front room, "The place is on fire!"

Doyle crawled on hands and knees into the front room where he found the carpet smouldering. He was helping Ronan to stop it from spreading when Reynolds called him from the landing. Still on hands and knees, he crept out to join his officer. Smoke was coming from under the door of the room where the Wilsons had stored their valuables, "Here, give me a hand," said Reynolds, and together they rammed the door with their shoulders, forcing it open. Most of the ceiling had fallen and a mattress on the bed was burning furiously. They dragged the suitcases on to the landing, put out the fire, and shut the door again. Doyle pointed out that he was getting short of ammunition.

"Don't worry," said Reynolds. "We'll have more men and plenty of ammunition soon. So get back to your position. In the meantime take this." He handed Doyle ten rounds, then left him and went down the stairs.

Doyle returned to his position and saw that some military had managed to cross the bridge and were now crouched behind the Canal wall in Warrington Place. Tom Walsh, who had crawled back into the room just below Doyle when he found the wrecked stairs being plastered with bullets, watched them come down along the near side of the Canal while the main body massed ominously just beyond the bridge, under cover of the parapet and the bridge wall. There were more shouts of "Surrender!" followed by a sudden rush from Warrington Place. One soldier had his hand raised to toss a bomb when Walsh shot him; the bomb fell from his hand and exploded in a burst of light. Walsh knew then that the end could not be far off. The military were so close now that the house seemed to be rocking from the bomb explosions. Somewhere behind him he heard George Reynolds shout, "Come on, lads, we can't do any more. . . . "

Up until this time the fire from Clanwilliam House had been extremely fierce and accurate. To the desperate military, trying to carry the narrow pass, it seemed as though a whole army of men had ensconced themselves in the house—trained riflemen, whose every bullet seemed to claim a victim. Some were convinced that the rebels were using a machine-gun, the casualties were so appalling. Lieutenant Hewitt's platoon, for example, had been reduced to two men. Lieutenant C. P. Elliot's had been cut to ribbons and Elliot himself severely wounded. All officers and the Sergeant-Major and N.C.O.s of "B" Company had been either killed or wounded. Colonel Oates decided to call up his reserve company—"C" Company—under Captain Frank Cursham, a Nottinghamshire solicitor. Captain A. B. Leslie-Melville, Battalion Adjutant, anxious to experience action, joined Cursham's men but had advanced only a few paces towards the bridge when he was severely wounded. Cursham was forced to retreat.

Captain Quibell now led a strong assault force, consisting of Captain L. L. Cooper and Lieutenant William Foster and his platoon, out through the back of the school and onto the Canal path almost opposite Robert's Yard. Here they were reinforced by Cursham and Captain Branston, Second Lieutenant Curtis, and the survivors of "C" Company (whose losses during the day had been trifling). The low Canal wall gave ample protection, but the field of fire was impeded by the advertisement hoarding. Rebel fire penetrated and inflicted casualties. After a brief halt here, Quibell decided to try and rush the bridge. To support him, Colonel Oates led six men along Northumberland Road towards the bridge and concealed them carefully behind stone steps.

Quibell shouted to Lieutenant Hewitt, crouched behind the stone-work on the Percy Place side of the bridge with the only two survivors of his platoon, and then rose to his feet and charged. Both Hewitt and Foster backed him up and were followed by "C" Company under Cursham and Branston.

In Robert's Yard, O'Donoghue and his men knew that they had reached their last gasp. It had been a tough, desperate day, if a glorious one. In the considerable heat they had not had a single drop of water to drink, and it was now almost eight o'clock in the evening. Exhaustion was setting in and in the brief lulls while the military regrouped it was easy to dwell on the full extent of their plight. O'Donoghue had watched Quibell's men coming across the yard walls of the house opposite, exposing themselves to his fire as they leaped to the ground to take up positions for the final assault. At such close range it was difficult to miss, and he almost felt revulsion at the slaughter. Still, he had to keep banging away at the hoarding behind which most of his attackers were sheltering.

Quibell's charge from behind the hoarding was carried through with bravery and determination. Even so he was stopped dead half-way over Mount Street Bridge. "It was a bad moment," Foster recalls. "All we could do was to sham dead and lie still. There were piles of dead and wounded all around me. So I picked up a dead man's rifle (officers carried revolvers only) and opened fire."

For a moment the fire from Clanwilliam House died away and Quibell leaped to his feet. "Up and at them, lads!" he shouted, and the party—cheering wildly, jumping over the dead and wounded, tripping and falling over widely strewn equipment—darted and weaved towards Clanwilliam House. They found the door heavily barricaded.

In the final rush Quibell had been slightly nicked by a bullet, so Foster took charge and began battering at a window. He found this also heavily barricaded, but finally managed to force a way into the darkened room. The house was rocking from the explosion of bombs hurled by the other officers. At the front door Captain Cursham tried to lob a bomb through the drawing-room window on the first floor, but missed, and the bomb, bouncing back off the sill, exploded on top of him, wounding him fatally. Inside, Lieutenant Foster tip-toed across the room towards the hall door.

In the upper back bedroom of Clanwilliam House, Jimmy Doyle was knocked almost senseless by a tremendous explosion—which brought part of the ceiling down. He recovered to find himself choking in the thick smoke filling the room. From outside the military were still shouting, "Surrender! Surrender!" Then he heard Ronan call out and staggered through the smoke into the front room. "I think the roof's on fire," said Ronan, pointing. But he was interrupted by a wild shout from downstairs. It seemed to come from Tom Walsh. "Come on!" Doyle said to Ronan, and they raced for the stairs.

Tom Walsh had been firing more and more desperately as the soldiers closed in on the house, and George Reynolds, standing on the landing behind him, emptied his revolver through the drawing-room window. He had risen to his feet to do it, a gesture hard to understand, for bullets had riddled the landing all day. Walsh heard a crash behind him and, glancing round, saw that Reynolds had fallen. He crawled over, calling out to the others, and found that Reynolds had been shot in the thigh and was bleeding badly.

When Doyle and Ronan got down the stairs, they saw Reynolds lying in a pool of his own blood just inside the drawing-room door, and Tom Walsh trying to staunch the bleeding. Doyle noticed two dead men over near the window—Patrick Doyle crumpled on his side and Dick Murphy propped up as though he were still living, clutching a rifle. He helped Walsh drag Reynolds, who was apparently dying, out on to the landing. Reynolds asked for water and Doyle crawled back into the room to get some while the Walshs tried to make the wounded man comfortable—Tom saying an Act of Contrition into his ear. The military were now cheering wildly outside. Doyle filled a cup from a dirty basin—the water was scummy with fallen plaster and dust—and then crept back and put it to Reynolds's lips. The dying man drank greedily. When the cup was withdrawn, he murmured, "God," followed by "Mick, Mick!" and then his head slumped to one side.

Even years later, Doyle could not exactly recall what happened to him after that, not, that is, until he found himself outside Clanwilliam House, lying flat on the grass close to a garden wall, the area behind him lit by flames. Tom Walsh, however, remembers that when Reynolds died (and he is certain that he was dead when they left him), they all went down into the kitchen, in the basement. Here they were trapped, because they had barricaded the back door. There was a quick way out, however; through a small window not much bigger than a foot square. They wriggled through this into the back garden, then climbed the garden wall and finally separated when they got to the far side.

Lieutenant William Foster's account of the last moments inside the doomed house differs in one important detail from the rebel version. Foster says that when he began to ascend the staircase from the hall downstairs, he saw a rebel standing on the half-landing at the turn of the stairs. "I am absolutely confident that a man stood on the half-landing. He was in civilian clothes and, I think, armed, but it was dark and I can't be sure he had a revolver. I certainly shot this man when he was standing and looking at me, and as far as I can remember he fired also." Foster shot from the hip, then bayoneted the rebel (who could only have been the wounded Reynolds) and finally, satisfied that he had killed him, plunged forward as far as the door of the drawing-room. In a hasty glance in, he saw two men crouched by the windows. He had the impression that they were still firing, so he rolled a Mills bomb across the floor and slammed the door shut. There was an explosion and when he opened the door again the two Sinn Feiners lay sprawled out on the floor and a great spout of flame was jetting from the centre of the room and striking into the ceiling where the bomb had burst a gas pipe. Behind him his men passed up the stairs, and he heard more bombs going off in the upper rooms. He himself went downstairs and out into the street and found, with the fighting over, that he was shaking like a leaf. Clanwilliam House was burning furiously and Major Rayner said, "Perhaps we ought to send for the Fire Brigade."

"How *do* you send for the Fire Brigade?" somebody asked, and Foster, struck by the sheer incongruity of Rayner's remark, broke into laughter.

Three of the surviving rebels—William Ronan and the two Walshs—were meantime making their way over one garden wall after another at the back of the houses in Lower Mount Street. They reached Love Lane finally and, in desperation, knocked on the door of a cottage. A young girl answered.

Eamonn Ceannt
(Edmund Kent)

Grace Gifford, who married Joseph Plunkett the night before his execution

British troops in the ruined interior of the G.P.O. after the Rising

Eamon de Valera

Countess Markievicz in her Irish Citizen Army uniform

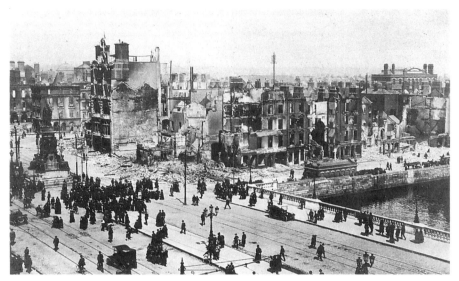

Two views of the destruction of Lower Sackville Street. The wide-angle shot was taken from the south side across O'Connell Bridge. The view below shows the O'Connell monument in the centre with destruction all around it. The camera is pointing down Eden Quay towards Liberty Hall and the Loopline Bridge, with the Custom House dome in the background.

In order to prevent the further slaughter of Dublin citizens, and in the hope of saving the lives of our followers now surrounded and hopelessly outnumbered, the members of the Provisional Government present at Head-Quarters have agreed to an unconditional surrender, and the Commandants of the various districts in the City and Country will order their commands to lay down arms.

P. H. Pearse
29th April 1916
3.45 p.m.

I agree to these conditions for the men only under my own Command in the Moore Street District and for the men in the Stephen's Green Command.

James Connolly
April 29/16

On consultation with Commandant Ceannt and other officers I have decided to agree to unconditional surrender also

Thomas MacDonagh

The Surrender of Headquarters.

The surrender order signed by Pearse and countersigned by James Connolly and Thomas MacDonagh

Prisoners being marched down Eden Quay following the collapse of the Rising

FOUR MORE SHOT

Edmund Kent Among the Executed

TWENTY OTHERS SENTENCED

The official notification issued to-day at the Headquarters Staff Office. Dublin, says:

The following are further results of trials by Field General Courtmartial:—
Sentenced to death, and sentences carried out this morning:—

> CORNELIUS COLBERT.
> EDMUND KENT.
> MICHAEL MALLON.
> J. J. HEUSTON.

All these four men took a very prominent part in the rebellion.
Sentenced to death, commuted to eight years' penal servitude:—

> JAMES O'SULLIVAN.

Sentenced to death, commuted to five years' penal servitude:—

> VINCENT POOLE.
> WILLIAM P. CORRIGAN.

Sentenced to death, commuted to three years' penal servitude:—

> JOHN DOURNEY.
> JAMES BURKE.
> JAMES MORRISSEY.
> MAURICE BRENNAN.
> GERALD DOYLE.
> CHARLES BEVAN.
> JOHN O'BRIEN.
> PATRICK FOGARTY.
> JOHN FAULKNER.

> MICHAEL BRADY.
> JAMES DEMPSEY.
> GEORGE LEVINS.
> JOHN F. CULLEN.
> J. DORRINGTON.
> W. O'DEA.
> P. KELLY.

Sentenced to ten years' penal servitude, seven years remitted.

> MICHAEL SCULLY.

Sentenced to two years' imprisonment, with hard labour, one year remitted:—

> J. CRENIGAN.
> WILLIAM DERRINGTON.

Acquitted and released:—

> JOHN R. REYNOLDS.
> JOSEPH CALLAGHAN.

EAMONN KENT, or Ceannt, was one of the signatories to the Proclamation issued by the rebels on Easter Monday. About two months ago he was prosecuted under the Defence of the Realm Act for certain utterances in the County Cork, but was discharged.

He was an official of the Dublin Corporation.

Mr. Kent was a man of intellectual attainments, and had a brilliant Intermediate course.

The long-drawn out announcements of executions horrified Irish public opinion.

In the long term the leaders of the Rising became national heroes. This series of stamps was issued on the 50th anniversary of the Rising.

A 1916 Veterans' Campaign Medal, showing the symbolic figure of the dying Cuchulain

A THING OF THE PAST.

JOHN REDMOND—"Bad luck to that infernal machine with the foreign name. Ever since it come on the road I have lost any fares I had. I can't afford to give the poor baste a feed of oats. I'm to blame meself. Me ould yoke is a bit slow, and it's out of date. I was wan time in comfortable circumstances."

Printed and Published by " Sinn Fein," 17 Fownes St., Dublin.]　　　　　[From " THE LEPRACAUN."

The immediate effects of the Rising saw Sinn Fein overwhelm the Irish Parliamentary Party in the general election of 1918.

"Can you give us something to cover our uniforms?" asked Ronan. From upstairs the girl's mother shouted, "Put them out, put them out, or we'll be shot!" So they carried on, climbing over several more garden walls until eventually they found a basement flat whose tenants were out. Here they found clothes—of a kind. Jim Walsh draped a lady's coat around his shoulders; Ronan dressed himself in a tramway-man's uniform, and Tom Walsh pulled on an overcoat. Thus crudely disguised, they took the risk of walking out into Lower Mount Street. Away up at Mount Street Bridge they could still hear bombs and shots going off. People crowded every door and window and Tom Walsh, sighting a friend, shouted that they were going to hide in nearby stables, and would he ask their mother to bring them some food and clothes.

They reached the stables and a little later their mother took them some food and civilian clothes. They changed, then left the stables and hid for a while in the grounds of a nearby convent, where they lay in the grass and listened to the girls singing "Hail Glorious St. Patrick." In the early hours of the morning they quit the convent grounds and found refuge with a friend, as had been arranged in the meantime by their mother.

James Doyle got safely away also, although he was fired at by the military as he ran through a garden. Near Merrion Square he was set on by a hostile crowd as he staggered blindly along the street. He managed to get away from them, only to collapse eventually near Stephen's Place. Here some people carried him into a house, removed his uniform, and dressed his wounds. James Grace hid in the kitchen of No. 25 until Clanwilliam House had fallen and then left it and hid in a woodshed; later that night he attempted to escape by swimming the Canal with his boots tied around his neck, but was challenged by military sentries and forced back into the woodshed, where he remained until found by a search party three days later.

Meanwhile Clanwilliam House blazed fiercely, lighting up streets for miles around. The house next door caught fire and the occupants, Mr. and Mrs. Mathis, who had crouched in terror in their cellar throughout the battle, sat on deck-chairs in their back garden and watched their home burn down. In the angry crimson glow, Brigadier Maconchy rode stiffly along Mount Street through picquet lines of troops with fixed bayonets stretching as far as Fitzwilliam and Merrion Squares, the crowds cheering madly and calling out for "The Gineral". In Powers Court, just off Lower Mount Street, officers and men were served gargantuan meals of Irish ham and scalding cups of tea by the celebrating residents.

In the meantime, scarcely three hundred yards away, panic gripped the rebels in Boland's Bakery and their comrades strung out along the railway line.

By seven o'clock in the evening the strange, unnatural quiet which had fallen over most of Dublin had begun to rest like an eiderdown upon Sackville Street itself. Sometimes when a figure staggered out into the open—a drunk, perhaps, who had forgotten about the curfew—a burst of firing would break the heavy silence. In the G.P.O., Pearse tried to cheer his men by reading out communiqués he had received from his subordinate Commandants in the city. These were universally optimistic in tone, but now few men were capable of responding to such artificial hopes. Realization that defeat was not only inevitable but imminent, had sunk into most of them and they felt it was only a question of time before the khaki hordes flung themselves upon the G.P.O.

In St. Stephen's Green, Mallin's men, cut off from General Headquarters and lacking information as to what was happening in the rest of the city, remained in good spirits, although shortage of food and a certain disorganization resulted in young rebels who were mere boys being left at their posts without food or relief for days on end. Fred O'Rourke, aged sixteen, for instance, was discovered in a faint by Citizen Army woman Maeve Ward and, on being revived, explained that he had had nothing to eat except a handful of biscuits since he left home on Monday morning. Mary Donnelly, after hauling herself through the holes in the walls a dozen times during the night to deliver food, discovered another youngster who had been existing on nothing but plum jam since Tuesday morning. The Countess, however, refused to let small details like this spoil her considerable satisfaction. As alert, lively, and blood-thirsty as ever, she declared ringingly, "Think of it! We've done more already than Wolfe Tone." As darkness crept over Dublin, the men and girls gathered in the big lecture-room of the College of Surgeons and, led by Joseph Connolly, sang rebel songs with contented cheerfulness.

Margaret Skinnider, a young Glasgow schoolteacher, was impatient with this kind of thing. She wanted to get at the enemy, and suggested that she and Joseph Connolly should ride past the Shelbourne on their bicycles and toss a few bombs through the windows.

"Too dangerous," smiled Mallin.

A little later, however, she talked him into allowing her to accompany a patrol to the Russell Hotel; orders were to get rid of a troublesome sniper on the roof. The patrol ran into trouble. The patrol leader, Councillor William Partridge, had just broken the glass front of a shop premises beside the hotel, which was on the corner of the Green and Harcourt Street, with the aim of getting on to the roof when a volley cracked out from the other side of the street. Margaret Skinnider was turning to speak to seventeen-year-old Fred Ryan, when he fell dead and she herself was hit and severely wounded. Partridge, with another member of the patrol, carried her to the corner of Cuffe Street, where they got help to carry her back to the Surgeons.

Mallin had no qualified medical men on his staff and gave orders that she was to be taken to the nearest hospital. She refused, however, and Miss Margaret Ffrench-Mullen had to bandage her up as best she could. In her subsequent delirium, Miss Skinnider heard someone declare, "That's the death rattle," and decided she was done for. A little later, when she heard big guns booming nearby, she thought: Oh, everything's all right now—it's the Germans, attacking the British.

Meanwhile, northward on the other side of the city, flames from the blazing Linenhall Barracks had lit up North King Street like broad daylight. It was easily the biggest fire Dublin had ever seen. The heat was such that neighbouring tenements and shops seemed inevitably doomed, especially when the Dublin Fire Brigade refused to turn out. Commandant Edward Daly, afraid that the conflagration would destroy the whole city, ordered his men to find fire hoses and tackle the blaze themselves. A search of the nearby North Dublin Union uncovered a few, and throughout the night the rebels fought the fire, despite constant and heavy military sniping.

Shortly before midnight Daly called a conference of officers to decide whether it would be wise to attack eastward in an attempt to break through the military lines in Capel Street and link up with the General Headquarters' garrison in the G.P.O. There was little to discuss; an attack under such conditions clearly had no hope of success, and there was nothing for it but to hold on and defend themselves with their last ounce of determination.

In the G.P.O., Pearse, Connolly, MacDermott, and Clarke took turns resting on mattresses placed behind the central counter on the ground floor. Here each, with the aid of a sleeping draught prepared by the medical section, slept for brief spells. Once, in the early hours of the morning, The O'Rahilly shook Connolly awake to tell him that the British were "stealing over the roofs in Henry Street." Connolly raised his head slightly and then commented laconically, "They are *not*," and went back to sleep like a man with no care in the world.

About nine o'clock on Wednesday evening, Lord Kitchener's secretary called on Lord French with a message that the Government desired to send a senior general of some reputation to Ireland and that the Army Council had therefore chosen Sir John Grenfell Maxwell. As C.-in-C., Egypt, Maxwell had done much to organize assistance for the troops in Gallipoli and had checked the one serious Turkish thrust in the Delta. French broke open the sealed letter and read:

"I am commanded by the Army Council to inform you that Lieut.-General Sir John Maxwell has been appointed G.O.C. forces in Ireland from 27th inclusive. His Majesty's Government desire that in this capacity Sir John Maxwell will take all such measures as may in his opinion be necessary for the prompt suppression of insurrection in Ireland and may be accorded a free hand in regard to the movement of all troops now in Ireland or which may be placed under his command hereafter and also in regard to such measures as may seem to him advisable under the Proclamation dated 26th April under the Defence of the Realm Act."

Ffrench immediately sent word to Maxwell who, idle since his replacement by Sir Archibald Murray, the former Chief of the Imperial General Staff, was known to have a slight chip on his shoulder, and arranged for him to call at 10.30 the next morning. Then, thoroughly on his mettle, the irascible little

Army chief telephoned the Prime Minister to inform him that he was holding the 60th Division in readiness to go to Queenstown and had also alerted
the cavalry at Aldershot.

That night Mr. Birrell left Holyhead for Dublin on the Mail Boat, accompanied by a large retinue of newspaper reporters.

The flames of Clanwilliam House licking into the sky, and the recollection of
the day-long booming of artillery had sown its due measure of demoralization among the men under de Valera's command: without waiting for orders,
for instance, Lieutenant Joseph Fitzgerald abandoned a row of small cottages
in Grand Canal Street as "a waste of time" after hearing—and accepting—a
rumour that Battalion H.Q. had abandoned the Bakery and taken to the
mountains. De Valera, his puttees discarded and his red socks showing up
brightly, moved up and down the line, from one shallow trench to another,
exhorting his men to remain in their positions and get ready to withstand
repeated bayonet charges. He felt certain that the military would now switch
their attention to the Bakery and the railway line and would attack continuously throughout the night after a short rest for regrouping. His desperately
fatigued men quickly flung up low banks of earth in front of the inadequate
trenches, but instead of occupying these holes, they stretched themselves flat
a few yards back from them, with the idea of catching the military napping
as they clambered over the earth banks and lunged with their bayonets into
the empty trenches.

Captain Simon Donnelly, however, more accurately aware of just how
exhausted most of the men were and—from his study of British military
textbooks—just how unlikely it was that the British would launch a night
attack, tried hard to get de Valera to cancel these dispositions. He had nothing like de Valera's faith in the capability and will of the men to withstand a
charge of cold steel. To Donnelly, these lads, gripping their strange assortment of rifles with a nervous energy, almost as though they thought the
weapons were about to bite them, jittery as young virgins when anybody
approached in the dark, were not at that moment the stuff of great heroes but
young fellows whose romantic notions of dying for Ireland could be easily
smashed by a determined charge and the terrifying glint of naked bayonets. "I
never had any faith in the men acquitting themselves well in a bayonet
charge," he insists today, "especially in the dark."

Towards dawn, when long hours had passed with no sign of a British
attack de Valera countermanded his earlier order and Donnelly brought the
men down off the railway line so that they could rest and eat before meeting
the stern challenge he was certain daylight would bring. As a measure of the
rebels' situation, officers and N.C.O.s passing down the line with these orders
had, in most cases, to kick awake the men who should have been on the alert.

At 2 a.m. the 2/6th South Staffordshire Regiment, part of the 176th Brigade
which had landed at Kingstown on the heels of the Sherwood Foresters,

moved forward from Ballsbridge under the command of Brigadier-General L. B. Carleton, and relieved the weary remnants of the Notts. and Derby lads who had battled so desperately and so bloodily all the previous day. These now retired upon Ballsbridge Showgrounds where, in the Agricultural Hall, Colonel Oates was pleased to find his "lost" Company ("D" Company) which had been left behind at Liverpool. With them was his second in command, Captain "Mickey" Martyn and, what was possibly of more immediate interest to him, his son, Captain J. S. Oates, O.C. "D" Company.

In the G.P.O., Commandant-General James Connolly, active and vigorous again after a short nap, sought to raise his men's spirits by getting them to sing the songs they usually sang on route marches. This annoyed Captain Michael Collins who, awakened from sleep by the noise, barked at Miss Carney, "If this is supposed to be a concert, they'll want that piano in the next room."

23

THE WEATHER—down the years it would be remembered through a mist of gold as "Rebellion Weather"—was superb. At 6 a.m. on Thursday, Volunteer Richard Humphreys, for example, woke to a spring morning as beautiful as any he could ever remember. All over Dublin trees and flowering shrubs were bursting into life and he could scent a wonderful effervescence in the air.

But unknown to Volunteer Humphreys, into this most pleasant city of venerable buildings and Georgian squares was stealing hunger. Compounded by chaos. The great Rebellion, far from being any longer a matter of mere curiosity, excitement, or even exhilarating danger, had become a nuisance to most of Dublin's citizens. There was no traffic in the streets. Within the military cordon there were no bread or milk deliveries. There was no theatre, no cinema. There was no time, indeed; for every public clock in the city had stopped—in need of rewinding. There were no newspapers. There was no work, no wages, no banks open, no separation allowances being paid, no postal services. All factories were closed; no ships had sailed in or out of the Port of Dublin since Easter Monday, save for troop transports or supply vessels. The street had not been swept. Waiters and cooks in hotels stood idle. In all the city perhaps only doctors and nurses carried on as usual—if at an accelerated pace. And over all lay the strange, unnerving stillness, as though the city had become a giant cemetery.

Hunger, of course, was the worst menace. In Commandant Daly's area, the people were still being fed, though inadequately. Bread was handed out sparingly every day under rebel supervision, to the people living around Monk's Bakery. But in de Valera's area, the military—under the impression that the shawlies, appearing at Boland's for the daily handout, were bringing in supplies to the rebels—opened fire to deter them. In the nature of things, they shot and wounded several, thus forcing de Valera to end the arrangement.

In the back streets, the poor grew desperate. One man, trapped in his home with five children to feed, took an axe and broke his way through the roofs of five neighbouring houses until he found something to eat. Shopkeepers riveted heavy planks to their shop fronts and stuck up notices saying: "This shop is sold out." In the Ringsend district a crowd of yelling women broke into a grocer's shop, beat up the proprietor, and dispossessed him of his entire stock. Unable to carry away heavy sacks of rice, they angrily broke them open and started flinging great handfuls at one another like guests at a wedding. In other areas shopkeepers tried to stave off attacks by selling foodstuffs well under normal prices. Some shopkeepers exhibited great kindness; one grocer-publican housed a dozen neighbours for the whole week of the Rebellion, feeding them regularly and accepting no payment.

The situation grew so bad that not even money could always buy food. People sidling up to hotel doors, prepared to pay anything for a meal, were asked, "Have you brought the food with you?" Inside conditions were sometimes chaotic and extremely uncomfortable. Several English and Scottish visitors, over for the Spring Show, spent most of the week cooped up in their hotels, eking out a bored existence with increasingly meagre meals. Doors and windows in the Gresham Hotel had been kept shut since Tuesday afternoon and the air grew stale and odious, worsened by the stench of the Lancers' dead horse outside, corrupting rapidly under the blazing sun.

From the suburbs, well-dressed men and women journeyed for miles into the surrounding countryside to bring back bread, sides of bacon, and vegetables. One clergyman arranged for a fleet of private cars to bring in supplies from Belfast for his parishioners. Some prices skyrocketed—butter rose to six shillings a pound, oranges sixpence each, bananas two shillings and sixpence a dozen. The military commandeered what meat there was available and tentative arrangements were made to distribute it to the population, once the rebels were crushed. Many troops had to subsist on short rations. In Trinity College, there was neither bread nor sugar by Thursday, and soldiers crowded into the kitchens where they were given hard ship's biscuits to munch on. In the College of Surgeons, the rebels were so short of food that a major tunnelling operation was begun to reach a nearby pastry shop.

Dublin had become a lunatic world. Ceremonial funerals, an important ingredient of the city's social life, were forbidden; only the driver and one mourner were allowed to accompany the hearse to Glasnevin. People on the outskirts of the city continued to play golf and tennis as though nothing out of the ordinary were happening. At Clontarf, a couple got married while a machine-gun swept the street outside. In Trinity College, soldiers played football on the tennis courts, grazed their horses on the immaculate lawns, slept in the quadrangles. In Charles Street, the dead lay unburied for three days. In the Castle, they buried seventy dead in a single night, all wrapped in sheets and thrown into a common grave. Death often came to those who least expected it. A shopkeeper was shot dead as he walked up the stairs carrying a glass of water to his sick wife. A nun was killed as she was shutting a convent window. A woman died simply of fright. A priest was shot fatally as he went to the aid of a wounded man. A girl was killed as she stood in her own doorway. A woman was shot through the hand as she sat at her own fireside. A woman patient propped up in a hospital bed was hit by three bullets which zipped through a window at the far end of the ward. A County

Court crier, raising his hand in the street to salute a friend, was shot dead because a military sniper thought he was about to throw a bomb.

All over the central fighting areas, rebels, soldiers, and dead civilians alike were buried in back gardens.

The Times thundered at Birrell, blaming him for the troubles because he had spent too much time in Chelsea's literary salons and had shown an aptitude for shelving his responsibilities. In the same issue the newspaper reported John Redmond's speech, declaring that "as for the overwhelming majority of the people of Ireland, the proceedings filled them with detestation and horror," and Sir Edward Carson's offer of the services of fifty thousand Ulster Volunteers "for the maintenance of the King's authority." The Russian newspaper *Novoc Vremya* headlined the news, "The New German Farce." The Germans on the whole played the story down. Under the small headline "Serious Disturbances in Dublin" the *Frankfurter Zeitung* commented: "These serious riots cannot be regarded as important for the course of the war, but they are certainly not child's play."

The morning waxed hot and still. On the roof of the G.P.O. men rolled over, breathed deeply, and cautiously raised their heads. The paving stones below, worn shiny, flung back a sharp light which hurt the eyes. Somewhere, away towards Jacob's, a heavy burst of firing broke the stillness, and a sudden tension gripped the defenders. All night long they had waited for the military to begin the assault; now they believed it must come at any moment and accordingly braced themselves. Behind them, to the north-west, the blazing Linenhall Barracks still sent fierce, billowing clouds into the clear sky.

At precisely ten o'clock, timed to the second by an officer's watch, a field gun barked and a shell landed in Lower Abbey Street. Connolly, believing—almost hoping—that this was the prelude to attack and that the main thrust would be across O'Connell Bridge from Trinity College, dispatched twenty men to reinforce his garrison in the Metropole Hotel. The solitary shell, however, indicated nothing of the sort. Instead, it inflicted a kind of damage none of the rebel leaders had ever thought of. Within moments of its landing, a thin spiral of smoke rose into the air from what appeared to be Wynn's Hotel, next door to the Royal Hibernian Academy. The shell had, in fact, crashed into the *Irish Times* printing office, setting fire to giant newsprint rolls stored there. Gradually huge flames leaped and flickered. From a vantage point on the roof of the G.P.O., Willie Pearse eyed the blaze and remarked, "That fire won't be easily stopped." He did not guess it then, but it was the end of Sackville Street. When it rose from its ashes, it would have become O'Connell Street—and much of its symmetry and grace would have gone forever.

Father John Flanagan had said Mass that morning to the smallest congregation he could remember. The Pro-Cathedral was closed to the public and there were only three other priests present. They had all been up most of the night preparing for the removal of the sacred books and vessels to a safer place, lest the Pro-Cathedral catch fire. A strong wind fanning the glowing embers of nearby Lawrence's toy-shop had sent showers of sparks floating over the church roof. Father Flanagan had telephoned the Fire Brigade, to be told surprisingly; "Our orders are that we're not to go out—even though further fires can be expected before the end of the week." Luckily, the wind had died away towards morning and the great church had been saved.

At 10.30 a.m. there was a knock on the presbytery door and Father Flanagan answered. It was a young lady. Highly agitated, she blurted out her request: "Would you come to the G.P.O., Father, there's a Volunteer dying?"

The priest's first reaction was to consider the request unreasonable. Two priests had already been stationed in Jervis Street Hospital, which lay just behind the G.P.O., specially to attend to the spiritual needs of the men in rebel G.H.Q. Still . . . He went back into the church to pick up the Viaticum, and, accompanied by a friend, set off for the Post Office by a circuitous route. The military allowed him to pass through their lines in Great Britain Street and near Moore Street without difficulty. But while negotiating the latter street, a sniper, whether military or rebel he was unable to tell, opened fire on them and his friend was shot dead. Father Flanagan, despite the bullets which continued to fly around him, knelt and anointed the dead man. Then, shaken, but still determined to fulfil his priestly duty if God so willed, he pressed on towards Henry Street where rebels spotted him and signalled him to enter through buildings at the rear of the Post Office. He was escorted through the crude holes which had been broken in the walls and into the great public office of the G.P.O. where, he wrote later, he found "as gay and debonair an army as I have ever seen." He was led to the wounded Volunteer and, after attending him, saw Pearse, who urged him to stay, pointing out that the men felt the need of a chaplain. Aware that it was essential not to compromise the Catholic Church by appearing to aid or comfort rebels, Father Flanagan at first refused, but in the end decided that his priestly duty overrode every other consideration, and stayed.

Even the most naïve no longer believed in victory. Yet the men garrisoning General Headquarters were still far from being dispirited. Their main anxiety, indeed, was that in some way or other they might be cheated of the chance to get a real crack at an English uniform. Far from experiencing the emotions of the defeated, a man turned to his comrades when another shell hit Lower Sackville Street, and remarked, "Isn't this great gas, boys?"

The fire in Lower Abbey Street had by this time begun to spread rapidly. Sparks caught the great barricade of furniture and newsprint rolls which Captain Tom Weafer's men had thrown up across the top of the street, and from here the flames jumped to Wynn's Hotel on the south side. Premises along both sides of the street were soon blazing furiously, the fire spreading both north and south. Taking advantage of this gap which opened a ready way into Sackville Street, the military began infiltrating until they were stopped by fire from the rebels under Lieutenant Oscar Traynor who, during the night, had tunnelled from the Metropole Hotel to Messrs. Manfield's premises on the corner of Middle Abbey Street. Traynor's men brought on themselves a double wrath—first, of the military in Lower Abbey Street and second, of the Canadians and Anzacs on the buildings at the corner of D'Olier and Westmoreland streets—by returning the fierce fire so effectively that the military advance was halted.

Meanwhile, in the cellars below the D.B.C. Restaurant, seventeen-year-old James O'Byrne took cover with the rest of his Company when artillery fire opened up again. Acrid smoke soon filled the cellar and above the noise of the big guns and the heavy rifle-fire outside, he could hear the crackle of burning wood. Rocked and shattered by the bombardment, O'Byrne and his comrades no longer knew what to do and could only turn in their extremity to the familiar refuge of prayer.

If the 2/6th South Staffords had attacked de Valera's headquarters at dawn, they almost certainly would have scattered the rebels like children. Rebel nerves, after a taut, jittery night, had reached breaking point, and actual physical weariness was such that when Volunteer Lyons attempted to report to Captain John MacMahon, his Company C.O. in the Bakery, he found him stretched out across an orange box like a carcase of dead meat. Several other officers and men lay on the cement floor, utterly exhausted. It would have taken little to demoralize them completely. A night spent watching the flames of Clanwilliam House and the scarlet glow that stained the rest of the Dublin sky, plus fresh information that more troops from England were arriving every moment, had flung the men into something like despair. There was the continuing lack of sleep and the never-ending strain of waiting for the English attack. Additionally, with dawn, came the knowledge that they were now cut off completely from General Headquarters and could not hope for help.

His officers, too, were beginning to be seriously worried about de Valera. Tall, lanky, feverish-eyed, "The Spaniard" was tensed and exhausted to an abnormal degree.

He had not slept (as far as anyone knew) since the opening of the Rebellion, and for the two days preceding it. None had been more conscious than he of the reckless and irresponsible nature of what Pearse and the I.R.B. proposed doing, and of its only too-inevitable end, an undertaking which appeared even more reckless, irresponsible, and inevitable because of the *Aud's* sinking and MacNeill's countermand. Officers, including Simon Donnelly, begged him to rest for a while, but he trusted no one, afraid that if he napped for even half an hour men would desert their posts or fall asleep. The sight of his strained and anxious figure did nothing to relieve the jitters which had been so bad during the night that a few men were shot by their own comrades simply for failing to give the correct countersign. De Valera himself narrowly missed death when he gave the wrong password.

These, then, were the young men who found themselves under artillery fire shortly before noon on Thursday. The attack began without warning. Suddenly there was a boom, followed by a whistling noise overhead, and a 1-pound shell landed heavily in the mud less than twenty yards from Boland's Bakery. It caused demoralizing consternation among the rebels, but it was at this juncture that Donnelly showed his real worth. He ordered a squad of men to erect a rough, shellproof shelter, using the flour bags stored in the Bakery, and withdrew all units from their exposed positions along the railway line. A second shell landed while his orders were being carried out, bursting the wall of the Bakery and blowing a bread van to pieces.

With commendable ingenuity, Irish Command—still short of the 59th Division's artillery, which did not arrive at Kingstown until the following day—had rigged up their own field piece, a quite admirable improvisation, if hardly on a par with Portal's armoured cars. They stripped a naval 1-pounder gun from the gunboat *Helga* and mounted it upon a lorry. Towed through the streets by blue-jackets the previous evening, the gun had been cheered by crowds eager to see a quick end to the nonsense and, towards the end of the battle of Mount Street Bridge, had been hauled into position in Percy Place. By the time it was ready for firing, however, Clanwilliam House had fallen. The gun remained in Percy Place all night, under guard, General Carleton's intention being to advance, with it in support, towards Trinity College first thing on Thursday morning.

24

THE DAY HAD begun in lively fashion for the as yet untried South Staffords, tough, unyielding men drawn from some of the most highly industrialized slums in the world; men whose horizons until now had stretched no farther than the great kilns and smelters, the pitheads and the slag-heaps of the Black Country; men, in short, who were prepared to put up with "no bloody nonsense" from the Sinn Feiners. English troops did not, of course, as yet feel hate for the rebels. This was to grow as the fighting got tougher and rebel tactics became less commendable to men trained for a different kind of warfare. It would seem mean and cowardly to hide behind a chimney stack or suddenly blast a man from an open window. It seemed even worse, perhaps, not to wear a uniform; to shoot down unsuspecting troops, then throw away your rifle and stroll out through the back garden with your hands in your pockets. Very soon every street, every house, almost every individual in Dublin—whether man, woman, or child—would begin to look like evil spawn to the South Staffords. Nobody, it seemed, could be trusted.

There were tales of troops breaking into houses from which there had been firing only to find them occupied, perhaps, by a grandmother or other innocent with a "Peter the Painter" rifle-pistol stashed under the bed. Catholic priests became highly suspect, supposedly having disgraced their cloth by signalling or acting as spies for the rebels. Almost any fairy-tale became credible. Even years later Captain G. J. Edmunds of the 2/6th Sherwood Foresters believed that a party of priests who attempted to pass his column in the Stillorgan Road were "Sinn Fein priests," anxious to cycle ahead and warn the rebels. Other priests were believed to have solemnly pronounced curses on the troops. Indeed, any sort of invented rubbish was thought authentic by men who discovered Dublin to be as strange as Timbuctoo (the sight of Catholics crossing themselves in the streets was regarded as a bizarre manifestation almost on a par with jungle voodoo), and who thought street-fighting a treacherous kind of warfare. The fact that a soldier, posted on the roof of a house in Lower Mount Street, eventually went off his head and began to slaughter passers-by indiscriminately is an indication of the tension under which troops had to fight.

However, at noon on Thursday, April 27th, 1916, the 2/6th South Staffords were still a calm and steady lot. But as the brilliant sun warmed the day, and

218

chased away the rebels' night terrors, their courage returned, and soon the Staffords were being heavily sniped. The shooting came from long-range positions in Boland's Mills—an immense grey structure towering over the Canal basin—and the complex of railway yards and buildings around it. In quick succession Lieutenant Halliwell was shot dead, Lance-Corporal Barratt was hit in the head, and Captain P. S. Bayliss was wounded. The men were forced to take cover behind the Canal wall and in the grounds of the school until something was worked out. Then houses along Lower Mount Street were rapidly taken over and, in an adoption of the rebels' own tactics, sharp-shooters were hidden behind chimney pots and on the roofs. Civilians were ordered to stay indoors. Those who ignored the instruction paid the penalty. Charles Hyland, for instance, who had spent all the previous day helping to carry the wounded into Sir Patrick Dun's Hospital, was shot dead on his own doorstep.

It was some time before the *Helga*'s gun could be brought to bear on what was generally understood to be the rebels' main position, because here, as with the 9-pounders opposite Kelly's the previous day, there was some difficulty with the recoil. Working rapidly, however, in the shade of spreading trees and enjoying a certain liberty because the nearest rebel post was four hundred yards away and rebel fire consequently inaccurate, the men eventually jacked out the paving stones and the gun was made ready. Its opening blast shattered what remained of the windows in Percy Place, and landed, apparently without much effect, among the rebel positions. After a suitable interval it was followed by a second.

It was the most critical moment of the week for de Valera; upon his behaviour now was to rest much of his later reputation as a soldier and a leader. Certainly with a man who had less confidence in himself, who was less intellectually vainglorious and less determined to make what heroes he could out of his unpromising raw material, the Boland's garrison might easily have scattered and broken. De Valera realized that it would not take much to batter down Boland's Bakery, an adequate-enough structure against rifle or machine-gun fire, but flimsy in relation to heavy gunfire, and that even a small-calibre shell would quickly demoralize his men. He called for a green flag and, when it was brought to him, he ordered Captain Michael Cullen and three men to occupy a tall disused distillery tower, some three or four hundred yards from the Bakery and perhaps the dominating landmark in the area. Before a third shell could be fired, Cullen and his men had hung the rebel flag from the top of the tower and had then hastily retreated down a spiral staircase to the ground floors.

The military at once took new bearings and another shell arced triumphantly into the cloudless sky. It missed the tower by several yards, however, and plunged into the Liffey near Sir John Rogerson's Quay, while de Valera danced up and down in high glee, shouting, "Hurray! What a rotten shot!" The burst landed in the water within feet of the *Helga*, at that moment lying alongside the Quay. It immediately led to one of those mad contretemps which inevitably appear to attend the English when they find themselves breathing in the pure, crystal air of Ireland. The *Helga*, believing herself under bombardment, replied with a salvo which also missed the tower by yards and fell just short of Percy Place. Nothing daunted, the 1-pounder had another go at the tower and once again missed—the shell following precisely the same trajectory as its predecessor and plunging into the Liffey so close to the *Helga* that it drenched the crew. As the gunner prepared for yet another go, Sergeant George Norton of the South Staffs., heard him remark, "If I miss again, it means tuppence off my pay!" Luck was with him this time, however, and the shell cracked heavily against the top of the tower, knocking the green flag askew and bursting a water tank, which showered its contents upon the defenders and almost drowned them.

De Valera was so delighted that the English had been fooled into firing on the wrong target that he ran up and down the railway line cheering like a schoolboy. The rank and file hardly shared his enthusiasm. For them the whole business was grim, and they wondered what would happen when the tower was finally demolished. This would obviously happen fairly soon, for after his initial lapses, the gunner in Percy Place had got his aim straight, and every time the gun boomed, great chunks of masonry plunged towards earth. The *Helga* caught on to what was happening and was finding the mark. But inexplicably, after less than a dozen shells had cracked stunningly into the tower, the bombardment ceased.

A few minutes later Volunteer Jackson was seen to stagger from the tower. To Captain Donnelly, who ran to meet him, he cried, "You must relieve us. Send someone else in there—we can't stick it!" Behind him emerged the rest of the party, all badly shaken. Donnelly told them to withdraw, but did not try to send another party in. The tower, in drawing off the heavy gunfire, had served its purpose, and the green flag, however askew, still flaunted defiantly. It was, morally, a victory.

As the lull continued, Donnelly decided an infantry attack must be following and ordered his men into positions to repel it. The South Staffords, however, were concerned only with continuing their advance into the city. This, according to their own reports, they found "arduous and perilous," in no way like fighting an open battle in France or among the ruins of Ypres or Albert. It was not until evening, in fact, that they felt confident enough to push forward in strength.

The bombardment of the tower had ended prematurely because the 1-pounder gun had been borrowed by the 2/7th and 2/8th Sherwoods. At daybreak, the two Battalions had received orders from General Lowe to march to the Royal Hospital at Kilmainham along the same route which their left wing had taken without incident the previous day. With that staunch old warrior, Colonel Oates, in command of the advance guard and the main body—including Brigade H.Q., Royal Engineers, and A.S.C., with the rest of the 2/8th and the remnants of the 2/7th following—the column set off from Ballsbridge Showgrounds intending to cross Leeson Street Bridge and proceed by the South Circular Road. They hoped to negotiate all this without fighting. No one expected a repetition of Wednesday's battle during the crossing of the bridge, but the 1-pounder was borrowed as a precaution, since there was a report that the Sinn Feiners were holding a few houses in the vicinity. The gun, as it turned out, was not needed.

All, indeed, went as well as had been anticipated until the column reached the vicinity of the South Dublin Union where, at Rialto Street, a flurry of shots stampeded the horses of the Royal Engineers. Colonel Oates and the advance guard had already passed the spot and were approaching Rialto Bridge when the shots were fired.

The Colonel at once called his second in command, Captain "Mickey" Martyn, and ordered him to clear Rialto Street and all buildings in the vicinity. Martyn was a short, dashing bundle of energy, imbued with the French spirit of *élan*, who had served with the first-line Battalion at "Plug Street" and Neuve Chapelle. While the Colonel was giving these orders, his son, Captain John Oates, who had gone scouting ahead with a small advance party, reported that he was being fired on from the front and also from a rhubarb field south-west of the bridge.

Colonel Oates halted the entire column, deciding that both flanks would have to be cleared before it was safe to allow the Brigade transport—a long column of vehicles—to risk the crossing. He ordered Captain Dimmock with "A" Company to clear the rhubarb field, brought "D" Company up to secure the line of advance along the South Circular Road, and stationed a platoon at the approach to the bridge where he established his Advanced H.Q. The 2/7th and 2/8th appear to have been gluttons for punishment: a short detour could have been made easily and action avoided.

As it was, Captain Martyn entered the Union grounds and began by investigating the Auxiliary Workhouse from which the firing appeared to be coming. He found the place deserted but from it, spotted a Sinn Fein flag flying above a fairly strong-looking building five or six hundred yards away. A sudden black puff of powder from one of its windows showed where the shooting really was coming from. Characteristically Martyn decided to have an immediate go at it. Even if he failed to take it, he reasoned, he would at least keep the Shinners occupied long enough to let the Brigade transport get through. He left a small party under Captain Oates near the Rialto Gate to give him covering fire, and led forty men across the open ground. The crossing was no picnic.

"I found a bullet in Dublin every bit as dangerous as a bullet in No-Man's-Land," recalled Martyn. "In some ways the fighting in Dublin was worse. In France you generally had a fair idea where the enemy was and where the bullets were going to come from. In Dublin you never knew when or from where you were going to be hit."

The fire from the Nurses' Home—for this was the building which Martyn had spotted from the Auxiliary Workhouse—was heavy and accurate and Martyn knew he was suffering casualties (one was Lance-Corporal Chapman, gamekeeper to the Duke of Newcastle), but he had no time to look round. In short rushes—advancing, dropping to return fire, then jumping up to make another short dash before flopping down again—the party advanced towards the great straggle of Union buildings lying between them and the Nurses' Home. In the meantime Brigadier Maconchy decided to risk sending a transport across the bridge to see what would happen. Reins gripped in one hand, rifle in the other, the Army Service driver galloped his horses towards the bridge. The animals strained eagerly and sparks flew as the iron-rimmed wheels skidded and bounced along the road, the transport swaying crazily. A volley of bullets sang over the driver's head and all around him, some piercing the wooden slats, but the horses never slackened. The lesson was clear though: the rest of the transport was not likely to get through without being severely damaged.

Captain Oates watched Martyn and his men vanish towards the first Union building and waited for some sign that they had come in contact with the rebels. Heavy fire from the main positions in the Nurses' Home continued, however, and Oates, with only his orderly, decided to reconnoitre and see what had happened to Martyn. Screened by the trees near the Canal wall, he managed to reach the building near which he had last seen Martyn and his men. He turned a corner and bumped into the platoon Martyn had borrowed from him. Martyn was not with them. They were in a long quadrangle, enclosed by tall stone buildings on either side and the Nurses' Home, with its republican flag hanging limply, still lay four or five hundred yards away.

Sergeant Walker reported that Captain Martyn had gone off alone to see if it were possible to get into the Nurses' Home. Even as he spoke, a window shot up and a rebel opened fire. Oates thought the men took the surprise well—at least they did not run away. Foolishly, however, they leaped from one side of the quadrangle to the other, with the muzzle moving after them as though they were attached to it by a piece of string.

"Come on, let's get inside!" shouted Oates, and raced towards a doorway at the corner of the quadrangle. The men followed him, and as they burst into the building, they bumped straight into Martyn. He rapidly explained that he had worked his way along the left flank of the Union through a series of workhouse wards until he was stopped by a brick wall and realized that there was no direct way from there into the Nurses' Home. He thought they should advance through the Maternity Hospital they were now in, for they would probably find windows overlooking the rebel positions.

"That sounds fine," agreed Oates.

"Right then," said Martyn. "Come on."

They advanced without difficulty through several maternity wards, their appearance creating a hubbub among the patients, and gained the windows overlooking the Nurses' Home. Here Martyn posted riflemen. A brisk exchange of shots, however, made him decide that they were unlikely to make progress by firing at heavily barricaded windows and hoping with luck to hit a Sinn Feiner. To the left of the Nurses' Home, directly facing them, lay a line of low buildings which appeared to be connected to it. "If we get in there, there must be a way into that building where the flag is," said Martyn. "I'm going across to recce."

Oates and the main body gave him covering fire, and Martyn, with a platoon in support, raced across the intervening ground under scattered fire. He returned shortly to explain that he had worked his way up through the low buildings—which were in fact an old people's ward—until he had come up against a blank wall.

"The only way through is to knock a hole in that wall," said Martyn. "Where can we find battering tools?"

Oates ordered Sergeant Walker to search for hammers and picks. Then, under covering fire, he and Martyn raced across the quadrangle, followed by the main body, two or three men at a time. Luckily the rebels proved to be "fairly poor shots" and there were no casualties. At the same time, an eight-man party made for the Bakehouse, just beyond the Nurses' Home, with the idea of enveloping the building on the right flank while Martyn enveloped it on the left. They were met by fierce, if again inaccurate rebel fire, but managed to reach their goal, although one man was shot dead as he entered the doorway and another was severely wounded. Two soldiers remained in the Bakehouse to give covering fire, while the other four crept around the side into a courtyard flanking the Nurses' Home. Here they dropped a bomb through a barred window of a building just behind the Bakehouse, killing one and wounding eight unfortunate members of the Union who had taken shelter in the dormitory there. On the left flank, meanwhile, Martyn and Oates had hurried through the Old People's Ward and reached the blank wall barring the way into the Nurses' Home. They waited until Sergeant Walker came up with a coalpick (hammer at one end, pick at the other) and got to work on the wall. It presented little difficulty, being only two bricks thick, and it was quickly weakened to a point where only a push was necessary to break through. At this point Martyn casually turned to Oates and said, "Would you nip back, John, and get some bombs?" Never dreaming what Martyn might be up to, Oates went back into the Old People's Ward for a box of bombs. He returned to find Martyn gone and only a big hole gaping in the wall.

"The blighter!" swore Oates softly, and ducked through the hole.

It was quite dark and noisome inside; the windows had been well barricaded and the place was still full of choking dust. At the far side of the room—it seemed to be an office—was an open door. As Oates started towards it, there came a shattering burst of fire from just beyond it and instinctively he flung himself to the floor. There was a sudden thumping noise at the door and a member of his platoon came charging through, a shocked, incredulous look on his face.

Good God—he's running away! thought Oates, and shouted. But the man stumbled blindly past him and fell headlong through the hole. Oates went after him. The soldier was lying stretched out on his face, quite still. Oates bent over him and found he was dead. He had been shot through the heart and must have been dead even as he charged through the door.

Oates rose quickly and tiptoed across to the door, where he halted. "I shall never forget that scene," he recalls. "I was looking into a lobby. To my right was the main door of the Nurses' Home, which had been blocked up with all sorts of rubbish. To my left was a wide doorway or archway—a kind of ornamental affair dividing the lobby. This had been barricaded with the most extraordinary conglomeration of everything you could possibly think of—sandbags, stones, rocks, furniture, mattresses. Opposite me was a door. It was open and I could see that it led into some kind of offices with a big barred window at the far end. 'Mickey' Martyn and Sergeant Walker were stretched flat on the floor just under the barricade with the Sinn Fein rifles sticking out of the barricade just over their heads. The rebels, apparently, were unable to depress them to the right angle. I saw Walker take the pin out of a bomb and try to throw it over from where he lay. Unfortunately there were only a few inches of space between the top of the barricade and the ornamental arch and it was not an easy thing to do. Instead of going over, the bomb hit the top of the barricade and fell back into the room. I thought 'My God—that's the end of them!' and I'm ashamed to say, I ducked back. Then I heard a tremendous explosion."

Miraculously Martyn and Walker still lived. When the bomb fell beside him, Martyn picked it up and threw it again. This time it sailed cleanly over the barricade and exploded on the far side. There was a great deal of shouting and yelling by the rebels, then sounds of running feet, followed by an almost absolute silence. Martyn glanced round the little lobby and took stock. Two of his men lay dead near the door. Then he saw Oates in the doorway.

"You damn fool!" he shouted. "Come on! If you stay there you'll get shot!"

Oates emptied everything he had at the barricade—an automatic Colt and a Ross rifle—and dived full length under it to join Martyn and Walker. Rebel rifles still poked through the barricade, but they were no longer firing. The three men waited for some sound or movement. After a few moments they heard a rustle and scraping, as though someone were dragging himself along the floor.

"We'll never get through this," whispered Martyn, indicating the barricade. "We'd better try the annexe," and he pointed to the door on the left. Oates nodded and they crawled through it on their stomachs. Once in the safety of the doorway they got to their feet and rushed towards the windows. If they got through them, they might, by creeping round the side of the Nurses' Home and entering it from the rear, successfully outflank the barricade. Martyn broke the window with his revolver and seized the bars. He shook them like a lunatic, but they held firm.

"Blast!" he swore. "It's no use—we'll have to go back and try some other way." Then, as they started towards the door, a simply tremendous firing broke out in the lobby. "It was completely indiscriminate firing," recalled Oates. "They were just blazing away across the room at nothing in particular as though they had lost their heads." The three men lay flat and crawled forward cautiously. There seemed nothing for it but to cross the lobby somehow, go back to the hole, and try to work their way around the outside of the Nurses' Home. Waves of suffocating cordite beat into their faces and they began to cough. Immediately another tremendous blast of fire swept the lobby.

At the beginning of this extraordinary battle, the Nurses' Home was occupied by exactly twenty-seven insurgent officers and men (sixteen more rebels occupied the buildings fronting James's Street, but they were not immediately involved in the fighting). From the beginning they had been under heavy strain. Nine sentry posts had to be manned nightly, and there were only twenty men available to do duty—Ceannt, Brugha, Cosgrave, the cook Doyle, a Red Cross man, and a man who had suffered a nervous breakdown being excused. By Thursday no one had had a proper sleep for days. Casualties, too, had been relatively heavy—eight men killed, a dozen wounded and more than a dozen captured. Morning, that Thursday, however, had been marked with a strange quietness. The city appeared to have relapsed into normality. Not a single shot had disturbed the serenity and people could be seen walking in the streets, or idly talking with their neighbours. It was so quiet, indeed, that the garrison had seized the opportunity to shave and freshen themselves up. A dispatch from Pearse shortly before noon had raised their spirits, too, so it was with a faint feeling of surprise that the first sounds of shots were heard shortly before 3 p.m. These, in fact, had been fired by rebels cooped up in Jameson's Distillery in Marrowbone Lane. Here one hundred and twenty men and their women auxiliaries were so confident of victory that they had even arranged a ceilidhe—an Irish dance—for the following Saturday night. It was these shots—from their sentries posted on the roof—which stamped-ed the Royal Engineers' horses.

When Captain Martyn began advancing across the Union grounds, the covering fire given him was so fierce and sustained that the men in the Nurses' Home found themselves pinned down and, for all practical purposes, unable to return it. Bullets streamed through the windows from all angles, stripping what remained of the plaster from the walls and ceilings, blasting window frames and cutting off each man from his fellows. Movement up or down the stairs became impossible. Martyn was thus able to gain his first objectives with little loss. It was only when he and his men began their rush across the courtyard in front of the Nurses' Home, one party heading for the Bakehouse, the other—under Martyn himself—making for the Old People's Ward, that the rebels were able to get in reasonable shots. Despite this, both parties gained their objectives with minimum losses.

The rebels had been holding out well, but now the military missed an excellent opportunity to bring the battle to a swift conclusion. Had the

Bakehouse party, when they dropped their bomb into the dormitory, continued along the wall of the building, they would have come upon a hole giving them access to the rebel positions along the James's Street frontage. Had they even, as an alternative, swung left, they would have taken the Nurses' Home in the rear, and could have captured the entire garrison with a minimum of trouble. As it was, they retreated to the Bakehouse.

The truth was that, at this moment, each side had gathered rather exaggerated ideas of each other's strength. The rebels, picking out the long column of transports and the two Sherwood Battalions through field-glasses, calculated that they were up against two thousand men, although in fact Colonel Oates had actually dispatched less than fifty men to deal with them. Martyn himself, from the outset eager for action and perhaps a trifle contemptuous of the opposition, had little or no idea of the rebel strength until a Union official (perhaps deliberately) told him that there were more than two hundred rebels holding out in the Home. This sobered him a trifle but failed to deter him, and although heavily outnumbered at the actual point of battle, he almost managed to pull it off. In fact, he would have, indeed, but for the sheerest ill-luck.

When he and his small party smashed their way into the lobby, Commandant Ceannt decided that all was lost. He had seen the military gain the Bakehouse and knew that his line of retreat was in danger. When the military also got into the lobby, Ceannt decided it was time to get out. Volunteer David Sears, who later wrote an account of what happened in the South Dublin Union, insists that there was no panic among the garrison. He says that he and the men with him received a definite order to evacuate the Nurses' Home and that their retreat was carried out in an orderly, if hurried, fashion. Lieutenant William Cosgrave, the Battalion Adjutant (later to become leader of the Irish Free State) who was on the rebel side of the barricade when Martyn broke in, also said that a definite order to retire was given to him. "It was given to me by Captain Douglas Ffrench-Mullen and I understood it was a definite order from Vice-Commandant Brugha who was upstairs and in a position to see where the British were." On the other hand, Section-Commander John Joyce, who was on the top floor, did not receive any order. He recalled that after he had been firing on the Bakehouse party for some time his ammunition ran low and, when he turned to ask for more, he discovered he was alone.

Ceannt left by the rear of the Nurses' Home just as Captain Martyn broke into the lobby and was met by the first fierce volley which killed three of his men. Sears says that Ceannt, realizing the full peril of the position, hurried off to call up the sixteen men in James's Street as reinforcements, and that this action, coinciding with panicky shouts of "The British are in!" was misunderstood by the rest, who thought the enemy had broken through the barricade. This, in turn, led to Brugha ordering a retreat. Whatever was the cause of the confusion, the rebels were already fleeing before Martyn tossed his bomb over the barricade and called on them to surrender.

It was a stroke of ill-luck for the military that Walker decided to throw the bomb. It killed no one. It did not cause the rebel retreat. But it wounded Cathal Brugha (Charles Burgess), the fierce, courageous little Vice-Commandant, who was the last man down the stairs (except for Joyce who was still busy firing away at the Bakehouse). As Brugha crossed the lower landing (which was roughly the same height from the ground as the top of the barricade), the bomb exploded. Small fragments hit him and as he collapsed in agony, Captain Oates, standing in the lobby doorway and raking the barricade first with his Colt automatic and then with his rifle, hit him again. Somehow, not a single shot proved fatal and although it was said of him years afterwards that "every time he walks, he jingles," Brugha was able to drag himself to the bottom of the stairs and crawl into a small kitchen opening off the passageway. He managed to turn over on to his stomach, and with his "Peter the Painter" rifle pointing at the barricade, prepared to hold off the military singlehanded.

This is how Joyce found him when he came down the stairs. Firing had ceased temporarily as Martyn, Oates, and Walker crawled towards the annexe.

Joyce bent over Brugha. "Good God! What's happened?" he asked.

"Oh, they've left," said Brugha laconically.

"But what about you?" asked Joyce.

"I'm staying here," said Brugha. He fumbled in his pocket and extracted a watch. "If you ever get out of here alive, will you give this to my wife?" he asked weakly. "Now, will you get me a drink of water?"

Joyce, pocketing the watch, rose and got water from the kitchen. While Brugha drank, there was a shout of "Surrender!" from the far side of the barricade. Brugha immediately fired a terrible burst in defiance. Then turning to Joyce he said, "You'd better go in after the others. Tell Ceannt I'll hang on here as long as I'm able."

Crouching low, Joyce darted past the foot of the stairs and doubled round to the rear of the Home and into the open courtyard. At the far side a hole had been broken in a wall; he went through it and found himself in the dormitory next to the Bakehouse where more holes in the wall led to the offices on James's Street. The rest of the Battalion were in the dormitory. When Joyce arrived, Cosgrave was arguing with Ceannt that the military had not, in fact, broken into the Nurses' Home and that they should return and continue fighting. Joyce told Ceannt that he had left Brugha lying desperately wounded and alone at the barricade, but that he would hold on for as long as possible. To Joyce's astonishment, Ceannt shook his head and wearily shrugged his shoulders.

"I got the impression that it was all up then," recalls Joyce. "I remember sitting down on a chair or sofa and thinking, 'This fellow Ceannt thinks it's the end.'"

Sears, who was present, admits that at this point the rebels felt so dispirited that they could only sit there and wait for the military to arrive. Ceannt said that they had all put up a good fight, that there was still no question of surrender, and that they would go on fighting to the last man. Then he led them in a decade of the Rosary, following which anybody who had cigarettes had a last smoke. "If the military had come in then," wrote Sears afterwards, "they could have raked us with fire and we were in no position to reply." As the military would have had to cross an open courtyard, this is a measure of the rebels' demoralization.

Then, while they sat gloomily around, their thoughts fixed on defeat, they heard someone singing "God Save Ireland," in short, intermittent snatches. One man ventured out to see who it was and returned shortly to report that it was Brugha, who had apparently dragged himself into a small yard at the rear of the kitchen. He had, in fact, propped himself up with his back to a wall and through the open back door had been able to enfilade the barricade at an angle of forty-five degrees. From time to time he fired at the barricade. When the military refused to charge over it, he began singing in defiance, repeatedly challenging them to come over and fight.

"That singing seemed to stir Ceannt from his lethargy," recalls Joyce. "It stirred every one of us, in fact. I remember Ceannt suddenly saying, 'Come on, boys,' and then the whole crowd of us rushed back. Some of us manned the barricade while others lay flat on the landing behind the partly erected barricade there, and from there we blazed away. Brugha had in fact saved us, for the military never got through."

Captains Martyn and Oates and Sergeant Walker scuttled back across the lobby to the safety of the small room they had entered through the hole long before the main body of the rebels had plucked up enough courage to return. From the annexe doorway Oates had plastered the barricade with bullets, while Martyn and Sergeant Walker scrambled across to the far side. Then Martyn, from the other side, gave cover to Oates. Safely across, the three men sat down in the small room to decide their next move. At brief intervals a burst of bullets in the lobby showed that the rebels [*this was Cathal Brugha*] were still there, and still quite aggressive.

"We decided that none of us felt brave enough to storm the barricade," remembered Oates. "Martyn said he would go back and report, and see if anything else could be done. He left me in the room with orders to see that the rebels didn't break out. I remained with about half-a-dozen men. It was growing dark and the lights had been turned on in the Old People's Home next door, where the rest of my platoon waited. I ordered these to be turned out so that we would not be caught in silhouette if the rebels broke out. And here we stayed. I had two boxes of Mills bombs. I placed my men round the walls and told them to keep their eyes fixed on the doorway and if they saw the slightest movement, to toss a bomb. For a long time everything remained quiet. Then suddenly there was a terrific burst of fire in the lobby [*this was when the rest of the rebels returned*] and I thought: Oh, well, here they come! It really sounded quite tremendous in that confined space and immediately my recruits bolted. I hadn't the sense to do the same . . . I just sat there with the two boxes of bombs between my feet. The easiest way to save my life, I decided, was to chuck a bomb into that lobby every two or three minutes. I had about forty-eight bombs in all and I calculated that that would keep me going long enough, anyway, for Martyn to come back. That is what I did. I felt sorry for the old people behind me in the Ward—the noise must have been horrible—but I never heard a sound from them. Every now and then these chaps kept firing into the lobby and then I'd give them another one. I'd got through one box and was half-way through the other, beginning to wonder what I was going to do next, when Martyn returned. He said, 'It's all right now—Brigade and the transports have got through—we've managed to keep these chaps so busy that they haven't had time to give trouble. Orders now are to withdraw.' So we decided to give the Sinn Feiners the rest of the box. We stood in the doorway and tossed the bombs at the barricade—possibly some went over, possibly most didn't. Then we went back into the Old People's Ward where I found Sergeant Walker and another stalwart called Negus looking thoroughly ashamed of themselves; when they realized that I'd stayed on, they'd come back. We rejoined the other men in the yard and made our way through the Union grounds back to Rialto Bridge and from there to the Royal Hospital. When we finally got there, everyone, of course, had gone to sleep long ago. So we dossed down in front of the altar in the Chapel and fell asleep."

It was then 10.15 p.m. Outside—away down towards Sackville Street and the centre of Dublin—the whole sky had turned blood-red.

25

BY EARLY AFTERNOON, the flames were relentlessly consuming Lower Abbey Street, but despite their spectacular nature, they were still moving slowly; the buildings, at least a hundred years old, were solid. By 2.52, however, with the cannonading continuing, the flames had reached Sackville Place, which meant that at least half the block between Lower Abbey Street and Nelson Pillar was on fire.

Captain Purcell, Chief of the Dublin Fire Brigade, looking through his field-glasses from the high tower of the Fire Station near the Custom House, watched it spread slowly along both sides of Abbey Street. Now and then, he would put down his glasses and clench and unclench his fists in anger. He was so furious at times that none of his men dared to approach him. He had been warned by the military that it would be dangerous for him to tackle the fires and he now watched the city he loved, which his courage and skill had saved more than once, perish in front of him.

To reporter John O'Leary, in his eyrie on Aston Quay, burning Dublin was a scene of a "grandeur almost indescribable," a tremendous holocaust of flame and smoke billowing into the air in such vast clouds that the street itself appeared to be dwarfed. Flames advanced from Lower Abbey Street towards the river, and he saw people emerge from the houses along Eden Quay like "terrified animals running before a forest fire." As they ran towards the Custom House, their tiny bundles joggling crazily up and down, gunfire ceased. He heard, floating across the river, the sound of the crackling and hissing flames, loud and roaring in the new silence. He saw a soldier knocking at doors along Eden Quay, and more people emerging. Another soldier appeared with a megaphone and O'Leary caught the echo of his flat voice, "Come out, come out!" One by one reluctant people—young and old, sick and infirm, strong and weak—came out and were escorted towards Beresford Place. And then the gunfire restarted. A violent boom shivered over the water and a puff of smoke rose into the air beside the G.P.O.

Two shells hit the *Freeman's Journal* building in Princes Street, falling short of the G.P.O. by scarcely twenty yards. Another shell screamed across the roof of the Metropole Hotel and crashed into the slates just above Volunteer Charles Saurin, on guard at a top-floor window. Dust and dirt billowed down the chimney into the room and yellow fumes swirled through the window. Spluttering and coughing, Saurin staggered into the corridor outside, as yet another shell hit the roof and a huge crack appeared in the wall beside Lieutenant Oscar Traynor. Saurin was again almost hit when a jet of machine-gun bullets, whipping in over the G.P.O. roof from Upper Sackville Street, scorched down the corridor. When the murk had finally cleared, Traynor ordered his men to evacuate the two top floors and left a man called Neale alone to keep watch in case the place caught fire. Neale, a Londoner, who spoke with a cockney accent, and, as a good socialist, addressed everyone as "comrade," perched nonchalantly on the top parapet, his legs dangling over Sackville Street, and studied the scene through his field-glasses as though it were a play.

With characteristic recklessness James Connolly risked the dangerous streets to set up fresh outposts in preparation for a last stand by the Army of the Irish Republic. Undismayed by the sight of flames all along Lower Sackville Street, he stumped energetically up Henry Street, placing some men in a warehouse there, others in O'Neill's pub in Liffey Street (to command the Mary Street and Denmark Street approaches), and then retraced his steps to supervise the building of a large barricade in Princes Street, the short cul-de-sac at the south side of the G.P.O. Here he was hit. Without allowing his men to realize that he had been wounded, he strolled casually back into the G.P.O. and walked around to the hospital section.

"Have you a screen here?" he carelessly asked McLoughlin, the medical student.

"There's one in that corner," said McLoughlin.

"Well, I want you for a moment," said Connolly, nodding to McLoughlin to follow him.

Behind the screen he took off his jacket. A bullet had pierced the upper flesh of his right arm. Captain Mahony was called quietly and he dressed the wound and bandaged it. This done, Connolly slipped on his jacket again, warning McLoughlin, "Now, don't say a word about this." Then he walked back into Princes Street as little concerned, apparently, as if he had nicked himself shaving.

Elsewhere in the G.P.O., a man went off his head and had to be locked up. Richard Humphreys, writing later, recalled the long-drawn-out tension of interminable hours of waiting. Desmond Ryan remembered voices calling out, "Go upstairs to meals," or "Two men are dying, be quiet." There were constant alarms that the military had begun their attack. Once almost the entire garrison rushed to the northern side of the building, with a few craning dangerously out of the windows to see, after someone had reported an armoured car coming down Henry Street. From the roof of the warehouse in Henry Street, Volunteer John Reid and his comrades opened fire on the monster. Bullets bounced harmlessly off its plating, until somebody tossed a bomb and stopped it.

At three o'clock, Connolly posted sentries and lined the rest of his men up on the marble floor of the main office, numbering them off as smartly as though they were still on parade. Pearse left his high stool and took his place beside him. Then Connolly stepped back a pace and Pearse began speaking. The armoured car, he announced, had been overturned by a bomb. All their principal positions were still intact; Commandant Daly had taken the Linenhall Barracks and captured twenty-three prisoners; the country was rising in support and a large body of Volunteers was marching on Dublin from Dundalk. Between thirty and forty police had been captured in an engagement at Lusk, and panic had been unleashed among the authorities, especially in the counties of Dublin and Meath. Wexford had risen and a column was marching on Dublin. Stocks of food had been found and the Dublin men would have no difficulty in holding on until the country forces arrived to relieve them. He ended by declaring that as the Irish Republic had held out for three full days, they were, by international law, entitled to the status of belligerents and the right to send a delegate to the Peace Conference which would follow the war.

It sounded almost like victory. Cheers rang out through the building and the men began singing *The Soldier's Song.* All fears of a military attack vanished and the men went back happily to their positions. Then, suddenly, from somewhere just off Upper Sackville Street, a field gun boomed briefly and shrapnel spattered over the roof, wounding several men. Connolly ordered everyone down at once and in their haste the men tumbled through the safety manholes (rough holes torn in the roof through which ropes had been lowered), and Humphreys saw some men ignore the ropes altogether and drop the whole distance of eighteen feet.

As this was happening, Mary Ryan saw The O'Rahilly, wearing a Tyrolean hat, parade with a small party of men in the rear courtyard. She watched him strut up and down, before warning them: "Let every man remember this—as custodians of the prisoners every man must keep in mind the honour of his country. Whatever happens to the rest of us—they must be our first concern."

The omens worsened. Pearse and Connolly, although both believing in the right of women to make a full contribution, decided that the moment had come when they must leave. They had been gay, helpful, brave, and unflinching. Louise Gavan Duffy, chief assistant to Quartermaster Desmond Fitzgerald, had not slept since Tuesday; had served tea, sandwiches, and hot meals even while the shelling was at its height. Peggy Downey had gone on cooking; Mae Murray had tended to the wounded. Long before other armies of the world would allow women to take places in the front lines, the Army of the Irish Republic accepted the principle that women were entitled to stand there if they so wished. Pearse, however, knew it was time they went and issued orders accordingly.

Peggy Downey, a fiery little Liverpool girl, refused to accept the order. "I'm going to see Mr. Pearse," she told Miss Gavan Duffy. "I insist on staying."

"So do I," said Miss Gavan Duffy.

"In that case, so do I," said Mae Murray.

All three saw Pearse, and demanded to be allowed to stay. The rebel Commander-in-Chief could not refuse them. "If that is what you want, then you have my permission to stay," he said, looking very pleased. Three other determined women were also permitted to stay: Winifred Carney—Connolly's secretary—and two young nurses, the Misses Elizabeth O'Farrell and Julia Grenan.

Disaster, when it came, arrived unexpectedly.

Connolly ordered a "Stand to" in the main office and then marched along the ranks and picked out thirty men, among them fifteen-year-old John MacLoughlin. He dismissed the rest and led the picked men into the court-yard, where he told young MacLoughlin that he was putting him in charge and had an important job he wanted carried out. The military, he thought, would attack from both ends of Abbey Street—moving up Lower Abbey Street from Capel Street or one of the bridges near the Castle. He wanted MacLoughlin to occupy the *Irish Independent* newspaper offices in Middle Abbey Street and prevent the military moving down it. Then he led the party into Princes Street and through a back alley-way to Middle Abbey Street.

It was because Connolly was short of officers that he was forced to place a boy of fifteen in charge of a vital outpost at this critical moment. MacLoughlin, as it turned out, proved an inspired choice—so far as anybody could have been in the circumstances. Tall and strong for his age, MacLoughlin had come to the notice of Pearse and Connolly when he was carrying dispatches to them from John Heuston and Commandant Daly in the early part of the week. He had talked good sense, had shown he possessed sound ideas, and seemed to have that energy and persistence which usually lifts a man to prominence. Among men of limited talents and abilities, the tall self-assured youth no longer seemed merely a fair enough choice. Connolly, anyway, seized on him thankfully. Telling ten men to occupy Lucas's Lamp depot, Connolly stepped from the shelter of the alleyway into Middle Abbey Street and beckoned MacLoughlin and the remainder of the party to make a dash for the *Independent* offices. Then, contemptuous of danger, he edged out to the kerb to watch. He saw them safely inside and had just turned towards the alley again when a bullet ricocheted wildly from the pavement and struck him in the ankle.

He fell and lay for a moment twisting with pain. Then realizing that he was alone and no one was likely to answer his cries, he began dragging himself along the alleyway, inch after agonizing inch. He covered exactly one hundred and ten yards before flopping into the gutter in Princes Street, where he was seen at last by his men, and carried into the Post Office.

To Captain John Mahony, I.M.S., it did not seem wrong or in any way disloyal to assist in the rebel hospital. As a prisoner of war he had the right to refuse, but his natural inclinations as a doctor led him to do what he could. Each night, after a spell in the hospital below, he was returned to the room on the second floor which he shared with Chalmers and King. When Connolly was brought in, bleeding heavily, Mahony immediately applied a tourniquet, while a rebel, like a magician producing a rabbit, wheeled up a bed. The bullet had smashed into the bone just above Connolly's ankle, and Mahony suggested to "The Chronic" that he improvise a splint from a piece of board. While McLoughlin and Volunteer James Ryan, a medical student whom MacDermott had put in charge of the "hospital," applied the splint, Mahony watched silently. Ryan was punctilious about Mahony's position and took care to have as little truck as possible with him in contrast to "The Chronic," who regarded himself as a neutral. It was to "The Chronic" that Mahony turned when he saw Connolly wince with pain. There was nothing to keep the torn ankle fixed and so the ends of the bones were protruding through the flesh.

"I couldn't stand that," recalled Mahony many years later. "I was, after all, first and foremost a doctor—so I asked McLoughlin ('The Chronic') if he had any way of giving an anaesthetic?" He produced some chloroform—or at least a compound of spirits and chloroform of a strength of one in two thousand.

"It would have taken a whole lake of that to put Connolly under," says Mahony, "and I began to understand why McLoughlin hadn't qualified after ten years of trying. 'Oh, that'll be alright,' he insisted, when I pointed out its inadequacies. Eventually Ryan sent a small lad for some chloroform and anaesthetic ether. Ryan administered this while I released the tourniquet, fished out the small fragments of broken bone and ligatured the small vessels. Then I fashioned a back splint with a footpiece, applied it, and gave Connolly an injection of morphia. When I'd finished, Desmond Fitzgerald came to me and said, 'You're not to go back to your friends tonight—you're to stay here in the hospital.' So they produced a mattress for me and I lay down on it. Some time later Connolly called me over, and eyeing me critically, said, 'You know, you're the best thing we've captured this week!'"

Although Connolly's spirit and courage remained as strong as ever, physically he grew weak. Despite the injection he twisted and turned restlessly throughout the night, and Harry Walpole, his bodyguard, heard him cry out once, "Oh, God, did a man ever suffer more for his country!"

At 4.30 that morning, the 2/5th and 2/6th Sherwood Foresters had left the Royal Hospital, Kilmainham, for Dublin Castle. During the night, the men had been quartered in the rare armoury of the hospital; the officers, in the little chapel among the exquisite carvings by Grinling Gibbons. Nearby, Kingsbridge station had been taken over as Battalion H.Q. (the colonels establishing themselves in the Directors' Boardroom) where a complex system of outposts was established by Captain Stebbing to protect the lines and railway sheds while snipers of the Royal Irish Regiment potted away at the South Dublin Union. Following an early meal of bully beef and tea, the two Battalions marched towards the Castle along a route protected by men of the Irish regiments, posted on roofs or the floors of houses. Camp was set up in

Castle Yard where the troops remained until late afternoon, amusing themselves watching snipers in Bermingham Tower operate against the Four Courts and Jacob's Biscuit Factory. Great drapes of canvas had been wrapped around the Tower to give cover and one sharpshooter had already been credited with over twenty victims.

Shortly after five o'clock the first units moved from the Castle down Parliament Street towards Grattan Bridge, where they were abruptly scattered by volleys from the Four Courts. Rebel command of the bridge threatened to disrupt the tying up of the two inner cordons—round the G.P.O. and the Four Courts. One of the armoured cars, therefore, was loaded with sharpshooters and, under heavy fire, drove along the Quay and set down its sixteen occupants in a churchyard opposite the Four Courts. Private Bob Bury of Ashbourne, Derbyshire, was one of the men who jumped from the "boiler." He flung himself flat on a moss-covered grave and opened fire from between two headstones. This manoeuvre helped to keep down the rebels' fire to some extent, but the bridge was still swept by bullets and crossing it was difficult. Eventually the armoured car towed a field gun into position at the corner of Essex and Exchange streets and began bombarding the Four Courts, registering four clean hits on the east wing.

Military tactics, of course, were distinguishable from rebel ones by a marked superiority of method. Each Sherwood Company was assigned a specific sector to work in. Captain Tompkins and "D" Company were allocated the area from Coles Lane to Sackville Street, Captain Edmunds with "A" Company a sector from Capel Street to Coles Lane, while "C" Company under Captain Jackson was made responsible for Upper Abbey and Liffey streets. Captain Orr and "B" Company were to contain the Four Courts itself. Once the first troops crossed Grattan Bridge, they began erecting barricades to prevent the rebels infiltrating. Captain Edmunds discovered an apparently inexhaustible supply of sacks in a factory in his sector and ordered them filled with earth (most hovels in the area were so poor that they had only earthen floors, which the troops hacked up). The improvised sandbags were then loaded into the armoured cars, which dropped them off at strategic points.

The "boilers" allowed the Sherwoods to work with almost utter impunity in the narrow, criss-crossed area of hovels and tenements. Each was capable of transporting a minimum of fifteen men at a time and their use counterbalanced, to some extent, the unorthodoxy of the rebels' own tactics. Shinners, the infantry had realized by now, might be hidden behind any of a couple of hundred chimneys and were exceedingly difficult to locate, telltale puffs of smoke from the rifles being rare; or they could be behind any curtained window. In the circumstances, the troops at times became jittery and trigger-happy. Private Thomas Fidler of Renishaw, Derbyshire, remembered one hectic ten-minute action in the gathering dusk that Thursday evening, when units of "A" and "B" Companies mistook each other for Shinners and began blazing away at each other.

The armoured cars, generally used only to transport men charged with holding key posts, would back up to houses on the corner of right-angled streets and disgorge troops armed with crowbars and hatchets for breaking in. They would then reload and drop more men at houses opposite, commanding the street along which they had just driven. In this way the cordon was slowly contracted. A first fruit was the release of the Lancers who had been holed up in the Medical Mission since Monday. At nightfall, however, operations ceased except where it was absolutely safe, as for example when the Royal Irish Regiment handed over their sector to "C" Company, Sherwoods. That night troops slept on the pavements, with sentries posted at each corner.

Towards midnight, flames from the burning Linenhall Barracks finally spread to the premises of Messrs. Moore and Alexander, wholesale druggists in Bolton Street, and the area became so brightly lit that it was possible to pick out a pin lying on the pavement. The highly inflammable materials exploded in a roar, creating a searing furnace which challenged the spectacular flames along Sackville Street. At intervals barrels of oil shot into the air like fiery rockets and burst into pieces with a sound like artillery.

Captain Purcell still retained a faint hope that somehow or other the tall D.B.C. building in Lower Sackville Street might withstand the flames. He watched Reis's, next door to it, go up and still the D.B.C. held fast. Then suddenly, a long time afterwards, an ominous light appeared in its upper lantern window and smoke and flames finally burst through the ventilators and windows. Within half an hour the roof had caught fire and the great lantern on top was encased in flames. "The whole made a weird sight," wrote Purcell afterwards. Reporter O'Leary saw the flames kiss the ball on the top of the pagoda-like dome, and for a while watched it stand high above the smoke and flame, thrown into relief by the scarlet clouds. "A scene of greater grandeur I have never witnessed, even in the cinema," he wrote. "It was only topped by the avalanche of flame and smoke that cascaded to the ground when the top itself collapsed." Richard Humphreys, watching from the G.P.O., saw the crash as "a gigantic waterfall of fire."

And still the fires raged on and spread. At 7.30 p.m. the façade of the Waverly Hotel fell with a terrible roar and a vast cloud of smoke, glistening with blazing embers, oozed into the street like volcanic lava, and billowed off into the sky, leaving behind a rubble of smoking brick. At 9 p.m. the whole dolorous magnificence was brought to a climax by the collapse of Hopkins & Hopkins, whose blazing fall crushed and melted down thousands of pounds' worth of gold and silver.

At 10 p.m. Hoyte's oil works opposite the G.P.O. burst into flames and a sheet of death-white fire spurted several hundred feet into the air with an explosion which shook the walls of the G.P.O. This was followed by what sounded like a heavy bombardment, as thousands of oil drums exploded over

Sackville Street. The light became so harsh and terrible that the men inside the G.P.O. had to shut their eyes. The heat struck them "like a solid thing," and across Sackville Street a million sparks floated in a starry cascade.

Long hoses snaked their way over the marble floors of the G.P.O. as windows and barricades were drenched time and again to keep them from catching fire. Men, dazed with the heat and the fearsome possibility that they would be burned to death, moved like sleep-walkers. With Connolly weak and suffering great pain, more and more of the actual direction of the battle devolved upon Tom Clarke and Sean MacDermott, who could not even boast military rank. Plunkett, courageously cloaking his own extreme pain and weakness, rose from the mattress where he had lain for most of the Rebellion and did what he could to relieve their burden. Once, staring out at the terrible fires, he remarked, "It's the first time it's happened since Moscow—the first time a capital has been burned since then!" which drew a weak, uncomprehending smile from some of the men, while others turned from him as though doubting his sanity. To Captain Mahony he seemed a weird apparition, striding about in a creased uniform, wearing a glittering bangle, big rings and, for some reason, a single spur jangling on one boot. As Mahony stood watching him, Quartermaster Fitzgerald approached and said, "Captain, I want you to know that we'll probably have to evacuate this position tomorrow. We're putting Chalmers and King down in the cellar for safety; if you manage to get away, you can tell your friends where they are."

Still the cordon contracted. Machine-gun and rifle-fire went on continuously throughout the night. Once an armoured car made a fleeting appearance in Westmoreland Street, as though it intended to cross O'Connell Bridge, but it soon retreated. Despite the harassment, Pearse strove desperately to keep a system of reliefs and duties going; even at the height of the bombardment, those off duty were glad to wrap themselves in a coat or blanket and, with their rifles beside them, stretch out on a shelf or a table or even on the floor.

And all the while the fire, creeping along the far side of the street and getting closer every second to the Imperial Hotel and Clery's, caused the temperature inside the G.P.O. to rise. It grew so hot, in fact, that when hoses were turned on to the coalbags and books which formed the window barricades—to prevent them catching fire—the water at once turned to steam. On the far side of the street a shining river of molten glass flowed along the pavement.

Suddenly a shout from across the street reached the G.P.O. and a figure was picked out, framed in a window of the Imperial Hotel. The cable line had long since been shot to pieces, so the man made a trumpet with his hands and shouted that the hotel had caught fire at the rear. "What are the orders?" he roared.

"Come over here, if you can," he was told.

In a moment four men were seen standing in the doorway of Clery's which occupied the ground floor. Pearse ordered the front door of the G.P.O. thrown open, and the four men dashed for it one by one. The last man across, who had wrapped himself in a mattress as protection, fell on his face in the middle of Sackville Street, and a great "Oh!" went up from the watchers in the G.P.O. The man lay still for a moment as bullets chipped pieces out of the roadway, then amid cheers, picked himself up and resumed his run. Ten minutes later the flames burst through the hotel windows.

The O'Rahilly stood beside young James O'Byrne watching the hotel burn down. "Do you know what they're doing that for?" he remarked quietly.

"Yes," said O'Byrne. "With that out of the way they can get a good bang at us."

"No," said The O'Rahilly sadly, "that's not the reason. It's to show you and me exactly what they think of poor old Ireland."

The great fear shadowing the mind of every rebel was that if he were captured by the military, he would be instantly put up against a wall and shot. This was what troubled Brennan Whitmore certainly, as he and his comrades slipped down a ladder from the Pillar Café into North Earl Street and, with Hoyte's oil barrels exploding spectacularly over their heads, doubled across the street to an alleyway on the far side. General Headquarters having neither confirmed nor countermanded his plan, he had decided to make a break for it on his own responsibility. They ran through the alleyway into Cathedral Street and then into Marlborough Street and Brennan Whitmore began to feel optimistic. "This is what Headquarters should be doing," he remarked to one of the aides, Volunteer Gerald Crofts.

He was handicapped, however, by the presence of the four Cumann na mBan ladies. Crofts suggested that they should be left in the Pro-Cathedral Presbytery. Brennan Whitmore agreed, so they stopped on their way past and rang the bell. The priest who came to the door said, "I presume you want sanctuary?"

"Well, it's not for ourselves, Father, but for these four girls," said Brennan Whitmore. The girls, however, were not willing to be left behind. Their protests were followed by a struggle, but eventually they were hustled inside and the priest slammed the door shut as Brennan Whitmore and Crofts ran off.

For the first five hundred yards or so all went well, but as Brennan Whitmore led his men across a street opening, a bullet caught him in the leg. Young Noel Lemass, who was running beside him, also collapsed, wounded. In the resulting panic, the men scattered. When Brennan Whitmore managed to drag himself to the shelter of a corner, he found he had only nine men left and only the vaguest idea of where he was. Nearby was a tenement and, helped by one of his men, he led the way into it. The place simply swarmed with women and children and, while they were trying to find a corner in which to hide, a man appeared and ordered them out. Brennan Whitmore told him to go to hell and led his men into the first unoccupied room he found. He told them to place the wounded Lemass on a bed and disposed the rest of them around the room with their backs to the wall. Warning them to keep a constant watch and waken him before daylight, he rolled under the bed. Within seconds he could feel the fleas biting, but he was so tired that, despite them, he was soon fast asleep.

Rebel nerves had reached breaking point. In the South Dublin Union, a man pointed a gun at Ceannt, threatening to shoot him. In Church Street, a young man flung himself to the floor of the Father Mathew Hall and screamed aloud for God to save him from all devils around him. It took six men to hold him down and two administrations of chloroform to quieten him. In Boland's, a man ran amok and shot a sentry, a popular city councillor called Peter Macken, and was, in turn, shot by a comrade.

From the roof of the College of Surgeons, the Countess Markievicz watched Dublin burning. "Think of it," she said to Chris Caffrey. "That's not Rome burning—but Dublin!"

A short distance away Professor O'Briain sat awestruck and then commented, "Lord, we are destroying the city."

From Killiney Hill, nine miles away, people could pick out Nelson atop his pillar.

In a cellar near the docks where he and several other "suspects" had been incarcerated by the military, Sean O'Casey laid down his volume of Keats and gazed at the scarlet stain spreading across the sky. One of the men playing cards followed his gaze for a moment and then said, "Christ help them now!"

Sparks showered down upon the roof of the G.P.O. as though from a cornucopia. With the building threatened by fire, Pearse ordered all bombs and grenades taken into the cellars. Again men drenched the walls and barricades with water. Yet for a while their efforts seemed useless. Dramatically, then, a breeze whipped in from the mountains and the flames were swept to the south-east away from the G.P.O.

Desmond Ryan sat down wearily on a barrel and gazed at the flames licking the sky. After a while Pearse sat down beside him, his face red and scorched under his upturned hat. They chatted idly for a while, then Pearse said, "We might all come through—perhaps."

"I've only one reason for wishing to survive," said Ryan. "Some day I'd like to write a book about this."

Pearse smiled, but remained silent for a moment. Then almost abruptly he asked, "It was the right thing to do, wasn't it?"

"Yes," said Ryan slowly, "yes, it was."

"Failure, of course, means the end of everything," said Pearse sadly, "the Volunteers, Ireland, all!" A shadow crossed his face as outside yet another building crashed. "Well, when we're all wiped out, people will blame us for everything, I suppose, and condemn us," he continued. "Yet if it hadn't been for this protest, the war would have ended and nothing would have been done. After a few years people will see the meaning of what we tried to do."

He fell silent again. Then, as another flurry of gunfire boomed down Sackville Street he suddenly seemed to come alive once more. "What a great man The O'Rahilly is," he said enthusiastically. "Coming in here with us although he's been against a Rising. You know, Emmet's [two hour] insurrection is as nothing to this. They will talk of Dublin in the future as one of the splendid cities—as they speak today of Paris. Dublin's name will be glorious for ever!"

Across the street, the whole front of Clery's and the Imperial Hotel crashed to the ground in a rending, tearing roar, and great tongues of fire leaped hundreds of feet high. Above the sound of the rushing flames the rebels all around them began to sing:

"Soldiers are we,
 Whose lives are pledged to
 Ireland!"

From the window of the Chief Secretary's Lodge in Phoenix Park, Augustine Birrell looked out and wept.

26

WHEN GENERAL SIR John Grenfell Maxwell, K.C.B., K.C.M.G., and his staff (it included Prince Alexander of Battenberg) sailed up the River Liffey at two o'clock on Friday morning, April 28th, 1916, the entire city of Dublin appeared to be given over to the holocaust.

"When we got to the North Wall," Sir John wrote later to his ailing wife, "it was not quite so bad, yet a great deal of that part north of the Liffey was burning. Bullets were flying about, the crackle of musketry and machine-gun fire breaking out every other minute. We were met by three motors and drove to the Royal Hospital. The tower is picquetted with soldiers and most of the rebels are in a ring fence and we are gradually closing in on them. I think that after tomorrow it will be clearer, but a lot of men will be knocked over. These infernal rebels have got a lot of rifles and apparently a fair supply of ammunition. Everything is hung up. No food or supplies of any sort can be got; it is not safe to walk into the town. Grafton Street and all the shop part has to be cleared of these infernal fellows."

Sir John, still vigorous and not entirely free of ambition at fifty-six, had arrived back in Ireland still smarting from what he considered the raw deal which had been handed him by the politicians. As C.-in-C. Egypt he had checked the Turk in his one serious advance into the Delta, and it was certainly not his fault that everything had gone wrong at Gallipoli. Why they had not left him to fight out the war on the terrain he knew best he would never know. In addition, they had left him languishing in idleness for almost a month since his return from Egypt. In a letter to his friend, Sir George Arthur, only a few days previously, he had allowed himself to give expression to the bitterness he felt: "I have been in a nursing home for the past ten days for a complete overhaul as it was thought I had a stone. But happily I am passed fit. I am idle and fear likely to be as the political people have got their knives into me." At one stage he had toyed with the idea of turning down the Dublin job—he could offer Lady Maxwell's ill-health as an excellent excuse— but mature reflection had convinced him that his career still might be advanced if he could deal with this affair quickly and efficiently. Within hours of his arrival, therefore, he issued a Proclamation:

> "The most vigorous measures will be taken by me to stop the loss of life and damage to property which certain misguided persons are causing by

their armed resistance to the law. If necessary I shall not hesitate to destroy all buildings within any area occupied by the rebels and I warn all persons within the area specified below, and now surrounded by H.M. troops, forthwith to leave such area under the following conditions: women and children may leave the area by any of the examining posts set up for the purpose and will be allowed to go away free. Men may leave by the same examining posts and will be allowed to go away free provided the examining officer is satisfied they have taken no part whatever in the present disturbances. All other men who present themselves at the examining posts must surrender themselves unconditionally together with any arms and ammunition in their possession."

Then, getting down to the sure military aspects of the problem, he confirmed Lowe's orders in relation to the operations in and around Sackville Street; ordered the 2/4th Lincolns (part of the 176th Brigade which had arrived during the night, bringing the 59th Division to its full complement) to fling an outer cordon around the entire southern suburbs of the city, and in the afternoon ordered the 2/5th and 2/6th South Staffs. to concentrate on reducing the Four Courts area, while the Sherwoods and the Irish Regiments dealt with rebel General Headquarters. He then interviewed the Lord Lieutenant and Mr. Birrell.

"They do not altogether appreciate being under my orders," he wrote Lady Maxwell, "but I told them I did not mean to interfere unless it was necessary and I hoped they would do all I asked them to. The Sinn Feiners are all over Ireland; when we have done with them in Dublin we will have to clear the outstations. But from all I can gather the nerve centre of the movement is in Dublin and in that part we have surrounded. I got your telegram. I am glad you are going on all right; mind, no setbacks and try to do what the doctor orders. It's strange being back in Dublin, living in the Royal Hospital [he had been Chief Staff Officer to the Duke of Connaught when the latter was C.-in-C. Ireland in 1902]. Since I began this letter a good deal has happened: I think the signs are that the rebels have had enough of it. I will know this for certain tonight."

To Maxwell all was as it should be. He had arrived on the scene promptly and all that it had been necessary for him to do was to give a few quick blasts on his trumpet and the walls had begun to fall down.

Dawn, in fact, had lighted a scene of destruction and desolation paralleled up to that time only by the ruined towns and cities of Northern France. To those familiar with newspaper photographs, Dublin overnight had become a second Ypres. Here rose up the same sliced, skeleton buildings, here spread the same acres of flattened and obscene rubble. Directly opposite the G.P.O. stood bare, blackened walls, smoke still wreathing around them. It was no longer possible to see as far as O'Connell Bridge. Now and then yet another wall would fall with a stupendous crash, shooting up a fresh shower of burning fragments and clouds of billowing smoke. Debris was scattered half-way across the street; steel girders hung twisted and blackened. The heat still remained and a heavy smell of burning cloth hung in the air.

To reporter O'Leary, bleary-eyed after a sleepless night, the most poignant sight of all was that of the stiff body of an old man lying across the tram tracks on O'Connell Bridge—shot down some time during the night—for this was the only figure of a human being amid the entire wasteland. The Post Office seemed even more majestic, more stately than ever in contrast to the ruin and devastation all about it. Above all it still flaunted the green flag and the green, white, and orange tricolour. Then he began to notice the military, singly and in twos and threes, creeping furtively across the bridge, probing for cover among the debris. Now comes the final assault, he decided, and braced himself for a thrilling bayonet charge.

Inside the G.P.O., a lull had set in. Breakfasts were served according to routine, and the women—who had been warned the previous evening that they would eventually have to go—prepared now to leave. Pearse, conscious that the end could not be far off, had spent the early hours of the day working on a manifesto, writing it with conscious irony, on Post Office notepaper bearing the Royal Arms of England in the top left-hand corner. In his own grandiose language he declared:

"Headquarters, Army of the Irish Republic,
General Post Office, Dublin,
28th April, 1916. 9.30 a.m.

The Forces of the Irish Republic which was proclaimed in Dublin, on Easter Monday, 24th April, have been in possession of the central part of the Capital since 12 noon on that day. Up to yesterday afternoon, Headquarters was in touch with all the main outlying positions, and, despite furious, and almost continuous assaults by the British Forces all those positions were then still being held, and the Commandants in charge were confident of their ability to hold them for a long time.

During the course of yesterday afternoon and evening the enemy succeeded in cutting our communications with our other positions in the city and Headquarters is today isolated.

The enemy has burnt down whole blocks of houses, apparently with the object of giving themselves a clear field for the play of artillery and field guns against us. We have been bombarded during the evening and night by shrapnel and machine-gun fire, but without material damage to our position, which is of great strength.

We are busy completing arrangements for the final defence of Headquarters, and are determined to hold it while the building lasts.

I desire now, lest I may not have an opportunity later, to pay homage to the gallantry of the soldiers of Irish Freedom who have during the past four days been writing with fire and steel the most glorious chapter in the later history of Ireland. Justice can never be done to their heroism, to their discipline, to their gay and unconquerable spirit in the midst of peril and death.

Let me, who have led them into this, speak, in my own, and in my fellow-commanders' names, and in the name of Ireland present and to come, their praise, and ask them who come after them to remember them.

For four days they have fought and toiled, almost without cessation, almost without sleep, and in the intervals of fighting they have sung songs of the freedom of Ireland. No man has complained, no man has asked 'Why?' Each individual has spent himself, happy to pour out his strength for Ireland and for freedom. If they do not win this fight, they will at least have deserved to win it. But win it they will, although they may win it in death. Already they have won a great thing. They have redeemed Dublin from many shames, and made her name splendid among the names of cities.

If I were to mention names of individuals, my list would be a long one. I will name only that of Commandant-General James Connolly, Commanding the Dublin Division. He lies wounded, but is still the guiding brain of our resistance.

If we accomplish no more than we have accomplished, I am satisfied. I am satisfied that we have saved Ireland's honour. I am satisfied that we should have accomplished more, that we should have accomplished the task of enthroning, as well as proclaiming, the Irish Republic as a Sovereign State, had our arrangements for a simultaneous rising of the whole country, with a combined plan as sound as the Dublin plan has been proved to be, been allowed to go through on Easter Sunday. Of the fatal countermanding order which prevented these plans from being carried, I shall not speak further. Both Eoin MacNeill and we have acted in the best interests of Ireland.

For my part, as to anything I have done in this, I am not afraid to face either the judgment of God, or the judgment of posterity.

(Signed) P. H. PEARSE
Commandant-General
Commanding in Chief, the Army of the Irish Republic and President of the Provisional Government."

Connolly, indeed, was still the guiding brain. He had slept fitfully during most of the night. With morning, and a realization that the end could not be put off much longer, his iron will asserted itself. "Put me on some kind of stretcher and take me into the front hall where I can resume command," he demanded.

James Ryan, the medical student who was officially in charge of the "hospital", demurred. So did Mahony and McLoughlin. Ryan stressed the gravity of his wound, but he brushed the objection aside. "It is more important that I give confidence to the garrison," he insisted.

He was lifted on to a small iron bed, therefore, and half-wheeled, half-carried into the front hall, where his reappearance, despite the obvious pain he was suffering, cheered the men immensely. Harry Walpole, his bodyguard, reporting for duty, found him reading a detective story. Connolly put down the book while Walpole lit a cigarette for him, then, exhaling luxuriously, he said, "A book like this, plenty of rest, and an insurrection—all at the same time. This certainly is revolution de luxe."

Yet the man refused to stay idle for long. He sent for Miss Carney and began dictating a dispatch to her which would prove his last. It contained little that bore resemblance to the facts, yet from Connolly's point of view, it performed its main function, which was to keep up the morale of his men. Her Webley beside her, Miss Carney typed the following order:

"Army of the Irish Republic
(Dublin Command)
Headquarters, April 28th, 1916.

To Soldiers,

This is the fifth day of the establishment of the Irish Republic, and the flag of our country still floats from the most important buildings in Dublin, and is gallantly protected by the officers and Irish soldiers in arms through the country. Not a day passes without seeing fresh postings of Irish soldiers eager to do battle for the old cause. Despite the utmost vigilance of the enemy we have been able to get information telling us how the manhood of Ireland, inspired by our splendid action, are gathering to offer up their lives, if necessary, in this same holy cause. We are here hemmed in because the enemy feels that in this building is to be found the heart and inspiration of our great movement.

Let us remind you of what you have done. For the first time in 700 years the flag of free Ireland floats triumphantly in Dublin City.

The British Army, whose exploits we are for ever having dinned into our ears, which boasts of having stormed the Dardanelles and the German lines on the Marne, behind their artillery and machine-guns they are afraid to advance to the attack or storm any positions held by our forces. The slaughter they have suffered in the last few days has totally unnerved them, and they dare not attempt again an infantry attack on our positions.

Our Commandants around us are holding their own.

Commandant Daly's splendid exploit in capturing Linenhall barracks we all know. You must know also that the whole population, both clergy and laity, of this district are united in his praises. Commandant MacDonagh is established in an impregnable position reaching from the walls of Dublin Castle to Redmond's Hill and from Bishop Street to Stephen's Green.

(In Stephen's Green, Commandant Mallin holds the College of Surgeons, one side of the square, a portion of the other side and dominates the whole Green and all its entrances and exits.)

Commandant de Valera stretches in a position from the Gas works to Westland Row, holding Boland's Bakery, Boland's Mills, Dublin South-eastern Railway Works and dominating Merrion Square.

Commandant Ceannt holds the South Dublin Union and Guinness's Buildings in Marrowbone Lane and controls James's Street and district.

On two occasions the enemy effected a lodgment and were driven out with great loss.

The men of North County Dublin are in the field, have occupied all the Police barracks in the district, destroyed all the telegram system on the Great Northern Railway up to Dundalk, and are operating against the trains of the Midland and Great Western.

Dundalk has sent 200 men to march upon Dublin, and in the other parts of the North our forces are active and growing.

In Galway, Captain Mellowes, fresh after his escape from an English prison, is in the field with his men. Wexford and Wicklow are strong and Cork and Kerry are equally acquitting themselves creditably. (We have every confidence that our Allies in Germany and kinsmen in America are straining every nerve to hasten matters on our behalf.)

As you know, I was wounded twice yesterday, and am unable to move about, but have got my bed moved into the firing line, and with the assistance of your officers, will be just as useful to you as ever.

Courage, boys, we are winning, and in the hour of victory, let us not forget the splendid women who have everywhere stood by us and cheered us on. Never had man or woman a grander cause, never was a cause more grandly served.

(Signed) James Connolly
Commandant-General, Dublin Division."

It all sounded magnificent; and really that was all that mattered. Victory, in the military sense anyhow, had never been possible, but every extra hour they held out, every additional English soldier who set foot in Ireland, every shell which wrecked another building was another step towards ultimate victory. Never more would the Citizen Army "and their pop-guns" be a subject for public merriment; no longer would those who dreamed of a separate Ireland be contemptuously regarded as cranks and visionaries—for the dreamers had finally proved themselves to be men of action. They had at long last made their noise in the world; and the louder it was, the more certain their eventual victory.

The coils flung round them by the military still contracted however, if more slowly and less spectacularly than on the previous day. The 5th Leinsters, the

Dublin Fusiliers, and the Ulster Composite Battalion along with dismounted troops of the Mobile Column held a tight arc stretching from the Castle along Dame Street and the Quays to Trinity College and the Custom House, and thence to Amiens Street station and Gardiner Street. In Great Britain Street, the Royal Irish Regiment held the line, gradually moving eastward as the 2/5th and 2/6th Sherwood Foresters filtered into the labyrinth of streets behind the G.P.O. Captain Jackson's "C" Company pushed in from Capel Street towards Abbey Street while "A" Company cleared Jervis Street and Denmark Street, and "B" Company set up a field gun in Great Britain Street at the junction of Coles Lane, which would prevent any rebel escape along Henry Street. Rapidly the ring fence round the G.P.O. began to bristle with barricades, machine-guns, artillery, and mortars: a machine-gun on the roof of the Rotunda Hospital at the head of Sackville Street, a mortar in Findlater Place just off the east side of Sackville Street, snipers as far down as the Gresham Hotel, a machine-gun on top of Purcell's on the D'Olier Street corner, a field gun in Westmoreland Street, and finally a machine-gun on the roof of Jervis Street Hospital.

The Sherwoods found their task distasteful. Casualties were persistent and the men were inclined to lose their tempers when they saw the terrible wounds caused by the rebel bullets. Operations were hampered, too, by the women of the neighbourhood, who in their eagerness to loot the shops in Henry Street continually cut across the line of fire. Every house in the area had to be thoroughly searched, and as many were filthy, the job became more and more of a nightmare.

Just before noon an 18-pounder had been dragged into position in Great Britain Street and aimed down Coles Lane straight at Arnott's, a big drapery shop at the rear of the G.P.O. in Henry Street. Private Thomas Fidler recalled that the Colonel shouted, "Open all windows in the area!"; that another officer misinterpreted the order and bawled, "Close all windows!"; and that someone else shouted, "Open those windows!" "While confusion reigned," said Private Fidler, "I remember the gun was fired off anyhow, and every bally window in the area was shattered." The military concern to avoid shattering windows in Great Britain Street was a trifle inexplicable in view of their bombardment of Arnott's, which was not even occupied by the rebels. The building caught fire immediately but was saved by its water-sprinkler system. Within a few minutes a small lake appeared in Henry Street.

In the Post Office the women and girls who were about to leave lined up in the main office where they listened, for the last time, to an address by Pearse. They deserved a foremost place in the nation's history, he told them; their bravery, their devotion and their heroism in the face of danger surpassed even that of the women of Limerick in the days of Patrick Sarsfield; without them, he insisted, the men could not have held out so long. And then, with the diffident awkwardness which characterized his relations with women, he shook each of them by the hand and said good-bye. Clutching their Red Cross flag, the women stepped out into Henry Street and with pale, anxious faces, set off to meet the military.

Upstairs in their prison room overlooking Princes Street, Lieutenants Chalmers and King crouched under the table while bullets ricocheted around the room, and wondered how they would get out alive; it seemed ironical that, having escaped thus far without having their throats slit, they might end by being shot by their own side. Three rooms away Constable Dunphy of the D.M.P. and the other military prisoners lay flat on the floor to avoid the machine-gun fire. Then The O'Rahilly, anxious for their safety, ordered them transferred to the cellars where they at least would have protection. The move did nothing to remove Chalmers's deep misgivings, although The O'Rahilly promised: "I give you my word that you'll escape with your lives." They were locked in a cellar where, in semi-darkness, they were able to feel the foundations tremble every time the artillery fired.

The bombardment, by now, had intensified. In Westmoreland Street the gunners were firing across O'Connell Bridge over open sights. They were finding it difficult, however, to get the exact range of the Post Office and kept smacking their shells into the Metropole Hotel beside it instead. To Volunteer Saurin, inside the hotel, the detonation sounded terrific, but in actual fact little damage was being done, the shrapnel splintering harmlessly over the roof. For a while, indeed, the main fury of the military assault seemed to be directed against the Metropole block (which extended from Manfield's shop on the corner of Middle Abbey Street to Princes Street). Even so Lieutenant Traynor's twenty-man garrison still held out in Manfield's, desperately stemming the advance of the military up Lower Abbey Street and also preventing any direct attack across O'Connell Bridge. Two machine-guns sprayed their positions incessantly, but the rebel fire remained dangerous. Once Lieutenant Traynor returned to the Metropole from Manfield's through the holes in the wall and declared, "Thank God. I can die now—I've just shot one."

In contrast to the rebels in other positions—especially in the College of Surgeons where they were experiencing real hunger—the men in the Metropole were at least able to enjoy good food. Saurin—ordered into the basement to help a G.P.O. forage party fill sacks with tea, flour, fruit, and bottles of preserves—found that the management had cannily locked the silver room and the wine cellar before leaving. Comrades sent to prepare a meal for the garrison high-spiritedly donned the uniforms of the chefs and enjoyed themselves clowning around. Yet despite the circumstances and the fact that they had a wide choice of meats available, they refused to prepare any meat dishes, remembering that it was a Friday and therefore, for Catholics, a meatless day. One man asked Saurin to go down to the store-rooms and send up some flour so that he could bake some bread. Saurin discovered in the semi-darkness a sack of what seemed to be flour and sent a sample up to the "chef." A few seconds later there was a whistle on the speaking tube from the kitchen and he answered it. It was Volunteer Joe Tallon, the "chef."

TALLON: Do you know what your sample is?
SAURIN: No.
TALLON: The same stuff as your head's made of—sawdust!

Back in G.H.Q. it dawned on Pearse and Connolly that the incredible was actually happening—that the military were not going to attack frontally. Even so, Connolly ordered an enormous barricade of coal-bags erected just inside the main entrance door. With its appearance, the rank and file realized how close they had come to the moment of truth and began to cast around for personal cover. Some, for the first time that week, thought of their families. A man beside Brian O'Higgins remarked that his wife was sick and he had six children, the eldest of whom, aged fourteen, was looking after them all. He wondered what was going to happen to them. On the roof the men recited the Rosary every half hour, between intervals of shrapnel fire.

At a few minutes past four o'clock Volunteer Joseph Sweeny instinctively ducked as he heard a shell whistling towards him, and something crashed on to the roof only a few yards from where he crouched. When he looked around, spurts of flame were shooting out in all directions. The roof, half-penetrated by an incendiary shell, had caught fire.

Captain Brennan Whitmore awoke to the intolerable bites of fleas and a roomful of military, standing poised with grenades in their hands. Befuddled with sleep, he instinctively opened fire on the young officer in charge—luckily missing him. The soldiers surprisingly failed to react, but the officer, angrily pointing to the burn on his sleeve, demanded, "Who fired that shot?" Nobody spoke. Glaring at the prisoners he again roared: "I'll have you all shot! Now, who fired that bullet?" Still nobody answered. Enraged, he ordered them out into the street, and told his sergeant to search them. "The young basket's off his head!" murmured the sergeant as he searched Brennan Whitmore. Behind them, from the steps of the tenement they had left, the crowd urged the soldiers: "Shoot them, the bloody Shinners!" The sergeant turned, saluted smartly, and reported. "No weapons, sir."

"Right, sarg'nt. Line them up on the other side there. And then shoot them."

At this a wild cheer broke from the tenement crowd.

The sergeant grimaced, but ordered "March!" and the dejected-looking rebels stepped forward. Brennan Whitmore had just begun to say a last prayer when a British captain came around the corner, and the sergeant shouted "Halt!"

"Where are you taking those men, Lieutenant?" asked the captain casually when he came up.

Angrily the lieutenant displayed the hole in his sleeve. "I was going to shoot them, sir."

The captain turned to the sergeant. "March these prisoners to the Custom House, sarg'nt."

"You lucky lot of baskets!" the sergeant murmured to Brennan Whitmore.

In the Custom House, they were imprisoned at the foot of an airshaft and guarded by two sentries. Some time later they were brought in small batches before a colonel of the Queen's Regiment, where their names, addresses, and occupations were noted. Brennan Whitmore tried to bluff his way out by saying that he was a Wexford journalist who had come to Dublin for the races on Easter Monday and had found himself caught in the Rising. The colonel, however, showed no inclination to accept this yarn.

The rebels could not complain of bad treatment. The military apologized for not being able to offer them better food, and said that they were living on iron rations themselves. Their officers wanted souvenirs of the Rebellion and Captain Frank Thornton had to part with his uniform buttons. Shortly afterwards the rebels were put through a second interrogation. Thornton's Volunteer contribution card was found and an officer wanted to know what it meant.

THORNTON: We contributed what we could to buy arms.

OFFICER: Do you seriously mean to tell me that you men have been saving out of your wages to buy rifles?

THORNTON: Yes.

OFFICER: Didn't your leaders get all the money they wanted from Germany?

THORNTON: Certainly not. Any German rifles we've got we paid for with our own money.

OFFICER: Well, I never could understand this damned country anyway!

Later an Australian sergeant came to the doorway and shouted obscenities at them. Then he asked, "'Ere, what about the German sniper?"

"We had no German snipers," insisted Brennan Whitmore indignantly. "By the way, you British had some pretty good snipers yourselves. We had a cable across Sackville Street and one of your fellows hit the canister from Trinity."

The Aussie gave a whoop. "Do you mean I got it?"

"You mean it was you?" asked Brennan Whitmore astonished. "Well, you didn't cut the cable, but you were within half-an-inch of doing so."

"Listen," said the Aussie, suddenly friendly. "I'll try to find you something to eat." Smiling happily he went away.

"You know, that fellow's crazy," said Thornton.

In a short time the Aussie returned carrying a big biscuit tin and a jug of cold tea.

"I'm sorry, but this is all I could scrounge," he apologized. "But anyway, here, take it," and added, "for Auld Lang Syne!"

Brennan Whitmore looked at the tin of biscuits—every one broken—at the jug of cold tea, and at the eager, friendly face of the Australian. Then he reached out for them. "For Auld Lang Syne," he said.

In Jacob's, the rebels simply sat and waited, itching for some kind of action. Behind the tall, solid walls, they could feel themselves impregnably positioned, although Major MacBride, the handsome, soldierly, divorced husband of the great beauty, Maud Gonne, thought the whole thing was "daft." "Why don't we fight them as the Boers did," he said, "instead of locking ourselves up in a whole lot of buildings?"

In the South Dublin Union, they watched a "funeral" taking place from the courtyard in front of the Nurses' Home. Ceannt had given the Union authorities permission to remove any military killed in the Bakehouse in Thursday's fighting. The rebels watched an old cart lumber away, carrying two plain coffins, never dreaming that inside one was a very live "corpse"—one of Martyn's men who had been cut off and was now being helped to escape.

In Boland's a new form of terror had seized upon the garrison. As Volunteer George Lyons wrote later: "You had a feeling that your comrades might go mad—or, what was even worse, that you might go mad yourself." No one was immune from suspicion. Captain Michael Cullen, who had been in charge of the party which had erected the flag on the distillery tower, began to talk a little wildly and was knocked on the head by Captain Donnelly. Worse, de Valera himself seemed almost exhausted. Lieutenant Joseph Fitzgerald tried to persuade him to rest for a while. "I can't," de Valera protested, "I can't trust the men—they'll leave their posts or fall asleep if I don't watch them."

"Look," said Fitzgerald, "I promise to sit beside you and if anything happens, waken you immediately."

On this understanding, de Valera lay down on the bed in the Grand Canal Dispensary and fell asleep almost immediately. Then he began to toss restlessly, disturbed by some nightmare. Suddenly, his face beaded with sweat, his eyes wild, he sat bolt upright and in an awful voice bawled, "Set fire to the railway! Set fire to the railway!"

Fitzgerald, afraid that de Valera had gone off his head, called other officers immediately. They managed to calm the overwrought commandant a little, but he still insisted that Westland Row station must be set on fire. Lieutenant John Quinn, in charge of the party occupying the station, thought the order was mad, but felt he had to obey it.

Bundles of paper soaked in whiskey were tossed into booking offices, waiting-rooms, and empty trains—and a good blaze had been started when Captain John MacMahon eventually persuaded de Valera to listen to reason and the fires were put out. De Valera quickly recovered his composure.

In the College of Surgeons the actual fighting was no longer the main problem. So long as you kept your head down and away from the windows, machine-guns could chip as many bricks as they liked out of the façade. The battle was now almost wholly one of wits. First, the military dressed a sniper in maid's uniform and placed him in a window of the Shelbourne where he enjoyed considerable success until a volunteer operating from the Turkish Baths discovered the ruse and shot him through the head. Then, the military rang up a shop held by the rebels, their snipers standing ready to shoot any man who lifted the receiver, which was beside a window. Captain MacCormack rose to the bait the first time the trick was tried, and only a crash tackle by Frank Robbins saved him.

Countess Markievicz remained brave and belligerent as ever, determined to hold out until the last man lay dead. Professor O'Briain recalls that her main worry was that she "had no stabbing weapon for close quarters work— I'll have to get a bayonet or sword or something," and Mallin's wry comment: "My, my, but you're very bloodthirsty!"

The main problem was food. Men fainted at their posts through lack of nourishment. Late in the afternoon O'Briain, who was posted in a house farther down the block, returned to the Surgeons and saw Miss Nellie Gifford in charge of the commissariat. "There are fourteen men over there starving, and I can't go back without something," he said desperately. Yet all she could spare him was a little rice. "And that," he recalled without relish, "was my first bite to eat since Tuesday."

27

NEXT TIME I'll make sure I'll get him, thought little John Reid. Crouched behind a sack of coal on the second floor at the Henry Street corner of the G.P.O., he had been carefully watching a head bob up and down at the parapet of the Gresham Hotel. He was so weary that he found it difficult to hold the barrel steady, to keep his finger tensed. He wanted to squeeze the trigger and just hope for the best. Yet he was determined to get that Tommy.

Beside him someone said quietly, "There's a fire." Reid glanced up at the glass dome. Flames were bursting forth, but before he could say anything an officer hissed fiercely, "Shut up!" Reid readjusted his sight, but his concentration was gone now and the bead wobbled wildly. He knew then that he would never get the Tommy.

Suddenly there was a tremendous uproar behind him, and when he looked around, men were charging across the floor, dragging great hoses which wriggled about like gigantic boa constrictors.

A babel of shouts and commands filled the Post Office and the encircling military, had they but known, could almost have thrown away their weapons and advanced with bare hands. Men wrestled to fix two lines of hose on to the hydrants and direct twin jets of water on to the fire. Sweating, cursing, and struggling, they formed several bucket lines and passed water along in a fearful race to douse the flames. Within ten minutes only a cloud of steam remained to show that there had been a fire, and everyone relaxed a little. Seconds later another incendiary shell struck the roof, shooting off a splash of flame. Amid renewed uproar, a hose was turned on and a strong jet of water smacked against the blaze. From his perch on the far side of the river, reporter O'Leary watched smoke rising like an Indian signal above the Post Office. Suddenly his eye caught a limping dog which ran across Sackville Street, shrieking madly—the only thing alive, it seemed to him, in all that desolation.

Pearse, with Joseph Plunkett at his heels, stumped through the smoke and water towards the new outbreak. Then he stopped short and in quick, jerky sentences, spoke to Plunkett. For once his air of quiet, calm confidence seemed to have deserted him—and he no longer moved among the rebels as a man loftily above the battle. His face was red and excited and the words tumbled from him in a stream. Plunkett, too, was excited and they both stood shouting at each other, oblivious of everything except the paramount need to restore order before panic set in among their men. It was the supreme moment for cool, highly disciplined thinking, for the firm word of command, which would freeze men in their tracks. Connolly could have done it. It was not, however, the role for which nature had cast Pearse. The uproar continued. The Irish temperament, sometimes wild and uncontrollable, was now, under pressure, showing its weakness. Humphreys recalls: "Everybody appeared to consider it his duty to give orders at the top of his voice while the fire gained ground very fast."

Yet Pearse, despite the difficulties and the handicap of his own nature, slowly managed to bring some order out of all this confusion. A large party was put to work dealing with the fire while the rest were peremptorily ordered back to the windows to hold off the enemy. The O'Rahilly, calm and not easily ruffled, helped Pearse a great deal, and for a while, as things gradually sorted themselves out, he became the effective director of operations. Through smoke and flooding water, parties made their way up ladders and, with picks and axes, hammered at the ceiling, breaking holes through which the hoses could be brought closer to the flames. One or two men toppled back, caught by a stream of bullets zipping through the windows as the military launched yet another barrage of machine-gun and rifle-fire. Twice bullets cracked into the plaster near Pearse's head as he watched his men struggle up a ladder gripping a wriggling, slippery hose.

At 4.45, O'Leary noticed that the cloud of smoke rising from the G.P.O. had assumed "dangerously large proportions." He could see the rebels out on the roof trying to deal with it, but they were finding it difficult to raise their heads because of the heavy machine-gun fire. Five minutes later he saw a great tongue of flame leap through the roof.

From the Telegraph Room on the top floor, glimpses of sky could be seen through the blazing gaps in the roof—there were now quite a number of them. On the roof itself a party led by Captain Michael O'Reilly daringly crawled along thin steel frames holding together the panes of the glass dome, guiding a hose towards the flames. "You didn't think about it," recalled O'Reilly (later chairman of Ireland's largest insurance company), "in fact you didn't realize until afterwards what a risk you'd been taking. The only thing that mattered was that the fire had to be put out."

As fast as they extinguished a blaze in one part of the roof, however, another shell landed a few yards away. One or two, or even three, fires might have been brought under control, but not a dozen. The rebels realized that the Post Office was doomed.

The fire ate fiercely through the roof in several different places, and slates, plaster and mortar showered down into the flood water, turning it into a great, slimy, coal-blackened lake. Bullets tore into the hosepipes and jets of water spouted like fountains; Humphreys saw one man holding on grimly to the hose as a spout drenched him from head to foot. Lines of men continued to pass buckets up the ladders to the men on the roof. It was all useless. Clouds of smoke filled the room, dirty, black choking stuff that had the men soon coughing badly. A whole side of the roof had caught fire now, and there was a rending, tearing noise as a huge lump of it crashed into the room below, scattering the fire fighters, who slipped and fell among the tangle of hoses and buckets, drenching themselves in filthy water. The very floor shook and a yell went up. "The floor's giving way!" Burning wood and charred plaster sizzled in the water and clouds of steam rose to mingle with the smoke. From a corner of the room Volunteer Sweeny kept firing at the military, who, taking advantage of rebel difficulties, were attempting an advance from the Parnell Monument.

"They must have thought we were done for," recalled Sweeny. "Our rifle-fire was returned by machine-guns, with interest, but we were well sand-bagged and loopholed and now and then we were able to get our heads up. They were firing from all round Upper Sackville Street and we could hear the chatter of a gun from somewhere near Amiens Street station. Fortunately the Pillar blocked their fire to some extent or they might have driven us out sooner."

And yet the military still showed no signs of making an assault. Now and then, when a khaki blur showed itself for an instant along Upper Sackville Street or on some rooftop, reporter O'Leary saw puffs of smoke issue from the burning Post Office, proving that the rebels were still defiant. At every barricade the military gripped their rifles harder and waited with tight nerves. At any moment, they believed, a mob of trapped and desperate men, driven by reckless fanaticism, would pour out of that blazing building and charge down upon them, determined to slaughter or be slaughtered. Meantime, they must wait and fight the gnawing tension; wait for the fire to drive out the rats.

At 5.30 p.m., Father John Flanagan, summoned with everyone else into the general sorting office as more and more fragments fell into the main public office, asked The O'Rahilly what was to happen to the wounded, now numbering sixteen. The O'Rahilly replied that he wanted them taken to Jervis Street Hospital. Captain Mahony, told to accompany the party, tried to persuade James Connolly to go with them.

"No, my place is with my men," answered Connolly brusquely.

At 6 p.m., led by Captain Martin O'Reilly, the party, consisting of Father Flanagan, Captain Mahony, the sixteen wounded men and twelve of the fifteen women who had stuck it out until then, started crawling through the tunnelled walls towards the Coliseum Theatre in Henry Street. A few men went with them to help carry the wounded, who were lifted on mattresses or blankets. Three women remained behind: two Red Cross nurses—blonde, pretty Elizabeth O'Farrell and the dark, petite Julia Grenan—and Connolly's indomitable secretary, Miss Winifred Carney, who when urged by Pearse to leave with the others, replied in curt, unladylike terms. Before ducking through the hole in the wall, Father Flanagan was approached by The O'Rahilly, who asked for a Last Absolution and blessing, saying, "Father, I'm afraid we'll never meet again in this world." Father Flanagan did as he was asked, and then, with a last look at a gallant and resolute face, stepped through the crude hole in the wall.

Through two intervening shops, across a roof (where they were exposed to military fire), then up a ladder, the party made their way in a slow, painful effort which lasted more than half an hour. They finally reached the Coliseum where, in the saloon bar, the wounded were made comfortable on a thick pile carpet, and Captain O'Reilly and Quartermaster Fitzgerald talked over what they should do next. Although the bar had been held by the rebels since Monday afternoon not a single bottle of beer or spirits had been touched, a point Father Flanagan noted with pleasure. Captain Mahony was impressed by Quartermaster Fitzgerald's determination to prevent any of the party from sampling the contents now, although in the circumstances he thought it would have been reasonable. Fitzgerald, however, sensitive to rebel honour, declared he would allow only non-alcoholic drinks to be taken.

Meanwhile, back in the Post Office, Pearse and Connolly had decided that their position was no longer tenable. The problem now was whether the onrushing flames would force them to leave while it was still daylight, or whether they might be able to hold on until darkness. More important was *where* and *how* they would go. The two Poole brothers offered to explore the sewers to see if an exit could be found that way, but were driven back by the filth. Pearse, after consulting his fellow members of the Provisional Government, finally announced that an attempt would be made to establish new Headquarters in Messrs. Williams and Woods', soap and sweet manufacturers in Great Britain Street, which was the nearest large building. A dash would be made from the side door in Henry Street and then up Moore Street to the factory. The O'Rahilly had volunteered to lead an assault party of twelve men in an attempt to reach Williams and Woods', seize the building and establish a route for the remainder of the Post Office garrison.

Towards seven o'clock, however, and before The O'Rahilly's charge could be mounted, the threat to the G.P.O. was suddenly intensified. The fire, which—due to the gallantry of the fire fighters—had been more or less confined to the front part of the Post Office, began to surge rapidly along both sides of the building, threatening to engulf everything. Flames roaring near the head of the ventilator shaft sent sparks floating into the basement where the gelignite and bombs had been lodged for safety when the fire first started. Captain Dermot Lynch led a party into the basement to remove the stuff to a safer place. Volunteers John MacLoughlin, John Reid, and Brian O'Higgins staggered along a passageway under Sackville Street to a courtyard in the rear of the building on the Princes Street side, carrying their dangerous burden. Other rebels, holding lighted candles, were stationed at short intervals to show them the way and guard against a collision or a fall, which might cause catastrophe. MacLoughlin found the job "hair-raising." The home-made bombs had been stored at the foot of the ventilator shaft and as The O'Rahilly flushed a steady stream of water up the spark-filled area, the three Volunteers scooped up armfuls. Once, as MacLoughlin stopped, The O'Rahilly momentarily lost control of the hosepipe and a staggering stream of water hit MacLoughlin full in the chest, crashing him to the ground with the bombs in his arms. In that dangerous instant he thought the end had come, but the drenching water must have affected the bombs; anyway none exploded. Then abruptly the water gave out and, as blinding fumes eddied from the ventilator shaft, The O'Rahilly ordered everyone to leave.

Upstairs he remembered Lieutenants Chalmers and King and the thirteen other prisoners locked in the cellars. He told Lynch, who immediately saw Connolly. The Commandant-General, directing operations from his bed beside the Henry Street exit, ordered that the prisoners should be placed in what was now the safest part of the building, a ferro-concrete rear annexe which had been added during the recent remodelling. Lynch left at once to attend to the transfer.

For Lieutenant Chalmers at least, his appearance was not a moment too soon. For almost three hours he and his fellow-prisoners had yelled themselves hoarse as smoke filtered along the passageway, and they realized that they were trapped in a burning building where the alternative facing them appeared to be a choice between horrible deaths. Chalmers could scarcely control himself as Lynch remarked soothingly, "It's all right now, boys," and led the highly-strung party into the Princes Street courtyard and then into a room where they were left temporarily in charge of, as Chalmers put it later, "a woman in male attire who flourished a big, loaded revolver and threatened us." Who that could have been is difficult to imagine, as none of the three women left in the building were so dressed. A little later the prisoners were escorted to the Henry Street exit where The O'Rahilly awaited them. Private Peter Richardson of the Connaught Rangers told reporters afterwards: "We were placed near the door where we could rush for our liberty. Then, shaking hands with each one of us in turn, The O'Rahilly said, 'Good-bye . . . I may never see you again. Good-bye and good luck to you.' Then the door was pulled open."

Chalmers led the party, with a Dublin Fusilier following close behind. He ran into the street, crossed into Henry Place opposite, and then turned a corner. He was running west towards Moore Street when a machine-gun opened up and caught him in the thigh. Beside him the Dublin Fusilier fell dead with a bullet in his head. Chalmers dodged about for a moment, utterly bewildered, until he was fired on again by a second machine-gun. He jumped over a low wall, followed by the rest of the party, and ran into an alleyway, where he collapsed and was carried into a cellar by a sergeant of the Royal Irish Regiment.

Behind them The O'Rahilly, gripping his Mauser pistol, walked from the Post Office, leading twelve smoke-begrimed, haggard-eyed men into Henry

Street. Here they lined up and listened to Pearse, who explained once again that their job was to establish new headquarters in Williams and Woods'. When Pearse finished, The O'Rahilly looked his men over and then told them briefly, "It will be either a glorious victory or a glorious death, boys," and, turning, led the way towards Moore Street.

All went well as they filtered slowly west towards the corner, taking cover in doorways, then darting forward for a few yards before again taking cover. Making as little noise as possible, they opened a way through their own barricade in Henry Street and scrambled through. At Moore Street corner they halted to sort themselves into two parties—The O'Rahilly explaining that he would lead the charge northward up Moore Street along the left-hand pavement, leaving the second party to advance at the double along the right.

The O'Rahilly and his party fanned out across the end of Moore Street and the Sherwood Foresters, massed behind a barricade at the top of the street where it ran into Great Britain Street, at once opened up on them. Men were hit, and Volunteer Charles Steinmayer, running along the right-hand side of the street, recalled that it was "a case of taking cover wherever it could be found—and this consisted of doorways about six inches deep." The charge did not get very far, being stopped within twenty-five yards. From the cover of a doorway, Steinmayer saw The O'Rahilly drop to the ground at the corner of Sampson's Lane, an opening on the left. He himself dived into a laneway on the right and took refuge in a tenement as another volley swept the street—it now seemed "humanly impossible for anything to get up that street."

Meanwhile The O'Rahilly dragged himself into Sampson's Lane where he was joined by a few men, while the others huddled in doorways in Moore Street or took refuge in Henry Place on the far side of the street. The military still blazed away mercilessly, raking Moore Street from one end to the other, but eventually there came a lull. At once the indomitable O'Rahilly rose to his feet and, firing blindly towards the barricade, led another advance up Moore Street. He cut across Moore Street as he ran, perhaps hoping to get into Sackville Lane, and regroup his men there; or possibly he wanted to draw the enemy fire on himself while his men charged on to the barricade. Whatever his reasons, his men responded bravely to his gallant leadership, but of his original party only a handful remained, and the military, reinforced by picked marksmen, cut them down easily with a withering fire. The O'Rahilly was hit. Wounded mortally, he collapsed at the entrance to Sackville Lane. Realizing that he had not long to live, he propped himself against a wall and scratched a last note to his wife. This read: "Written after I was shot. I was hit leading a rush. I got more than one bullet I think."

Within a few moments silence fell over the empty street. When it became clear that the rebels would no longer attack, Captain G. J. Edmunds sent a sergeant down to search The O'Rahilly's body. The man brought back the note The O'Rahilly had written to his wife, and Connolly's last order, copies of which were immediately sent to General Maxwell.

More than two-thirds men who went out with The O'Rahilly on his last charge ended up as casualties.

In those last hours inside the burning Post Office, the thoughts of Joseph Plunkett had turned often to Grace Gifford, the artist daughter of a Dublin solicitor whom he might have married on Easter Sunday. In his breast pocket—as he and Pearse made a last tour of the blazing building, calling together the few men still at their posts—lay a short note and his Will, bequeathing her everything "of which I am possessed and may become possessed." In the main hall he stopped and asked Winifred Carney, "Will you do something for me?"

Miss Carney had not particularly admired him—his bizarre get-up and his strange, almost histrionic manner had caused her to make uncomplimentary remarks about him to Connolly earlier in the week, to which the rebel leader had replied that Plunkett "is such a brilliant military man that I don't care how he dresses." But his behaviour throughout the Rebellion, his courage and his cheerfulness despite his weakness and pain, had gradually won her sympathy and she allowed him to slip the filigree bangle from his wrist and put it on hers. Then he took from his finger one of the great antique rings—which had particularly roused her ire—and pressed it, along with the note, into her hand, asking her if she would deliver them to Grace Gifford. Miss Carney promised she would and he went on towards the Henry Street exit, where Connolly waited on his couch, Clarke and MacDermott by his side.

There was still spirit left in the rebel army. Most of them looked brave as they listened to Pearse's last words to them, his exhortation to "go out and face the machine-guns as though you were on parade." Captain Mahony, recalled from the Coliseum because a man had fallen over Connolly's foot and smashed the "cradle" (Mahony fixed it), saw them gather around their Commander-in-Chief and stand calmly as if they were still on manoeuvres. "I found it impressive," recalls Mahony. "I could see no panic, no obvious signs of fear—and in the circumstances that would have been excusable, for parts of the building were already an inferno and the roof and ceilings had already given way in places. To me, in that hasty moment, it seemed that Pearse, in the way he held them all together, was a gifted leader and a man supremely fitted to command. Then I went back to the Coliseum."

The men in the Metropole had joined the Headquarters garrison by now and Charles Saurin remembers how they sang defiantly as they edged towards the exit. The words of *The Soldier's Song* which had gripped their imagination (it has since become the National Anthem of the Republic of Ireland) were roared out with all the fervour of men who intended to go on resisting stubbornly, however often they were beaten. This was the human spirit at its most obstinate, expressing a particular inheritance, centuries of resistance to England and the determination to be free. The song rose above the noise of the flames, and, from the front of the building, the constant explosion of small-arms ammunition and the home-made bombs which, perhaps fortunately for themselves, they had never had a chance to use. There was a good-natured patience about the men. They were crowding towards the door when a shotgun went off accidentally and hit Volunteer Andrew Furlong's ammunition pouch. It exploded, sending bullets in every direction—nine pierced Furlong's leg. Beside him, the strange cockney socialist called Neale, swayed and fell against Saurin. "Can't you stand away and let a fellow lie down?" asked Neale gently. He was laid on a pile of mail-bags and Lieutenant Traynor asked, "Are you badly hurt?" to which Neale replied wryly, "I'm dying, comrade."

When young John MacLoughlin reached the door, Pearse and MacDermott were explaining the route to Williams and Woods' factory. This was the first MacLoughlin had heard of the plan and he protested that the factory, and indeed the whole of Great Britain Street, had been in the hands of the military since Thursday. He knew of this personally, for he had sneaked through the area on his way to the G.P.O. from Commandant Daly's headquarters following the fall of the Mendicity Institution.

"Why don't we go up Henry Street, through the markets and on into the Four Courts?" he suggested.

Pearse considered this, while someone shouted, "Stop The O'Rahilly—he's gone into Moore Street with some men."

Unhesitatingly MacLoughlin darted through the door and ran across into Henry Place opposite. He reached Moore Street just as The O'Rahilly and his men were being cut to pieces. He turned, to discover that most of the garrison, led by Captain Michael Collins with a drawn revolver, had followed him. It was dusk now and in the quickening darkness the burning Post Office, the flames licking so high that they threatened to cremate Nelson himself, looked an awesome sight to young MacLoughlin.

With the rebels in the streets the military now opened up in real earnest. Among the fleeing men order and discipline were fast disappearing in the confusion. Some followed MacLoughlin and Collins up Henry Street; others, obeying the strict instructions of their Commander-in-Chief, dashed towards Moore Street and, turning the corner, ran straight into the blazing guns of the military, most of them being hit. The rest ran wildly across into Henry Place and then around the corner towards Moore Street, but were stopped at the bottom of Moore Lane (parallel to Moore Street) because it was under machine-gun fire from the roof of the Rotunda Hospital.

While Collins sought refuge for his men in the houses along Moore Street, MacLoughlin grabbed an officer's sword and took over command at the bottom of Moore Lane. When he ordered the men to search for materials to make a barricade, they found a motor-van in a nearby yard and pushed it into position barring the mouth of the Lane. It wasn't much use as protection, but it partially screened the men as they ran across the opening. Some of them, scared to run the gauntlet, broke into O'Brien's mineral water premises nearby, others into stables. Still others, seeing their comrades hit by the machine-gun bullets, cowered in the laneway, too terrified to move. Plunkett, coming up behind them, drew his sword and rallied them on. "Don't be afraid, don't be cowards, any of you. On, on, on!" Clarke and MacDermott took up positions in the lane as fresh arrivals, frightened by the intense machine-gun fire, scattered madly, and shouted at them to behave like men. Amid all the confusion, young MacLoughlin stood out like a rock, and seeing that the men were ready to obey him, MacDermott shouted, "You're the only one who seems to know where we are—you'd better give the orders around here."

Few of the men had any idea where they were going. Someone shouted at Volunteer John Nunan to "go into the warehouse," and he climbed into O'Brien's mineral water store, where he stayed until the firing died down. James Ryan found himself clambering aimlessly over the roofs, but got down finally into a courtyard at the rear of Moore Street, from where he was able to rejoin the main party.

Volunteer Kevin O'Carroll was hit in the leg and carried into the nearest house, filled with hysterical women. This was the home of the McKane family—mother and father and fourteen children. For two days the family had huddled together in a tiny cottage, the last house in a row of workmen's cottages in Henry Place, crouched under the beds, saying their Rosaries and growing more and more hungry. They had not dared to go out after seeing a looter shot and his body thrown up on a barricade by the military. Elizabeth, then ten, recalled years later how the "boys came up in twos and threes while we were all kneeling saying our prayers."

"My father jumped up when he heard the commotion in the yard," she remembered. "A rifleman, without waiting for him to open the door, broke the glass panel. It was terrible. The rifle went off and pierced my father's shoulder—he was carrying the baby in his arms at the time—and went straight through him and hit my eldest sister Bridget in the forehead, killing her instantly. I remember my mother getting to her feet, looking completely stunned—everything had happened so suddenly."

Pearse and Connolly were still in the Post Office. Connolly, despite his pain, insisted on staying with Pearse until the rest of the garrison had got safely away. Finally he allowed them to carry him out on a stretcher, the faithful Miss Carney hovering by and a young boy, proud to be of service to his general, walking beside the stretcher, shielding Connolly's body from bullets. Smoke had by now clouded Henry Street; so black and thick, Joseph Sweeny recalled "that it was almost impossible to see your finger in front of your face." He was with the last party to hurry across. Behind him came the two Red Cross nurses, Elizabeth O'Farrell and Julia Grenan, who were escorted to the safety of Henry Place corner by Pearse himself. He returned to check that there was no one left in the burning building. By then, floors were collapsing spectacularly, heaving giant tongues of fire into the glowing night, beams were falling and interior walls crashing down. Pearse, standing alone for a moment amid all the terror and the beauty, stared at the ruin, symbolic in a way of all his hopes. As he turned to leave, a small party stumbled from a hole in the wall, led by Captain Michael

O'Reilly and Willie Pearse, who had been helping to carry the wounded to the Coliseum Theatre. Willie went out first, followed by the Commander-in-Chief himself, Volunteer Patrick Colwell, and Captain O'Reilly.

At the bottom of Moore Lane, where the screening barricade had been made larger, Miss O'Farrell slipped and fell as she ran across. She was helped up and led into Cogan's, a grocer's on the corner of Henry Place and Moore Street, where she found Connolly, Plunkett, Clarke, and MacDermott. Connolly lay on his stretcher in the middle of the floor, his face white and shadowed with pain. She knelt beside him and asked how he felt.

Connolly: "Bad—the soldier who wounded me did a good day's work for the British Government."

When Pearse reached the bottom of Moore Lane, he, too, slipped and fell— and in exactly the same spot as Miss O'Farrell, but he jumped up immediately and safely reached Cogan's. Mrs. Cogan told the rebels they could have a ham she was boiling, and then vanished with her family into the cellar. When the ham had been cooked, Miss Carney portioned it out among the famished men, kneeling to feed Connolly. MacDermott took an egg from a box, bored a hole in it and sucked it. Two rebels stood on guard at the windows, which had been barricaded, and another stood guard at the door. Then Miss Carney collected small personal possessions from each of the men for their wives or their mothers. When she bent over one young boy, he asked her nervously, "Do you think we'll win? . . . You see, I've never been in a rebellion before."

"Neither have I," said Miss Carney, and smiled.

Outside MacLoughlin and Plunkett worked frantically to build a barricade at the junction of Henry Place and Moore Street. In the glare of the Post Office flames the rebels were an easy target and there were casualties. Strangely, the military still made no attempt to come to close grips.

From the far side of the Liffey, reporter O'Leary watched, absorbed, as the G.P.O. continued to burn spectacularly. "The fire," he wrote, "grows and grows, seems to bubble over as heaps of glowing debris crash over the granite walls and through the flame-eaten windows. High above the doomed building, the Republican flag flutters in the stifling atmosphere of smoke. Leaping flames lick and kiss the pole on which it hangs. With my field-glasses, I can see the letters IRISH REPUBLIC scorch to a deep brown. Now and then the flag is buried as thousands of fragments of burning paper belch up as it were from a volcano. Now it begins to hang its head as if in shame. At 9 p.m. the G.P.O. is in ruins, its granite walls look like the bones of a skeleton skull. Its core is nothing but smouldering debris. The fluttering of the flag grows feebler. In the dimness of the night I see it give an occasional flutter, as if revived by a gust of air. At length at 9.51 p.m. the staff supporting it begins to waver and in a second falls out towards the street. The Sinn Fein fortress is no more."

In Cogan's, Pearse ordered a party of men to start breaking through the wall towards Great Britain Street, then held a brief council of war. A decision was taken to give the boy, MacLoughlin, high military command.

"He should hold my rank," insisted Connolly, impressed as were MacDermott and Plunkett with the boy's vigour and energy and his evident qualities of leadership. In their predicament, overwhelmed but reluctant to admit defeat, they considered the youth capable of lifting some of the burden from their exhausted shoulders. Pearse, too, perhaps remembered Cuchulain, the boy hero of ancient Ireland. There was no alternative, anyway. Connolly was *hors de combat*, as was Plunkett, despite his display of courage. Clarke and MacDermott were not military men, while Pearse himself was almost spent. MacLoughlin received news of his appointment soberly and immediately suggested that everyone should get as much sleep as possible, so that they would be ready for what the morning might bring. As accommodation downstairs was crowded, Pearse and his brother went upstairs, where they spread two blankets on a table and lay down on them. MacLoughlin went outside and posted sentries at the barricade, checked the positions of all the men and then retired himself, bedding down under the table on which the Pearse brothers slept.

At the barricade, John Nunan hunched wearily beside Volunteer Frank Kelly and Captain George Plunkett and listened to a wounded man moaning on the far side of Moore Street. They listened to his faint cry: "Water, water!"

"That must be one of our lads," whispered someone.

"Give me your water bottle, Frank," said Plunkett.

Kelly slipped it from his shoulder. "Keep me covered," said Plunkett, "but don't fire unless you have to." He edged his way through the flimsy barricade and bending low, ran towards Sampson's Lane. A volley crashed out immediately and sparks flew where the bullets hit the street. Plunkett dived into the laneway where Nunan, by the glare of the fires, saw him bend over a prone figure. He watched Plunkett lift the man on to his shoulders and start back. A few ragged shots blew dust from the bricks; then the firing ceased as the military realized Plunkett was rescuing a wounded man. When Plunkett reached the barricade, Nunan saw with surprise that the wounded man was not a rebel but a British soldier. Plunkett dumped him unceremoniously over the barricade and gasped out: "Here, take him—I want to get his rifle." Nunan and Kelly pulled the wounded man in while Plunkett jinked his way across the street again. This time the military fired on him with all they had, but he reached the far side, grabbed the rifle and managed to dash back safely.

In the Coliseum, meanwhile, Father Flanagan and Quartermaster Fitzgerald, watching the flames advance, decided that the time had come to try to reach Jervis Street Hospital. Neither was familiar with the theatre and they had difficulty finding any way out other than the main exit into Henry Street. Eventually they found a door leading to Princes Street. Father Flanagan placed himself at the head of a little procession which, Red Cross flags held high, wended its way along an alleyway, climbed over a burning barricade, and emerged cautiously into Middle Abbey Street. Here it was fired upon, but when the Red Cross flag had been waved several times, Captain Orr of the Sherwood Foresters stepped forward with drawn revolver and shouted, "Bearer of flag and one other advance and parley." Father Flanagan gestured to Captain Mahony, who flung back his coat to show his khaki jacket; then they both stepped forward.

In Moore Lane, Mrs. Thomas McKane, hysterical following the death of her daughter Bridget and the wounding of her husband, Thomas, ran towards the British barricade, waving a white sheet over her head.

"Get back for God's sake, or we'll fire!" shouted a Tommy.

"My husband! My husband!" yelled Mrs. McKane. "I must get a priest!" She continued running towards the barricade and a rifle cracked, the bullet tugging at her sleeve. "Get back," yelled the Tommy. "Get back, you silly bitch!"

"My husband!" screamed the half-crazed woman. "I must get a priest." And she kept on running.

"For Christ's sake, sir, what shall we do?" shouted the Tommy desperately.

"Use your head, man," barked the officer. "Stop firing at once!"

28

CERTAINLY BRIGADIER-General Lowe, the tall, austere officer who continued to conduct field operations despite the arrival of Maxwell, ought to have realized that North King Street was the worst place that could have been chosen through which to draw the northern boundary of the inner cordon around the Four Courts. As early as Easter Tuesday, small probing operations had shown that the rebels, in considerable strength, were well bedded down in the area. A Red Cross ambulance, trying to get through to the Richmond Hospital on Thursday, had been fired on from a barricade, and an armoured car, cautiously pushing forward early that (Friday) morning, had been liberally sprayed with Mauser bullets. It was clearly a place to be wary of; perhaps first encircled and then worked over thoroughly before troops were sent in.

Maxwell ordered otherwise. Left with two North Staffs. Battalions on his hands at Kingstown, he decided to bring up the South Staffs. from Mount Street and give them the task of finally making the cordon link-up through North King Street. Orders given to Lieutenant-Colonel Henry Taylor of Wolverhampton, C.O. of the 2/6th South Staffs., were to press westwards from Capel Street and join with the 2/5th South Staffs. advancing eastwards from Queen Street. Taylor left Trinity College about five o'clock in the evening, marching his Battalion over Butt Bridge, skirting the Post Office area by way of Gardiner and Great Britain streets and eventually halted at the junction of Bolton and Capel streets. From the Sherwood Foresters he learned that North King Street was too strongly held by the rebels to allow for an unsupported infantry assault. He would need to call up the armoured cars. At 5.45 p.m. he took over the Bolton Street Technical Schools as a base of operations and ordered a rifle party on the roof to open fire on the rebel barricades. The arrival of one armoured car allowed him to commence serious operations. The car opened the attack by rolling slowly forward and depositing assault parties in several houses along the street. Behind it advanced the infantry, pouring fierce and indiscriminate fire into all the houses before entering and occupying them. Civilians who had not followed General Maxwell's instructions to leave the area were shepherded back to the Technical Schools for safety.

Two hundred yards up North King Street, Volunteers Thomas Sherrin, William Murphy, William Hogan, John Williamson, and John Dwan watched the "tank" slew across the street and fire a broadside at them. They returned the fire, but saw their bullets rattle harmlessly against the armour plating. It was the beginning of the most vicious and most sustained fighting of the whole week, although casualties were to be well below those at Mount Street Bridge, due largely to the less open nature of the ground and because most of the battle was fought in darkness. The employment of the armoured car also helped to keep casualties down, as did Colonel Taylor's decision to adopt rebel tactics, and tunnel through houses. For both sides the fighting rapidly became an edgy, nerve-testing battle, fought out in an unusually narrow street, with men firing from behind bedroom windows or chimney pots.

The focal point turned out to be "Reilly's Fort"—an empty public house at the corner of North King and Church streets, where a green flag still hung defiantly from the lance of the dead British trooper. These premises commanded a stretch of North King Street some two hundred yards long. Opposite Reilly's, across North King Street, was a barricade. Two hundred yards down on the right-hand side, and at a slight bend in the road, lay Beresford Street. Towering over it was Jameson's Malt House and Granary, from whose top floor Volunteer Frank Shouldice and two other insurgents had command of the whole area. Out of sight around the bend, and on the left-hand side, lay Coleraine Street and it was at a barricade here that Sherrin and his comrades met the first onslaught of the South Staffs. As night fell, their battle became a lonely, desperate fight against spitting flashes of fire from each side of the street (which was all they could see of the enemy) and the constant roar of the armoured car, whose engine revved loudly as it advanced and then reversed to back up against a door.

Inside the armoured car rebel bullets created a terrible racket. Sergeant Sam Cooper of "B" Company, 2/6th South Staffs., remembered how "Every bullet clanged and jarred through your head. It wasn't possible to fire back, either—you couldn't discharge a rifle in that confined space." Nor did the car guarantee complete invulnerability. "I remember we backed up to a pub as bullets rattled madly against 'the tank'—and one fellow broke a window and we all poured out. It wasn't until daylight we discovered one fellow had been hit apparently just as he got out. He was lying dead under a window."

For the military, on the whole, the fight was sheer nightmare. The Shinners were foxy, shadowy foes, ready to fight dirty; they would use anybody, old women, young girls, old men, boys. Sergeant Cooper remembers that the worst thing was the strain of staring out into North King Street from a pub window, scanning the rooftops constantly, peering into the night until his eyeballs felt like footballs. He recalls: "One young fellow was certain we were being fired on from behind a chimney. I kept watch, but could see nothing. I had hardly left the window for a second when he yelled out, 'They're firing from behind that chimney'—so we let them have it. We riddled the chimney stack, knocking every pot to hell and eventually bringing the whole lot tumbling down. A complete waste of ammunition—there wasn't a Shinner in sight."

Progress was slow. From the high Malt House, Frank Shouldice, lying out on an iron platform at the top of the outside stairway, poured down an accurate fire on the houses along the north side of the street, picking out his targets by the answering flashes of their rifles. Sherrin and his comrades blazed away in a terrible fury. Once when the armoured car ventured too near, they tossed a handful of grenades at it, and caused it to retire. They themselves faced a constant hail of bullets. Somehow none of them was hit, although annihilation clearly could be only a matter of time. Small parties of military had begun to work their way along the rooftops in an attempt to lob heavy hand grenades down on the barricade. Caught in the heavy, relentless rebel fire, this proved suicidal and the grenades fell in front of the barricades, exploding brilliantly, but harmlessly.

By midnight Colonel Taylor's gains were precisely nil. The rebel barricade still held. Thousands of rounds of ammunition had been poured out wildly and recklessly into the flickering night by his young recruits. Faced with failure, Colonel Taylor decided that the only way to beat the rebels was to adopt their own tactics. He sent a strong party to tunnel through some houses with the idea of outflanking the barricade. Then, about 2 a.m., the armoured car struggled up to within thirty yards of the barricade and a party armed with picks and crowbars broke into No. 172 North King Street, a house owned by Mrs. Sally Hughes, where twenty neighbouring families had taken refuge.

If the struggle so far had been a hard frightening battle for the men forced to fight it, it now became a matter of pure terror for the impoverished inhabitants. General Maxwell had warned that anybody who remained within the battle zone did so at his own risk, but since Easter Monday only the rebel writ had run in North King Street and few people were aware of their risk. Some who learned of it elected to remain anyway in what they took to be the safest place they could stay—their own homes. Early in the week the rebels had tried to persuade most inhabitants to move to the nearby North Dublin Union, but except with people living in houses which were entered and fortified, this attempt was not successful. Now, into the midst of these frightened people crashed the South Staffords, infuriated by their own slow progress, and with a lust for blood in their hearts.

"We heard the soldiers banging at the street door," testified Mrs. Ellen Walsh later. "Mr. Hughes called out to his wife, 'Don't open the door, Sally, we shall all be killed.' But as the soldiers kept thundering at the hall door, Mrs. Hughes at length opened it. 'You are just in the nick of time, we were going to blow you up,' shouted the first soldier through the door. We then heard a voice cry, 'Are there any men in this house?' Immediately about thirty soldiers . . . ran at us like infuriated wild beasts or like things possessed. They looked ghastly and seemed in a panic. There was terrible firing going on outside in the street . . . and an armoured car was near the door. One of the soldiers with stripes on his arm seemed in command. He shouted, 'Hands up!' and they presented their rifles at us. We all stood round the room in groups, and my husband

and Mr. Hughes seemed petrified at the wild looks and cries of the soldiers and stood motionless with their hands clasped in front of them. . . . The man in command shouted, 'Search them,' and they searched the two men and the two boys. At the same time the others rushed about the house, furiously searching everywhere. They thrust their bayonets through a feather tick . . . and ripped it to bits, and stabbed the furniture in a hunt for ammunition.

One of our men said, 'There was no one firing from this house.' The corporal with stripes said, 'Not firing, eh?' and pointing to a rip in his hat said, 'Look what a bullet did for me. I nearly lost my life.' The women and children were then all ordered down into the back kitchen and my poor husband and Mr. Hughes were brought upstairs. We were locked in the kitchen. I shall never forget the horror of it. Some time after I heard a voice upstairs crying, 'Mercy! Mercy! Don't put that on me!' and someone resisting as if being tied up, or having his eyes bandaged. The old man [a lodger] in the upper room close by heard my husband crying, and as they killed them he heard his last words: 'O, Nellie, Nellie, jewel!'"

And so the episodes known in Dublin as "The Massacres of North King Street" began.

At the barricade, young John Dwan fell with a bullet through his head. William Hogan lifted the inert body on to his shoulders, crawled back to the entrance of Coleraine Street where he laid his friend down and stood guard until stretcher-bearers could be found to take him to hospital. By now the hammering of picks as the Staffs. tunnelled through the houses could be heard above the rifle-fire and Sherrin and his comrades, realizing the military's intentions, decided to retreat. They crawled one by one towards Coleraine Street where, once under cover, they doubled round by a back lane to Church Street, and rejoined Lieutenant Jack Shouldice and his men in Reilly's. Behind them the South Staffs. continued to fire upon the deserted barricade until at length, realizing it was no longer manned, they rushed forward and occupied it. In Reilly's Fort, they heard a constant breaking of glass and smashing of woodwork and the excited shouting of orders as the military battered their way into more and more houses. Now and then a star-shell would rocket into the night, bathing the scene in a weird, blue light.

At Commandant Daly's Headquarters in the Father Mathew Hall, eighty yards from Reilly's Fort, priests from a nearby church listened to the confessions of the rebels, and afterwards administered Holy Communion. Addressing the men, a priest explained: "The situation at present is very grave and we all know that if the military break in, there will be no mercy shown to anyone. I want you all, therefore, to offer your lives to God as a willing sacrifice for Ireland, if it is so needed. I will stay with you to the end." He had scarcely finished speaking when an unexpected sound came floating in from the street outside. It was the sound of the men at the barricades singing.

Firing ceased abruptly as the astonished South Staffords listened to a rebel song drift over the barricades, sung with all the fervour of patriotic hearts.

The voices rose defiantly into the sudden quietness of the night. As the song ended, the South Staffords poured volley after volley into the darkness in a fury of frustration. The rebels replied with two songs: *The Boys of the West* and *The Green Flag*. Each time the South Staffords ceased firing until the song had finished, then unleashed a further furious storm of lead. The rebel reply was an outburst of ironical cheers and yet another song.

"Frank McCabe sang a most inappropriate song," recalled Volunteer Thomas Sherrin. "It was called *The Bucket of Mountain Dew*. It runs:

On yonder little hill,
There's a darling little still
Its smoke curling up to the sky.
And it's easy to tell
By the whiff and the smell
That there's poteen, me boys,
Close by.

For it fills the air
With a perfume rare,
And betwixt both me and you,
As home we roll,
We'll drink a bowl,
Or a bucket
Of the Mountain Dew.

Oh, we certainly sang good-ho that night!"

Colonel Taylor, short and slightly pompous, did not appreciate the concert. As dawn began to light the grey streets, he sent his angry troops charging over the captured barricade in an impatient effort to finish the job. It was twelve hours since he had seized the Bolton Street Technical Schools and ordered his men down North King Street and in that time they had managed to advance barely two hundred yards—casualties, fortunately, had been light. Now four platoons of "C" Company, led by Major J. Sheppard, went into the charge with bayonets thrust determinedly forward.

They were met by the concentrated fire of seven riflemen in Reilly's pub. In the narrow street, bedded down behind their loopholed windows, big sacks of maize and meal protecting their heads, the rebels had ample time and opportunity to pick out their men. A sheet of heavy, killing bullets stopped Sheppard's men dead. Sheppard himself fell wounded. His men, scattering for cover, dashed into Beresford Street where, high above their heads, Volunteer Frank Shouldice waited for them.

"Our fellows at Reilly's were firing into them, and some more from six cottages then being built on waste ground on our left. About fifteen Tommies turned into Beresford Street right under me. I was on the iron platform and all I had to do was fire down upon them. One by one we knocked them all over. It was a terrible slaughter, and to this day I can't understand why they decided to rush things." Thus Frank Shouldice.

"If they'd kept boring through the walls, creeping up on us gradually, we'd have stood no chance," said Sherrin. "Some officer, however, clearly lost his head and sent those lads out to their death."

Captain Fionan Lynch and Lieutenant Jack Shouldice, who had been touring posts all night, had just come down from the Malt House when the South Staffs. launched their charge. "When the last of those fellows was knocked over, we leaped over the barricade in Beresford Street and ran out into the road and picked up their rifles and ammunition. One young fellow, still alive, was moaning pitifully for his mother, but what could I do to help him?" said Jack Shouldice.

Still the battle raged on. Lieutenant Shouldice worked his way back into Reilly's to reinforce the other riflemen. The military pushed their way from one house to another, aided by a heavy covering fire from the houses through which they had tunnelled. On the other side of the street they reached the corner of Beresford Street. Shouldice and his men blanketed the street with fire, taking turns when their rifles got too hot to hold. The interior of Reilly's was a shambles. Worse, the sacks of meal and flour used to loophole the windows were pierced by bullets and the contents poured out, leaving them with no protection. "We weren't frightened," recalled Sherrin. "We were simply past being frightened by then." Their ammunition, however, was running low.

"On two occasions I sent messengers down to the Father Mathew Hall to bring back supplies," recalled Lieutenant Shouldice, "but neither could get back. By this time we were under heavy fire not only from the frontal attack by the 2/6th South Staffs., but also from the 2/5th South Staffs., advancing at our rear from Queen Street through Smithfield. They had a machine-gun with them and constantly swept the roadway outside. Shortly after 7 a.m. I sent young Patrick O'Flanagan out in a last desperate attempt to get fresh ammunition. We were almost exhausted physically, and we hadn't had a decent meal or anything to drink for some time, but we were still determined to keep fighting as long as the stuff held out."

Young O'Flanagan reached the Father Mathew Hall and was on his way back when Shouldice saw him halt briefly, then dash suddenly into the road. He was more than half-way to Reilly's door when Shouldice saw him trip. "Then I saw him falling forward, carried on by his own impetus." When Shouldice got down into the hallway to help him, the boy lay dying in the doorway. The ammunition pouches he had collected lay in the roadway, just out of reach.

By 9 a.m. it was all over in Reilly's. Shouldice took a vote among his men, then lined them up in the hallway, and during a momentary lull they made a run for it.

They were half-way across the street before the military began shooting, but they flung themselves to the pavement and scrambled furiously on their hands and knees to safety.

With a shout of triumph the Staffords swept forward victoriously. Captain Percy Bayliss, of Wolverhampton, rushing ahead impetuously with his platoon, became isolated from the main body. From both ends of Church Street the rebels swept the crossing with bullets. Colonel Taylor, his brow black as thunder, strode up North King Street followed by his orderly. For sixteen damned hours, now, he had struggled fiercely to take this wretched slum and still the Battalion was hung up. Warily he approached the crossing. And there, straight in front of him, ruffling slightly in the breeze, a green flag hung mockingly.

29

AT DAWN THE main army of rebels cut off in Moore Street commenced burrowing again through the houses towards Great Britain Street. In Cogan's, the three rebel women prepared a scrappy meal for the members of the Provisional Government, after which the whole party moved forward through the holes in the wall as far as Hanlon's fish shop at No. 16. The holes had been broken through at different levels and the job of getting Connolly's stretcher up and down flights of stairs and through the holes was laborious. For Connolly, whose foot had turned gangrenous, every step of the way meant torture. It was decided that he could go no further and a halt was made at No. 16. Here, in the back parlour of a fishmonger's shop, the final Headquarters of the broken Army of the Irish Republic were established. The five leaders, Pearse, Connolly, Plunkett, Clarke, and MacDermott, along with Pearse's young brother, flopped down wearily wherever there was room. Near Connolly were placed four wounded men, including the British prisoner rescued by George Plunkett.

A field gun thundered somewhere in Sackville Street and the leaders and their principal officers held a last council of war. Asked to outline the position as it appeared to him, MacLoughlin, the boy commandant, said he thought the important thing was to escape from Moore Street before the military realized exactly where they were and how weak they had become. Once they found out, the troops were certain to set fire to Moore Street and as the rebels ran from the flames, they would be mown down without mercy. He thought there was no hope of breaking through the barricade at the top of Moore Street; the way to go, he suggested, was down Henry Street, through the old Ormonde markets and then on to the Four Courts. If twenty men, well-armed and with bombs, were first to hurl themselves in a diversionary charge against the British barricade, they would distract the military's attention long enough to allow the rest to break out from the houses and dash across the street into the laneways opposite. From there, they could filter into Capel Street and on to the Four Courts. Scouts might be sent ahead to contact Commandant Daly and a strong escort party provided to secure a link-up. The leaders listened in silence while the boy put forward his ideas. When he had finished, Pearse asked, "How many lives would we lose?"

MacLoughlin replied: "Twenty to thirty in Moore Street. If the British are in strength in Denmark Street, most of us probably will not get through. But in any event, we're simply doomed if we stay here."

There was silence. Then the leaders leaned forward, their heads almost touching, and in low, careful tones, began talking over the merits of the plan. Pearse raised his hand finally and, clearing his throat, said that they were all agreed; the plan seemed worth trying. MacLoughlin went among the weary men, asking for twenty volunteers and, when he had found them, they set to work to bore a way through the intervening houses to Sackville Lane. From here, only twenty yards short of the British barricade, they would mount their diversionary charge. Some hours later, when they had finally broken into the last house, MacLoughlin carefully stepped into the lane to reconnoitre. The dead body of The O'Rahilly lay on its back, face up to the sky, two of his men crumpled up nearby. MacLoughlin tiptoed to the corner and peered cautiously around. He was followed closely by Sean MacDermott, weeping a little at the sight of The O'Rahilly. Then a rebel shouted that they were both wanted urgently back in No. 16.

When they returned to the house, they were told that the plan had been called off. An incident had occurred which had decided Pearse that surrender was necessary. Robert Dillon, licensee of The Flag, a public house in Moore Street, his premises set on fire by a burning fragment from the G.P.O., had ventured out into the street with his wife and daughter, carrying a white flag. The military had chopped them down mercilessly under the very eyes of Pearse, who turned away sickened.

When MacDermott and MacLoughlin entered the room, Pearse asked the boy, "Will the retreat not involve the loss of civilian life? Won't it be bound to lead through populous districts, whatever route we take?"

"I'm afraid it will," said MacLoughlin.

"In that case, will you issue cease-fire orders to last for the next hour," ordered Pearse abruptly.

Stunned, MacLoughlin, without speaking further, quit the room to pass on the order. When he returned, some fifteen minutes later, old Tom Clarke, his face sad and haggard, beckoned him over to sit beside him. Miss Carney, still cheerful, made them both a cup of tea. Then Clarke gently broke the news that the decision had been made to ask for terms and that a messenger had been sent out to treat with the military. MacLoughlin stared astonished and Clarke added thoughtfully, "Perhaps we ought to go on with your plan and fight it out, for terms or no terms, probably we'll all be killed anyway."

"Deep gloom settled over the place," wrote MacLoughlin later. "No one spoke; the only sound was the groaning of the wounded soldier. On the wall above the fire-place was a lithograph of Robert Emmet, standing defiantly in the dock. Underneath it was a caption which said: 'Until my country takes its place among the nations . . . let no man write my epitaph.'"

Although by now they had the ruined Post Office invested on all sides, still the military seemed to have no inkling at all as to the real plight of the rebels. General Maxwell remained in Dublin Castle, while Lowe refused to put a foot outside Trinity College. So uninformed, indeed, were the military of the real state of affairs that Colonel Hodgkin, C.O. of the 2/6th Sherwood Foresters, summoned Captain G. J. Edmunds to Battalion H.Q. in Great Britain Street and ordered him to take one hundred men and report to Colonel Owens of the Royal Irish Regiment.

"The position is, Edmunds," explained the Colonel briskly, "that the Royal Irish are getting ready to assault the Post Office to try and take it, and they need some extra men to help out. So take a hundred chaps and report to Colonel Owen in Summerhill at once, will you, there's a good fellow?"

In Sackville Street a shell crashed through the upper storeys of the Metropole Hotel, and sent a loud, reverberating echo sighing away down the ruined, desolate street. Not even a bird moved any longer. Thin smoke still wisped into the air from the smouldering Post Office, whose flagpole hung crazily askew, the scorched green flag hanging down in sorrowful defeat. Machine-gun bullets ate viciously into the façade of the empty hotel. Again and again the artillery rumbled, the shells picking great holes in the deserted buildings. Soon reporter O'Leary noticed the first traces of fire eating its way along the Metropole roof. Fanned by a breeze, the flames gained strength and once again smoke clouds drifted across Sackville Street, obscuring for long intervals the figure of Nelson.

In No. 16 Moore Street, Pearse and Connolly talked together long and earnestly in low tones. At last Pearse arose from the wounded man's couch and spoke to MacDermott, who turned and asked Miss O'Farrell to obtain a white flag. She left the room to search for a Red Cross insignia, and MacDermott went into the house next door where he discovered Captain Michael O'Reilly shaving.

"Can you get us a white flag of some sort?" asked MacDermott.

O'Reilly took a large white linen handkerchief from his breast pocket. "Will this do?" MacDermott nodded, his face grey. Quietly he tied the handkerchief to a stick, then handed it back to O'Reilly, who went to the front door and stuck the "flag" out. A volley of bullets caused him to duck back. In the silence which followed O'Reilly again stuck the handkerchief out. This time he waved it gently, and the military did not fire. MacDermott beckoned Miss O'Farrell forward, and the young woman, holding her Red Cross flag, walked out into the street. It was 12.45 p.m.

The nurse stood for a moment gazing up the street towards the barricade and waving her flag. A shout came from the military, telling her to come forward. Defiantly, the young woman started walking. At the barricade hands stretched out to assist her. Slightly out of breath, she jumped down on the far side, and demanded to see the general.

She was brought before Colonel Hodgkin, to whom she explained that she had been sent by Mr. Pearse, who wished to treat with them.

"How many girls are down there?" asked Hodgkin brusquely.

"Three," replied Miss O'Farrell.

"Well, take my advice and go down and bring the other two girls out of it," said the Colonel shortly.

He was about to help her back over the barricade when he changed his mind and said, "No. Don't go; you'd better wait—I suppose this will have to be reported." He called another officer and told him to escort Miss O'Farrell along Great Britain Street. The nurse walked along the street passing Tom Clarke's shop, and then stopped outside either No. 70 or 71, while the escorting officer called for the C.O.

In a short time Colonel Portal came out, and there was the following dialogue:

O'FARRELL: The Commandant of the Irish Republican Army wishes to treat with the Commandant of the British forces in Ireland.
PORTAL: The Irish Republican Army?—the Sinn Feiners, you mean.
O'FARRELL: No, the Irish Republican Army they call themselves and I think that is a very good name, too.
PORTAL: Will Pearse be able to be moved on a stretcher?
O'FARRELL: Commandant Pearse doesn't need a stretcher.
PORTAL (turning to another officer): Take that Red Cross off her and bring her over here and search her—she's a spy.

The officer obeyed. The Red Cross insignia was taken off her arm, then off her apron. Then the officer took her into the hallway of a nearby bank and searched her. Satisfied that she had no concealed arms, he took her into Tom Clarke's shop where she was held prisoner.

In No. 15 Moore Street, Julia Grenan knelt in the hallway and said a prayer for the safety of her friend. When she had finished, she rose to her feet and went over to Sean MacDermott. Hesitantly she asked him, "Will they shoot her?"

"Ah, not at all," said MacDermott comfortingly, patting her on the arm. He turned away and went into the next house, No. 16. A few minutes later she heard Connolly call out to her and went through the hole in the wall to the wounded leader's bedside.

"Now, don't be crying for your friend," said James Connolly soothingly; "they won't shoot her. She may be away for some time, but don't worry, they won't shoot her."

In Trinity College, General Lowe's telephone rang. It was Dublin Castle on the line to say that a Red Cross nurse had come to the Moore Street barricade with a verbal message from Pearse, saying he wished to treat as to terms of surrender—the girl had been detained pending further orders. Lowe at once left for Great Britain Street, accompanied by Captain H. de Courcy Wheeler.

"General Lowe treated me very gentlemanly," wrote Miss O'Farrell afterwards. "I gave him the message and he said he would take me in a motor-car to the top of Moore Street. I was to go back to Mr. Pearse and tell him that 'General Lowe would not treat at all until he would surrender unconditionally,' adding that I had to be back in half an hour as hostilities must go on."

Colonel Portal then wrote a note to this effect, which General Lowe signed, and they both took her in a motor-car as far as Moore Street. Here she was permitted to go back over the barricade again to rebel headquarters at No. 16. She delivered the messages, explaining that she had to be back within half an hour.

"The situation was discussed and then I was sent back with a written message," she goes on. "I went back to the top of Moore Street where General Lowe was waiting in the car. He was vexed because I was a minute over the half hour coming, but I pointed out that I wasn't by my watch. Then one of the officers set his watch by mine. I did not know what was in Mr. Pearse's note [he had requested terms for his men, although not for himself], but General Lowe's reply was 'Go back and tell Mr. Pearse that I will not treat at all unless he surrenders unconditionally and that Mr. Connolly follows on a stretcher.'" Lowe then warned her that unless she and Mr. Pearse were back within half an hour he would resume hostilities. Once more she returned to Moore Street carrying this message, and the members of the Provisional Government held a short council. "Then Mr. Pearse decided to go back with me," added Miss O'Farrell.

No one spoke in the little parlour as the Commander-in-Chief, his face more sombre than any of those present could remember it, shook everyone there by the hand for what they sensed might be the last time. MacLoughlin had the impression that Pearse did not altogether believe that this was a final good-bye, but felt that he would be permitted to return and make whatever arrangements were thought necessary. The women wept bitterly and Miss Grenan pressed Rosary beads on Miss O'Farrell. Then the two stepped out into the street—Pearse tall and still commanding in presence, Miss O'Farrell blonde and diminutive, trotting briskly beside him.

At exactly 2.30 p.m. officially (Miss O'Farrell's watch, however, said 3.30) General Lowe received the rebel commander on the British side of the barricade at the top of Moore Street. Lieutenant King, who had been held prisoner in the Post Office, was called forward to identify Pearse, but said he could not as he had not seen him there.

"Were you in the G.P.O.?" asked King.

"Yes," answered Pearse briefly.

"Well, I didn't see you there."

Pearse, a trifle irritated by this nonsense, did not answer but simply took off his sword and handed it to Lowe. The general took it and then said, "My only concession is that I will allow the other Commandants to surrender. I understand you have the Countess Markievicz down there?"

"No, she isn't with me," said Pearse shortly.

"Oh, I know she's down there," said Lowe sharply.

"Don't accuse me of speaking an untruth," replied Pearse, somewhat heatedly.

"Oh, I beg your pardon, Mr. Pearse, but I do know she's in the area."

"Well, she's not with me, sir."

At a loss for a moment Lowe then suggested that Miss O'Farrell should be detained by the military for the night in order that she could take Pearse's surrender order round to the other rebel commandants.

"Will you agree to this?" asked Pearse, turning to the nurse.

"Yes, if you wish it," replied Miss O'Farrell.

"I do wish it," said Pearse slowly and sadly, and shook her hand. She watched him as he was led away, escorted by General Lowe's son and another officer.

Lowe, accompanied by Captain Wheeler, drove off towards Sackville Street, the car carrying Pearse, with an armed bodyguard standing on the running-board, following immediately behind. Then the two cars disappeared from sight round the Parnell Monument. As Miss O'Farrell stood there, her head bowed in misery, she heard a military officer remark, "It would be interesting to know how many German marks that chap has in his pocket."

In Moore Street, the small party left behind sat together in strained and anxious silence. After a while MacLoughlin crossed to Connolly's bedside. "What do you think will happen?" he asked the wounded leader. "Oh, I think those of us, including myself, who have signed the Proclamation, will be shot. Some good, however, might come from what we have done," said Connolly. He advised MacLoughlin not to reveal his rank. "You're a young man; you'll be able to pick up the thread; men such as you will be needed." As the Commandant-General spoke, MacDermott gently laid a hand on young MacLoughlin's shoulder and led him away. As they left the room, the young man saw Miss Carney kneel at Connolly's bedside, weeping bitterly, asking, "Is there no other way?"

CONNOLLY: "No—I couldn't bear to see my brave boys burned to death—there is no other way." He called for the medical student, James Ryan, and asked to be prepared for the journey. A stretcher was brought in and Connolly gently lifted on to it and then carried into the house next door.

Meanwhile Pearse had been driven to the Headquarters of Irish Command at Parkgate where, on arrival, he was ushered before General Maxwell. The interview, according to Maxwell's biographer, Sir George Arthur, "was both short and stern. Pearse seemed stunned by the thought of what he had brought on his followers, and unhesitatingly yielded to the demand to write and sign notices ordering the various 'commandos' to surrender unconditionally." The instrument of surrender read:

"In order to prevent the further slaughter of Dublin citizens, and in the hope of saving the lives of our followers now surrounded and hopelessly outnumbered, the members of the Provisional Government present at Headquarters have agreed to an unconditional surrender, and the Commandants of the various districts in the City and Country will order their commands to lay down arms.

(Signed) P. H. Pearse
29th April, 1916, 3.45 p.m."

This done, Captain Wheeler was instructed to go to the Red Cross Hospital in Dublin Castle where by this time Connolly had been taken and to obtain his counter-signature. When Wheeler arrived, Connolly had already been put to bed and was under medical care. Wheeler read out Pearse's statement and explained that General Lowe thought he—Connolly—should endorse the order as far as his own comrades were concerned. Connolly scribbled: "I agree to these conditions for the men only under my own command in the Moore Street District and for the men in the Stephen's Green Command. (Signed) James Connolly, April 29/16."

Copies of both orders (written on the same piece of paper) were then taken to Miss O'Farrell to deliver to Moore Street along with a written note telling the men how they should surrender: "Carrying a white flag, proceed down Moore Street, turn into Moore Lane and Henry Place, out into Henry Street and around the Pillar to the right-hand side of Sackville Street; march up to within a hundred yards of the military drawn up at the Parnell Statue, halt, advance five paces and lay down arms."

When the nurse reached Moore Street with these orders, there were still some hotheads who wanted to fight on. They were quietened however, by Tom Clarke, who pointed out that he had given his life to the struggle and was satisfied as things were; he thought Ireland "would be all right in the future." Thereupon MacDermott and MacLoughlin rounded up most of the men in the backyard of No. 16, and MacDermott, looking as though he might break down at any moment, read Pearse's letter aloud, stumbling over the words, then haltingly adding some of his own: "I am proud of you. You have made a great fight. It is not our fault that you haven't won. You were outclassed, that is all."

It was evening before all the wounded were placed on stretchers on the pavements. The Moore Street shops were closed and shuttered; the bodies of the dead lay where they had fallen. Together MacDermott, MacLoughlin and Captain Michael O'Reilly marshalled the fit men into ranks in the middle of the street. O'Reilly was ordered to lead the way, carrying the white flag.

He set off at the head of fifty men, the main body following. When the latter, led by MacLoughlin, flanked by Willie Pearse and Sean MacDermott, reached Sackville Street, they saw no sign of O'Reilly's party. O'Reilly, with that instinct for farce which somehow obtruded on even the most dramatic moments of the insurrection, had taken the wrong turning and had gone marching past the burned-out G.P.O. and the still blazing Metropole Hotel towards O'Connell Bridge, where he proceeded to lay down arms to an astonished military party advancing to meet him from Westmoreland Street. After a short parley O'Reilly's men picked up their arms again, and O'Reilly led them back up Sackville Street to rejoin the rest of the rebel army. Drawn up on each side of the street in front of the Gresham Hotel were two hundred and fifty or three hundred rebels. The command rang out: "Step five paces forward and deposit your arms!"

As the order echoed down the great, devastated thoroughfare, where every principal building had been either destroyed or was still burning, where the dead horses of the Lancers, killed six long days ago, still lay stinking in obscenity, the haggard, weary, hungry, and bedraggled army threw down its arms angrily and stepped back five paces to stand weaponless at the mercy of the conquerors.

The attitude of the military towards their beaten adversaries hardly smacked of generosity. Officers and men, on the whole, believed that the rebels were in the pay of the Germans, doing their dirty work for them, and considered that they deserved little better treatment than to be placed against a wall and shot. Rebellion, even if not fomented by Germany, was a heinous crime, too, and certainly no authority anywhere had ever been known to treat those who attempted to suborn it with anything but the most excessive harshness. In England, in Highland Scotland, and, of course, in Ireland itself, rebels throughout the centuries had always been mercilessly punished by the Crown. A rebel's life was forfeit, as were his goods and possessions. Only the most naïve might have imagined that they would be accorded the honoured treatment prescribed by international law for recognized prisoners of war.

Physically, the military behaved most correctly. Rebel complaints of ill-treatment can be whittled down to a series of insults delivered almost entirely by a single officer. Typical of this man's attitude was a sneer directed at Sean MacDermott. "So you've cripples in your army!" To counter-balance this kind of childishness there were generous gestures. One officer walked behind the line of prisoners murmuring, "If you men have any incriminating papers, tear them up quietly and drop them in the gutter behind you." Again, as the rebels were marched to the grounds of the Rotunda Hospital (a small plot of greensward opposite the Parnell Monument), Joseph Plunkett, hardly able to walk, swayed and almost fell. A soldier gave him a rough shove forward and threatened to bayonet him, only to have a sergeant pull him fiercely by the arm and bark angrily, "Do your duty and do no more; *that's* not your duty."

By 10 p.m. some four hundred rebels (including Daly's men from the Four Courts who had by this time surrendered) had been squashed into this small plot of ground. (A small detachment of Daly's men, under Volunteer Patrick Holohan, were cut off in North Brunswick Street and had refused to surrender although, at the urgings of the Capuchin monks of the district, they had agreed to a truce while confirmation of Pearse's order was brought to them). Here, as the night came down and a bitterly cold wind swept Sackville Street, the main body of the rebel army squatted, crushed close together, with ample time to look back on its errors. Fires still smouldered, or burst intermittently into life along the great street. Armoured cars rattled past every now and then and there was a constant stream of Red Cross ambulances "gliding by silent as ghosts." At intervals Tommies would gather up rebel arms and trot away with them. An officer, examining a Howth gun, remarked as he fingered a Mauser bullet, "You know, this damn thing would kill a bally elephant!" From the roof of the Rotunda, a machine-gun stood trained throughout the night, while a ring of bayonets encircled the plot. The Misses Grenan and Carney sat on the grass beside Sean MacDermott and sucked compressed food lozenges he gave them, which "tasted awful."

In the early hours the quiet, well-behaved officer in charge was relieved by Captain Lea Wilson, a dark-browed, florid-faced, thick-lipped Irishman, a little the worse for drink. Wilson began to hurl insults at them. "He strides around looking for looters and threatening to have us all shot and telling us not to smoke, not to stand up, and not to lie down and, if we want lavatories, use the beds provided and lie down in both," Desmond Ryan wrote later. "He roars madly at his own men and issues contradictory orders. Rushes at this man and that shouting he'll have them shot. Strikes matches and holds them in the faces of the men and shouts 'Anyone want to see the animals?' He bends over Plunkett and snatches a document from his inner pocket: 'Ah, his Will! He certainly knew what he was coming out to get!' He snatches a whistle from Willie Pearse, has another man's Red Cross armlet ripped away with bayonets. 'You're a nice specimen of an English gentleman!' snarls an exasperated victim. He yells at Clarke: 'That old bastard is the Commander-in-Chief. He keeps a tobacco shop across the street. Nice general for your ✱✱✱✱ army.' One Volunteer mutters: 'A dark night, a dark lane, a stout stick—and that fellow!'" (Three years later Michael Collins had Wilson shot during the War of Independence.)

At nine o'clock on Sunday morning, thoroughly miserable, stiff and half-frozen after their night in the open, the rebels were lined up in Sackville Street and told to start marching. Wilson, in a fit of rage, had confiscated MacDermott's walking stick during the night. MacDermott pleaded that, without it, he would be unable to keep up with the others and so was permitted to march by himself under separate escort. As for the rest, an eye-witness in the Gresham Hotel who saw them march down Sackville Street that morning has left this description of the scene:

> "It's a sight I shall never forget. That thin line, some in the green uniform of the Volunteers, others in the plainer equipment of the Citizen Army, some looking like ordinary civilians, the others looking mere lads of fifteen, not a few wounded and bandaged, and the whole melancholy procession wending its way through long lines of khaki soldiers. But down-hearted— no! As they passed, I heard the subdued strains of the scaffold song of many an Irishman before them—'God Save Ireland.' Dockers, labourers, shop assistants, all conditions of men; all have the same look of defiance which will haunt me to my dying day. Whatever else they were, they were not cowards. If they had been at the front and accomplished what they had accomplished in the face of such odds, the whole Empire would have been proud of them, and the whole world ringing with their praises."

This was a lone voice, a lone view. As the prisoners marched towards Richmond Barracks, crowds stood at the kerbsides to hoot and jeer them. "Shoot the traitors!" they cried, "Bayonet the bastards!" In one of the poorer quarters, the shawlies pelted them with rotten vegetables, the more enthusiastic disgorging the contents of their chamber pots over the beaten, yet somehow still undefeated, men. Some of this popular hostility can be explained by the fact that Easter Week 1916 was the first anniversary of the second Battle of Ypres, in which the Dublin Fusiliers had suffered very heavy losses. For instance, the 2nd Battalion of the Dublins had had over 500 officers and men killed or wounded on 24 April 1915 alone. The Rising broke out exactly a year later: many women were therefore mourning the first anniversary of a loved one's death.

The G.P.O. and the Four Courts had fallen. Patrick Pearse had surrendered and lay captive in Arbour Hill Barracks. Connolly was in the hospital in Dublin Castle. The people of Dublin flocked into the city to see the still smouldering ruins and hunt for souvenirs, while the City Fathers totted up the cost of it all, and General Maxwell prepared his court-martials. Yet the Rebellion was still not over. Commandants Ceannt, MacDonagh, de Valera, and Mallin had not yet surrendered. Escorted by Captain Wheeler, Nurse O'Farrell, a brave and lonely little figure, set off through areas where bullets still flew, carrying the instrument of surrender. She went first to Boland's Bakery, where de Valera, who did not know her personally, refused at first to believe its authenticity. She left, not knowing whether he intended to surrender or not. Here, as with other commands, there were men who wanted to go on fighting and the authority of de Valera and his senior officers was openly flouted by a few diehards who supported Lieutenant John Guilfoyle and his plan to escape to the mountains and carry on fighting. In the end, on the plea that only by surrendering immediately were they likely to save de Valera's life, they gave in. De Valera, escorted by Cadet Mackay, a military prisoner, left the Bakery, stopped the first respectable person he saw—Dr. Myles Keogh of Sir Patrick Dun's Hospital—and informed him that he wished to surrender. Keogh immediately passed the message on to Trinity College.

De Valera made two memorable remarks that morning. To the military officer who took his surrender he said, "Shoot me if you will, but arrange for my men." And then to the people gathered in Lower Mount Street to watch his men lay down their arms: "If only you'd come out with knives and forks!"

Commander MacDonagh surrendered only after a good deal of discussion, insisting that, as Pearse was being held prisoner, the Commander-in-Chief was acting under duress in issuing his order. An interview was arranged with General Lowe by the Capuchin friar, Father Augustine, after which MacDonagh drove to the South Dublin Union to see Ceannt and talk over the position. In the end both surrendered at the same time.

Father Augustine also played a vital part in securing young Holohan's surrender, thus saving the South Staffords the distasteful task of winkling him out. After seeing Pearse in Arbour Hill and securing a copy of the surrender order written in the Commander-in-Chief's own hand, the monk was permitted to pass through the embattled lines to see Holohan. In the face of such a document, the desperate young rebel reluctantly laid down his arms.

Constance Markievicz remained gay and utterly fearless right to the last. She and Michael Mallin marched right out of the side door of the College of Surgeons together and together surrendered to Captain Wheeler. Then she took off her great Mauser pistol-rifle and bright bandolier, raised them to her lips, kissed them, and then handed them over.

"I can place a motor-car at your disposal, madam," said Wheeler, with great courtesy.

"No," she answered, still defiant, and with all the pride and dignity of a lady of the Big House, added, "I shall march at the head of my men as I am Second-in-Command, and shall share their fate."

Epilogue

ONE THOUSAND THREE hundred and fifty-one people had been killed or severely wounded—officially. One hundred and seventy-nine buildings in central Dublin, enclosing sixty-one thousand square yards, had been irrevocably ruined and the cost, in terms of the monetary values then existing, was two and a half million pounds sterling. One hundred thousand people—approximately one-third of the total population—had to be given public relief.

It was a time for wisdom. Had General Sir John Maxwell, in the last analysis, been something more than an unimaginative soldier, he might have understood that from the Imperial point of view, the way to treat the insurrectionary leaders was to make them look ridiculous. Had he, in effect, spanked them and sent them home with a stern warning to be good boys in the future, Britain might well have avoided the disasters of the years which followed—which ate into the fabric of the Imperial idea as surely as any German Army. The consequences were immense; not least among them the continual fostering by Irish-Americans of the traditional dislike felt by the United States for colonialism.

Yet, all in all, perhaps it was asking a little too much to expect Maxwell to foresee any of this. Possibly almost any man, placed suddenly in his position, faced with the precedents he had to face, would have done very much as he did. The sentences he confirmed were hardly barbaric and he allowed the leaders to die a soldier's death when he might so easily have hanged them as common felons. Against the charges that the courts-martial were set up and carried through with an almost indecent haste, is to be set the fact that, while the menace of a German invasion remained, time was of the essence. Rebels and rebellion must be crushed, and the quicker it is done, the better. Perhaps the real irony lay in the fact that by executing Pearse and his comrades in the way that he did, Maxwell was only doing what they really wanted him to do. Only in death, most of them knew, could they achieve victory.

Pearse, MacDonagh, and Clarke were shot at dawn on the morning of Wednesday, May 3rd, 1916, in the yard of Kilmainham Jail. In his court-martial speech Pearse went to some lengths to refute the suggestion that the insurrection had been financed with German gold as was genuinely believed by most people at the time:

"I desire in the first place to repeat what I have already said in letters to General Sir John Maxwell and Brigadier General Lowe. My object in agreeing to unconditional surrender was to prevent further slaughter of the civilian population of Dublin and to save the lives of our gallant fellows, who, having made for six days a stand unparalleled in military history, were now surrounded and (in the case of those under the immediate command of headquarters) without food. I fully understand now, as then, that my own life is forfeit to British law, and I shall die very cheerfully if I can think that the British Government, as it has already shown itself strong, will now show itself magnanimous enough to accept my single life in forfeiture and to give a general amnesty to the brave men and boys who have fought at my bidding. In the second place I wish it to be understood that any admissions I make here are to be taken as involving myself alone. They do not involve and must not be used against anyone who acted with me, not even those who may have set their names to documents with me. (The Court assented to this.)

I admit I was Commander-General Commander-in-Chief of the forces of the Irish Republic which have been acting against you for the past week and that I was President of the Provisional Government. I stand over all my acts and words done or spoken in these capacities. When I was a child of ten I went down on my knees by my bedside one night and promised God that I should devote my life to an effort to free my country. I have kept that promise. First among all earthly things, as a boy and as a man, I have worked for Irish freedom. I have helped to organize, to arm, to train, and to discipline my fellow countrymen to the sole end that, when the time came, they might fight for Irish freedom. The time, as it seemed to me, did come and we went into the fight. I am glad that we did, we seem to have lost, we have not lost. To refuse to fight would have been to lose, to fight is to win, we have kept faith with the past, and handed a tradition to the future. I repudiate the assertion of the prosecutor that I sought to aid and abet England's enemy. Germany is no more to me than England is. I asked for and accepted German aid in the shape of arms and an expeditionary force, we neither asked for nor accepted German gold, nor had any traffic with Germany but what I state; my aim was to win Irish freedom; we struck the first blow ourselves but I should have been glad of an ally's aid.

I assume I am speaking to Englishmen who value their own freedom, and who profess to be fighting for the freedom of Belgium and Serbia. Believe that we too love freedom and desire it. To us it is more desirable than anything else in the world. If you strike us down now we shall rise again and renew the fight. You cannot conquer Ireland; you cannot extinguish the Irish passion for freedom; if our deed has not been sufficient to win freedom then our children will win it by a better deed."

On the morning of his execution Pearse wrote to his mother:

"My dearest mother,

I have been hoping up to now it would be possible to see you again, but it does not seem possible. Good-bye, dear mother. Through you I say good-bye to 'Wow? Wow' [a sister], Mary Brigid, Willie, Miss B., Michael, cousin Maggine and everyone at St. Enda's. I hope and believe Willie and the St. Enda's boys will be all safe.

I have written two papers about financial affairs and one about my books which I want you to get. With them are a few poems which I want added to the poems in MS. in my bookcase. You asked me to write a little poem which would seem to be said by you about me. I have written it, and a copy is in Arbour Hill barracks with other papers.

I have just received Holy Communion. I am happy, except for the great grief of parting from you. This is the death I should have asked for if God had given me the choice of all deaths—to die a soldier's death for Ireland and for freedom. We have done right. People will say hard things of us now, but later on will praise us. Do not grieve for all this but think of it as a sacrifice which God asked of me and of you.

Good-bye, dear mother, may God bless you for your great love to me and for your great faith and may He remember all you have so bravely suffered. I hope soon to see papa, and in a little while we shall all be together again. I have not words to tell you of my love for you and how my heart yearns to you all. I will call to you in my heart at the last moment.

Your son,
Pat."

The poem to which he refers was called *The Mother*.

I do not grudge them; Lord, I do not grudge
My two strong sons that I have seen go out
To break their strength and die, they and a few,
In bloody protest for a glorious thing,
They shall be spoken of among their people,
The generations shall remember them,
And call them blessed!

Little of what Tom Clarke had to say—if he said anything much—has survived to us. To his court-martial judges he announced that he would do the same again if spared. To his wife, on the last night of his life, he said, "I am to be shot at dawn. I'm glad it's a soldier's death I'm getting. I've had enough of imprisonment."

MacDonagh wrote his own epitaph:

His songs were a little phrase
Of eternal song
Drowned in the harping of lays
More loud and long

His deed was a single word
Called out alone
In a night where no echo stirred
To laughter or moan

But his song's new soul shall shrill
The loud harps dumb
And his deed the echoes fill
When the dawn is come.

At midnight the news was broken to MacDonagh that he would be shot at dawn. His wife was not able to get to him but his sister, a nun, found him in "a dank, vile cell" lighted by the butt of a candle. He had already confessed by the time she arrived, had had Holy Communion, and had written to his wife. When his sister entered the cell and saw that there was no water, she asked the sentry, "Will you give him some water to wash in?" The sentry, acting under orders, refused. MacDonagh's sister then handed him a Rosary which had belonged to their mother and he put it around his neck. "I hope they will give me this when it is over," she said. "Ah, no," he said quietly, "they will shoot it to bits." (They did not—only four beads were shot away and the Rosary was eventually returned to his sister.)

In his court-martial speech MacDonagh said:

"Gentlemen of the Court-martial. I choose to think that you have but done your duty, according to your lights, in sentencing me to death. I thank you for your courtesy. It would not be seemly for me to go to my doom without trying to express, however inadequately, my sense of the high honour I enjoy in being of those predestined in this generation to die for the cause of Irish freedom. You will, perhaps, understand this sentiment, for it is one to which an Imperial poet of a bygone age bore immortal testimony: 'Tis sweet and glorious to die for one's country.' You would all be proud to die for Britain, your Imperial patron, and I am proud and happy to die for Ireland, my glorious Fatherland."
(A member of the court): "You speak of Britain as our Imperial patron."
(MacDonagh): "Yes, some of you are Irishmen."
"And what of your Imperial patron; what of Germany?"
"Not if Germany had violated and despoiled my country and persisted in withholding her birthright of freedom."
(President): "Better not interrupt the prisoner." (The prisoner bowed.)

"There is not much left to say. The Proclamation of the Irish Republic has been adduced in evidence against me as one of the signatories; you think it already a dead and buried letter, but it lives, it lives. From minds alight with Ireland's vivid intellect, it sprang; in hearts aflame with Ireland's mighty love it was conceived. Such documents do not die. The British occupation of Ireland has never for more than one hundred years been compelled to confront in the field of fight a rising so formidable as that which overwhelming forces have for the moment succeeded in quelling. This rising did not result from accidental circumstances . . . "

The rest of the manuscript, whose authenticity has been questioned, but which is accepted as wholly true by MacDonagh's family, is missing.

Late the same night, Mr. Stoker (the Grafton street jeweller who had been standing outside the General Post Office when Joseph Plunkett had headed the rebel charge into it) was just about to close his shop when "a taxi stopped at the front door and a beautiful young woman stepped out and asked me to show her some wedding rings. The best, as she put it, that money could buy. She had a thick veil, but I could see that her eyes were red with weeping and, noticing continuous convulsive sobs as she spoke, I ventured to ask the reason. It was then that she revealed the terrible tragedy she was about to suffer. 'I am Joe Plunkett's fiancée,' she said. 'We are to be married in prison tomorrow morning, an hour before his execution. Oh, I can't tell you how I love him and he loves me. We belong to each other. And even if we are together for only a single hour I mean to marry him in spite of everything in order to bear his name through life.'"

The "beautiful young woman" was Grace Gifford. At 1.30 a.m. on May 4th, 1916, she was led into the small chapel of Kilmainham Jail and stood waiting until the ailing Joseph Plunkett was brought in, in handcuffs, and led up beside her before the altar. Owing to a lighting failure, the marriage was performed by the Reverend Eugene MacCarthy by the light of a single candle, held by a British soldier, while twenty soldiers, with bayonets fixed, lined the walls of the chapel. Immediately after the ceremony the couple were separated, but before Plunkett's execution at dawn, the bride was allowed to see him for a further ten minutes. During those last few minutes fifteen soldiers stood guard in the cell, and the time was regulated to the second by a soldier who stood by with a watch.

At dawn Plunkett, Commandant Edward Daly, Michael O'Hanrahan (MacDonagh's second in command at Jacob's) and Willie Pearse were all shot together.

The gallant Major John MacBride died alone on May 5th. On the same day, the death sentence on the Countess Markievicz was commuted to life imprisonment. The Countess affected the deepest chagrin at this decision. However, in his memoirs William Wylie, the prosecuting counsel at the courts-martial, insists that her performance in court was craven. He quoted her as saying: "I am only a woman and you cannot shoot a woman." He commented that "she crumpled up" and that "she was literally crawling", adding that the memory of her conduct revolted him.

On the following Monday morning, May 8th, four more men were executed—Eamonn Ceannt, Michael Mallin, J. J. Heuston, and Cornelius Colbert; nineteen other death sentences were commuted to varying terms of imprisonment.

On Thursday, May 11th, the death sentence passed on de Valera was commuted to one of life imprisonment.

Finally, on Friday, May 12th, Sean MacDermott and James Connolly were shot—the last men to pay the supreme penalty.

These last two executions shocked public opinion as none of the others had. The earlier ones had taken place while most Irish people were still stunned and still full of resentment against the rebels. But as penalty followed penalty a feeling of revulsion set in; the belief took hold that the Government was indulging in an orgy of revengeful bloodletting. Strong voices were raised in protest; the United States Senate requested the President to transmit to the British Government an expression of "their hope that Great Britain would exercise clemency in the treatment of Irish political prisoners generally." Redmond and the Orange leader, Carson, appealed for clemency in the House of Commons. "No true Irishman calls for vengeance," said Carson magnanimously. "It will be a matter requiring the greatest wisdom and the greatest calmness in dealing with these men. Whatever is done, let it be done not in a moment of temporary excitement but in a moment of deliberation."

When eventually Irish Command announced that de Valera had been spared the death sentence (Maxwell had taken into account de Valera's American birth and also William Wylie's opinion—privately expressed—that he was not very important and was unlikely to make any trouble in the future!), there was general relief and a feeling that wisdom and statesmanship were likely to heal the breach rapidly. The rebellion, after all, had been crushed; its principal leaders were dead. True, Connolly lived, but the man had been severely wounded, and one thing was certain—he would never again lead another military rising. And who, anyway, could shoot a wounded man?

The people of Ireland were stunned to learn that General Maxwell could—and from that moment on he and the nation he represented earned their hearty opprobrium; even today his name is still execrated as "Bloody" Maxwell. The shock was the more severe because, on the day before Connolly's execution, an official announcement had stated: "The trials by court-martial of those who took an actual part in the rising in Dublin are practically finished. . . . "

The last persons, outside his jailers and executioners, to see MacDermott alive were the two Ryan sisters, Mary and Phyllis, who later married men well known in modern Ireland. Phyllis became Mrs. Sean T. O'Kelly; Mary, the wife of General Richard Mulcahy. In her contemporary account of the last meeting, Mary Ryan wrote: "The last time I saw him [MacDermott] was in his prison cell at Kilmainham Jail at three o'clock on the morning of May 12th. He was shot at 3.45 on the same morning. . . . The cell was small with walls whitewashed. There was a raised board in the corner—a plank bed. There was a small rough table near a light on which was placed a tall, brass candlestick. . . . On the plank bed were a couple of soiled blankets. MacDermott had a smile on his face. He was cheerful. There were two soldiers there all the time. He sat on the plank bed discussing the revolution. He told of the insults hurled at them by the British after they'd laid down their arms—the inhuman treatment in Richmond Barracks. He did not complain—almost as if he did not expect better treatment. He preferred to talk of casual matters, asking about different people we knew, enjoying little jokes almost as though we were in Bewleys [a well-known Dublin coffeehouse]. The most pathetic scene was where he tried to produce keepsakes for different girl friends of his we mentioned. He sat down at the table and tried to scratch his name and the date on the few coins he had left and on the buttons which he cut from his clothes with a penknife reluctantly provided by a young officer who stood by. His beautiful head bent assiduously over the work. At three o'clock on the arrival of the prison chaplain, we bade farewell. He had a beautiful head, black hair with deep blue eyes, dark eyebrows and long lashes. Illness had left him lame and somewhat delicate—he often looked tired and frail. He had wonderful charm. He had worked and planned for Irish independence since boyhood. . . . His last words, aside from prayers, were 'God save Ireland.' At four o'clock, when the shooting was done, a gentle rain began to fall—the tears of Dark Rosaleen."

James Connolly's daughter, Nora, has left an account of the last days of her father as he lay wounded in Dublin Castle, uncertain as to his fate.

"On Tuesday [May 9th] I went with mother. There were soldiers on guard at the top of the stairs and in the small alcove leading to Papa's room. They were fully armed and as they stood guard they had their bayonets fixed. In the room there was an R.A.M.C. officer with him all the time. His wounded leg was resting in a cage. He was weak and pale and his voice was very low. Mother asked was he suffering much pain. 'No, but I've been court-martialled today. They propped me up in bed. The strain was very great.' She knew then that if they had court-martialled him while unable to sit up in bed, they would not hesitate to shoot him while he was wounded. Asked how he had got the wound he said: 'It was while I had gone out to place some men at a certain point. On my way back I was shot above the ankle by a sniper. Both bones in my leg are shattered. I was too far away for the men I had just placed to see me and was too far from the Post Office to be seen. So I had to crawl till I was seen. The loss of blood was great. They couldn't get it staunched.' He was very cheerful, talking about plans for the future, giving no sign that sentence had been pronounced an hour before we were admitted. He was very proud of his men. 'It was a good clean fight. The cause cannot die now. The fight will put an end to recruiting. Irishmen will now realize the absurdity of fighting for the freedom of another country while their own is enslaved.' He praised the women and girls who fought. I told him about Rory [Connolly's son: the boy had been arrested with other rebels but had given a false name and was released along with all other boys under sixteen]. 'He fought for his country and has been imprisoned for his country and he's not sixteen. He's had a great start in life, hasn't he, Nora?' Then he turned to mother and said: 'There was one young boy, Lillie, who was carrying the top of my stretcher as we were leaving the burning Post Office. The street was being swept continually with bullets from machine-guns. That young lad was at the head of the stretcher and if a bullet came near me he would move his body in such a way that he might receive it instead of me. He was so young-looking, although big, that I asked his age. "I'm fourteen, sir," he answered. We can't fail now.'

"I saw father next on Thursday, May 11th, at midnight. A motor ambulance came to the door. The officer said father was very weak and wished to see his wife and eldest daughter. Mama believed the story because she had seen him on Wednesday and he was in great pain and very weak, and he couldn't sleep without morphine. Nevertheless she asked the officer if they were going to shoot him. The officer said he could tell her nothing. Through dark, deserted, sentry-ridden streets we rode. I was surprised to see about a dozen soldiers encamped outside Papa's door. There was an officer on guard inside the room. Papa turned his head at our coming.

"'Well, Lillie, I suppose you know what this means?'

"'Oh, James, it's not that—it's not that!'

"'Yes, Lillie. I fell asleep for the first time tonight and they wakened me at eleven and told me that I was to die at dawn.' Mamma broke down and laid her head on the bed and sobbed heart-breakingly. Father patted her head and said: 'Don't cry, Lillie, you'll unman me.'

"'But your beautiful life, James. Your beautiful life!' she sobbed.

"'Well, Lillie, hasn't it been a full life and isn't this a good end?' I was also crying. 'Don't cry, Nora, there's nothing to cry about.'

"'I won't cry, Papa,' I said.

"He patted my hand and said: 'That's my brave girl. . . .'

"He tried to cheer Mama by telling her of the man who had come into the Post Office during the Rising to try and buy a penny stamp. 'I don't know what Dublin's coming to when you can't buy a stamp at the Post Office. . . .'

"The officer said: 'Only five minutes more.' Mama was nearly overcome—she had to be given water. Papa tried to clasp her in his arms but he could only lift his head and shoulders from the bed. The officer said: 'Time is up.' Papa turned and said good-bye to her and she could not see him. I tried to bring Mama away but I could not move her. The nurse came forward and helped her away. I ran back and kissed Papa again. 'Nora, I'm proud of you.' Then the door was shut and I saw him no more. . . .

"(Later) We saw Father Aloysius who had attended him in Kilmainham. 'How did they shoot him . . . how could they shoot him?' asked Mama. 'He couldn't sit up in his bed.'

"'It was a terrible shock to me,' said Father Aloysius. 'I'd been with him that evening and I promised to come to him this afternoon. I felt sure there would be no more executions. Your father was much easier than he had been. I was sure that he would get his first real night's rest. The ambulance that brought you home came for me. I was astonished. I had felt so sure that I would not be needed that, for the first time since the Rising, I had locked the doors. And some time after two I was knocked up. The ambulance brought me to your father. I'll always thank God as long as I live that He permitted me to be with your father until he was dead. Such a wonderful man—such a concentration of mind. They carried him from his bed in an ambulance stretcher down to a waiting ambulance and drove him to Kilmainham Jail. They carried him from the ambulance to the jail yard and put him in a chair. . . . He was very brave and cool. . . . I said to him, "Will you pray for the men who are about to shoot you?" and he said: "I will say a prayer for all brave men who do their duty." His prayer was "Forgive them for they know not what they do . . . " and then they shot him.'"

Adding fuel to the flames of anger and resentment sweeping the country were "the atrocities"—first the rampaging personal acts of Captain Bowen-Colthurst and second, the behaviour of the 2/6th South Staffordshire Regiment, in the course of the savage fighting in North King Street. Allegations of at least six cases of cold-blooded murder were to be levelled against Bowen-Colthurst; fifteen against the South Staffs.

Army authorities might very effectively have dampened down the Bowen-Colthurst affair had it not been for the intervention of Major Sir Francis Vane who, as he put it, was "alive to the good name and reputation of the British Army" and was convinced that Bowen-Colthurst's behaviour well warranted official investigation and censure. He first made it his business to protest to General Friend, Colonel Kennard, and Major Price at Dublin Castle, insisting that Bowen-Colthurst be relieved from command pending an investigation. The three men responded by deprecating "the fuss" he was trying to make, Price adding, "Some of us think it was a good thing Sheehy-Skeffington was put out of the way, anyway." So, early in May, Vane crossed to London and visited the War Office and on May 3rd interviewed Lord Kitchener, who assured him that he would send a telegram ordering Bowen-Colthurst's arrest.

Maxwell, alleged Vane later, simply ignored Kitchener's telegram; not only that—instead of dealing with Bowen-Colthurst, he took action against Vane, depriving him of his rank and dismissing him the service. Skeffington's widow carried on the campaign for redress until eventually she was received by the Prime Minister, Mr. Asquith, who expressed himself as horrified at the allegations against Bowen-Colthurst but even more horrified at the suggestion that General Maxwell was assisting the resident military authorities in Dublin to hush up the case. "I confess I do not and cannot believe it. Does anyone suppose that Sir John Maxwell has any object in shielding officers and soldiers, if there be such, who have been guilty of such ungentlemanly, such inhuman conduct? It is the last thing the British Army would dream of."

When Mr. Asquith crossed to Ireland himself, a few days later, however, he found that the British Army, as it was constituted in Ireland anyway, was unfortunately quite capable of "inhuman conduct" and General Maxwell or his subordinates only too anxious to hush up anything unpleasant. As a result, Captain Bowen-Colthurst was formally court-martialled on June 6th and after a number of witnesses had testified to his character and behaviour before and after the Skeffington affair, he was found guilty, but insane, and incarcerated in Broadmoor Criminal Asylum.

No unprejudiced person could possibly attach blame to an army because it was unfortunate enough to have at least one lunatic—or near-lunatic—in its ranks. Resentment primarily arose—and still lingers in Ireland—because the Army authorities, by refusing to act promptly against Bowen-Colthurst, appeared to condone his behaviour. Asquith and Maxwell, however, soon found themselves deep in the mire of something a great deal more unpleasant. This time a whole Battalion of English troops, it was alleged, were involved. Sent across to Dublin to act as the guardians of authority and upholders of the law, the 2/6th South Staffs. had behaved like barbaric savages in North King Street. No less than fifteen innocent civilians, it was alleged, had been bayoneted to death during military operations in the area—fifteen men who, despite protests and expostulations, despite the pleas of their family, were dragged away and either shot or bayoneted simply "because they [the military] were determined to wreak vengeance on the helpless inmates whom they found in the houses."

Although stories of the horrors alleged to have occurred were rife in the city from May 1st, it was not until the bodies of two victims whom members of the South Staffs. had buried in a cellar were dug up that the authorities were forced to take note. The inquest was adjourned to give Colonel Taylor an opportunity to be represented, but he consented merely to forward a statement saying:

"I cannot discover any military witnesses as to the manner in which the two men, Patrick Bealen and James Healy, met with their deaths, but I cannot believe that the allegations made at the inquest can be correct. To the best of my knowledge and belief, during the military operations in Capel Street and King Street, which lasted from 6 a.m. on Friday, 28 April until the truce was declared on the afternoon of Saturday, 29 (and which were, in fact, continued for some hours after that by the rebels in that area) only those houses were entered by the military which the exigencies of the case rendered actually necessary, and no persons were attacked by the troops other than those who were assisting the rebels and found with arms in their possession.

The premises, No. 177 North King Street, were indicated to me as one of the houses from which the troops had been repeatedly fired upon, and the troops were also continually fired upon both during the night of the 28th April and the whole of the following day from the distillery, at which the deceased man, James Healy, was stated to have been employed. The operations in the portion of King Street, between Linenhall Street and Church Street, were conducted under circumstances of the greatest difficulty and danger for the troops engaged, who were subjected to severe fire, not only from behind several rebel barricades, which had been constructed across King Street and other barricades in Church Street and side streets, but practically every house in that portion of King Street and other buildings overlooking it.

Strong evidence of these difficulties and dangers is afforded by the fact that it took the troops from 10 a.m. on the 28th April until 2 p.m. on the 29th to force their way along King Street from Linenhall Street to Church Street, a distance of some 150 yards; and that the casualties sustained by the regiment (the great majority of which occurred at this spot) numbered five soldiers, (including two Captains) wounded, eleven N.C.O.s and men killed and twenty-eight wounded.

I am satisfied that during these operations the troops under my command showed great moderation and restraint under exceptionally difficult and trying circumstances."

The Coroner's court saw things in a different light. They returned a verdict as follows: "We find the said Patrick Bealen died from shock and haemorrhage, resulting from bullet wounds inflicted by a soldier, or soldiers, in whose custody he was, an unarmed and unoffensive prisoner. We consider that the explanation given by the military authorities is very unsatisfactory, and we believe that if the military authorities had any inclination they could produce the officer in charge."

It was clearly impossible now to simply bulldoze a way through the affair. In a statement to the *Daily Mail,* General Maxwell tacitly admitted that brutalities had been committed: "Possibly some unfortunate incidents, which we should regret now, may have occurred . . . it is even possible that under the horrors of this attack some of them 'saw red'; that is the inevitable consequence of a rebellion of this kind."

Inevitably there was an inquiry. An elaborate identification parade was laid on at Straffan camp, outside Dublin, where the whole Battalion was paraded, and the wives and mothers of the dead men were invited to pick out the soldiers who had committed the alleged crimes. They were unable to identify any one—and certainly in the case of Bealen and Healy this would have been difficult as the two culprits who had shot the men and then buried them in the cellar were safely back in England, having been got out of the way quickly on the orders of their company officer. One of the culprits was a Corporal Bullock, the other a sergeant who lived long in quiet retirement.

The latter was the man referred to in a letter sent by Maxwell to Lord Kitchener: "In one case a sergeant acted like a madman, the redeeming feature being that he reported what he had done. It must be borne in mind that there was a lot of house to house fighting going on, wild rumours in circulation, conflagrations, and, owing to the darkness, a good deal of 'jumpiness.' With young soldiers and under the circumstances, I wonder there were not more."

Despite this, announcing the result of the inquiry to the House of Commons, the Prime Minister said: "The conclusion arrived at after a full hearing in all the cases was that the deaths occurred in the course of continued and desperate street and house to house fighting which lasted for nearly two days and in which soldiers were constantly exposed to sniping from windows and the roofs of houses. There can be little doubt that some men who were not taking an actual part in the fighting were in the course of the struggle killed by both rebels and soldiers. But after careful inquiry it is impossible to bring home responsiblity to any particular person or persons."

So there it was; between them, the Army and Government had managed to get all the skeletons safely, as they thought, locked away in a cupboard. It mattered not that ordinary Irish people—who desperately wanted to believe that English "atrocities" had ended with the disappearance of the redcoats and the solution of the agrarian difficulties of the nineteenth century—now began to feel that the English leopard could never change his spots and that the only compatible solution for Ireland, if she was ever to enjoy any kind of peace, was to go along with the republicans and cut all connecting links.

Of the other actors in the drama of the Rebellion, Lord Wimborne, Mr. Birrell, and Sir Matthew Nathan handed in their resignations almost immediately after the cessation of hostilities and on the eighteenth of May a formal Royal Commission of Inquiry began its sittings in Westminster. In its findings, the Commission exonerated Wimborne from all blame, and partially exonerated Sir Matthew, but added: "We consider that he did not sufficiently impress upon the Chief Secretary during the latter's prolonged absences from Dublin the necessity for more active measures to remedy the situation in Ireland." They found Mr. Birrell "primarily responsible for the situation that was allowed to arise and the outbreak that occurred."

This left Maxwell undisputed Lord of Ireland, a position which he no longer really relished. He constantly agitated against the Government's policy of oscillation between conciliation and coercion, demanding that they at least make up their minds which policy they wished to employ. He himself favoured the appointment of an executive who would "meet a warm-hearted people half-way in redressing grievances." He expressed himself as disgusted with the poverty and squalor he found in Dublin, which "could be easily prevented" and emphasized the evil of allowing absentee landlordism to continue in other parts of the country. Finally he blamed all the trouble on the Government's pusillanimity in allowing Carson to form the Ulster Volunteers, naming this as the primary cause of the Rebellion and the growing unrest which succeeded it.

It would seem, certainly, that he grew more and more anxious to undo as much as he possibly could the damage he himself had caused by executing fifteen rebels. But such was the virulence of the campaign against him both in Ireland and in England that by October he was no longer in a position to exercise any further influence on Irish affairs. The Government terminated his appointment in Ireland and as a clear mark of their disapproval of the way he had handled affairs there, relegated him to the relatively unimportant post of G.O.C. Northern England. For the man who, both in the Middle East and Ireland, had enjoyed almost the status of a pro-consul, it was a bitter disappointment. He had washed the Government's dirty linen for it, and this was his thanks. . . . Thus, in bitterness and disappointment, ended his career.

Not that Pearse or Connolly would really have wanted that. In sentencing them to death, he had only done what they wanted him to do—he had made them glorious martyrs.

And that, in the end, would free Ireland.

Bibliography

Arthur, Sir George. *General Sir James Maxwell*. London, 1932.

Barker, Ernest. *Ireland in the Last Fifty Years—1866–1916*. Oxford University Press, 1917.

Barr, F. *History of the Great War*. London.

Boyle, J. F. *The Irish Rebellion of 1916, a brief history*. 1916.

Brennan, Robert. *Allegiance*. Dublin, 1950.

Bromage, Mary C. *De Valera and the March of a Nation*. London, 1956.

Burca, Seamus de. *The Soldier's Song*. The story of Peadar O'Cearnaigh. Dublin, 1957.

Callwell, C. E. *Field-Marshal Sir Henry Wilson; his life and diaries*. London, 1927.

Catholic Bulletin. *Easter Week and After. Eye-Witness accounts biographies*. 1916.

Carty, James. *Ireland—from the Great Famine to the Treaty of 1912*. Dublin, 1951.

Clarke, Kathleen. *Revolutionary Woman*. Dublin, 1991.

Clarke, Thomas J. *Glimpses of an Irish Felon's Prison Life*. Dublin, 1922.

Collins, Michael. *The Path to Freedom*. Dublin, 1922.

Colum, Padraic. *Poems of the Irish Revolutionary Brotherhood*. Boston, 1916.

Colum, Padraic. *Life of Arthur Griffith*. Dublin, 1959.

Colum, Padraic and Others. *The Irish Rebellion of 1916 and its Martyrs*. 1916.

Colvin, Ian. *The Life of Lord Carson*. London, 1934–36.

Connolly, James. *Labour in Irish History*. Dublin, 1910.

Curry, Charles E. *Sir Roger Casement's Diaries*. Munich, 1922.

Devoy, John. *Devoy's Post Bag, 1871–1928*. Dublin, 1948–53.

"Dublin's Fighting Story". Told by the men who made it. Tralee, 1949.

Dudley Edwards, Owen and Fergus Pyle. *1916: the Easter Rising*. London, 1968.

Dudley Edwards, Ruth. *Patrick Pearse: the triumph of failure*. London, 1977.

Dudley Edwards, Ruth. *James Connolly*. Dublin, 1981.

Duggan, John P. *A History of the Irish Army*. Dublin, 1991.

Dwane, David T. *Early Life of Eamon de Valera*. Dublin, 1922.

Ervine, St. John. *Craigavon, Ulsterman*. London, 1949.

Ervine, St. John. *The Irish Rebellion*. "Century Magazine," New York, 1917.

Fitzhenry, Enda C. *Nineteen-Sixteen, An Anthology*. Dublin, 1935.

Forbes, Lady Angela. *Memories and Base Details*. London, 1921.

Fox, R. M. *History of the Irish Citizen Army*. Dublin, 1943.

Fox, R. M. *Green Banners*.

Griffith, Arthur. *The Sinn Fein Policy*. Dublin, 1907.

Gwynn, Denis. *The Life and Death of Roger Casement*. London, 1930.

Gwynn, Stephen. *John Redmond's Last Years*. London, 1919.

Henry, R. M. *The Evolution of Sinn Fein*. Dublin, 1920.

Hobson, Bulmer. *A Short History of the Irish Volunteers*. Dublin, 1918.

Holt, Edgar. *Protest in Arms, 1916–23*. London, 1960.

"Irish Times". *Sinn Fein Rebellion Handbook*. Dublin, 1917.

"Irish War News". *The Irish Republic*. Vol. 1, No. 1. Dublin, Tuesday, April 25th, 1916.

Johnstone, Tom. *Orange, Green and Khaki: the story of the Irish regiments in the Great War, 1914–18*. Dublin, 1992.

Le Roux, Louis N. *Patrick H. Pearse*. (Translated by Desmond Ryan.) Dublin, 1932.

Le Roux, Louis N. *Tom Clarke and the Irish Freedom Movement*. Dublin, 1936.

Lloyd George, David. *War Memoirs*.

Lynch, Dermot. *The I.R.B. and the 1916 Insurrection*. Dublin.

Lyons, F.S.L. *Ireland Since the Famine*. London, 1971.

MacArdle, Dorothy. *The Irish Republic*. Dublin, 1951.

MacCann, John. *War by the Irish*. Dublin, 1946.

MacColl, Rene. *Roger Casement. A New Judgment*. London, 1956.

MacLoughlin, Sean. *Memories of the Easter Rising*. Dublin, 1948.

MacManus, M. J. *Eamon de Valera, a biography*. Dublin, 1944.

Martin, Rev. F. X. *MacNeill on the 1916 Rising*. Irish Historical Studies, Dublin, 1966.

Midleton, Earl of. *Ireland, dupe or heroine?* London, 1932.

Monteith, Robert. *Casement's Last Adventure*. Dublin, 1953.

Norway, Mrs. H. *The Sinn Fein Rebellion As I Saw It*. Dublin, 1916.

O'Brien, Nora Connolly. *The Unbroken Tradition*. New York, 1918.

O'Brien, William. *The Irish Revolution and How it Came About*. London, 1923.

O Broin, Leon. *The Chief Secretary: Augustine Birrell in Ireland*. London, 1969.

O Broin, Leon. *Dublin Castle and the 1916 Rising*. London, 1970.

O Broin, Leon. *Revolutionary Underground: the story of the Irish Republican Brotherhood*. Dublin, 1976.

O Broin, Leon. *W. E. Wylie and the Irish Revolution, 1916–1921*. Dublin, 1989.

O'Connor, Frank. *The Big Fellow*. London, 1937.

O'Casey, Sean. *The Story of the Irish Citizen Army*. 1919.

O'Faolain, Sean. *De Valera*. London, 1939.

O'Faolain, Sean. *Constance Markievicz*. London, 1934.

O'Faolain, Sean. *The Story of Ireland*. London, 1943.

O'Hegarty, P. S. *The Victory of Sinn Fein*. Dublin, 1924.

O'Kelly, J. J. *Cathal Brugha*. Dublin, 1942.

O'Malley, Ernie. *On Another Man's Wound*. London, 1936.

O'Rahilly, Aodogán. *Winding the Clock*. Dublin, 1991.

Pearse, Mary Brigid. *The Home Life of Padraig Pearse*. Dublin, 1935.

Philips, W. Alison. *The Revolution in Ireland, 1906–23*. London, 1923.

Redmond-Howard, L. G. *Six Days of the Irish Republic*. 1916.

Royal Commission. *On the Rebellion in Ireland*. London, 1916.

Ryan, A. P. *Mutiny at the Curragh*. London, 1956.

Ryan, Desmond. *The Man Called Pearse*.

Ryan, Desmond. *Remembering Sion*. London, 1934.

Ryan, Desmond. *James Connolly, his life*. Dublin, 1924.

Ryan, Desmond. *The Rising*. Dublin, 1957.

Sheehy-Skeffington, Hanna. *British Militarism as I have Known It*. Tralee, 1946.

Spindler, Karl. *The Mystery of the Casement Ship.* Berlin, 1931.

Stephens, James. *The Insurrection in Dublin.* Dublin, 1916.

Taaffe, Michael. *Those Days are Gone Away.* London, 1959.

Taylor, Rex. *Michael Collins.* London, 1958.

Tierney, Michael. *Eoin MacNeill: scholar and man of action.* Ed. F. X. Martin, Oxford, 1980.

"Times, The". *The Times History of the War.* Vol. 7, 1916.

Townshend, Charles. *Political Violence in Ireland: government and resistance since 1848.* Oxford, 1983.

Vane, Sir Francis. *Agin the Government.* London.

Von Papen, Franz. *Memoirs.* London, 1952.

White, J. R. *Misfit, An Autobiography.* London, 1930.

THE FOLLOWING BRITISH MILITARY HISTORIES HAVE ALSO BEEN CONSULTED:

Oates, Lt.-Col. W. C., D.S.O. *The Sherwood Foresters in the Great War. The 2/8th Battalion.* Nottingham, 1920.

Bradbridge, Lt.-Col. E. U. *Fifty-Ninth Division, 1915–18. A compilation.* Chesterfield, 1928.

Edmunds, Capt. G. J. *The 2/6th Battalion, The Sherwood Foresters, 1914–18.* Chesterfield, 1960.

Meakin, Lieut. Walter. *The 5th North Staffords, 1914–19.* Longton (Staffs.), 1920.

THE FOLLOWING HELPED WITH THEIR RECOLLECTIONS:

Insurgents

Beaslai, Piaras. Four Courts.

Byrne, James. Sackville Street.

Brady, Joseph. Jacob's Biscuit Factory.

Buttner, Patrick. St. Stephen's Green.

Canny, Joseph. North Circular–Cabra Roads.

Cabbrey, Chris. St. Stephen's Green.

Cavanagh, Maeve. Liberty Hall.

Collins, Maurice. North King Street.

Cosgrave, William. South Dublin Union.

Daly, Frank. Four Courts.

Dillon, Mrs. Thomas (*née* Plunkett). Sackville Street.

Donnelly, Simon. Boland's Bakery.

Doyle, James. Mount Street Bridge.

Dowling, Sean. Roe's Distillery.

Duffy, Joseph. Kimmage Garrison.

Duffy, Louise Gavan. G.P.O.

Fitzgerald, Lt. James. Boland's Bakery.

Guilfoyle, Joseph. Boland's Bakery.

Hanratty, Mrs. Emily. Dublin Castle.

Hayes, Senator Michael. Jacob's Biscuit Factory.
Hogan, Liam. North King Street.
Holohan, Garry. Magazine Fort.
Joyce, John. South Dublin Union.
Lane, Edward. Jacob's Biscuit Factory.
Moloney, Helena. Dublin Castle.
Morkan, Eamonn. Four Courts.
Morkan, Mrs. Eamonn. Four Courts.
Mulcahy, General Richard. 5th Battalion.
Mulcahy, Mrs. Mary. G.P.O.
Murphy, Fintan. G.P.O.
Nicholls, Harry. St. Stephen's Green.
Nolan, Peter. Boland's Bakery.
Nunan, Sean. G.P.O.
O'Briain, Professor Liam. St. Stephen's Green.
O'Donoghue, Denis. Mount Street Bridge.
O'Flanagan, Frank. Church Street Bridge.
O'Kelly, Fergus. Wireless School, Sackville Street.
O'Reilly, Michael. G.P.O.
O'Rourke, Frederick. Jacob's Biscuit Factory.
Regan, Lawrence. Four Courts.
Reid, J. Sackville Street.
Robbins, Frank. St. Stephen's Green.
Ryan, Desmond. G.P.O.
Sherrin, Thomas. North King Street.
Shouldice, Lieut. J. North King Street.
Shouldice, Frank. North King Street.
Skinnider, Margaret. St. Stephen's Green.
Sweeny, Major-General J. G.P.O.
Walsh, Thomas. Clanwilliam House.

British Forces

Col. J. S. Oates, D.S.O. 2/8th Sherwood Foresters.
Col. M. C. Martyn, D.S.O. 2/8th Sherwood Foresters.
Captain Frank Pragnell. 2/7th Sherwood Foresters.
Major W. Foster. 2/7th Sherwood Foresters.
Captain C. O. Langley. Adjutant, 2/6th South Staffs.
Captain Godfrey Tallents. Staff, 177th Brigade.
Lieutenant Norman Bladen. North Staffs.
Captain G. J. Edmunds. 2/6th Sherwood Foresters.
Lt.-Col. B. D. Shaw. 2/5th South Staffs.
Captain G. H. Mahony, Indian Medical Service.

Other Ranks

Shelley, J. E., Sergeant. 2/6th South Staffs.
Norton, George, Sergeant. 2/6th South Staffs.
Butlin, W. 2/6th South Staffs.
Hands, Horace, Sergeant. 2/6th South Staffs.
Spires, A. 2/6th South Staffs.
Capewell, A. 2/6th South Staffs.
Gutridge, A. 2/6th South Staffs.
Guttridge, J., Sergeant. 2/6th South Staffs.
Cooper, S., Sergeant. 2/6th South Staffs.
Walker, Thomas. 2/6th South Staffs.
Shenton, A. 2/5th North Staffs.
Billington, A. 2/5th North Staffs.
Booth, Doughlas. 2/5th North Staffs.
Myett, J. 2/5th North Staffs.
Lovatt, John. 2/5th North Staffs.
Rhead, P. B. 2/5th North Staffs.
Boulton, Bertram F. 2/5th North Staffs.
Sargeant, A. 2/5th North Staffs.
Bufton, Frederick. 2/5th North Staffs.
Mellor, J. R., Sergeant. 2/6th Sherwood Foresters.
Brown, H. A. 2/6th Sherwood Foresters.
Wilson, F. 2/6th Sherwood Foresters.
Fidler, T., M.M. 2/6th Sherwood Foresters.
Broomhead, A. 2/6th Sherwood Foresters.
Boram, Bernard. 2/6th Sherwood Foresters.
Shepherd, J. 2/6th Sherwood Foresters.
Rowland, J. 2/6th Sherwood Foresters.
Bury, R. S. 2/6th Sherwood Foresters.
Hubbuck, Oscar, Sergeant. 2/6th Sherwood Foresters.
Slack, A. E., Sergeant. 2/6th Sherwood Foresters.
Reynolds, George. 2/7th Sherwood Foresters.
Church, Arthur. 2/7th Sherwood Foresters.
Reynolds, S. 2/8th Sherwood Foresters.
Ibberson, G., Sergeant. 2/8th Sherwood Foresters.
Lynch, John. 2/5th Leicestershire Regt.
Dakin, H. H. 2/5th Leicestershire Regt.
Watson, H. 2/5th Leicestershire Regt.
Coxon, B. 2/5th Leicestershire Regt.
Perbedy, H. 2/5th Leicestershire Regt.
Glover, B. 2/5th Leicestershire Regt.
Bradford, H. 2/4th Leicestershire Regt.
Kerr, D. 2/4th Leicestershire Regt.
King, C. A. 2/4th Leicestershire Regt.
Stodd, Albert. 2/4th Leicestershire Regt.
Gedry, S. 2/4th Leicestershire Regt.
Shenton, T. A. 2/4th Leicestershire Regt.

Reedman, W. 2/4th Lincolnshire Regt.
Lilley, H. 2/4th Lincolnshire Regt.
Hubbard, G. H. 2/4th Lincolnshire Regt.
Walton, H. W. 2/5th Lincolnshire Regt.
Doughty, H., M.M. 2/5th Lincolnshire Regt.
Boot, A. J. North Midland Field Ambulance.
Tunley, W. S. North Midland Field Ambulance.
Bennett, A. North Midland Field Ambulance.
Jones, W. B. 2/5th Sherwood Foresters.
Hill, E. 2/5th Sherwood Foresters.
Cowley, J. Royal Artillery.

Civilians

Patrick Doyle.
Maurice Linnane.
The Misses Elizabeth and Rose McKane.
Mrs. Rose McKane.
Joseph O'Gorman.
Patrick Nolan.
Joseph O'Byrne.

THE FILES OF THE FOLLOWING NEWSPAPERS AND PERIODICALS HAVE ALSO
BEEN CONSULTED:

The Times.
The Irish Times.
Dublin Saturday Post.
Gaelic American.
Daily Mail.
An t-Oglac.
An Phoblacht.
Illustrated London News.
The Sphere.
The Graphic.
New York Times.
Sunday Press.
Irish Press.
Irish Independent.

Index